The Mysteries
of Consciousness

ALSO EDITED BY INGRID FREDRIKSSON

*Aspects of Consciousness:
Essays on Physics, Death and the Mind*
(McFarland, 2012)

The Mysteries of Consciousness

Essays on Spacetime, Evolution and Well-Being

Edited by INGRID FREDRIKSSON

McFarland & Company, Inc., Publishers
Jefferson, North Carolina

LIBRARY OF CONGRESS CATALOGUING-IN-PUBLICATION DATA

The mysteries of consciousness : essays on spacetime, evolution and well-being / edited by Ingrid Fredriksson.
  p. cm.
Includes bibliographical references and index.

ISBN 978-0-7864-7768-5 (softcover : acid free paper) ∞
ISBN 978-1-4766-1690-2 (ebook)

1. Consciousness. 2. Physics. 3. Evolution.
I. Fredriksson, Ingrid, editor.

QC6.4.C57M97 2015   128'.2—dc23   2015030620

BRITISH LIBRARY CATALOGUING DATA ARE AVAILABLE

© 2015 Ingrid Fredriksson. All rights reserved

No part of this book may be reproduced or transmitted in any form or by any means, electronic or mechanical, including photocopying or recording, or by any information storage and retrieval system, without permission in writing from the publisher.

Cover image: *Besides and Beyond* © Annica Andersson

Printed in the United States of America

*McFarland & Company, Inc., Publishers
Box 611, Jefferson, North Carolina 28640
www.mcfarlandpub.com*

To my Mother and Father in heaven,
the infinite Universe and our Consciousness forever

I have my body and
I am consciousness—Pim van Lommel

Acknowledgments

I am very grateful to every contributor in this book and also for the opportunity to attend the international conference in Stockholm 2006, which awoke my great interest in consciousness. Since that time I have visited every "Toward a Science of Consciousness" conference and many of the "Science and Non Duality" conferences held around the word. In Salzburg 2007 I first met Karl Pribram and listened attentively to his excellent speech.

This book's aim is to pursue a new paradigm, and I am very grateful to all the people that have contributed this book in various ways.

I also thank my family, my translators Richard Lawes and Yarrow Cleaves, and Annica Andersson for the art on the cover.

To all, both named and unnamed, my heartfelt thanks.

Table of Contents

Acknowledgments   vi

Introduction   1

Part I. Physics, Spacetime and Near Death Experiences

Six Protocols, Neuroscience and Near Death: An Emerging Paradigm Incorporating Nonlocal Consciousness
   STEPHAN A. SCHWARTZ   5

Conscious Spacetime: An Outline to Experiential Monism
   JAN PILOTTI   21

The Psi-Track and Other Unexplained Energy Fields
   GÖTE ANDERSSON   55

Part II. From the Evolution of Life to DNA: The Universe We Can't See with Our Eyes

The Role of Consciousness in the Origin and Evolution of Life
   ALLAN EMRÉN   83

DNA Consciousness: From Theory to Science
   JOHN K. GRANDY   116

Do Consciousness and Electrons Exist in Water?
   INGRID FREDRIKSSON   149

The Non-Local Universe Is the Conscious Universe
   MENAS C. KAFATOS, HYEJUNG LEE *and* KEUN-HANG SUSAN YANG   178

Part III. How to Feel Well in Your Brain and Heart

What Is Love? The Physical Cosmology of Spiritual Union
   RICHARD L. AMOROSO   195

Consciousness in the Third Millennium
   AMNA AL FAKI, M.D., *and* INGRID FREDRIKSSON   221

Table of Contents

The Need for an Existential Holism
    ALF E. SJÖBERG   243

Thinking Matters: Well-Being, Mindfulness and the Global Commons
    JANET McINTYRE-MILLS   263

Systematic Mental Training: Effects on Brain, Mind and Reality
    LARS-ERIC UNESTÅHL   293

About the Contributors   317

Index   319

Introduction

When Hippocrates (c. 460–c. 370 BC) was consulted by the philosopher Demokritos, Hippocrates diagnosed him as "too healthy." Demokritos had a disposition that he commonly called "cheerfulness" or "confidence." He enjoyed life and had learned to control his consciousness.

Once again, we've started considering consciousness in ways that go beyond the clinical approach. It has been widely believed hundreds of years that humans, and all living things, possess something that might be called spiritual, and that we are not limited to the purely physical, trapped within our bodies. Thanks to technology and extensive research, we are now starting to explore life on the non-local and microscopic levels. We are made up of 100 trillion cells, all communicating with each other via chemical and electrical systems, we are truly masterpieces, and consciousness seems a miracle.

The purpose of this work is not to clarify what consciousness is, but it is to push consciousness toward a new paradigm in science.

One of Einstein's partners in discussion was the physicist from the University of London, David Bohm. Another of Bohm's discussion partners was Karl Pribram, a neurophysiologist at Stanford University. Bohm and Pribram's theories, considered together, provide a profound new way of looking at the world: Our brains mathematically construct objective reality by interpreting frequencies that are ultimately projections from another dimension, a deeper order of existence that is beyond space and time; the brain is a hologram enfolded in a holographic universe. Researchers in Japan have now provided mathematical evidence that the holographic principle might be true and the holographic paradigm is real.

This work is pushing toward a new paradigm, a perspective also espoused by Stephan A. Schwartz. He mentions that 13 million people have reported a near death experience (NDE), but the number is much larger because many people do not immediately report experiences. A story from Pim van Lommel, heard by myself and Stephen A. Schwartz, illustrates the dynamic in play: At an academic conference on NDEs a few years ago a respected cardiologist stood up and said, "I've worked as a cardiologist for 25 years now, and I've never come across such absurd stories in my practice. I think this is complete nonsense; I don't believe a word of it." Whereupon another man stood up and said, "I'm one of your patients. A couple of years ago I survived a cardiac arrest and had an NDE, and you would be the last person I'd ever tell."

In Einstein's four-dimensional spacetime space and time are relative, but measurements in spacetime are absolute, the same for all observers. So spacetime is an objective reality and seemingly ontological, more basic than space and time. The past events, the now and all future events exist at once in spacetime. Consciousness is not localized in the brain but in body and spacetime. Jan Pilotti's essay further explores time and space.

The last essay in the first part, by Swedish author Göte Andersson, is "The Psi-Track and Other Unexplained Energy Fields." It is a marvelous essay detailing the phenomenon of personal energy fields. All living creatures seem to have these unknown energies, discovered by the author in 1987, indicating that there is a holistic principle in nature.

Part II is about the small things from the universe that we can't see with the eye. Intelligent life should not be able to appear anywhere in merely 14 billion years. As we are here, however, there has to be some mechanism that makes intelligent life possible, unless we are created and developed in a supernatural way. Allan Emrén's essay offers a scientific, and different, story of the creation.

John K. Grandy's essay has three notable parts to it. The first is the history and background of the theory of DNA consciousness and how this term emerged. The second part objectifies DNA as a degree of consciousness. This is done on three dynamic levels that have been verified scientifically. The third part is a scientific outline of how DNA gives rise to human consciousness, provides a continuum of this biological process of consciousness, and takes part in the erosion of the cognitive processes later in life. These are referred to as the three neurogenetic phases of human consciousness. Collectively, these three parts of the essay help validate the transition of DNA consciousness from a theoretical proposal to a science.

In every living being and organism there is an entire world as amazing as the one we see around us. In our body there are 100 trillion cells, and DNA that extends 10,000 kilometers. The base pairs in our DNA are held together by hydrogen. Maybe the hydrogen bonds in DNA's base pairs constitute our immune system and our consciousness! There is water in the cells, and between them, and while large molecules have to go through membrane proteins to enter the cells, small molecules like H_2O and O_2 can pass through the cell membrane without difficulty. In the spaces between the brain cells at the end of every neuron are synapses, the basic unit of a brain cell, where chemical charges build up. In the same space dendrites—tiny filaments of nerve endings communicate with other neurons, sending out and receiving their own electrical wave impulses. This, together with the quantum hologram and non-local consciousness, provides an explanation and an exciting developmental phase in the illusion in which we live, as Ingrid Fredriksson writes. Consciousness appears to exist in everything that has DNA.

Menas C. Kafatos, Hyejung Lee and Keun-Hang Susan Yang talk about the non-local universe. Their essay explains that quantum theory opened the door to consciousness but did not provide a solution, except hints of what the next steps might be. The issue of consciousness presents a clear embarrassment to modern science.

Part III begins with "What Is Love? The Physical Cosmology of Spiritual Union" by Richard L. Amoroso. Now that the physical basis of consciousness or the cosmological nature of the mind-body interaction has been discovered, it is possible to describe the scientific basis of love. What is the soul, what is life, what is intelligence, and especially what is love, and why does it take a whole cosmology to adequately describe it? These are some of the questions that noetic science can begin to answer. It would take a whole volume to completely describe the physical cosmology of love, thus in this essay the author gives only a brief description as a way of introducing what is to come.

Consciousness has no accepted or recognized specific scientific definitions. Yet there are constantly many trials by philosophers, scientists and other workers to define and disclose the mystery and genesis of consciousness and its cause and effect—not only upon our existence as human beings, but also its effect upon the universe, and the question of whether it is fundamental to universal existence as a whole.

Consciousness is a subjective awareness of self-being and surroundings. As a definition, though, this is lacking, as we need a testable theory that is biological, physical and coherent to explain consciousness.

Amna Al Faki and Ingrid Fredriksson write about intelligence of the heart together with intelligence of the brain, which offers a feasible approach to explaining the biological phenomenon of consciousness. In Eastern philosophy the brain, especially the fore brain, is also considered a cognitive organ so a new approach and new definition based upon the brain and heart will explain consciousness.

As a society we are stressing ourselves out for the purpose of having more and more things and more and more information. This is merely the physical-material part of life. Consciousness is a matter of the spiritual-existential part. Both are equally important. In yogism and Buddhism, one goes beyond thinking to direct realization and experience in the field of introspective observation. Consciousness is able to receive information there about the significance of the bliss of love and wisdom for fellow humans. Alf E. Sjöberg discusses these subjects in his essay.

What is consciousness? If it is more than the firing of an assemblage of neurons in our brain how does it relate to mindfulness? What is the link between mindfulness, well-being and the global commons? These questions are asked in the penultimate essay by Janet McIntyre-Mills. The last essay is about the philosophy, principles and applications of systematic training of self-hypnosis, called Integrated Mental Training (IMT), utilized and studied by the author of the essay, Lars-Eric Uneståhl.

Part I. Physics, Spacetime and Near Death Experiences

Six Protocols, Neuroscience and Near Death
An Emerging Paradigm Incorporating Nonlocal Consciousness

STEPHAN A. SCHWARTZ

It has been more than six decades since Gilbert Ryle, Waynflete Professor of Metaphysical Philosophy at Oxford, coined the phrase "The Ghost in the Machine," in his book *The Concept of the Mind,* as a way of criticizing what he saw as Descartes' absurd mind-body dualism.[1] Since then the nature of consciousness has been largely explored only from the assumption that it was an as yet not understood neurophysiological process entirely resident in the organism. Its inherent physicality became an ironbound axiom. However, a growing body of experimental research now challenges this and a fundamental transition is underway in science. Still a minority position, it is nonetheless the trend direction in a wide range of disciplines, from medicine to biology to physics. Whole new sub-disciplines have emerged driven by the results of this research since Ryle's dismissive words.

This work is pushing toward a new paradigm, one that is neither dualist nor monist, but rather one that postulates consciousness as the fundamental basis of reality. Max Planck, the father of Quantum Mechanics, framed it very clearly in an interview with the respected British newspaper *The Observer* in its January 25, 1931, edition. Context is always important, and Planck understood very well that he was taking a public position, speaking as one of the leading physicists of his generation, through one of Britain's most important papers. He did not mince words: "I regard consciousness as fundamental. I regard matter as derivative from consciousness. We cannot get behind consciousness. Everything that we talk about, everything that we regard as existing, postulates consciousness."[2]

Two corollaries flow from Planck's assertion: First, the existence of Nonlocal Consciousness, an aspect of consciousness independent of space time and not resident in an organism's physiology. Second, that all consciousnesses are interdependent, and interconnected.

One sign of the power of this trend is that most scientists performing research concerning consciousness tend to cite in their papers only work within their own discipline, or a closely related one. Physicists rarely cite physicians, and physicians rarely cite physicists.

As a result separate literatures dealing with consciousness, both local and nonlocal, are developing independent of one another. It is only when seen collectively, however, that the emerging paradigm this research is producing becomes clear, that being a paradigm incorporating Nonlocal Consciousness.

The validation of Planck's perception proceeds on four fronts, which we will discuss below.

The Neurosciences

One group of disciplines focuses on the local mind: the neurosciences, which are concerned with the physiological mechanics of an organism's consciousness. These scientists are often not interested in nonlocal consciousness and, indeed, may believe it could not exist. Yet by pushing forward to the edge of the physical, they have begun to unravel how the nonlocal becomes local in spite of themselves because nonlocal awareness projects itself into the physiology of their consciousness research. Beginning in 2003, and continuing with a shifting list of collaborators, Mark Jung-Beeman has steadily sought to understand the neurobiological process of insight: the aspect of consciousness that solves problems that cannot be worked out with the intellect alone.[3] His studies have yielded many insights, most notably: "We observed two objective neural correlates of insight. Functional magnetic resonance imaging revealed increased activity in the right hemisphere anterior superior temporal gyrus for insight relative to non-insight solutions."[4]

Radiologist Andrew Newberg at the University of Pennsylvania, using standard imaging technologies, focused on monitoring the brain activity of spiritual practitioners as they exercise their practice, scanning the brains of nuns, Sikhs, and Buddhists. His research detected changes in their brains and he reported, "Meditation involves attentional regulation and may lead to increased activity in brain regions associated with attention such as dorsal lateral prefrontal cortex (DLPFC) and anterior cingulate cortex (ACC)."[5] Out of this and other work has arisen the subdiscipline of Neurotheology. It has left Newberg with the view that "it is important to infuse throughout the principles of neurotheology the notion that neurotheology requires an openness to both the scientific as well as the spiritual perspectives."[6]

Taking the physiological to its limits and showing consciousness directly affecting material reality at a distance—nonlocal perturbation—Jeanne Achterberg's therapeutic intention studies show changes in the brain of the recipients towards whom a healer has expressed therapeutic intention. "Each healer selected a person with whom they felt a special connection as a recipient for Therapeutic Intention. Each recipient was placed in the MRI scanner and isolated from all forms of sensory contact from the healer. The healers sent forms of (TI) that related to their own healing practices at random 2-minute intervals that were unknown to the recipient. Significant differences between experimental (send) and control (no send) procedures were found (p = 0.000127). Areas activated during the experimental procedures included the anterior and middle cingulate area, precuneus, and frontal area. It was concluded that instructions to a healer to make an intentional connection with a sensory isolated person can be correlated to changes in brain function of that individual."[7]

At the Division of Nuclear Medicine, Department of Radiology at the University of Pennsylvania, a team led by J.F. Peres, and including Newberg, have explored Nonlocal Perception—the acquisition of information that could not be known by reason of shielding, distance, or time. They "focused on the spiritual experiences involving dissociative states such as mediumship, in which an individual (the medium) claims to be in communication with, or under the control of, the mind of a deceased person," and writes messages."[8] This is what used to be called Automatic Writing, a technique involving nonlocal consciousness that has previously produced well thought of novels and poetry,[9] been used to winning chess games,[10] and in the reconstruction of Glastonbury Abbey.[11]

In the Peres team's protocol they "examined ten healthy psychographers—five less expert mediums and five with substantial experience, ranging from 15 to 47 years of automatic writing and 2 to 18 psychographies per month—using single photon emission computed tomography to scan activity as subjects were writing, in both dissociative trance and non-trance states. The complexity of the original written content they produced was analyzed for each individual and for the sample as a whole. The experienced psychographers showed lower levels of activity in the left culmen, left hippocampus, left inferior occipital gyrus, left anterior cingulate, right superior temporal gyrus and right precentral gyrus during psychography compared to their normal (non-trance) writing."[12]

Quantum Biology

Quantum biology, another new subdiscipline posits: Life is a molecular process; molecular processes operate under quantum rules. Thus, life must be a quantum process. Experimental evidence is beginning to accumulate that this quantum view of life processes is correct. U.C. Berkeley chemist, Gregory S. Engel, led a team that ingeniously found a way to directly detect and observe quantum-level processes within a cell using high-speed lasers.[13]

In early 2012 a team led by Neill Lambert at the Advanced Science Institute, RIKEN, and Yueh-Nan Chen of the Department of Physics and National Center for Theoretical Sciences, National Cheng Kung University in Taiwan, published a meta-analysis review of the Quantum biology literature to that date.

"Before the twentieth century," they wrote, "biology and physics rarely crossed paths. Biological systems were often seen as too complex to be penetrable with mathematical methods. After all, how could a set of differential equations or physical principles shed light on something as complex as a living being? In the early twentieth century, with the advent of more powerful microscopes and techniques, researchers began to delve more deeply into possible physical and mathematical descriptions of microscopic biological systems.... The pace of progress in this field is now rapid, and many branches of physics and mathematics have found applications in biology; from the statistical methods used in bioinformatics, to the mechanical and factory-like properties observed at the microscale within cells."

Their conclusion: "Recent evidence suggests that a variety of organisms may harness some of the unique features of quantum mechanics to gain a biological advantage. These features go beyond trivial quantum effects and may include harnessing quantum coherence on physiologically important timescales."[14]

This work is of enormous importance because it is building step-by-step to the most refined quantum physicality. But even its most ardent exponents recognize it has not given us the fullness of the mind. It has not answered what C.U. Smith of the Vision Sciences Laboratory at Aston University calls the "hard problem"—the neural correlates of consciousness (NCC). Smith examined "the work of prominent modern investigators:

J.C. Eccles/Friedrich Beck; Henry Stapp; Stuart Hameroff/Roger Penrose and David Bohm and their attempts to show where in the brain's microstructure quantum affects could make themselves felt. Smith reluctantly concluded that none have neurobiological plausibility."

Neuroscientists Jeffrey M. Schwartz and Mario Beauregard working with physicist Henry Stapp have also recognized this:

> Neuropsychological research on the neural basis of behavior generally posits that brain mechanisms will ultimately suffice to explain all psychologically described phenomena. This assumption stems from the idea that the brain is made up entirely of material particles and fields, and that all causal mechanisms relevant to neuroscience can therefore be formulated solely in terms of properties of these elements. Thus, terms having intrinsic mentalistic and/or experiential content (e.g. "feeling," "knowing" and "effort") are not included as primary causal factors. *This theoretical restriction is motivated primarily by ideas about the natural world that have been known to be fundamentally incorrect for more than three-quarters of a century* [emphasis added].[15]

In a lecture in 1944, near the end of his life looking back, Planck said, "As a man who has devoted his whole life to the most clear headed science, to the study of matter, I can tell you as a result of my research about atoms this much: There is no matter as such. All matter originates and exists only by virtue of a force which brings the particle of an atom to vibration and holds this most minute solar system of the atom together. We must assume behind this force the existence of a conscious and intelligent mind. This mind is the matrix of all matter."[16]

For Wolfgang Pauli, it was equally straightforward, "It is my personal opinion that in the science of the future reality will neither be 'psychic' nor 'physical' but somehow both and somehow neither."[17]

In the next generation of physicists, Oliver Costa de Beauregard observed, "Today's physics allows for the existence of so-called 'paranormal' phenomena.... The whole concept of 'non-locality' in contemporary physics requires this possibility."[18]

Einstein himself, who understood that every word he said or wrote would be viewed as historic, had no problem writing, "A human being is a part of the whole, called by us 'Universe,' a part limited in time and space. He experiences himself, his thoughts and feelings as something separated from the rest a kind of optical delusion of his consciousness. This delusion is a kind of prison for us, restricting us to our personal desires and to affection for a few persons nearest to us. Our task must be to free ourselves from this prison by widening our circle of compassion to embrace all living creatures and the whole of nature in its beauty. Nobody is able to achieve this completely, but the striving for such achievement is in itself a part of the liberation and a foundation for inner security."[19]

Researchers have begun to explicitly consider how the nonlocal becomes local. Frecska and Luna, of the National Institute for Psychiatry and Neurology in Budapest, present a neuro-ontological interpretation of spiritual experiences: The prevailing neuroscientific paradigm considers information processing within the central nervous system as occurring through hierarchically organized and interconnected neural networks. The hierarchy of neural networks doesn't end at the neuroaxonal level; it incorporates subcellular mechanisms as well. When the size of the hierarchical components reaches the nanometer range and the number of elements exceeds that of the neuroaxonal system, an interface emerges for a possible transition between neurochemical and quantum physical events. "Signal nonlocality," accessed by means of quantum entanglement, is an essential feature of the quantum physical domain. The presented interface may imply that some manifestations of altered states of consciousness, unconscious/conscious shifts have quantum origin with significant psychosomatic implications.[20]

Nonlocal Consciousness Research

The third front exploring Planck's assertion is work that explicitly studies nonlocal consciousness through experimentation. These studies fall basically into two categories: Nonlocal Perception, the acquisition of information that could not be known through psychological sense perception, and Nonlocal Perturbation, consciousness directly affecting matter, including therapeutic intention/healing.

Today there are six stabilized parapsychological protocols used in laboratories around the world exploring these two categories of phenomena. Under rigorous double or triple blind, randomized and tightly controlled conditions, each of these six has independently produced six sigma results. Six sigma is one in a billion—1,009,976,678—or the 99.9999990699 percentile.

These six protocols each has its own literature. The results of all these studies are based on the sessions being double or triple blind and properly randomized, and that a pre- agreed analysis, including statistical evaluation for variance from chance, be part of the process. That is, we don't need to get bogged down in antiquated arguments about sleight-of-hand, secret cuing, and the like, although this remains a staple of nonlocal consciousness research criticism. This kind of criticism stopped being apposite several decades ago. As far back as the mid–90s, after studying the data from just one of these four protocols, remote viewing, stalwart denier University of Oregon psychology professor Ray Hyman had to grudgingly admit, "…the experiments [being assessed] were free of the methodological weaknesses that plagued the early … research … the … experiments appear to be free of the more obvious and better known flaws that can invalidate the results of parapsychological investigations. We agree that the effect sizes reported … are too large and consistent to be dismissed as statistical flukes."[21]

In each case there is also a large enough body of research from enough different institutions, done by enough researchers that we have some idea of the process and how successful it can be. The studies, as I have noted, break down into two categories: Nonlocal Perception, and Nonlocal Perturbation.

Nonlocal Perception

Remote Viewing

A double or triple blind protocol in which a participant is given a task that can only be accomplished through nonlocal perception, the acquisition of information that could not be known with the normal physiological senses because of shielding by time or space or both. Sitting in a room 2,000 miles away, in answer to the question, "Please describe the current circumstances and conditions of the target couple, you couldn't know they were, at that moment standing beneath a waterfalls in the mountains of Colombia standing next to the water surrounded by greenery, watching two flying parrots. But nonlocal perception can and has provided just such information many thousands of times under conditions that even skeptics have had to acknowledge are impeccable.[22]

Ganzfeld

A protocol similar in intent to remote viewing in which an individual in a state of sensory deprivation provides verifiable information about film clips being shown at another location.[23]

Presentiment

A measurable psychophysical response that occurs before actual stimulation, such as the dilation of a participant's pupils while staring at monitor screen before the pictures appears.[24] Or, it is a change in brain function before a noise is heard.[25]

Retrocognition/Recognition

Many protocols also involve time dislocation to the past or future to be successful. It is routine today to do remote viewing experiments in which the session data is collected and judged against a randomly chosen target set before the target in that set is randomly selected.

In 2011, Italian experimental psychologist Patrizio Tressoldi, of the University of Padova, a scientist of the next generation too young to be involved with the remote viewing or Ganzfeld work of the 1960s through 2000, went back through all of the nonlocal perception research, both Ganzfeld and remote viewing, as well as anticipatory studies analyzing the data using both classical and Bayesian statistics. He stated explicitly that he accepted the famous phrase "extraordinary claims require extraordinary evidence," often attributed to Carl Sagan but probably coined by University of Michigan sociologist Marcello Truzz.[26] Tressoldi said the aim of his study was to "present a quantitative review of the evidence which is: mind may have non-local properties, that is, that some of its functions i.e. perceptual abilities may extend beyond its local functions, and beyond the space and time constraints of sensory organs. This quantitative review will be presented using both a classical frequentist and a new Bayesian meta-analytic approach."[27] His results can be seen in the tables below.

Table 1

Meta-analysis	N. studies	N.participants	Fixed ES (0.95 CI)	Z	Random ES (0.95 CI)	Z	Bayes factor (H1/H0, 2-tailed)	File drawer effect
Ganzfeld[1]	108	3650	0.12 (0.11-0.14)	19.36	0.13 (0.09-0.17)	6.39	18861051*	357§
ASC[1]	16	427	0.12 (0.09-0.15)	8.63	0.11 (0.03-0.19)	2.86	0.04764247	13§
Anticipatory responses[2]	26	890	0.21 (0.15-0.27)	8.7	0.21 (0.13-0.29)	5.3	$2.891308e^{+13}$	87#
Normal SC[1] (free response)	14	1026	-0.015 (-0.03-0.005)	-1.48	-0.03 (-0.06-0.002)	-1.84	0.02924606	-
Normal SC[3] (forced choice)	72	69726	0.007 (0.006-0.007)	16.2	0.011 (0.006-0.015)	4.88	0.003162905*	187§

[1]Storm et al. 2010[2];Mossbridge et al., 2012[3]; Storm et al., 2012; *one study excluded because N participants = 1; §Darlington and Hayes's (2000) formula; #Orwin's (1983) fail-safe N.   From Tressoldi

Table 2

Meta-analysis	N. studies	N.participants	Fixed ES (0.95 CI)	Z*	Bayes factor (H1/H0, 2-tailed)	File drawer effect
Dunne and Jahn (2003)	Not defined	366	0.34 (0.19-0.49)	6.3	25424503838	849**
Milton (1997)	78	1158	0.16 (0.10-0.22)	5.7		866**

*Stouffer $Z = \Sigma z/\sqrt{\text{Number of studies}}$; **Rosenthal's fail-safe N   From Tressoldi

Nonlocal Perturbation

Random Event/Number Generator (REG/RNG) Influence

The REG protocol is actually two major protocols. The first constitutes studies in labs where an individual intends to affect the performance of a physical system, such as a random number generator.[28]

Global Consciousness Project

The second is the Global Consciousness Project (GCP). Psychologist Roger Nelson of the Princeton Engineering Anomalies Research group studied the individual data coming out of the PEAR studies and understood the implication. Looking at the individual results in his lab he asked: Might it be possible that a mass of people having an individual but linked experience, some major highly emotional world event, could collectively produce a nonlocal perturbation effect?

To answer the question he designed and set up a worldwide constantly running coordinated network of computer-linked random number renerators (RNGs). If there were indeed non-random patterning he would have a measure of social awareness. Consciousness linked nonlocally expressing itself as a social awareness. And watching the data from events like the death of Princess Diana, the Japanese tsunami, or Nelson Mandela's funeral, that's what he saw.

Nelson describes it this way: "Subtle interactions link us with each other and the Earth. When human consciousness becomes coherent and synchronized, the behavior of random systems may change. Quantum event based random number generators (RNGs) produce completely unpredictable sequences of zeroes and ones. But when a great event synchronizes the feelings of millions of people, our network of RNGs becomes subtly structured. The probability is less than one in a billion that the effect is due to chance. The evidence suggests an emerging noosphere, or the unifying field of consciousness described by sages in all cultures. Coherent consciousness creates order in the world."[29,30]

I am giving a slightly expanded description of this project compared with the others because it represents a new stage in nonlocal consciousness research. Whether neuroscience or parapsychology, most protocols address only the functioning of individuals. The Global Consciousness Project extends individual change in consciousness to its nonlocal social level demonstrating its interlinkage and interdependence.

The GCP data is cumulative and publicly available. It lists hundreds of events in which an hypothesis predicting an event has been advanced and the subsequent results: Significant, Predicted Direction, Opposite, and Opposite and Significant. The most recent event was the death of Nelson Mandela. The data records the timeframe; the hypothesis source; the number of REGs recording it; the Z-score; and the probability. For Mandela, that was: 2013/12/05; many people hypothesize; 45 REGs reporting; a Z-score of 2.238; and a probability of 0.013. From the GCP website:

> The two following figures represent the history of our formal hypothesis testing. The first shows the Z-scores for more than 459 formally specified events in an ordinary scatterplot. While there is a noticeable positive bias, it is not easy to see its significance. Yet the odds against chance of this meanshift over a database this size are about a hundred billion to one.
> The second figure displays the same data as a cumulative deviation from chance expecta-

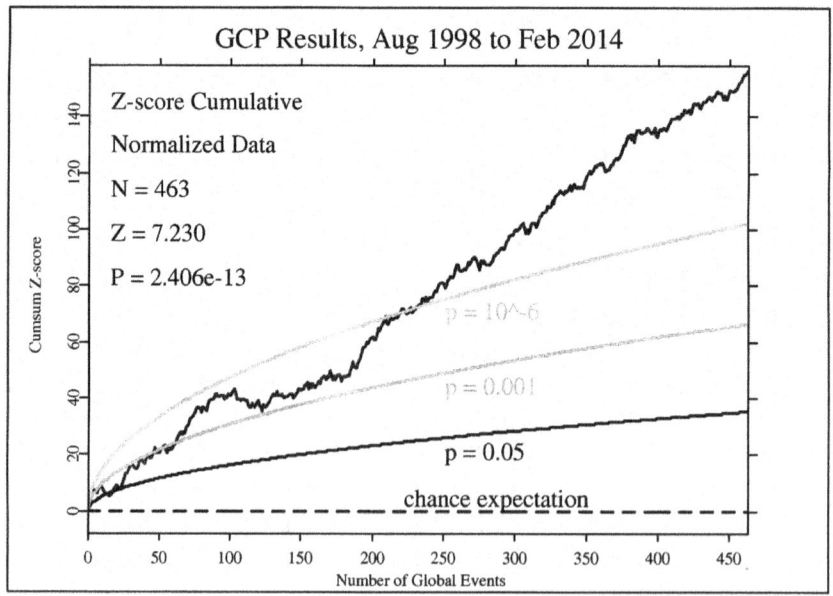

tion (shown as the horizontal black line at 0 deviation). Truly random data would produce a jagged curve with no slope, wandering up and down around the horizontal. The dotted smooth curves show the 0.05 and 0.001 and 0.000001 probability envelopes that indicate significant versus chance excursions. This figure can be compared with a "*control distribution*" using simulations of the event series.

The jagged red line shows the accumulating excess of the empirically normalized Z-scores relative to expectation for the complete dataset of rigorously defined events. The overall result is highly significant. The odds against chance are much greater than a million to one.[31]

A seventh protocol has also reached this level, although the results, at this stage, are still subject to differing interpretations:

STARING

A physiological response evoked by being the target of focused awareness.[32]

Since these protocols have the same fundamental methodology and collectively seek to study nonlocal consciousness, I believe they are best understood as one body of research.

To give some context: the six sigma effect each of these protocols has demonstrated is considerably more powerful than that of 81 milligram aspirin regimes that constitute a foundation of hypertensive disease treatment. If you are middle-aged, or older, and particularly if you are a man, you may well be taking an 81-miligram tablet every day— one of more than 40 million Americans. Jessica Utts, Chairman and professor of statistics at University of California, Irvine, decided to explore just exactly what the difference was between the "aspirin" effect and that achieved in nonlocal research. Her study compared databases from two protocols, remote viewing and Ganzfeld, against the aspirin database. Writing in the *Journal of Scientific Exploration* she said:

> In summary, how are the remote viewing and Ganzfeld results different from the antiplatelet and vascular disease conclusions?
> - The psi experiments produced stronger results than the antiplatelet experiments, in terms of the magnitude of the effect. There is a 36 percent increase in the probability of a (result) over chance, from 25 percent to 34 percent. There is a 25 percent reduction in the probability of a vascular problem after taking antiplatelets.
> - The antiplatelet studies had more opportunity for fraud and experimenter effects than did the psi experiments.
> - The antiplatelet studies were at least as likely to be funded and conducted by those with a vested interest in the outcome as were the psi experiments.
> - In both cases, the experiments were heterogeneous in terms of experimental methods and characteristics of the participants.

All of this leads to one interesting question: Why are millions of heart attack and stroke patients consuming antiplatelets on a regular basis, while the results of the psi experiments are only marginally known and acknowledged by the scientific community? The answer may have many aspects, but surely it does not lie in the statistical methods.[33]

Near Death Experience Research

The fourth research area is the study of Near Death Experiences (NDEs.) These often deeply moving experiences have emerged as a field of study incorporating both neuroscience, and laboratory clinical protocols.

NDEs have been explicitly reported—no interpretive analysis required—at least as far back as the fourth century BCE. In the tenth book of his *Republic*, Plato tells the story of "Er the son of Armenius, a Pamphylian by birth. He was slain in battle, and ten days afterwards, when the bodies of the dead were taken up already in a state of corruption, his body was found unaffected by decay, and carried away home to be buried. And on the twelfth day, as he was lying on the funeral pile, he returned to life and told them what he had seen in the other world. He said that when his soul left the body he went on a journey with a great company...."[34]

Since Er, there have been so many published accounts of near death experiences that they constitute an independent literature numbering into the thousands of titles. But as large as that number has become, it is just the medical literature's manifestation of a deeper point: Recent well-conducted studies reveal that about 4.2 percent of the American public has reported a near death experience. The population in the U.S. is a bit more than 315 million. So over 13 million people have reported having an NDE. To give that context, it is equivalent to all the Jewish people, all the Mormons, and Muslims as well, and most of the Buddhists, and that is likely but a fraction of it. The near death experiencer population is almost certainly much larger than 13 million because research has also revealed many people do not immediately report experiences. Often they don't speak of it at all until years or decades later, which is a problem for researchers, and why prospective studies, such as that of Dutch cardiologist Pim van Lommel published in the *Lancet* (2001), are so important.[35]

Experiencers initially often keep quiet for fear of being ridiculed, or embarrassed. As one experiencer noted, "I couldn't talk about it, or I would have been committed to an institution."[36] Cherie Sutherland, a visiting research fellow in the School of Sociology at the University of New South Wales, a near death experiencer herself, did a study which showed that "when people tried to discuss the NDE, 50 percent of the relatives and 25 percent of friends rejected the NDE, and 30 percent of nursing staff, 85 percent of doctors, and 50 percent of psychiatrists reacted negatively."[37]

Van Lommel tells this wonderful story to illustrate the dynamic in play: At an academic conference on NDEs a few years ago a respected cardiologist stood up and said, "I've worked as a cardiologist for 25 years now, and I've never come across such absurd stories in my practice. I think this is complete nonsense; I don't believe a word of it."

Whereupon, another man stood up and said, "I'm one of your patients. A couple of years ago I survived a cardiac arrest and had an NDE, and you would be the last person I'd ever tell."[38]

Even when they do speak, experiencers often don't quite know what to say. Based on hundreds of reports, it is easy to see that the experience is so powerful and often so foreign to the experiencer's view of reality, that it takes many years of inner processing to fully come to terms with what happens to them. "It had such a profound effect on the rest of my life: the timelessness that I experienced; the knowledge that my consciousness will survive outside my body. It was enough to destabilize my life."[39]

Two things have happened in medicine that makes it clear this area of research is going to grow. First, clinical practice in hospitals around the world has been sensitized to near death experiences so more are being recorded. Second, near death experiencers will increase in number thanks to increasingly sophisticated acute care medicine and cardiopulmonary resuscitation. And the growing number of survivors will produce social pressure to understand what death is. This is already what makes books on the subject bestsellers.

University of Virginia Division of Perceptional Studies researchers, Ed and Emily Kelly sum it up this way:

> the central challenge of NDEs lies in asking how these complex states of consciousness, including vivid mentation, sensory perception, and memory, can occur under conditions in which current neurophysiological models of the production of mind by brain deem such states impossible. This conflict between current neuroscientific orthodoxy and the occurrence of NDEs under conditions of general anesthesia and/or cardiac arrest is head-on, profound, and inescapable. In our opinion, no further scientific or philosophic discussion of the mind-brain problem can be fully responsible, intellectually, without taking these challenging data into account.[40]

Director of Perceptual Studies Bruce Greyson, who is also the Carlson Professor of Psychiatry & Neurobehavioral Sciences at UVA, has been researching NDEs for decades, and it has left him with this:

> A close examination of NDE research trends strongly suggests, as I have noted, that near death experiencers are growing in number thanks to evermore sophisticated acute care medicine and cardiopulmonary resuscitation; and that with medical staffs in hospitals around the world increasingly sensitized to NDEs, more are being recorded; and, more are occurring under highly controlled and monitored circumstances. One would assume that if NDEs were just a neurophysiological phenomenon this close control and scrutiny would result in the emergence of an explanatory materialistic model of these events incorporating, as Greyson et al. noted, "all relevant data, not just data supporting the a priori assumption that NDEs must be reducible to known neurophysiology.[41]

Such has not been the case.

NDEs are not double-blind randomized experiments in the same way a remote viewing experiment or a presentiment study is, although they can be prospective. They have, however, something very important to say that extends our understanding of the nonlocal domain. If NDEs cannot be explained entirely by physiology because the brain is not functioning at all, or sufficiently to account for the sensorial and cognitive awareness that occurs, then it explicitly requires nonlocal consciousness. What is the source of the information experiencers bring back? What accesses it? Both the six protocols and NDEs invoke nonlocal consciousness, but only NDEs do so with a clinically dead brain. Treating both streams of research collectively enriches both, and allows the nature of the NDEs to be assessed in the context of, and benefiting from, the insights derived from the six sigma laboratory protocols I have already described.

Conclusion—Two Models

At present, models of consciousness can essentially be subdivided into two distinct broad categories. Models of the first type are physicalist models holding all consciousness as being contained within an organism's neuroanatomy. Models of the second type are nonlocal models, historically conceived of as esoteric/spiritual/or religious, and distinguished by the assumption that a significant aspect of consciousness is not limited to the neuroanatomy, hence nonlocal.

Physicalist models assume the causality principle, use standard logic, and are based on high-quality reproducible experimental data. These models typically offer a plausible mechanism to account for the data. They basically follow the Cartesian analytic method and hold the view that science by deconstructing and analyzing a problem into simple parts that can be considered individually and, then, re-assembled to yield an understanding of the integrated whole. In essence, this mechanistic approach implies that consciousness is nothing but biological processes. Obviously all of this lies within the space-time domain.

The models of the second type, universal to almost all human cultures, are by their nature holistic and non-reductionist. They all include the idea that the whole is more than the sum of its physical parts, and that consciousness encompasses more than can be explained by space-time. These models also universally recognize that understanding this aspect of consciousness requires both analysis and direct experience. In describing their experiences individuals persistently talk about "timeless-time" and "spaceless-space" in describing their experiences.

When we look at *both* classes of models a number of salient questions arise:

- Is there a reality behind each of these two classes of models of consciousness?
- Are these two realities distinct and separate from each other or do they overlap?
- Is it possible to use our standard scientific method to develop models that account for the second "non-scientific" transcendent reality as well?
- What would be an appropriate scientific methodology that would allow one to start developing such a unified theoretical model?

Kuhn, who coined the term paradigm recognized that paradigms can and should change because eventually they simply fail to explain observed phenomena. Eventually anomalies accumulate that the paradigm cannot encompass, and these inadequacies force the paradigm into crisis. Kuhn saw this process of change as revolutionary not evolutionary saying, "Successive transition from one paradigm to another via revolution is the usual developmental pattern of mature science."[42]

In fact, he saw it changing for precisely the reasons I have discussed. He notes, "No ordinary sense of the term 'interpretation' fits these flashes of intuition through which a new paradigm is born. *Though such intuitions depend upon the experience, both anomalous and congruent, gained with the old paradigm, they are not logically or piecemeal linked to particular items of that experience as an interpretation would be* [emphasis added.]"[43] He goes on to say, "Scientists then often speak of the 'scales calling from the eyes' or of the 'lightning flash.'"[44]

It is one of the great ironies of science that its heroes are not just revolutionaries because of the quality of their insights. They are also revolutionaries because of the source, mechanism unknown, from which their information derives. At the deepest level the process by which the information is obtained is as revolutionary as the information itself.

John Mihalasky invokes intuition as an overt explanation, but tentatively,[45] and Kuhn notes only that it represents a change in gestalt, a change in "beingness." "Normal science," he says, "ultimately leads only to the recognition of anomalies and to crises. And these are terminated not by deliberation and interpretation, but by a relatively sudden and unstructured event like a gestalt switch." Scientists, Kuhn states, then often speak of the "scales falling from my eyes" or of the "lightning flash" that "inundates" a previously obscure puzzle, enabling its components to be seen in a new way that for the first time permits its solution." To someone interested in the field of nonlocal informational interactions this wording is virtually identical to that used by healers, remote viewers, spiritual pilgrims, and great artists.

It is not easy to become an historical figure of global and lasting proportions; even presidents and popes are forgotten in time. A notable percentage of the singular people who do reach this plateau describe their contribution as deriving from an experience of an altered state of consciousness, one of whose hallmarks is a sense of connection with a greater whole and a timeless spaceless awareness.

The Indian mathematician Srinivasa Ramanujan, with almost no formal training, produced insights into the nature of numbers of such profundity that pure mathematicians still work to understand them nearly a century after his death. These moments of genius, came to him, as Robert Kanigel explains, "It was the goddess Namagiri, [Ramanujan] would tell friends, to whom he owed his mathematical gifts. Namagiri would write the equations on his tongue. Namagiri would bestow mathematical insights in his dreams."[46]

Perhaps the most ironic example of dreams as a part of the pattern is the account of René Descartes. On Saint Martin's eve (November 10th) 1619, in Neuberg, Germany, he had an experience which led to what he called "a wonderful discovery."[47] From it he formulated "a marvelous science," a world view whose hallmark was its commitment to the primacy of the intellect; a view which has dominated how technological cultures have thought about the world ever since. What was this wondrous experience? It was that most non-intellectual of events: a series of three dreams.

And here is Johannes Brahms speaking of his state of consciousness while composing:

> In this exalted state I see clearly what is obscure in my ordinary moods; then I feel capable of drawing inspiration from above as Beethoven did.... Those vibrations assume the form of distinct mental images.... Straightaway the ideas flow in upon me ... and not only do I see distinct themes in the mind's eye, but they are clothed in the right forms, harmonies, and orchestration. Measure by measure the finished product is revealed to me when I am in those rare inspired moods.... I have to be in a semi-trance condition to get such results—a condition when the conscious mind is in temporary abeyance, and the subconscious is in control, for it is through the subconscious mind, which is part of the Omnipotence that the inspiration comes.[48]

Compare that with the autobiographies and biographies of saints such as St. John, St. Francis, and St. Teresa. They are filled with passages that sound much like Brahms or the experiences of remote viewers. Often, as in the case of the Virgin Eustochium of Padua (1469 CE), the linkage with the nonlocal is explicit: She "showed in her childhood signs of being beset by certain influences of a strongly poltergeist type."[49] And like the reports from geniuses and remote viewers, the accounts of saints again stress a sense of connection with something other than oneself. Of Beatrice of Ornacieu (c. 1309 CE) it was reported "As we are accustomed to find in mystics who have many visions and other sensible communications with the unseen...."[50]

One can see the obvious similarities in these descriptions. We know them as moments of genius, religious epiphany, psychic insight, or near death experiences. Many are the source of historic change, and they have a fundamental unity: the experience of nonlocal consciousness, modulated by intention and context. Two hundred years of reductive materialism has failed to explain them. They do, however, become comprehensible once nonlocal consciousness is recognized.

Based on the research being carried out across the spectrum of the sciences, I believe there are four relevant descriptors helping to define what the new paradigm might look like. They are:

1. Only certain aspects of the mind are the result of physiologic processes.
2. Consciousness is causal, and physical reality is its manifestation.
3. All consciousnesses, regardless of their physical manifestations, are part of a network of life which they both inform and influence and are informed and influenced by; there is a passage back and forth between the individual and the collective.
4. Some aspects of consciousness are not limited by the space time continuum, and do not originate entirely within an organism's neuroanatomy.

Two papers from the European Organization for Nuclear Research (CERN), one of the world's largest and most respected centers for scientific research, have recently been published. Each is roughly 30 pages in length. Nineteen of those pages are the single-spaced list of approximately 6,000 names—the researchers who support the findings of the CERN experiments. The papers conclude there is a one-in–300-million chance that the Higgs Boson does not exist, thereby validating the theory on why elementary particles have mass. It is by this collective assessment that the elusive Higgs Boson has been recognized as real.

Given the levels of evidence, how is this disparity possible between the reception of the Higgs Boson discovery compared with nonlocal consciousness research? The short answer, I think, is that we are seeing a demonstration of how culturally mediated science is. The Higgs Boson discovery is based on a less than a six sigma result yet, because it confirms a theoretical prediction and pretty seamlessly fits into established physics it is accepted. In contrast the nonlocal consciousness research with results better than six sigma, because we do not yet have a satisfactory explanation as to how these phenomena happen, is not. The objection is fundamentally cultural, not scientific. For all that the data will not be denied forever, and a new paradigm is emerging.

NOTES

1. Ryle, G. *The Concept of the Mind*. Oxford: Hutchinson Edition: Oxford University Press, 1963.
2. Interview with Max Planck. *The Observer*. January 25, 1931.
3. Bowden, E.M., Jung-Beeman, M. Aha! Insight experience correlates with solution activation in the right hemisphere. *Psychon Bull* Rev. 2003 Sep; 10(3):730–7. PMID: 14620371.
4. Jung-Beeman, M., Bowden, E.M., Haberman J., Frymiare, J.L., Arambel-Liu, S., Greenblatt, R., Reber, P.J., Kounios, J. Free in PMC Neural activity when people solve verbal problems with insight. PLoS Biol. 2004 Apr; 2(4):E97. Epub 2004 Apr 13. PMID: 15094802.
5. Baron Short, E., Kose, S., Mu, Q., Borckardt, J., Newberg, A., George, M.S., Kozel, F.A. Regional brain activation during meditation shows time and practice effects: an exploratory FMRI study. Evid Based Complement Alternat Med. 2010 Mar; 7(1):121–7. doi: 10.1093/ecam/nem163. Epub 2007 Dec 27. PMID: 18955268 [PubMed].
6. Newberg, A. *Principles of Neurotheology*. Burlington, VT: Ashgate, 2010.

7. Achterberg, J., Cooke, K., Richards, T., Standish, L.J., Kozak, L., Lake, J. Evidence for correlations between distant intentionality and brain function in recipients: a functional magnetic resonance imaging analysis. J Altern Complement Med. 2005 Dec; 11(6):965–71. PMID:16398587.

8. Peres, J.F., Moreira-Almeida, A., Caixeta, L., Leao, F., Newberg, A. Neuroimaging during trance state: a contribution to the study of dissociation. PLoS One. 2012; 7(11):e49360. doi: 10.1371/journal.pone. 0049360. Epub 2012 Nov 16.

9. Braude, S. Immortal remains: the evidence for life after death. Lanham, Md.: Rowman & Littlefield, c2003.

10. Neppe, V.M. A detailed analysis of an important chess game: Revisiting "Maróczy versus Korchnoi." *Journal Soc. Psychical Research*, 2007, 71:3, 129–147.

11. Eisenbeiss, W., Hassler, D. An assessment of ostensible communications with a grandmaster as evidence for survival. *Journal Soc. Psychical Research*, 2006, 70:2, 129–147.

12. Schwartz, S. *The Secret Vaults of Time*. New York: Grosset, 1978, pp. 1–56.

13. Panitchayangkoon, G., Hayes, D., Fransted, K.A., Caram, J.R., Harel, E., Wen, J., Blankenship R.E., Engel G.S. Long-lived coherence in photosynthetic complexes at physiological temperature. Proc Natl Acad Sci USA. 2010 Jul 20; 107(29):12766–70. doi: 10.1073/pnas.1005484107. Epub 2010 Jul 6. PMID: 20615985.

14. Lambert, Neill, Chen, Yueh-Nan, Cheng, Yuan-Chung, Li, Che-Ming, Chen, Guang-Yin, Nori, Franco. Quantum biology. *Nature Physics* 9:10–18 (2013. doi:10.1038/nphys2474). 09 December 2012.

15. Schwartz, J.M., Stapp, H.P., & Beauregard, M. (2005). Quantum physics in neuroscience and psychology: A neurophysical model of mind-brain interaction. *Philos Trans R Soc Long B Biol Sci*, 360(1458), 1309–1327.

16. Planck, M. "Das Wesen der Materie" Florence, Italy (1944). *Archiv zur Geschichte der Max-Planck-Gesellschaft*, Abt. Va, Rep. 11 Planck, Nr. 1797.

17. Pais, A., & Pauli, W.E. (2000). *The genius of science*. Oxford, England: Oxford University Press.

18. *De Beauregard O.C. The paranormal is not excluded from physics. J Sci Exploration. 1998; 12:315–320.*

19. Einstein, A. Letter dated 1950, quoted in H. Eves Mathematical Circles Adieu, Boston: Prindle, Weber and Schmidt, 1977.

20. Freska, E., & Luna, L.E. (2006). Neuro-ontological interpretation of spiritual experiences. *Neuropsychopharmacol Hung*, 8(3), pp. 143–153.

21. Hyman, R. (1995). Evaluation of program on "anomalous mental phenomena." In M.D. Mumford, A.M. Rose, & D.A. Goslin (Eds.), An evaluation of remote viewing: Research and applications. Chptr 3, pp. 62–96. Washington, D.C.: The American Institutes for Research (AIR). Retrieved from www.lfr.org/LFR/csl/library/AirReport.pdf. Accessed: 10 August 2012.

22. Tressoldi, P.E. (2011) Extraordinary claims require extraordinary evidence: the case of non-local perception, a classical and Bayesian review of evidences. *Frontiers in Psychology*, 2:117. doi: 10.3389/fpsyg. 2011.00117.

23. Williams, B.J. (2011). Revisiting the Ganzfeld ESP Debate: A Basic Review and Assessment. *Journal of Scientific Exploration*, 25, 4, 639–661.

24. Radin, D. Electrodermal Presentiments of Future Emotions. *Journal of Scientific Exploration*. 18:2:253–273.

25. Mossbridge, J., Tressoldi, P.E. and Utts, J. (2012). Predictive physiological anticipation preceding seemingly unpredictable stimuli: a meta-analysis. *Frontiers in Psychology* 3:390. doi: 10.3389/fpsyg.2012. 00390.

26. Truzzi, M. An extraordinary claim requires extraordinary proof. On the Extraordinary: An Attempt at Clarification, Zetetic Scholar, Vol. 1, No. 1, p. 11, 1978.

27. Tressoldi, P. Extraordinary Claims Require Extraordinary Evidence: The Case of Non Local Perception, a Classical and Bayesian Review of Evidences. *Frontiers in Psychology*. 10 February 2011, pp. 1–10.

28. Bösch, H., Steinkamp, F., Boller, E. (2006). Examining psychokinesis: The interaction of human intention with random number generators—A meta-analysis. *Psychological Bulletin*, 132, 497–523.

29. Nelson, R.D., Radin, D.I., Shoup, R., Bancel, P.A. Correlations of Continuous Random Data with Major World Events. *Found Phys Letters* 2002; 15:537–550.

30. Nelson, R. and Bancel, P. (2011). Effects of mass consciousness: changes in random data during global events. Explore, 7:373–383.

31. Global Consciousness Project. Formal Results: Testing the GCP Hypothesis. http://teilhard.global-mind.org/results.html#alldata. Accessed: 27 December 2013.
32. Schmidt, S., Schneider, R., Utts, J.M., et al. (2004). Distant intentionality and the feeling of being stared at: Two meta-analyses. *British Journal of Psychology*, 95:235–247.
33. Utts, J. The Significance of Statistics in Mind-Matter Research. *Journal of Scientific Exploration*. 1999. 13:4:615–638.
34. Plato. Republic X,614 b,c,d.
35. van Lommel, P., van Wees, R., Meyers, V., Elfferich, I. Near-death experience in survivors of cardiac arrest: a prospective study in the Netherlands. *Lancet* 2001; 358: 2039–45. *See Commentary page 2010.*
36. Van Lommel. p. 62.
37. Sutherland, C. Transformed by the Light: Life after a near death experiences. Random House Australia.
38. Van Lommel, p. xxx.
39. Van Lommel, p. 47.
40. Kelly, E. and Kelly, E., Crabtree, A., Gauld, A., Grosso, M., and Greyson, B. *Irreducible Mind*. Rowman & Littlefield: U.S. & UK, 2007.
41. Greyson, B. The Psychology of Near-Death Experiences and Spirituality chptr. 33 in *The Oxford Handbook of Psychology and Spirituality* ed. Lisa Miller Oxford: Oxford University Press, 2012, pp. 514–527.
42. Kuhn, p. 12.
43. Kuhn, p. 122.
44. Kuhn, p. 121.
45. Mihalasky, J. ESP: Can It Play a Role in Idea-Generation? *Mechanical Engineering*, Dec. 1972.
46. Kanigel, R. *The Man Who Knew Infinity*. New York: Washington Square Press, 1992; p. 36.
47. Adams, C., and Tannery, P. Oeuvres de Descartes. *(Vie de Descartes. vol. XII)*.
48. Abell, A.M. Talks with the Great Composers. G.E. Schroeder-Verlag: Garmisch-Parten-Kirchen, 1964, pp. 19–21.
49. Butler's Lives of Saints. Edited by xx, p. 325 (xxxx).
50. Ibid., p. 324.

Bibliography

Braude S. *Immortal remains: the evidence for life after death*. Lanham, MD: Rowman & Littlefield, c2003.
Einstein, A. Letter dated 1950, quoted in H. Eves *Mathematical Circles Adieu*. Boston: Prindle, Weber and Schmidt, 1977.
Kelly, E., A. Crabtree, A. Gauld, M. Grosso, and B. Greyson. *Irreducible Mind*. Lanham, MD: Rowman & Littlefield, 2007.
Newberg A. *Principles of Neurotheology*. Burlington, VT: Ashgate, 2010.
Pais, A., and W.E. Pauli (2000). *The Genius of Science*. Oxford, England: Oxford.
Ryle, G. *The Concept of the Mind*. Oxford: Hutchinson Edition: Oxford University Press, 1963.
Truzzi, M. An extraordinary claim requires extraordinary proof. On the Extraordinary: An Attempt at Clarification, *Zetetic Scholar*, Vol. 1, No. 1. University Press 1978.

Conscious Spacetime
An Outline to Experiential Monism

Jan Pilotti

The evolution of physics led to the important discovery of spacetime in Einstein's theory of Special Relativity and to the problems of determinism vs. chance, particle or wave and non-reality vs. non-locality in Quantum Mechanics. Relativity and QM are not easily unified. The mind-brain problem is still unsolved. A unified possible view is to take consciousness as fundamental besides matter and energy and beyond brain. Consciousness, phenomenal properties, are described in an extension of special relativity to a six-dimensional spacetime, three space and three time dimensions, which also supports a realistic interpretation of quantum mechanics.

Theoretical Physics and Some Crucial Experiments

Classical Physics

The word physics comes from Greek *physis*, nature, and the Greeks speculated about what they experienced in nature. They theorized about the world consisting of four elements and sometimes a fifth Aether[1] or, as Democritus, of atoms, indivisible small parts. Their concept of causes was in the Aristotelian four types of causes (including the final cause), more elaborated yet speculative as not based on experiments. The concept of force was based on the observation that material objects stopped quickly if not some "force" forced them to continue to move.

With Galileo Galilei (1564–1642) the experimental method was introduced as a basis for our knowledge about Nature. However thinking and interpretation of experiments was and still is necessary. As for example when Galilei formulated the modern concept of force as related not to velocity but to change in velocity, acceleration. This seems to contradict direct experience as objects stop, but in an idealized situation without friction the object will continue its movement without the need of any force. This is a way to define force, which led to a mathematically useful theory when Isaac Newton (1642–1727) formulated the laws of motion. But as Einstein clearly states, "this law of inertia cannot be derived directly from experiment, but only by speculative thinking consistent with observation."[2]

Newtonian Mechanics

Newton also formulated the law of universal gravitation $F_g = G\frac{Mm}{d^2}$ describing the forces F_g between any material bodies with masses M resp. m at distance d.

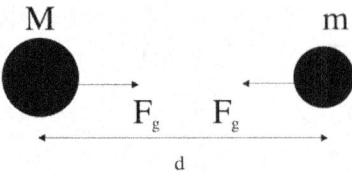

This together with his laws of motion, e.g., F= m·a (a=acceleration) made it possible in 1680s to describe and predict the fall of the apple, the tidewaters, the movements of the moon around the earth and the planets around the sun and sun and moon eclipses. This theory is very accurate and powerful and the theory could even predict where to find a new planet, Neptune.

With this Newtonian classical mechanics the movements of bodies or particles could be described in detail. If the masses, positions and velocities of all particles were known as initial data together with all the forces acting on the particles all their history and all their future movements could be exactly calculated in principle. This is the mathematical root to the statement that Newtonian mechanics is deterministic, that is the history and acting forces already determine all future movements.

Particles in Space and Time

Particles can most easily be visualized as small billiard balls. They follow a straight path if no forces act on them and they bounce with predictable results when they hit a wall or another object.

To describe the location of a particle we need three numbers, three space coordinates (x, y, z), related to our worlds three-dimensional space with length, breadth and height. An event is what happens where and when, so we also need time t as the fourth coordinate, e.g., the meeting of two particles at (x, y, z, t).

We can use different coordinate systems or frames for the description of particles and their movements but it is easy to translate the measurements done by observers in different frames. If frame S' (x,' y,' z') moves with velocity v along the x-axes in frame S (x, y, z) the relations between the space coordinates (x, y, z) resp. (x, y, z') for a particle measured in the two different frames are mathematically described by the Galilean transformation (GT) x = x'+ vt y=y' z=z' which also includes t=t'. Thus also x'= x-vt.

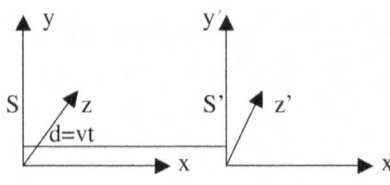

That t=t,' i.e., the time is the same for all frames is presupposed as time according to Newton is absolute and given by God. This Galilean transformation is also verified by experiments.

The formulas x = x'+ vt and x'= x − vt gives by mathematical differentiating with respect to t=t' the relation between the velocity w of a particle measured in S and the velocity w' measured in S,' namely w = w'+ v or w' = w – v. That is, velocities are added or subtracted. Experiments verify this exact law of subtraction or addition of velocities.

Already in Newtonian physics we have the Newtonian or Galilean Relativity saying that the laws of physics look the same in all systems of a special kind, so called inertial frames,[3] and the coordinates in different inertial frames are related according to the Galilean transformation.

If we study bouncing billiard balls and draw a picture of it, it will be rather messy. The numbers indicate the position at the times 0, 1, 2 and 3.

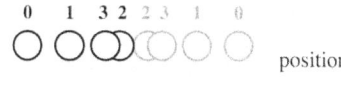

We can point in the directions of length, breadth and height but we cannot point in the direction of the fourth dimension, time. But we can yet picture the movement in a diagram of motion where we draw time, as if it was a space dimension. We draw the balls at time 1 "one stair up" and for time 2 "two stairs up" etc. and get a position vs. time diagram which is much easier to study.

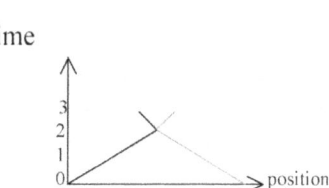

Waves

Classical physics also studies waves. Water waves are the propagation of movement of the water surface, mainly up and down. For sound waves the particles in the air move back and forth for small distances but no particle moves the whole way, e.g., from mouth to ear. Mathematically the function y=f(x) is displaced, without changing form, to the right the distance a if x is replaced by x–a (and to the left if x is replaced by x + a) and thus the function y=f (x–v·t) will describe a wave traveling to the right with velocity v, as the distance traveled in time t is v·t.

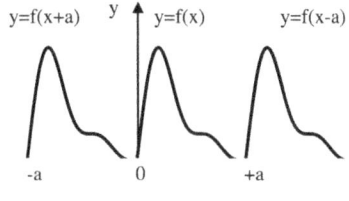

Special so-called harmonic waves can be described with a sinusoidal function y=Asin k(x–v·t) which also can be written $y = A \sin 2\pi(\frac{x}{\lambda} - f \cdot t)$ where A is the amplitude, e.g., the height of a water wave, λ and f are wavelength resp. frequency and related as $\lambda \cdot f = v$. Frequency is how many full periods or cycles run during a second and wavelength is the distance in space after which the pattern starts repeating itself.

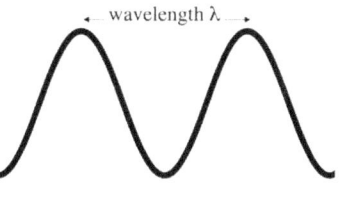

Waves show special characteristics when they hit hindrances. They bend around edges, diffraction, and create special interference patterns when

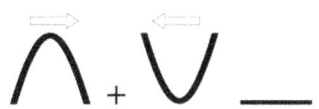

Gives Constructive Interference

Gives Destructive Interference

e.g., passing two holes or slits. This is due to combination of waves strengthening or canceling each others' actions.

The easiest way to see this is dropping stones in water. For one stone we get circles spreading over the surface. For two or more stones we get a beautiful pattern when the waves combine.

These phenomena of diffraction and interference distinguish, in classical physics, particles from waves. For example, if many particles hit a wall with two slits we get just two bands of particles on a screen behind the wall but for waves we will get a series of bands, the interference pattern.

What Is Light?[4]

During the Greek time the focus was to explain sight. Some as the Pythagoreans thought that the eye sent out an invisible fire and Euclid talked about rays of sight but not rays of light. Newton mainly advocated a corpuscular, particle, view of light, which explained color, reflection and refraction and straight path, but not interference. Huygens showed the mathematics of how wave theory could explain diffraction and interference, but not the straight path. But Newton also discovered "Newton's rings," which is an interference phenomenon and tried to create an association between waves and corpuscles "the motion of a projectile and the propagation of periodicity." But this theory was too far ahead of his time and remained embryonic. Young showed 1802 that light passing two narrow slits gave many bands of light and dark, which is an interference phenomenon. He got support from Fresnel who also showed that a wave theory could explain straight path. So a wave theory now explained all known phenomena of light, so light was now considered as a wave. But what kind of wave?

Electricity and Magnetism

About 500 BC discoveries of both magnetic force and static electrical force were made. Both could counteract gravity and both differed drastically from gravitation, as they have two qualities, attraction and repulsion.

During the era of exploration of the world by sail (in 13th–15th centuries) when the compass was used in the Occident, sailors noted that the compass rotated vigorously when lightning was seen, so lightning has something to do with magnetism.

Benjamin Franklin suggested in 1750 that lightning bolts could be electrical as they looked like the electrical sparks, though very huge. He put up a kite with a conducting wire, and when a lightning bolt hit the kite, which was connected to an electroscope, this was charged, supporting the theory that lightning was of an electrical nature.

Thus lightning has both electrical and magnetic effects, so the question of the nature of the relationship between electricity and magnetism came about. At that time electricity could only be mechanically produced by friction and induction, and gave short-lived sparks.

Galvani, a professor of anatomy, in 1762 used a machine to produce sparks; his assistant, examining a dead frog, saw that the leg of the frog jerked as an electrical spark was produced. Galvani made the supposition, which later proved to be correct, that muscles reacted through electricity and that there must exist intrinsic animal "magnetism" or electricity, which was discharged and caused the contraction.

Volta, a physicist, argued against this, suggesting that the electricity which made the leg jerk was not in the animal but produced by a pincette made of two metals. To prove this he constructed with two metals the first electrical battery, Volta's pile, which produced a continuous electrical current.

Hans-Christian Oersted in 1820 could now perform his famous experiment showing how an electrical current through a wire produced magnetic forces, not like a magnetic bar but in circles around that wire. According to Einstein[5] this was the first step away from the mechanistic view where all forces was directed along the line between the objects.

Michael Faraday in 1831 discovered the converse phenomenon: changing magnetic force could give electrical current, magnetic induction, now used to produce electricity.

Faraday also introduced the concept of a field for magnetic and electrical forces; a field can perhaps most easily be visualized of as a distribution of "possible forces." Faraday believed in a Divine Unity pervading all and perhaps this belief in something spiritual, non-material, helped him to formulate the concept of fields, which are active but not material.

Faraday's pupil, James Clark Maxwell,[6] was a brilliant mathematician and would synthesize the experimental facts about electricity and magnetism in his famous equations. Solving these showed electromagnetic waves moving, for example E(x-ct) and B(x-ct), in direction of x-axis, with the velocity in vacuum $c = \frac{1}{\sqrt{\mu_0 \varepsilon_0}} \approx 3 \cdot 10^8 ms^{-1}$ that is the same as that of light now derived from purely electrical ε_0 (0 for vacuum) and purely magnetic μ_0 measurements showing a deep connection between electromagnetism and light,

AND GOD SAID

$$\nabla \cdot E = \frac{\rho}{\varepsilon}$$

$$\nabla \cdot B = 0$$

$$\nabla \times E = -\frac{\partial B}{\partial t}$$

$$\nabla \times B = \mu\sigma E - \mu\varepsilon \frac{\partial E}{\partial t}$$

AND THERE WAS LIGHT

Before Einstein it was thought that light waves and other electromagnetic waves traveled in the ether with velocity c. But as velocities are added or subtracted electromagnetic waves and light in vacuum would thus have the special velocity c only relative the ether frame and other velocities in all other frames moving, as the earth, in the ether. Michelson and Morley experimentally tested this proposition in 1887. However all experiments gave null result—the velocity of light is the same in all frames (in a vacuum)!

Different hypotheses to explain this were suggested, for example that the earth dragged the ether, but this ought to affect how we could see the stars and thus didn't fit other observations. Lorentz had the hypothesis that material bodies, when moving in the ether, shrank in the direction of movement because the forces between atoms were affected in an exact degree as to cancel all measurable effects of movement relative the ether. It was not unphysical but a little ad hoc, as Lorentz's theory also meant that moving clocks showed time slowing down and that the mass of bodies increased when moving, in contradiction to classical Newtonian physics. Lorentz gave mathematical formulas for this, which were changed by Poincaré to a form of transformations of space and time coordinates, $x' = \frac{x - vt}{\sqrt{1 - v^2/c^2}}$ $t' = \frac{t - vx/c^2}{\sqrt{1 - v^2/c^2}}$ y'=y z'=z.

These yet-named Lorentz transformations (LT) also explained Lorentz's shrinking or length contraction.

But it was Einstein who gave a more basic physical ground for LT, as will be further discussed.

Unsolved Problems in Classical Physics

The idea that matter is constituted of atoms, indivisible parts, was given support by chemistry in the end of 18th century. But no one then knew what the atom was. Matter can be electrically charged by friction and electricity was first thought of as some type of fluid. Experimenting with electrically charged so-called "cathodic rays," Thompson, in 1897, argued that these rays were instead very small negatively charged particles—"corpuscles." As matter and atoms are mostly electrically neutral there must also be positive parts. Thomson also found that the mass of these corpuscles, now known as electrons, are thousands of times lighter than whole atoms, so he advocated the so called "plum pudding model of the now no longer indivisible atom," where the negative electrons lie as "raisins in a cake" of positive charge. Firing at atoms with positively charged alpha particles, Rutherford showed that these passed right through the atom if it didn't hit a very small part in the center. So the positive charge is in a very tiny center, the nucleus, whereas the negative electrons were in a bigger area. However, as positive and negative charges attract each other, the electrons would be drawn into the center and the atom would collapse. Then it was thought that if electrons move around the nucleus like planets around the sun there could, as in the solar system, be a balance between outwardly directed centrifugal forces and inwardly directed forces, electrical resp. gravitational. Unfortunately Maxwell's electrodynamics show that charged particles accelerating—changing speed or, as with electrons, changing the direction of velocity—emit radiation and thus lose energy, and will also in this model fall into the center—the atom collapses. Why the constituents of matter, the atoms, are stable could not be explained in classical physics.

Maxwell's equations show a whole spectrum of electromagnetic radiation, with different wavelengths or frequencies. A classical problem was the distribution of energy for different frequencies in radiation from an object called a black body. The classical theory of electromagnetic radiation gave a result which fits experiment only for low frequencies but give increasing energy for higher frequencies with a total amount of infinite energy, the so-called ultraviolet catastrophe. This was another problem not solved in classical physics.

Modern Physics

Albert Einstein and Max Planck started the revolution in physics leading to the Theory of Relativity and Quantum Mechanics, which have radically changed our view of physics and reality.

Einstein's Theory of Special Relativity[7]

Instead of seeing it as a problem that we couldn't measure different velocities for light in different frames moving relative to each other, it was Einstein's genius to postulate that the velocity of light in vacuum is the same in all (inertial) frames, irrespective of their relative movements. This was contrary to every other known physical phenomenon and all experimental verifications that these phenomena followed the law of addition or subtraction of velocities and thus had different velocities in different frames. Einstein now proposed against all other experiences that this is nevertheless not valid for light! Using this new hypothesis together with a generalization of the principle of relativity, to include electromagnetism, Einstein in 1905 radically changed our view on space and time. The two postulates are:

1. The velocity of light, in vacuum, is always the same for all observers in uniform movement relative to each other.

2. All physical laws are the same in all inertial frames.

Einstein could now logically and mathematically derive the coordinate transformations, the relations between the measurements of coordinates for events in inertial frames moving relative to each other. These formulas were the same as Poincaré has suggested, the so called Lorentz transformations (LT), and different from GT, but now shown to be the necessary consequence from two basic postulates. Now Maxwell's equations are the same in all inertial systems, but Newton's laws of mechanics have to be changed for high velocities but are still good approximations for low velocities in daily life.

The mathematically stringent derivation can be found in textbooks.[8] Here I will give a simplified presentation, which yet shows the basic physical arguments.

Derivation of Lorentz Transformations

Einstein looked at a beam of light passing from A to B from the perspective of two different frames S and S' which can be chosen so the event of the beam passing A is given the same four coordinates for length, breadth, height and time (0,0,0,0) in both S and S.' But if S' moves with velocity v along x axis in S they will measure different coordinates for the event of light passing the point B that is (x, y, z, t) and (x,' y,' z,' t'). Pythagoras' theorem says that for a right-angled triangle the relation between the hypotenuse h and the sides x and y are $h^2=x^2+y^2$. Using this two times in three dimensions for the distance d between the points A(0,0,0) and B(x ,y, z) we get $d^2=x^2+y^2+z^2$. Distance is also velocity times time that is d=ct where c is the velocity of light.

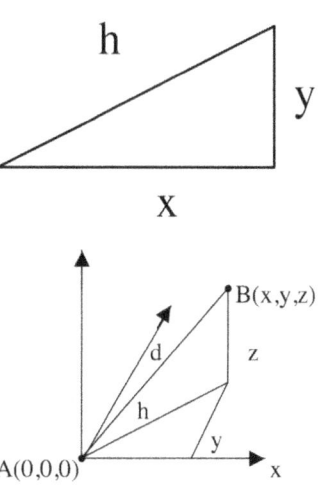

Squaring gives $d^2=c^2t^2$ and so $d^2=x^2+y^2+z^2=c^2t^2$ that is $x^2+y^2+z^2-c^2t^2 =0$ for two events on a light beam. As according to Einstein's postulate the velocity of light is the same in any inertial frame so even for the events in S' we get $x'^2+y'^2+z'^2-c^2t'^2 =0$ with same c! It can be strictly mathematically shown also using the physical arguments of homogeneity of time and isotropy of space and symmetry that $x^2+y^2+z^2-c^2t^2=K(x'^2+y'^2+z'^2-c^2t'^2)$ and that $x'^2+y'^2+z'^2-c^2t'^2= K(x^2+y^2+z^2-c^2t^2)$ with same K which together gives $K^2=1$.

This equation has two solutions $K=\pm\sqrt{1}$, i.e., K=1 and K=-1 as also (-1)•(-1) =1. Thus we have $x^2 + y^2 + z^2-c^2t^2= \pm (x'^2 + y'^2 + z'^2 - c^2t'^2)$.

As Rindler rightly argues this must be valid even if the velocity between the frames goes to zero and then S and S' will be the same, and we have identity, so we must discard the minus sign and now get $x^2+y^2+z^2-c^2t^2= x'^2+y'^2+z'^2-c^2t'^2$.

Rindler now mathematically proves that the transformations between the coordinates must be linear (that is just involving x, y, z and t and not x^2 etc.) He further shows that we can choose the orientation of S and S' so y'=y and z'=z as in the Galilean transformation, thus leaving $x^2 -c^2t^2= x'^2-c^2t'^2$. As the frame S' moves with velocity v along x-axis in S x'=0 must imply x=vt so we can set x'=B(x-vt) and also linearity gives t'=Cx + Dt where B, C and D can depend on v. Now simple college calculus leads to the Lorentz transformations between measurements of the coordinates of same events in different frames S' (x,' y,' z,' t') and S (x, y, z, t) and the relative velocity v between S' and S

$$x' = \frac{x-vt}{\sqrt{1-v^2/c^2}}$$ Cf. GT x'= x—vt

$$t' = \frac{t-vx/c^2}{\sqrt{1-v^2/c^2}}$$ t'=t

y'=y   y'=y
z'=z   z'=z

Einstein's postulates thus led to a totally new view of space and time. He called the theory "*the theory of relativity,*" because it shows that not only velocity is relative, which we already knew since Galilei, but also that space, length (objects become shorter when moving, length-contraction), time (goes slower, time-dilation), mass (increases) and simultaneity at different places also are relative. They have different values or are not the same for different observers mowing relative to each other. Experiments verify these effects but they are significant only for high velocities near the velocity of light. For velocities small compared with the velocity of light v^2/c^2 and v/c^2 are near to zero and LT will be near to GT. Therefore it gives the same results as in the old Newtonian physics for daily life, as our ordinary velocities are almost zero compared with the velocity of light in a vacuum, where c=300 000km/s. That is 7.5 turns around the equator of the earth in one second!

SPACETIME

Einstein pondered calling it the theory of the absolute, as the theory also shows what is absolute: the velocity of light in vacuum and the four-dimensional spacetime "distance" or intervals between two events (x_1, y_1, z_1, t_1) and (x_2, y_2, z_2, t_2) defined as $s^2 = c^2(t_2 - t_1)^2 - (x_2 - x_1)^2 - (y_2 - y_1)^2 - (z_2 - z_1)^2$. That is, irrespective of their relative movements, the spacetime intervals are the same for all observers, but it can be "split," projected, in different ways in space and time. Consider a stick of a certain length, which have different length in projections on different axes. This even has physical effects as the stick can pass a smaller hole if it has an angle to the hole. But the important difference is that in the theory of relativity it is a blend of space and time not just different lengths and it seems not easy to have a picture of it. (See end section).

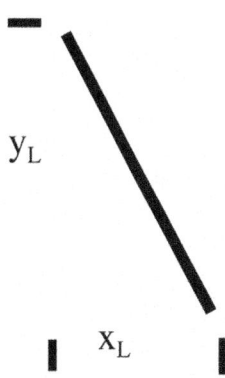

This feature of spacetime is well described by Minkowski. "Henceforth space by itself, and time by itself, are doomed to fade away into mere shadows, and only a kind of union of the two will preserve an independent reality."[9]

The four-dimensional spacetime is absolute but space and time taken separately is relative so spacetime is an objective reality and seemingly ontological more fundamental than space and time.

Petkov[10] argues for the objective reality of a four-dimensional spacetime. He claims to show that "if the world and the physical objects were three-dimensional, none of the kinematic relativistic effects" [as length-contraction, time-dilation, relativity of simultaneity] "and the experimental evidence supporting them would be possible." Petkov thus concludes that spacetime is ontologically four-dimensional.

That is, all past events, all events now and all future events exist at once in spacetime. Fig. 12 and 13 now get a new deep ontological meaning.

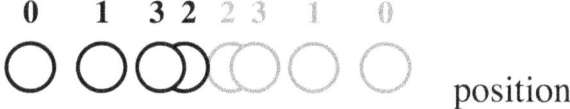

The four-dimensional spacetime is unchanging but we experience it as three-dimensional objects changing in time. Plato's definition of time seems appropriate: Time is a moving image of eternity.

Einstein's argument[11] for v<c. Einstein showed that the energy increased according to the formula[12] $E = \frac{m_0 c^2}{\sqrt{1-v^2/c^2}}$ and as the graph shows it is needed an infinite amount of energy to reach velocity of light and even impossible to come over it.

But light in vacuum travels with c! Yes, but light doesn't start from zero and accelerates but is "born" with that velocity c, "a flying start."

Therefore Einstein's theory doesn't exclude particles with superlight velocity if they are "born" with that velocity. However they cannot slow down to velocities lower than c. This was

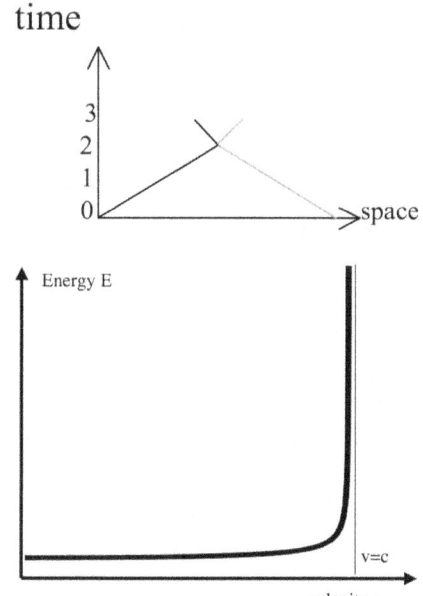

argued for already in the 1960s[13] and even if it of course was unclear what this superlight phenomena could be it was at that time thought of as particles and even given the name "tachyons" from Greek "tachy," meaning fast.[14]

Tachyons have not been found in experiments. In one such search Alväger and Kreisler[15] used $E = \frac{m_0 c^2}{\sqrt{1-v^2/c^2}}$ even for v>c and rearranged it to $E = -\frac{im_0 c^2}{\sqrt{v^2/c^2-1}}$ and argued that it is no problem that the tachyons (seem to) have imaginary rest-mass im_0, $i = \sqrt{-1}$, as they never can be at rest in our systems so it is not directly measurable. Seems possible but a little ad hoc due to the singularity at v=c. There is yet another approach which seems to be more in the spirit of the special theory of relativity and therefore perhaps less ad hoc.

Possible Extensions of Einstein's Theory of Relativity

In 1969 Parker[16] showed a mathematical possibility to describe superlight velocities in two dimensions, one space and one time dimension, but explicitly stated it was not possible in his way for our four-dimensional space-time.

In the beginning of the 1970s, at least four different researchers[17] independently discovered the possibility to describe phenomena with superlight velocity in agreement with Einstein's special theory of relativity if some extensions were made: either allowing imaginary numbers in the generalized Lorentz transformation for superlight velocities or real-valued transformations but in a six-dimensional space-time. Cole has also showed how in this six-dimensional spacetime, with three space dimensions and three time dimensions, you can predict the dark matter,[18] which according to many cosmologists is needed to explain the higher rotation velocity of galaxies. As matter and energy are equivalent and can be transformed into each other it is perhaps possible to describe even dark energy in this theory. Cole also shows that in six-dimensional spacetime the electrical field gets extra components and also a totally new field.[19] Fields have energy so again perhaps a possibility for dark energy. Matter is to some extent more extended in space, more "space-like," whereas energy is "driving force" for processes in time, so more "time-like," so it seems possible that three time dimensions could allow more "time" for energy (cf. also one of Heisenberg's uncertainty relations, $\Delta E \, \Delta t \geq h/2\pi$).

Basic Argument for Extending Einstein's Special Relativity to Six-Dimensional Spacetime[20]

If tachyons exist it is conceivable that many tachyons, which have the same velocity v>c relative some ordinary inertial frame (OIF) S, would all be at rest relative to each other and therefore it is conceivable to think of a "tachyonian" rigid frame (TIF) $_tS_v$ with the velocity v>c relative to S.

If we can observe tachyons, that is giving real coordinates to them in our frames, seemingly there must exist transformations between OIF and TIF with only real coefficients, as the coordinates for tachyons in their own frames also are real. But the ordinary LT doesn't work as they give imaginary numbers for v>c.

So either we cannot observe tachyons or there must exist real transformations other than the ordinary LT.

Generalization of the Principle of Relativity—Again—Now to v>c

If we generalize the special principle of relativity to be valid for all inertial frames, even those with v>c, it can still, interestingly, be formulated exactly as before.

Postulate 2: All Physical Laws Are the Same in All Inertial Frames

The other postulate about the velocity of light =c in all frames is also unchanged. Now we can exactly follow Rindler and as above come to
$$x^2 + y^2 + z^2 - c^2t^2 = \pm (x'^2 + y'^2 + z'^2 - c^2t'^2).$$
The argument to discard the "−" sign, that is identity when velocity goes to zero, is now not valid as we look for transformations to velocities >c. So we now chose the minus sign. It is not clear how to use the argument of homogeneity in time and isotropy in space for v>c, so without full justification we as a start simplify to two dimensions, which worked for v<c, and get $x^2 - c^2t^2 = -(x'^2 - c^2t'^2)$. Now the same argument as before seems valid, that as the frame S' moves with velocity v along x-axis in S, x'=0 must imply x=vt, so we can set x'=B(x-vt) and also linearity gives t'=Cx + Dt where B, C and D can depend on v. Now simple college calculus leads to the Generalized Lorentz transformations[21]
$x' = \dfrac{x - vt}{\sqrt{v^2/c^2 - 1}}$, $t' = \dfrac{t - vx/c^2}{\sqrt{v^2/c^2 - 1}}$ now real valued only for v>c!

But for the full expression $x^2 + y^2 + z^2 - c^2t^2 = \pm (x'^2 + y'^2 + z'^2 - c^2t'^2)$ there is now a more basic reason not to choose the minus sign, given by my teacher Dr. Lars Söderholm. The expressions on both sides of = are so called quadratic forms and according to the law of inertia for quadratic forms[22] you must have the same signature, or numbers of + and − signs on both sides, if the transformation shall be of a real value, i.e., it will not have to use any imaginary or complex numbers.

When there is no sign as in front of x^2 it means a +. For the two dimensional simplification we thus have the signature +− and thus in signs +−= ± (+ −). Using + in ± we get "+ −" = "+ −" and using − in ± we get " +−" = "−+" but both work, as the signature is just the number of plus and minus signs, not the order.

But for the four-dimensional case the signatures for the forms on both sides is + + + −. So we have + + + − = ± (+ + + −). Now the + in ± gives "+++−" = "+++−," which is okay but the − in ± now gives +++− = −(+++−), that is "+++−" = "− − − +," not the same signature. So for four dimensions the transformation must have imaginary numbers in them, which of course is possible[23] but needs some thinking about how to interpret them, as imaginary numbers are not simple physics, e.g., what is a length of 5i or the time duration 8i?

The formulas for two dimensions describing relations valid for v>c, yet simply following from the same arguments as Einstein used, was thrilling: it seemed we have this world of matter, the light world and a world beyond light. A solution was simple yet speculative. To be able to use the minus sign without changing the signature we could add two "minus-dimensions" thus in signature + + + − − − = ± (+ + + − − −). Now both signs work. Cole[24] very elegantly presented the case for both v<c and v>c for six as well as eight dimensions. Here I present the idea of six dimensions: + in ± gives "+ + +− − −" = "+ + +− − −" $x^2 + y^2 + z^2 - c^2t^2 - c^2t_2^2 - c^2t_3^2 = x'^2 + y'^2 + z'^2 - c^2t'^2 - c^2t_2'^2 - c^2t_3'^2$ and ordinary LT for v<c with two extra "time-like" dimensions, which for v<c can be shown to just transform into themselves as $t'_2 = t_2$ and $t'_3 = t_3$, thus leaving the rest of LT unchanged.

And − in ± gives "+ + +− − −" = "− − − + + +," yet the same signature and from $x^2 + y^2 + z^2 - c^2t^2 - c^2t_2^2 - c^2t_3^2 = -(x'^2 + y'^2 + z'^2 - c^2t'^2 - c^2t_2'^2 - c^2t_3'^2)$ we get Generalized LT in six dimensions.[25] $x' = \frac{x-vt}{\sqrt{v^2/c^2-1}}$, $t' = \frac{t-vx/c^2}{\sqrt{v^2/c^2-1}}$ as for two dimensions but also $y'=ct_2$, $z'=ct_3$, $t_2'=\frac{y}{c}$, $t_3'=\frac{z}{c}$. As argued above, even if tachyons exist, for us to be able to observe them there seemingly must exist a real transformation and thus more dimensions, so we have symmetry in positive, space-dimensions and negative "time"-dimensions, e.g., a six-dimensional spacetime. Of course, how to interpret these extra dimensions and "time-space interchange" is not straightforward.

However, most physicists haven't accepted these theories as it allows faster than light velocities, and thus allows the reversal of the order between cause and effect. This challenges a very basic dogma of science. My interpretation of these extra dimensions and reversal of cause and effect, perhaps surprisingly, relates to a new view on consciousness. But first some notes about quantum mechanics and the brain-mind problem.

Quantum Mechanics

Max Planck in 1901 found a mathematical formula which solved the ultraviolet catastrophe and which thus described black body radiation in full agreement with all experiments.[26] In constructing this formula he mathematically described the interaction of matter and electromagnetic radiation in the form of discrete energy "quanta" (Latin for amount) hv where v is the frequency of the radiation and h a physical constant found by experiment and now called Planck's constant. Planck himself at first considered that quantization was only "a purely formal assumption," so it didn't contradict Young's view that light was not particles but a wave and thus thought to be a continuous phenomenon. In 1904 another phenomena was studied, the so-called photoelectrical effect. When a light beam hit a metal surface in an evacuated tube, like a photocell, the energy in the light releases electrons from the surface and their energy could be measured. However it was the color of the light, or more physically the frequency of the electromagnetic wave, and not its intensity, which determined the energy of emitted electrons. E.g., for a special metal, red light would give no emitted electrons at all irrespective of how much the intensity, and thus the total energy, of the red light was increased. But for blue light, which has higher frequency, electrons are emitted even if the light had low intensity and it is also an almost instant effect. This cannot be explained if light is a continuous wave! Again it was Einstein who, in 1905, formulated the solution. He extended the idea from Planck and introduced the quantum as a real physical entity, so light travels in discrete quanta of energy, by Einstein called photons, and with the energy proposed by the formula of Planck, E=hv. So for low frequencies the energy in a photon is too small to release an electron from the metal surface but for higher frequencies the energy is enough to release an electron. Thus, quantum physics was born. But not without labor pains.

Young had, 100 years earlier, proved that light must be described as a wave because it showed interference and now Einstein showed that in the photoelectrical effect light must be described as discrete particles, photons. Whereas the special theory of relativity was from its birth a fully developed and logical consistent theory, the quantum ideas were more contradictory, and it took many years to become an accepted theory. It is now a mathematically exact theory confirmed by all experiments and, e.g., IT technology, and as the famous quantum physicist John S. Bell said, it works FAPP, "for all practical purposes."[27] But Bell warns us to fall in the "FAPP trap."[28] From the start and even now the foundations of quantum mechanics are still debatable.[29] About this complicated matter I will just give some comments.

From Bohr's Model of the Atom to de Broglie's Matter Waves

Bohr pondered the problem with the planet model of the atom and its classical instability. He used a vast amount of data from spectroscopy, which showed that each substance has its "fingerprint" in the specific light frequencies ν it radiates or absorbs. So there couldn't be just any amount of energy, as E=hν, in the interaction between atoms and light; there had to be specific amounts. That is, the energy in this interaction is not a continuous variable, but has discrete or quantized values. So Bohr now used quantization laws for angular momentum L=nh/2π n=1, 2, 3, etc., to just allow certain orbits and proclaimed that the classical theory about accelerated electrons sending out energy is not valid for the electrons in the atom in *these* orbits—and the atoms are thus stable! Light is only emitted when an electron changes from a larger orbit with higher energy to a smaller with lower energy; the opposite applies for absorption. A totally new explanation was needed, one that gave a description that explained the stability of atoms, fit all the spectroscopic data for the hydrogen atom and also gave a theoretically calculated correct value of an experimentally measured constant. Louis De Broglie was, during the First World War, a signaler, and became interested in electromagnetic signals and physics. Einstein showed that light which earlier was seen as waves also must be described as particles, or photons. De Broglie in his 1924 dissertation[30] suggested that nature ought to be symmetric and that what we ordinarily think of as particles also has wave qualities. His own words are illuminating:

> When I began to consider these difficulties I was chiefly struck by two facts. On the one hand the Quantum Theory of Light cannot be considered satisfactory, since it defines the energy of a light-corpuscle by the equation W=hν containing the frequency ν. Now a purely corpuscular theory contains nothing that enables us to define a frequency: for this reason alone therefore we are compelled in the case of Light to introduce the idea of a corpuscle and that of periodicity simultaneously.
>
> On the other hand determination of a stable motion of electrons in the atom introduces integers; and up to this point the only phenomena involving integers in Physics were those of interference and of normal modes of vibration. This fact suggested to me the idea that electrons too could not be regarded merely as corpuscles but that periodicity must be assigned to them also. In this way, then, I obtained the following general idea, in accordance with which I pursued my investigations: that it is necessary in the case of Matter, as well as of radiation generally and Light in particular, to introduce the idea of the corpuscle and of the wave simultaneously; or in other words, in the one case as well as in the other, we must assume the existence of corpuscles accompanied by waves. But corpuscles and waves cannot be independent of each other."[31]

De Broglie made, "based on an understanding of the relationship between frequency and energy … the assumption of existence of a certain periodic phenomenon of a yet to be determined character ... attributed to each and every isolated energy particle...."[32] From this idea and Einstein's special relativity he derived[33] for "the wave of an electron" the wavelength $\lambda = \frac{h}{p}$ (where p is mass times velocity of the electron), which was experimentally confirmed in electron diffraction in 1927.

Electrons accompanied by "guiding" waves also gave a physical interpretation of Bohr's rules for allowed electron orbits as only orbits, with the length of a whole number of wavelengths could exist, as these give constructive interference, whereas all other values cause destructive interference.[34]

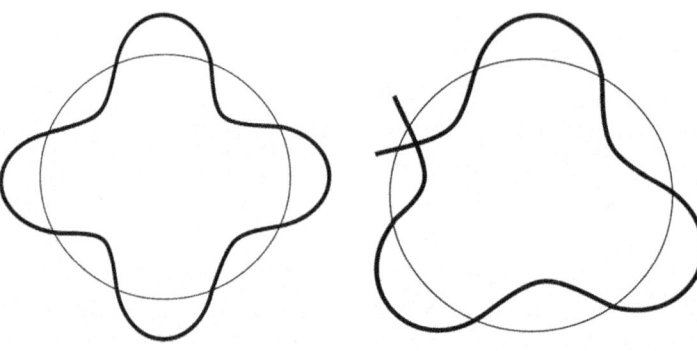

Circumference $2\pi r = 4\lambda$ Circumference $2\pi r \neq n\lambda$

Schrödinger's Wave Mechanics— And Many Interpretations

Schrödinger developed the idea about the wave nature of matter, "but removed the trajectories [for particles] from de Brogile's theory and produced a purely undulatory 'wave mechanics.'"[35] With Schrödinger's wave equation $-\frac{h^2}{8\pi^2 m}(\frac{\partial^2 \psi}{\partial x^2} + \frac{\partial^2 \psi}{\partial y^2} + \frac{\partial^2 \psi}{\partial z^2}) + V(r) \cdot \psi = i\frac{h}{2\pi}\frac{\partial \psi}{\partial t}$ one can correctly calculate the discrete states, at first for the hydrogen atom. However the equation gives many possible solutions, e.g., of the position of an electron; that is, the future position of an electron could not be definitely known, as in Newton's deterministic mechanics. So how is this wave function Ψ related to the real world? At a meeting in Solvay[36] in 1927 de Broglie presented "pilot-wave theory," whereby *real particles are guided by waves* given by a guiding equation. For a group of particles he also described how the wave gave probabilities for electrons *being in a spatial area*, not just probabilities of *finding* them there. Born, in his early papers where he presented the probability interpretation of the wave function, suggested that guided by the wave function, particles move in such a way that the distribution of their positions is given by the modulus squared of the wave function.[37] But then came the idea that *only the probability for different possible locations could be known* and that particle trajectories are not knowable and even non-existent. That the *wave function was the complete description of reality* came to be viewed as the correct interpretation. Schrödinger and Einstein were not satisfied with that, and thought that quantum mechanics was not complete.

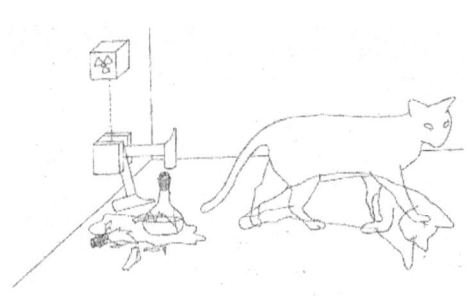

Schrödinger's cat (Artist Petra E.E.).

To show this Schrödinger introduced

his famous cat[38] that will die when an atom decays. The decay of a radioactive atom is a random process and is described by quantum mechanics with a wave function that is a sum, *a superposition*, of waves for the different possibilities, a wave for an *intact atom* and a wave for a *decayed atom*. A version of Copenhagen interpretation says that the atom is in a mixed state of an intact and a decayed atom until an observation, a measurement, is made, when one possibility become real, "a collapse of the wave function," to just one of the possibilities. It sounds odd, but perhaps possible on quantum level. But if the wave function was a complete description of the state that is valid also for ordinary objects, the cat is in a state between living and dead—until an observer looks and thus makes one possibility become real. In this interpretation seemingly objective reality doesn't exist before our measurement. "The hallmarks of orthodox quantum theory are the denial of determinism and, more importantly, the denial of an objective reality."[39] Most physicists seem to either not bother (the FAPP-trap) or adhere to this view. Others instead think that whenever different possibilities exist, *all* possibilities become real, but in totally separate and different worlds—the so called many world interpretation. So the relation between possibility and reality is strange. But there are also other interpretations. "Bohmian mechanics is a realistic quantum theory. It happens to be deterministic, which is fine but not an ontological necessity. The **merit of Bohmian mechanics** is not determinism, but **the refutation of all claims that quantum mechanics cannot be reconciled with a realistic description of reality**."[40]

The Swedish mathematician Tomas Blomberg has formulated a realistic stochastic (random) quantum theory where states are replaced by events.[41] In these realistic views the cat is either alive or dead without any observation or measurement.[42]

Double Slit Experiment and Another Strange View

When waves pass a double slit we get many bands in an interference pattern. Now we can also send one particle, a photon or an electron, one at the time at the double slit. Each particle always hit the analyzing screen at a small "point like" area. Yet after some time and many particles have passed an interference pattern of many bands emerges.[43]

This is described as a paradox and one of the basic mysteries of QM, "impossible, absolutely impossible, to explain in any classical way."[44] On one hand we have *particles, each passing through just one slit*; on the other hand we have bands of an interference pattern indicating *waves passing through both slits*. Physicists ask, "How can something pass through just one slit and both at the same time?" It doesn't fit our daily life experiences. Some physicists say that it is inconceivable how "single particles" can give such an interference pattern, but yet give "the explanation" that the particle in some way passes through both the slits, a split particle being at two places at the same time, then interfering with itself. Sounds a bit weird but as we have seen we must be open-minded to new discoveries. However what is really inconceivable is that many physicists seem not to know or ignore that there exists a simple theory, which explains this experiment in a conceivable way. John S. Bell writes about this "pilot wave" picture:

> While the founding fathers agonized over the question "particle" *or* "wave" de Broglie [in] 1925 proposed the obvious answer "particle, *and* wave." Is it not clear from the smallness of

the scintillation on the screen that we have to do with a particle? And is it not clear, from diffraction and interference patterns, that the motion of the particle is directed by a wave? De Broglie showed in detail how the motion of the particle, passing through just one of the two holes in screen, could be influenced by waves propagating through both holes. And so influenced that the particle does not go where the waves cancel out, but is attracted to where they cooperate. This idea seems to me so natural and simple, to resolve the wave-particle dilemma in such a clear and ordinary way, that it is a great mystery to me that it was so generally ignored. Of the founding fathers only Einstein thought that de Broglie was on the right lines ... it was rediscovered ... [and] more systematically presented in 1952 by David Bohm."[45]

We can now reinterpret Young's double slit experiment. He showed we could calculate the interference pattern for light passing two slits from the mathematical model of waves. But he didn't show that light has no particle character! His experiment was not accurate enough to show that and of course even in his experiment the effect on the screen was built up by particles, directed by a wave. It was the presupposition from classical physics that wave and particle exclude each other that led to the wrong conclusion that light was only a wave. So actually there has never been a real contradiction between particle and wave views of light, for as de Broglie, Bohm and Bell argue, it is particles directed by a wave! De Brogile's insight was to see the symmetry that even all particles also have a wave quality. But again—what kind of wave?

Bell's Inequality and Bell's Theorem

This is Bell's most revolutionary contribution. He took up the so-called EPR paradox in which Einstein, Podolsky and Rosen described a thought experiment that might show that quantum mechanics was not complete. Wiseman[46] writes,

> I suggest that Einstein's argument, as stated most clearly in 1946, could justly be called Einstein's reality-locality-completeness theorem, since it proves that one of these three

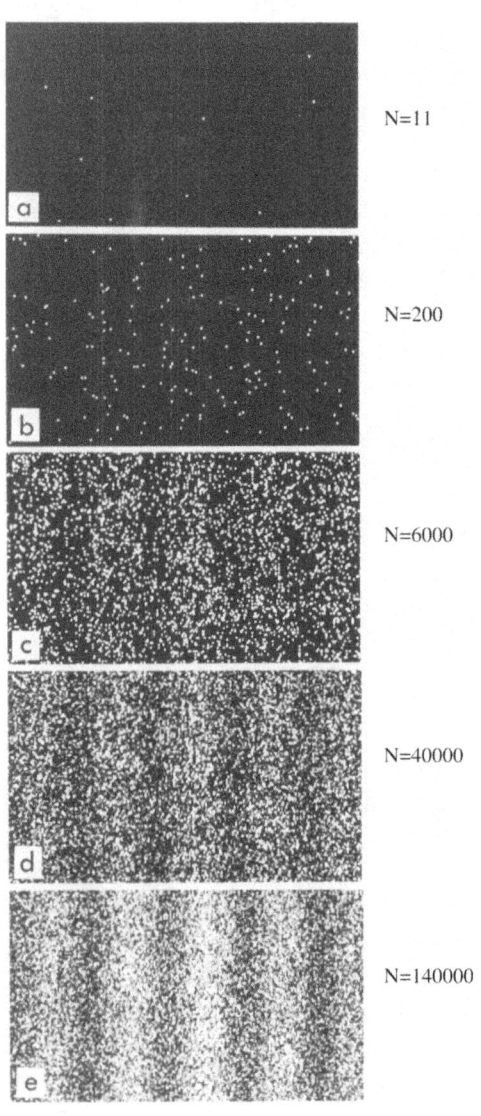

Results of a double-slit-experiment performed by Dr. Tonomura showing the build-up of an interference pattern of single electrons. Numbers of electrons are 10 (a), 200 (b), 6000 (c), 40000 (d), 140000 (e) (courtesy Dr. Tonomura).

must be false. Einstein's instinct was that completeness of orthodox quantum mechanics was the falsehood, but he failed in his quest to find a more complete theory that respected reality and locality. Einstein's theorem, and possibly Einstein's failure, inspired John Bell in 1964 to prove his reality-locality theorem. This strengthened Einstein's theorem (but showed the futility of his quest) by demonstrating that either reality or locality is a falsehood. This revealed the full non-locality of the quantum world for the first time.

Weisman also notes that already de Brogile's theory showed aspects of non-locality.[47] Bohm already (in 1951) clearly showed the even stronger result that at the quantum level the universe is an indivisible whole, a concept known as quantum indivisibility.[48]

Wiseman also writes that Bell's work has been misinterpreted as to show that there is no possibility for so-called hidden variables. But Bell points out that Bohm has presented exactly such a view "with the help of which the indeterministic description could be transformed to a deterministic" one, but it is nonlocal![49] And Wiseman[50] again:

> To conclude, the results of the Bell-experiments leave only two possibilities:
> (i) the world is non-local—events happen which violate the principles of relativity [violates local causality, that is, allow superluminality; cf. Wiseman p. 80, JP].
> (ii) objective reality does not exist—there is no matter of fact about distant events.
> Although consistent, the second option does seem very close to solipsism, "the view or theory that only the self really exists or can be known." Even if solipsism cannot be refuted, it can certainly be attacked on ethical grounds. As Karl Popper wrote pointedly, "any argument against realism which is based on quantum mechanics ought to be silenced by the memory of the reality of the events of Hiroshima and Nagasaki." Compared to solipsism, the proposition that relativity is not fundamental, and that the world is non-local, seems the lesser of two evils. This was certainly Bell's position, and is even seen as inevitable by some philosophers; Maudlin says "I have argued that the [following is] unequivocal: Violation of Bell's inequality can be accomplished only if there is superluminal information transmission."

Quantum Mechanics—A Conscious Interpretation

Wiseman argues that we have a choice—non-locality or non-reality, but many seem to choose the latter even if it is close to a solipsism. Is it the dogma that nothing can go faster than light that is so strongly held? But there exist generalizations of Einstein's theory of special relativity, which explicitly allow superluminal phenomena and are thus seemingly also supported by Maudlin's analysis.[51]

Also, Henry Stapp[52] claims he has proved the Bell inequality using only the assumption of locality and therefore the result of Bell-experiments actually show that it is locality that must be false. Of course one can say reality is also false but there is no need to, so why choose a view so devastating for science and life? Cushing,[53] professor in both physics and philosophy, argues in his book about the contingency of the Copenhagen interpretation, that if Einstein had known the result of Bell-experiments he had chosen reality even before his own local theory of relativity.

So the problems of QM with particle vs. waves and non-reality vs. non-locality seem to have a good solution: particles and waves together with reality and superluminal non-locality. But what about determinism vs. chance, which is another problem in QM?

Newtonian mechanics is said to be deterministic, in that the movements of particles are fully determined by the initial parameters and the forces of the system, while quantum mechanics is nondeterministic[54] as it just can give probabilities for the locations of the particles and measurements of other variables in the future. But Newtonian mechanics cannot in our daily life predict the future location of objects, which actually are totally unpredictable if we don't exclude the effect of the activity of other persons, whose intentions Newtonian mechanics cannot describe! On the contrary, intentional beings put a strong limit to the determinism of classical Newtonian mechanics, which thus in no way can be a support for the view that consciousness is something determined. That we with great success can use Newtonian mechanics for accurate predictions about ordinary material objects, for example apples and planets, can be interpreted as that it is easy in practice with these objects to differentiate and exclude the situations where intentions which cannot be described in the model can have an effect on the outcome, in short to differentiate between matter and intentional beings. If I know the weight of an apple and my force on it and other forces, e.g., gravity, in the system I can exactly predict the orbit of the thrown apple. But if some living person catches the apple, takes a bite and throws it in a new direction, this cannot be foreseen at all. Of course a brain researcher can argue that brains are material and all that brains do are determined and predictable. Such a theory doesn't exist yet and probably must be based on QM, and thus again not fully predictable. However we now in daily life have a class of phenomena where we know that *Newton's determinism* doesn't work due to possible involvement of intentional beings.

That quantum mechanics is nondeterministic, e.g., regarding the decay of radioactive atoms, can thus, by analogy, be interpreted as that on a quantum level matter and intentional quality are inseparable; that is, matter has an intrinsic intentional quality. This might at first sound absurd but Bertrand Russell has, in his Russellian monism, on other grounds, proposed that the intrinsic properties of the physical are or constitute phenomenal properties (conscious experiences, qualia), as a way to solve the notorious body-mind problem. If radioactive atoms are seen to have some intentional quality as, e.g., to decide when they shall decay, this gives another realistic solution to the Schrödinger cat paradox. Because then both the condition of the atom and the cat is determined by the atom's intentional action and exist as real all the time even if no one observes or can predict their conditions. So in this view reality exists independent of our observing it or not, and it also emphasizes a respect for the intentions of all intentional beings. This seems to me less absurd and more near a psychological and humanly useful interpretation than one version of the Copenhagen interpretation where objective reality is denied,[55] and than the many-world interpretation. For if as in the many world interpretation all possibilities became equally real, in one world I behave nicely as Dr. Pilotti but in another world I misbehave as Mr. Hyde. What is then my responsibility for my actions? The interpretation presented here respects intention and choice as causal and thus preserves the moral responsibility for our actions and seems to me to be more in unison with Plato's ideal of the Truth and the Good. And perhaps also the Beautiful?

If elementary particles have some intentional quality could it be that this quality is related to the waves that guide the particles? So that the Ψ wave in QM is not related only to chance but also to the intentional aspect of consciousness?[56] De Broglie's idea of both particle and wave might also be interpreted that we on quantum level have an analogue to the body-mind interaction.

Another point supporting this is that we never in physical reality see a superposition, the simultaneity of two incompatible material states. However in consciousness we can have ambivalence, e.g., two different and sometimes even opposite feelings and thoughts at the same time. We can think of a both living and dead cat but not experience both at once in physical reality. That we have superposition for waves and in QM might support that the quantum wave Ψ is also and perhaps more related to consciousness. But why then does bulk of matter follow Newtonian mechanics—why does it behave as without intentions if all parts have intentions? We come back to that.

Unification of Theory of Relativity and Quantum Mechanics

Einstein extended the theory of relativity to accelerated, non-inertial frames, the so-called theory of general relativity, and could thus explain gravity in a curved spacetime, but this theory has been difficult to unify with quantum mechanics.

Theories that seem to unify GR and QM are string theory or M-theory, which uses extra space dimensions. Not so many have worked with extra time dimensions. Bars[57] has done so but argues that more than two time dimensions will create more problems with the violation of causality and "ghosts," quantum states with negative probability, which he argues must be discarded. I am not so sure.

Dirac unified special relativity and QM for electrons and from $E^2 = m^2c^4 + p^2c^2$, thus $E = \pm\sqrt{m^2c^4 + p^2c^2}$, predicted the "positron," the anti-electron, a positively charged particle with the same mass as the electron but with a negative energy state, which later was found in experiments. He also wrote" that negative energies and probabilities should not be considered as nonsense. They are well-defined concepts mathematically, like a negative of money."[58] And perhaps "ghosts" indicate the conscious aspect related to QM?

However, there are problems already in unifying SR and QM. As we saw above, QM is non-local and one way—and as Maudlin argues a necessary way—to accomplish that is to allow superlight phenomena. The six-dimensional extension of special relativity with three time dimensions does this. But I think there is an even more basic contradiction between four-dimensional SR, SR4 and QM.

As shown above, spacetime is an objective reality and as Petkov describes, in a static four-dimensional spacetime, "the entire history of every object is realized and given once and for all,"[59] which seems to be a deterministic view and thus seemingly contradicts the indeterminism of QM. Petkov has an interesting yet also speculative suggestion[60] to resolve that, but here I will show that it is also seemingly possible to solve in SR6. We can picture the four-dimensional spacetime of three space and one time dimensions as a line symbolizing the one time dimension but where every point is the whole world[61] in three space dimensions at that time: All past events, all events now and all future events exist at once and all is seemingly determined, which seemingly contradicts QM.

But in the six-dimensional spacetime[62] with three space- and three time-dimensions the picture changes dramatically. Now we have a three dimensional "timebox" where again every point is a whole world in three space dimensions at a certain "three-dimensional time-point."

40   Part I. Physics, Spacetime and Near Death Experiences

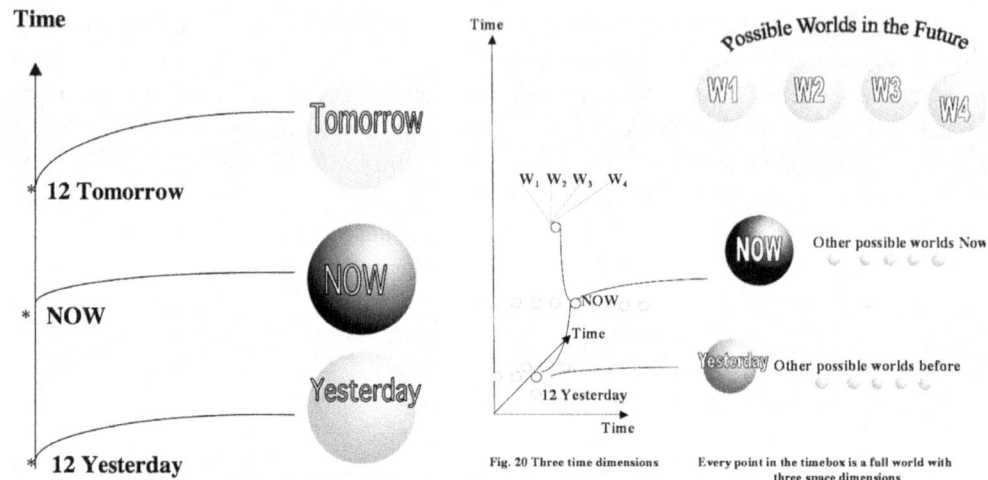

| One dimensional Time | Three dimensional space. The whole world at different points of time | Three time dimensions | Every point in the timebox is a full world with three space dimensions |

One time dimension

The six dimensional spacetime is supposed exists at once, like the four-dimensional spacetime but now there are many possible worlds, many possibilities as in QM. (Two time dimensions would be enough for this but seems not to allow the also needed superlight velocity.)

However, first about the mind-brain problem.

What Can a Brain Really Do?

After more than a hundred years of research, the "decade of the brain" and modern techniques for imaging the living brain, there is not even a hint of how we can explain or describe how a brain process could be or create an experience! It is not just details but the fundamentals which are lacking. Even neuroscientists who believe that the brain "produce" consciousness, admit that "No one has produced any plausible explanation as to how the experience of the redness of red could arise from the action of the brain."[63]

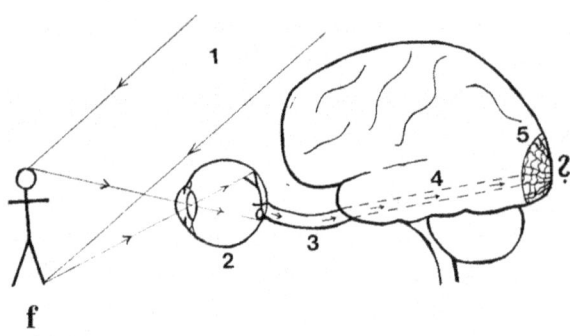

"White light" 1 reflecting on a "red" figure f. 4–5 just schematic of all complex actions in the brain.

This is a good example of the philosopher David Chalmers' point: "The really hard problem of consciousness is the problem of *experience*," such as *hearing* the sound of a clarinet, *seeing* the quality of deep blue, *thinking* about Christmas and *feeling* joy. "What unites all these states [of experiences] is that there is something it is like to be in them." Terms such as "phenomenal consciousness," "qualia," "conscious experience" and "first-person perspective" are used for these *subjective experiences*. "The easy problems are those of explaining cognitive and behavioral functions, such as discrimination, integration, and verbal report, ... by specifying a *mechanism* that performs the function. Here, neurophysiological and cognitive modelling are perfect for the task." But "what makes the hard problem hard and almost unique is that it goes *beyond* problems about the performance of functions.... A further unanswered question may remain *why is performance of these functions accompanied by experience?*" So according to Chalmers, "the usual methods of cognitive science and neuroscience fail to account for conscious experience.... To account for conscious experiences, we need an *extra ingredient* in the explanation ... something new."[64]

Chalmers then discusses the mental-physical relation in what he argues are the most important metaphysical views of consciousness: three "broadly reductive views, which see consciousness as a physical process that requires no expansion of a physical ontology" and three "broadly nonreductive views, according to which consciousness involves something irreducible in nature and requires expansion or reconception of a physical ontology."

Chalmers "think[s] that each of the reductive views is incorrect, while each of the nonreductive views holds some promise."[65]

If arguments against reductive views of consciousness are correct we must have further fundamentals, and consciousness involves something novel and fundamental in the world. In physics, space, time, mass and charge are taken as fundamentals and are not further explained. Instead, one takes them as basic and gives a theory of how they relate to everything else in the world. Chalmers suggests "that a theory of consciousness ... as everything in physical theory is compatible with the absence of consciousness ... take experience itself as a fundamental feature of the world, alongside mass, charge and space-time."

Chalmers asks how these novel fundamental phenomenal (or protophenomenal) properties relate to the already acknowledged fundamental properties of the world, which Chalmers here, at first, seems to mean as only those invoked in microphysics. He expects "some sort of fundamental principles—psychophysical laws—connecting physical and phenomenal properties"[66] but points to "an immediate worry that microphysical aspect of the world are often held to be causally closed, that is every microphysical state has a microphysical sufficient cause. How are phenomenal properties to be integrated with this causally closed network"? He sees three main options:

- *Interactionism-dualism* "deny the causal closure of the microphysical holding that there are causal gaps ... filled by a causal role for phenomenal properties."
- *Epiphenomenalism-dualism* "accept the causal closure of the microphysical and hold that the phenomenal properties play no causal role with respect to the physical network."
- *Monism (Russellian)* "accept that the microphysical network is causally closed but hold that phenomenal properties are nevertheless integrated with it and play a causal role ... constituting the intrinsic nature of the physical."

Chalmers doesn't claim any of these to be unproblematic but suggests that all are without clear fatal flaws.

Sometimes **interactionism-dualism** is discarded because "distinct physical and mental states could not interact since there is no causal nexus between them." Here Chalmers argues that this is also the case "for any fundamental causal interactions including those in physics." Yet "the most influential objection to interactionism is that it is incompatible with physics." Interestingly Chalmers himself argued thus[67] but has now changed his mind: against the claim that the microphysical is causally closed the non-deterministic aspect of quantum mechanics and collapse of wave function at measurement appears quite compatible with an interactionist interpretation. "[It is] natural to suggest that a measurement is precisely a conscious observation and … causes a collapse,"[68] by which a possibility in QM will be realized.[69] Chalmers admits that such interpretation of QM is controversial but writes about the irony that "in fact philosophers reject interactionism on largely physical grounds (it is incompatible with physical theory) while physicists reject an interactionist interpretation of quantum mechanics on largely philosophical grounds (it is dualistic). Taken conjointly these reasons carry little force, especially in light of the arguments against materialism elsewhere."

In Russellian monism, phenomenal or protophenomenal properties are located at the fundamental level of physical reality. Bertrand Russell argued, according to Chalmers,

> that physics characterizes physical entities and properties by their relations to one another and to us … (but) says nothing about the intrinsic nature of these entities and properties … (two) metaphysical puzzles … what are the intrinsic properties of fundamental physical systems? (and) … how can phenomenal properties be integrated with the physical world? Phenomenal properties seem to be intrinsic properties that are hard to fit with the structural-dynamic character of a physical theory and arguably they are the only intrinsic properties that we have direct knowledge of. Russell's insight … perhaps the intrinsic properties of the physical world are themselves phenomenal properties. Or perhaps … constitute phenomenal properties. If so then consciousness and physical reality are deeply connected.[70]

Chalmers admits that Russellian monism is "speculative and … [may] sound strange at first hearing. Many find it extremely counterintuitive to suppose that fundamental physical properties have phenomenal properties." On the other hand, as I argued, it supports a realistic interpretation of QM if allowing intrinsic intentionality. Chalmers concludes about Russellian monism, as for epiphenomenalism, that it is "not clear strangeness yields any strong objections … (and) the view seems to be compatible with all evidence and there is no direct evidence against it."

But there are principal problems. "Our phenomenology is unified, bounded and differentiated … and seems to have a single subject of experience." This is "a version of the combination problem for panpsychism" and we "have a good understanding of principles for physical composition but no real understanding of the principles of phenomenal composition." Chalmers says this is the most serious problem and an open question if it can be solved or not. "The only way … would seem to be in combination with a denial of microphysical closure holding that there are **fundamental dispositions above the microphysical level which have phenomenal properties as their grounds….**"[71] Thus it is almost like interactionism-dualism but the latter even "involves **fundamental causation above the microphysical.** This will involve a more radical view of physics, but might have the advantage of avoiding the combination problem."[72] I ponder if this fundamental causation above the microphysical could be the answer to why the bulk of matter still follows the Newtonian mechanics even if all the atomic parts have their own intentional quality. A sort of "group consciousness," where the parts "agree to behave" as a macroscopic object to make our daily life as it is?

Chalmers again: "Overall, Russellian monism promises a deeply integrated and elegant view of nature. No one has yet developed any sort of detailed theory in this class and it is not clear if such a theory can be developed. However there appear to be no strong reasons to reject this view." He concludes: "It is often held that even though it is hard to see how materialism could be true, materialism *must* be true since the alternatives are unacceptable." But Chalmers argues there are "at least three prima facie acceptable alternatives to materialism," i.e., interactionism, epiphenomenalism and panprotopsychism, "each of which is compatible with a broadly naturalistic (even if not materialistic) worldview and none of which has fatal problems." He also in a footnote discusses the choice between substance dualism and property dualism. He is neutral on that but "certainly not opposed to substance dualism (construed as the existence of fundamental nonphysical individuals) and there are some considerations (including issues about the combination problem and the unity of consciousness) that tend to favor it."[73]

Memory—Where Is It?

It is now and then claimed that at last we have found the engram, the memory storage in the brain.[74] But that claim seems to depend on lack of differentiation between (a) *episodic memory* of *unique events*, for example our first love, (b) *semantic memory*, learned knowledge (a and b equal *declarative*, or verbalized, memories) and (c) *nondeclarative*, *procedural memories* for our *learned ability* e.g., how to ride a bike or play the piano.

It is only for the last category of learning that we have studies showing the creation of new couplings between brain cells, as in Aplysia trained for a new conditioned response by repetition. But we cannot study episodic memory of unique events in animals as they can't talk about them. However, we know from humans that injuries to the brain can affect memory but you can't tell if it affects storage of memory or the possibility to retrieve it. There are persons, called savants, who have special gifts. One boy could play a piece of piano music after hearing it just once. Seemingly the unique event could directly be used as a procedural memory without training or repetition.

It is discussed in the literature if eidetic memory, "photographic memory," really exists but the Russian psychologist Luria[75] has reported a striking example about "S." Most of us can remember 5 to 9 numbers but S could remember 70 numbers after just hearing them once, and even after 15 years, and he could repeat them in any order. I think S's memory is best described as a very detailed episodic memory and not as a learned semantic memory, as it was enough for him to see or hear the items just once. "Episodic memory is memory for events in one's life that have specific location in time and space.... Episodic memory may be regarded as part of a more general ability to engage *in mental time travel*, which involves imagining the future, as well as the past."[76]

Models for memory have varied, from Aristotle's "impressions in wax" to tape recordings to computer memories. With analogy to our wireless connection to all data on the Internet, it would be enough to store the links for retrieval in the brain while the data or memory exists elsewhere. But where? Spacetime is ontologically real and all past events still exist in spacetime. So a species that in evolution learns to use this "spacetime library" for memories[77] will probably have an advantage over those that have to use their brains for the storage of *all* data. Even mental time travel and experiences of the future[78] can be interpreted as direct experiences of existing future in real spacetime.

Near Death Experiences (NDE)

People can, when near death, have extraordinary experiences, seeing themselves and what is happening around them, seemingly from a point outside their body (an out of body experience, or OBE). There are not as many veridical[79] NDEs as reported but enough to consider them. There are cases in which people were born blind yet during NDE have what seem to be visual experiences.[80] There are a lot of possible hypothetical, "normal" explanations, including fraud, recitation of common facts, guided hallucinations, etc. A Finnish philosopher[81] admits the difficulty of explaining "genuine" cases and posits it must be hallucinations plus information gleaned through a not yet discovered physical field. Of course this is possible, but ad hoc. Perhaps taking these NDE- and OBE-experiences at their face value we can find a new clue to explain even ordinary experiences? Moody reports upon the review of one's life during an NDE: "[Some] recall no awareness of temporal order at all. The remembrance was instantaneous; everything appeared at once and they could take it all in with one mental glance."[82] Here I summarize Morjani's[83] very long NDE: "Total awareness, I could see everything at the same time and it was not limited by distance and not limited by time either … [it] felt as if everything was happening at once. Past, present and future, it all felt like it was happening simultaneously."

I will argue that the near-death experience where people can see their "whole life" at once can be interpreted as that they experience the time dimension as space and thus experience the four-dimensional spacetime where everything which has happened, happens and will happen exists at once. Spacetime then is not only physically real and ontologically fundamental but also open for direct conscious experience.

There are also cases of seemingly precognitive visions,[84] but then all is seemingly predetermined, which seems to contradict nondeterminism in quantum mechanics and even more important our direct experience of our ability to choose. Can this have some connection to the mathematically possible extension of special relativity to six dimensional spacetime? Consider these NDE experiences of more dimensions: "Taking geometry, they always told me there were only three dimensions.… There are more. And of course our world—the one we are living in now—is three-dimensional, but the next one definitely isn't. And that's why it's so hard to tell you this. I have to describe it to you in words that are three dimensional,"[85] "I next realised that my vision included not only 'things' in the ordinary three-dimensional world but also 'things' in these four or more dimensional places that I was in.… Everything in the three dimensional space existed in the fourth dimension and also in the fifth dimension, and I at the time quite clearly understood what was meant."[86] In six-dimensional spacetime with three time dimensions the picture changes dramatically and now we have many, perhaps infinite, possibilities for the future.

Possibilities, Reality and Choices

In this view, which of the possible worlds that will become real depends on choices of all intentional beings, as the simplified figure shows. Dependent on A's and B's independent choices, to be at home or to go to a concert, one of the four possible worlds will be physically real in our three-dimensional world in space, while the other possibilities will continue to exist as non-realized possibilities. There is a significant difference between possibility and reality. Hegel said that which is real must have been possible, but that which is possible might happen to be real but doesn't need to happen to be real.[87]

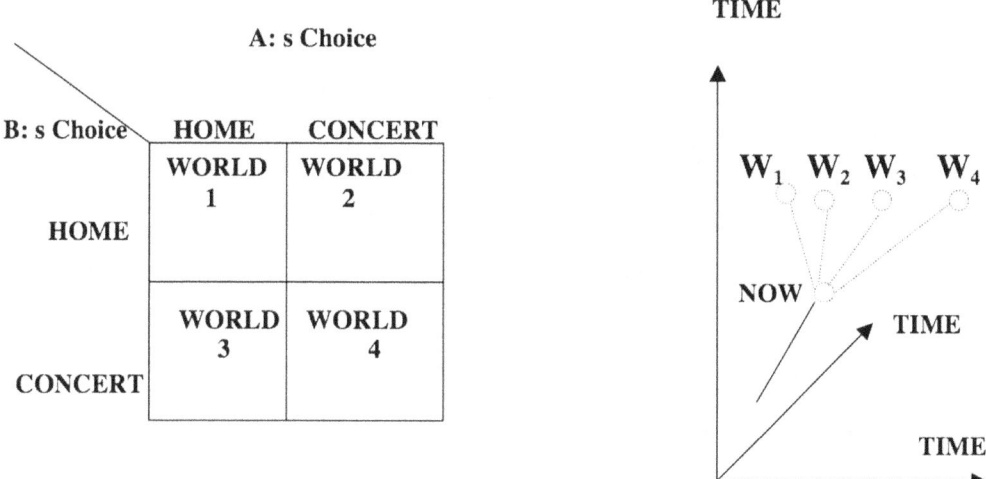

Choices of Possibilities Decide Reality

Where Are Our Experiences?

One fundamental problem of consciousness is the relation between processes located in the brain and the location of our experiences. In physics we can (almost) exactly locate material objects in space and time.

But there seems to be no consensus about the location of thoughts, e.g., the thought that you will eat something after reading this. Brain materialists claim that the thought is in your brain because thoughts are brain processes,[88] which actually begs the question. Other philosophers claim that the thoughts are where you are, but that it is meaningless to locate the thought to some part of the body,[89] e.g., the brain or stomach (a possible candidate for thoughts of eating?). Still other philosophers claim that the thought, the mental, doesn't seem to be possible to locate in space at all.[90] So it seems to be a difference of category between material brain processes and thoughts. What about sensory experiences?

Look for Your Self

You are now reading a book. Where is the book located? I think you will agree that the book is somewhere in front of your head and eyes. Where is your visual experience of the book located? Take time to look. If you say "in my brain or in my eyes," I must ask you how you then can see that there is a book out there in front of your eyes? Forget all you have heard and learnt and look again. If you still claim that the visual experience is in your brain/eyes you perhaps, as some do, claim that you can still see that the book is in front of your eyes and head because you have learnt to interpret or experience your brain process in that way. But *how*? Georg von Békésy[91] claims this "projection" to be learned and that it has a survival value, which perhaps explains why we developed it. But again, *how*? The neurophysiologist Benjamin Libet[92] said that this automatic subjective referral of our sensory experiences to the space is mysterious.

More Than the Brain

Alva Noé, philosopher and neuroscientist, writes "the brain is not the thing inside you that makes you conscious, ... we've been thinking about consciousness the wrong way—as something that happens in us, like digestion—when we should be thinking about it as something we do, as a kind of living activity."[93]

Riccardo Manzotti, researcher in consciousness, also questions the common view that our experiences are representations of the world inside our brain. He points to the chain of physical and causal continuity from the object in the world to the sense organs and all brain processes, and suggests that the whole chain, not just the end part (in the brain) is identical to our conscious experience.[94]

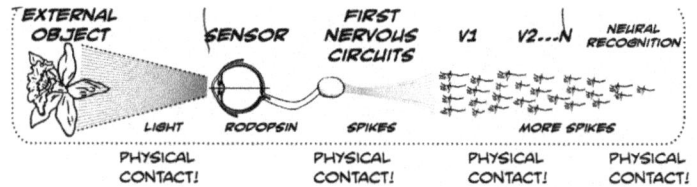

Conscious Experience (© Riccardo Manzotti).

He also argues that "Reality and the mind share the same ontological status.... Our access to the world is understood, to a greater or lesser extent, to be direct rather than mediated, representational or illusory."[95]

Consciousness in Spacetime[96]

It seems to me that Manzotti is on the right line. I have never had a sensory experience which I could localize as an experience *in* my brain, and I doubt that any one else has. To me it seems that all my sensory experiences are outside the brain, in the body or in the space around me. Touch is in the body where I feel the touch. Taste is in the mouth and smell is in the nose. Hearing and sight, is out there in the space around the body. Neither do I *experience* any brain processes at all in my brain related to sensory experience. Rather it seems to me that the most important aspect of sensory experiences is located in the matter or events in spacetime outside the brain. Sensory experiences, I suggest, are mainly located in the experienced matter, as events in the space now, the space-aspect of spacetime.

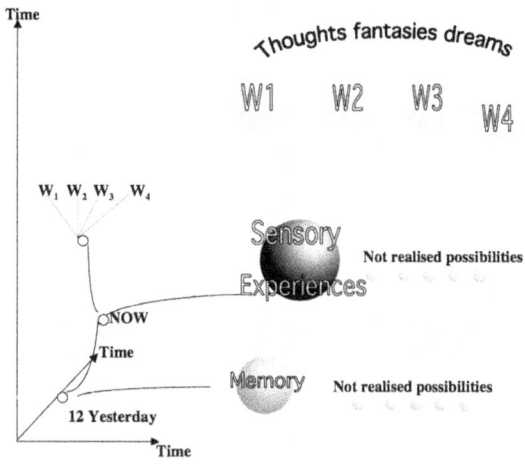

Six dimensional Spacetime   **Consciousness**

Mental experiences as thoughts, fantasies and dreams are outside space now, in time, the time-aspect of spacetime, and identical with events in possible worlds in the six-dimensional spacetime, which haven't been realized in the past, are lost possibilities for the now or can be realized in the future. Abstract thoughts and semantic memory can be interpreted as speech in a possible world. Episodic memories are earlier realized events in spacetime and wrong episodic memories are when we mistake a not-realized possibility for a realized possibility. Emotions can be construed as tensions between memories, the realized world (including the body) and frightening or hoped-for possible worlds. For ordinary experiences the brain is our "anchorage" in spacetime, defining from what focus we experience spacetime. In the presented view the changes in sensory organs and the brain don't create our experiences but are the traces of how our consciousness is brought in contact with events or possible worlds in the six-dimensional spacetime outside our brain.

Relativity of Cause and Effect from a First- and Third-Person Perspective.

A thought about the future is thus interpreted as a future possibility, which exists in the future of spacetime, because in spacetime all that can happen

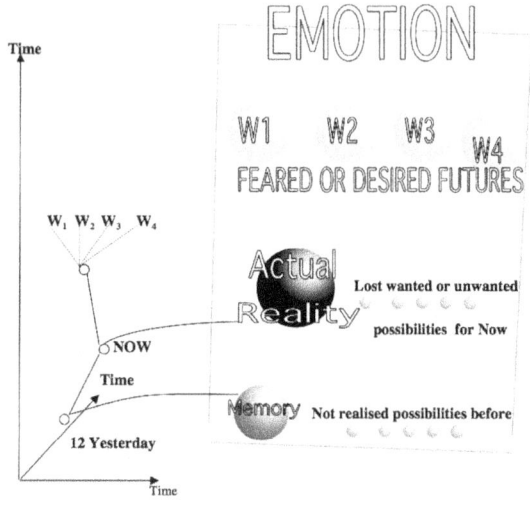

Six dimensional Spacetime   **Emotion**

already exists. When I write this sentence on my computer it is an adequate description for another person, the so-called *third-person perspective*, to state that processes in my brain are the causes of the movement of my arms and fingers to touch the keyboard causing the text on the screen. But in my own perspective, the *first-person perspective*, it is an equally adequate description to state that it is my focus on the thought, equal to my mental picture of the text on the screen in a possible future world, which causes the writing. That is, the order between cause and effect is relative and dependent on the perspective of the observer. Concerning consciousness, reversal of the order between cause and effect is an asset, as it seems to explain part of the difference between third-person and first-person perspectives. As superluminal causality admits frames where the order between cause and effect is changed, I think the example shows a possible relation between conscious causality and superluminal causality.

Conscious Experience as Fundamental

It seems quite reasonable, as Chalmers argues, that to explain conscious we need an extra ingredient, something new and "to take experience itself as a fundamental feature of the world, alongside mass, charge and space-time." Conscious experience is thus not further explained, but is also the only intrinsic property we have direct knowledge of. What is needed is a theory of how the new fundamental, conscious experience, relates to everything else in the world. Chalmers argues that we can expect "fundamental principles—psychophysical laws—connecting physical and phenomenal properties" (Chalmers 2010, 125).

Six-dimensional spacetime seems "physical enough" as coupled to the physical theory of special relativity, but "unphysical enough" to also possibly connect to phenomenal properties. It is suggested that all matter, not only microphysical, and all events and processes in six-dimensional spacetime, have intrinsic aspects with phenomenal properties as their grounds and that it might be possible to develop a more detailed description in six dimensions than the very sketchy outline given here. In summary, sensory experiences are seen as mainly located in the experienced matter outside brain, as events in the now, the space-aspect of spacetime, or sometimes as in distorted experiences in another possibility outside the now.

Mental experiences as thoughts, fantasies and dreams are in time, the time-aspect of spacetime, and identical with events in possible worlds in the six-dimensional spacetime. These possible worlds exist all at once in six-dimensional spacetime and are possible in the sense that they could have been or can become a physical real material world, but are also always possible to experience as mental. Memories are mainly earlier events in spacetime. Intentions or choices affect which possibilities will become real. What is in the now a sensory experience, that is "located in matter," is in the next moment a memory, outside the now, that is mental. A thought is mental, as a possibility in the future which can be realized and thus become material. So matter and mental can transform into each other and can be seen as a space- or time-aspect of Spacetime, a sort of "Conscious Monism."

If it is right that all events and processes in six-dimensional spacetime have aspects with phenomenal properties as their grounds, it is perhaps even possible to experience these events directly, without sensory organs and brain. Most scientists suppose that the brain is necessary for *all possible experiences* and probably think this is self-evident. But is it so clear? All our experiences when we are awake are accompanied with our body with its brain. However in dreams and even more so in out-of-body-experiences this connection to the body is not experienced as self-evident. Also, it seems that there is no experience or experimental data (in this life) which can falsify the hypothesis that the brain is necessary for all possible experiences,[97] which thus seems more as a belief than a scientific hypothesis. Therefore the question of the necessity of the brain for all possible experiences seems quite open. Thus it is possible, as a hypothesis, taking OBE at face value (especially those with an NDE where monitoring of brain activity shows no or very low activity),[98] indicating that under special circumstances it is possible to have direct experiences of events in spacetime without the mediation of sense organs and processes in the brain. This seemingly supports that events and processes in spacetime have aspects with phenomenal properties as their grounds.

Where Am I?

What integrates all experiences to a unified and single subject of experience? Maudlin writes:

Violation of Bell's inequality does not require superluminal matter or energy transport. Violation of Bell's inequality does not entail the possibility of superluminal Signalling. Violation of Bell's inequality does require superluminal causal connections. Violation of Bell's inequality can be accomplished only if there is superluminal information transmission [2013, 221].

So what "moves" faster than light and seemingly exists in the superluminal realm, seems to be more than matter, energy or signals but instead information and causality. To me this sounds like experiences and will or intention, which are conscious qualities. So perhaps also this can be seen to support that consciousness is fundamental, more than matter and energy and also related to the superluminal realm? So I, who experiences information and have or express will, causality, am seemingly more than energy and matter, more than time and space, possibly spacetime?

When for example we listen to music we don't hear a sequence of separate tones but "a *whole structure* that is in some sense 'timeless,'"[99] which can be interpreted as "I integrate over spacetime." This might also suggest why music is so important because it brings us in contact with our expanded consciousness in spacetime, ourselves, "I."

There is but one spacetime, so in this view just one I, the unification of consciousness. I think Schrödinger[100] is quite right when pointing out "the empirical fact that consciousness is never experienced in the plural, only in the singular" thus suggests some kind of "unification of minds or consciousnesses."

It seems easier from one consciousness to explain many: individuality is due to projections into different points of view, focused in body and brain, which gives different aspects of sensory experience and mental events. This might reverse the combination problem of panpsychism, which Chalmers sees as a major problem, and perhaps make it easier. This is perhaps also related to Bohm's "Indivisible Unity of the World (1951, 166). "The essential features of the implicate order are … that the whole universe is in some way enfolded in everything and that each thing is enfolded in the whole."[101]

50 Part I. Physics, Spacetime and Near Death Experiences

An illuminating analysis of the relation between ego and the One I, LOGOS, is also given by the philosopher Ashok Gangadean.[102] He also shows that awakening of a global consciousness and illumination is necessary for the survival of humanity and our beautiful planet.

• I Am Spacetime  ⊂ LOGOS

Notes

1. References to relevant Internet sites and where parts of or whole books can be downloaded, on and some further comments on http://www.drpilotti.info/eng/essaysonconsciousness.html.
2. Einstein, A., and Infeld, L. 1938, p. 8.
3. See note 8.
4. De Brogile, L. 1939, pp. 123–130.
5. Note 2, p. 88.
6. Turok, N. 2012, pp. 32–47.
7. Einstein, A. 1905.
8. Rindler, W. 1960, 2006.
9. Minkowski, H. 1908, pp. 75, 83.
10. Petkov, V. 2005, pp. 6, 122.
11. Pilotti, J. 2011c. "Einstein's argument for v<c" and "Possible extensions of Einstein's theory of relativity" reprinted with permission of the publisher.
12. $E = mc^2$ but m increases as $m = \frac{m_0}{\sqrt{1 - v^2/c^2}}$.
13. Bilaniuk, O.M.P., Deshpande, V. K., Sudarshan E.C.G., 1962; Tanaka, S., Progr. Theoret. Phys. 1960; Feinberg, G. (unpublished).
14. Feinberg, G., 1967.
15. Alväger, T., Kreisler, M. 1968.
16. Parker, L., 1969.
17. Recami, E., Mignani, R., 1974, Cole, E.A.B., 1977, Pavsic, M. (unpublished) http://www-f1.ijs.si/~pavsic/ExtenRel71.pdf. Pilotti, J. (unpublished) http://www.drpilotti.info/eng/sixdimensioinal-relativity.html.
18. Cole, E.A.B., 2000.
19. Cole, E.A.B., 1980.
20. Pilotti, J., unpublished.
21. See note 25.
22. Shilov, G. E. 1961, p. 122.
23. Recami, E., Mignani, R. 1974.
24. Cole, E.A.B. 1977.
25. Actually ± in all formulas; see notes 24 and 1.
26. Planck, M. 1901, Turok, N. 2012, p. 61.
27. Bell, J.S. 2004, p. 214.
28. Rosenblum, B., Kuttner, F. 2006, p. 140.
29. Bacciagaluppi, G., Valentini, A. 2009.
30. De Broglie, L. 1924.
31. De Broglie, L. 1939, pp. 168–69.
32. Ibid. Note 30, p. 1.
33. Ibid. Note 31, pp. 169–171.
34. Ibid. Note 30, chap. 3.
35. Ibid. Note 29, p. 37.
36. Ibid. Chap. 2, 11 and pp. 373.
37. Dürr, et al. 2013. Introduction. p. 6.

38. Schrödinger, E. 1935. Allori, V., Zanghi, N. 2001.
39. Ibid. 1935. Note 37 pp. 1–2.
40. Dürr, D., Teufel, S. 2009 pp. 9–10. David Bohm in 1952 "rediscovered" de Brogile's pilot wave theory and presented his "causal" or "ontological" theory. Bohm, D., Hiley, B.J. 1993.
41. Blomberg, T. 1987.
42. Allori, V., Zanghi, N. 2001 pp. 7–8.
43. Tonomura, et al. 1989. From Dr. Tonomura via internet but he doesn't necessarily endorse my conclusion. Also cf. Dr. Quantum and Holland, P. 2000.
44. Feynman, R., quoted in foreword by Tim Maudlin, p. vi, note 37.
45. Bell, J.S., 2004. p. 191. Original Bell, J.S. 1986. See also Holland, P. 2000.
46. Wiseman, H.M. 2006. p. 79.
47. Ibid. pp. 80–81.
48. Bohm, D. 1951 p. 166.
49. Bell, J.S. 2004 pp. 14–20, quote p. 160. Bell, J.S. 1966. Note 39.
50. Ibid. Note 46, p. 86.
51. Maudlin, T. 2013 p. 221.
52. Stapp, H. 2004, p. 88–92.
53. Cushing, J. 1994.
54. The Copenhagen interpretation describes only probabilities, and thus a nondeterministic view with chance. Bohm's mechanics are deterministic, even if not an ontological necessity (note 40). Blomberg's theory (note 41) is stochastic but does not exclude a "deeper" causal level. My view here is that in either case a deeper causal level can be related to consciousness, intentions.
55. See Note 39.
56. Pavsic, M. 2001. 12.1.
57. Bars, I. 2010.
58. Dirac, P. 1942.
59. Petkov, V. 2005. p. 152.
60. Ibid. p. 160.
61. Simultaneity is relative so there is actually no universal now and observers in relative movement have different views on which set of events in spacetime that constitute the whole world for a given time, but the difference is negligible for ordinary distances and velocities. The argument is still valid for each observer.
62. Boyling, J.B, Cole, E.A.B. 1993, also extend QM to six dimensions on other grounds. Chen, X. (2008) uses three time dimensions, but in another way, to unify SR and QM.
63. Crick, F., Koch, C. 2003.
64. Chalmers, D. 2010.
65. Ibid. p. 104.
66. Ibid. p. 125.
67. Chalmers, D. 1996. p. 156 and 2010, p. 128.
68. Note 64, p. 127.
69. Note 56, p. 316.
70. Note 64, p. 133.
71. Note 64, p. 137.
72. Ibid.
73. Note 64, p. 139.
74. Hurley, D. 2012; Purves, et al., 2012, pp. 697–98.
75. Luria, A.R. 1987.
76. Zelazo, P.D. 2007, pp. 576–77.
77. Strömberg, G. 1940/1970 p. 191.
78. Campbell, J. 1999.
79. Sabom, M. 1981, 1982.
80. Ring, K., and Cooper S. 1999.
81. Rosing, H. 1982.
82. Moody, R. 1973/1976. pp. 64–65.
83. Moorjani, A. 2012.
84. Ring, K. 1982.

85. Note 82, p. 26.
86. Geddes, A. 1937.
87. From Haveman, R. 1964.
88. Smart, J.J.C. 1981.
89. Schaffer J.A. 1968.
90. Cornman J.W. 1968.
91. v Békésy, G. 1967.
92. Libet, B. 1976.
93. Noë, Alva. 2009.
94. Manzotti, R. 2009, 2011.
95. Manzotti, R., and Pepperell, R. 2012.
96. Strömberg, G. 1970, Pilotti, J. 1987, 2011a–c and references therein.
97. Yet I have in Pilotti 2011c argued that there could be a possibility to falsify brain-materialism by studying the number of dimensions we can experience.
98. Van Lommel, P. 2010.
99. Pylkkänen, P. 2007. p. 96.
100. Schrödinger, E. 1969. pp. 140, 139.
101. Bohm, D. and Hiley, B.J. 1993. p. 382.
102. Gangadean, A. 2012.

References

Allori, V., Zanghi, N. (2001) What Is Bohmian Mechanics? Int. J. of Theoret. Physics 43, 1743–1755 (2004).
Alväger, T., Kreisler, M. (1968). Quest for Faster-Than-Light Particles. Physical Review 171, pp. 1357–1361.
Bacciagaluppi, G., Valentini A. (2009). Quantum Theory at the crossroad. Reconsidering the 1927 Solvay Conference. Cambridge: Cambridge University Press.
Bars, I., Terning J. (2010). Extra Dimensions in Space and Time. New York: Springer.
Bell, J.S. (1966). On the problem of hidden variables in quantum theory. Rev. Mod. Phys. 38, pp. 447–52. Also in Bell (2004).
Bell, J.S. (1986). Six possible worlds of quantum mechanics. Proceedings of the Nobel Symposium 65: Possible worlds in Arts and Sciences. Stockholm. Also in Bell (2004).
Bell, J.S. (2004). Speakable and Unspeakable in Quantum Mechanics. Cambridge: Cambridge University Press.
Bilaniuk, O.M.P., Deshpande, V.K., Sudarshan E.C.G. (1962). "Meta" Relativity. Am. J. Phys. 30, pp. 718–723.
Blomberg T. (1987). Principles of Deductive Theoretical Physics: A proposal for a general deductive physical theory based on successive Confidence estimates on Quantum Mechanical wave functions. Outline of a mathematical theory. In press.
Bohm, D. (1951) Quantum Theory. New York: Dover Publications Inc.
Bohm, D., Hiley, B.J. (1993). The Undivided Universe. London, New York: Routledge.
Boyling, J.B., and Cole, E.A.B. (1993) Six-Dimensional Dirac Equation. Int. J. Theoretical Phys. 32, pp. 801–812.
Campbell, J. (1999). Mind's past, present and future. New York: Framtider International, pp. 21–24.
Chalmers, D.J. (1996). The Conscious mind: In search of a Fundamental Theory. New York: Oxford University Press.
Chalmers, D.J. (2010). The Character of Consciousness. New York: Oxford University Press.
Chen, X. (2008). Three Dimensional Time Theory: To Unify the Principles of Basic Quantum Physics and Relativity. http://arxiv.org/abs/quant-ph/0510010.
Cole, E.A.B. (1977). Superluminal Transformations Using Either Complex Space-Time or Real Space-Time Symmetry. Il Nuovo Cimento, 40A, pp. 171–180.
Cole, E.A.B. (1980). New Electromagnetic Fields in Six-Dimensional Special Relativity. Il Nuovo Cimento, 60A, pp. 1–12.
Cole, E.A.B. (2000). Prediction of dark matter using six-dimensional special relativity. Il Nuovo Cimento, 115B, pp. 1149–1158.
Cornman, J.W. (1968). The Mind-Body problem. In Cornman J.W., et al. (eds.), Philosophical Problems and Arguments. London: Macmillan Company.

Crick, F., Koch, C. (2003). A framework for consciousness. Nature Neuroscience 6, no. 2, pp. 119–126.
Cushing, J. (1994). Quantum Mechanics. Historical contingency and the Copenhagen hegemony. Chicago: University of Chicago Press.
De Brogile, L. (1924). Recherches sur la théorie des quanta. English translation On the theory of quanta.
De Brogile, L. (1939). Matter and Light. The New Physics. New York: W.W. Norton.
Dirac, P. (1942). The Physical Interpretation of Quantum Mechanics. Proc. Roy. Soc. London (A 180), pp. 1–39.
Dürr, D., Teufel, S. (2009) Bohmian Mechanics. The Physics and Mathematics of Quantum Theory. Berlin, Heidelberg: Springer-Verlag.
Dürr, D. et al. (2013). Quantum Physics without Quantum Philosophy. Berlin, Heidelberg: Springer-Verlag.
Einstein A. (1905). Zur Elektrodynamik bewegter Körper. English translation: Electromagnetic Phenomena in a System Moving with any Velocity less than that of Light. In Einstein, et al. (1923/1952).
Einstein, A., Infeld, L. (1938/2007). The Evolution of Physics. From early concepts to relativity and quanta. New York: Simon & Schuster.
Einstein, A., Lorentz, H., Weyl, H., Minkowski, H. (1923/1952). The Principle of Relativity. New York: Dover Publications.
Feinberg, G. (1967). Possibility of Faster-Than-Light Particles. Physical Review 159, pp. 1089–1105.
Gangadean, A. (2012). The importance of transpersonal literacy in the emergence of awakened global consciousness: our maturation as a species. Lecture at Eurotas 2012.
Geddes, A. (1937). A Voice from the Grandstand. Edinburgh Medical Journal 44, pp. 365–84.
Haveman, R. (1964). Dialektik ohne Dogma? Naturwissenschaft und Weltanschauung. Reinbek: Rowohlt.
Holland, P. (2000). The Quantum theory of motion. An account of the de Brogile-Bohm Causal Interpretation of Quantum Mechanics. Cambridge: Cambridge University Press.
Hurley, D. (2012). Memory lives. Discover (April) pp. 30–37.
Libet, B. (1978). Cerebral correlates of conscious experiences. INSERM Symp. no. 6. Amsterdam: North-Holland Publ. Comp.
Luria, A.R. (1987). The Mind of a Mnemonist. New York: Harvard University Press.
Manzotti, R. (2009). A Process Oriented Externalist Solution to the Hard Problem. Cartoon, with fig. 27, published here with kind permission of the artist. http://www.consciousness.it/RM_Cartoons.php.
Manzotti, R. (2011). The Spread Mind. Seven Steps to Situated Consciousness. Journal of Cosmology, 14: 4526–4541.
Manzotti, R., Pepperell, R. (2012). The New Mind: thinking beyond the head. AI & Society. Knowledge, Culture and Communication 24 (1), 1–12.
Maudlin, T. (2011). Quantum Non-Locality and Relativity. Oxford: Wiley-Blackwell Publishing.
Minkowski, H. (1908). "Space and time" (lecture).
Moody, R. (1973/1976). Life after life. New York: Bantam Books.
Moorjani, A. (2012). Dying to be me. New York: Hay House Inc.
Noë, A. (2009). Out of our heads. Why you are not your Brain and other lessons from the biology of Consciousness. New York: Hill and Wang.
Parker, L. (1969) Faster-Than-Light Inertial Frames and Tachyons. Phys. Rev. 188, pp. 2287–2292.
Pavsic, M. (2001). The Landscape of Theoretical Physics. A global view. London: Kluwer Academic Publisher.
Petkov, V. (2005). Relativity and the nature of Spacetime. Heidelberg: Springer.
Pilotti, J. (1987). "Consciousness and the brain" (in Swedish). In Jacobson, N.-O., Ed. "Nytänkande." Stockholm: Norstedts.
Pilotti, J. (2011a). What can a brain really do? Mind-body question is either undecidable or materialism is false. Paper presented at Towards a Science of Consciousness, Stockholm. Pilotti, J. (2011b). Mind-body problem either undecidable or materialism is false. Relevance for treatment or suicidal intention. Poster at 14th International Conference for Philosophy and Psychiatry, Gothenburg.
Pilotti, J. (2011c /2012). Consciousness and Physics. Towards a scientific proof that consciousness is in Space-time beyond the brain. J. Transpersonal Research. Vol. 3, 123–34.
Planck, M. (1901) Ueber das Gesetz der Energieverteilung im Normalspectrum. Annalen der Physik, vol. 4, pp. 553.
Popper, K.R. (1974). The Logic of Scientific Discovery. London: Hutchinson.

Purves, D., et al. (eds.). (2012). Neuroscience 5th ed. Sunderland: Sinauer Ass. Inc.
Pylkkänen, P. (2007). Mind, Matter and the Implicate Order. Berlin-Heidelberg: Springer.
Recami, E., Mignani, R. (1974). Classical theory of tachyons (Special relativity extended to superluminal frames and objects) (a preliminary review). Riv. Nuovo Cimento, 4, pp. 209–290.
Rindler, W. (1960). Special Relativity. Edinburgh: Oliver & Boyd.
Rindler, W. (2006) Relativity. Special, General and Cosmological. London: Oxford University Press.
Ring, K. (1982). Precognitive and Prophetic Visions in NDE. Anabiosis vol. 2:1, pp. 47–75.
Ring, K., Cooper, S. (1999) Mindsight: Near death and out of body experiences in the blind. Palo Alto, CA: Institute of Transpersonal Psychology.
Rosenblum, B., Kuttner, F. (2006). Quantum Enigma. Physics Encounters Consciousness. London: Oxford University Press.
Rosing, H. (1982). "Medvetandets filosofi" (in Swedish). Helsingfors: Schildts.
Sabom, M. (1981). The near-death experience: Myth or reality. Anabiosis 1:1, pp. 44–56.
Sabom, M. (1982) Recollections of Death. A medical investigation. New York: Harper & Row.
Schafer, J.A. (1968). Philosophy of Mind. Englewood Cliffs, NJ: Prentice-Hall.
Schrödinger, E. (1935) . Die gegenwärtige Situation in der Quantenmechanik (The present situation in quantum mechanics). Naturwissenschaften. 23: pp. 807–812; 823–828; 844–849. Schrödinger, E. (1969) What Is Life & Mind and Matter. London: Cambridge University Press.
Shilov, G.E. (1961) An introduction to the theory of Linear spaces. Englewood Cliffs, NJ: Prentice-Hall.
Smart, J.J.C. (1981). Physicalism and emergence. Neuroscience vol. 6, pp. 109–113.
Stapp, H. (2004). Mind, Matter and Quantum Mechanics. Berlin-Heidelberg: Springer.
Strömberg, G. (1940/1970). The Soul of the Universe. North Hollywood: Educational Research Institute.
Tanaka, S. (1960). Theory of Matter with Super Light Velocity . Progr. Theoret. Phys. (Kyoto) 24 (1) pp. 171–200.
Tonomura et al. (1989). Am. J. Phys. 57, pp. 117–20.
v Békésy, G. (1967). Sensory Inhibition. Princeton: Princeton University Press.
Van Lommel, P. (2010). Consciousness Beyond Life. The Science of the Near-Death Experience. New York: Harper One.
Turok, N. (2012). The Universe Within. Toronto: Anansi.
Wiseman, H.M. (2006). From Einstein's theorem to Bell's theorem: a history of quantum non-locality. Contemporary Physics, Vol. 47, No. 2, March-April 2006, 79–88.
Zelazo, P.D., et al. (eds.). (2007). The Cambridge Handbook of Consciousness. Cambridge: Cambridge University Press.

The Psi-Track and Other Unexplained Energy Fields

GÖTE ANDERSSON

Preface

More than twenty years have passed since the author discovered and thereafter started investigating an energy phenomenon which is unfamiliar in normal science. It is still truthful to claim that these phenomena are repeatable under single-blind test conditions and even to high degree, double-blind.

In 1987 I discovered that a person can establish a remarkable type of energy field on another being, object and even to a distant place. Research has shown that the energy field can be established over considerable distances. I have named the energy field the psi-track, with regard to the fact it probably belongs to the psi-area. To carry out a final classification of its nature is at the present time difficult to perform.

Further forward in this essay is an account of how a person with an extraordinary ability and perception could actually see the psi-track plus other notable energy phenomenon with the naked eye. Numerous variations of the experiment, together with the said individual, were 100 percent repeatable even during strict double-blind conditions. I will return to this subject later, but first I will present another method used for detection of psi-tracks.

The Use of a Biophysical Method (Dowsing)

The background to my discovery of the psi-track is as follows:

My father Arthur Andersson, now unfortunately deceased, was in his earlier days a very dependable, experienced and trusted dowsing man. As a young boy I often accompanied my father when he had been asked by others to search for an underground water source using his dowsing rod. The fruits of his searches for water always ended in favorable wells. Often skeptics will argue that water, i.e., ground water, is virtually everywhere and that using a dowsing rod as a means to seek water is pointless pseudoscience. No professional dowser would claim to be able to detect deep lying ground water, rather only seams of water closer to the surface (water veins) and these are not to be found everywhere. A skilled dowser is able to pinpoint a water vein to within inches, even without signs in the ground or from the terrain as to the probability of water being there.

In years past, wells were dug by hand and because of this it was of great importance to employ the services of an experienced dowser. Today drilling machines are used to bore holes to great depths in order to reach ground water, therefore the services of skilled dowsers are no longer needed to such a degree. Water flows are also found in areas with karst (caves in the ground with water streams) landforms and can be readily detected with a dowsing rod. Leif Engh, a researcher in geophysics studied a typical karst area on the island of Gotland, Sweden, and made tests using geophysical instruments (slingram and VLF, very low frequency) and georadar to detect underground areas of small caves and streams. Engh is not actually a dowsing researcher but he had the idea to test if a dowser could get a reaction in the same place as the instruments. The notable result was that more than half of the 30 dowsers actually got a reaction in exactly the same places as the instruments. There were no clues of any kind as to the karst nature of the area visible to those involved with the testing.[1]

The dowsing phenomenon has been criticized, almost as far as to say to be ridiculed, by the skeptics. The reason for this is that they haven't bothered to closely scrutinize the phenomenon; rather, they have dismissed the whole field. The skeptics have not understood that it is the dowsers themselves who are sensitive to external energy stimulants, resulting in muscular tensions that influence their reactions. It is the wrists of the dowser that control the rods or other implements, and no respectable and serious water diviner would claim it to be some mysterious force responsible for the movement.

When it comes to detecting water veins it is not unreasonable to think that the water which circulates in the earth's magnetic field becomes faintly conductive of electricity, it is probably this electricity that the dowser senses. Another possible alternative is that the spot of perception is the place where a deviation in the magnetic field occurs. The latter theory concerning deviation in the earth's magnetic field and the sensitive dowser's reactions can be plausible, at least in certain cases. Here I would like to mention an interesting experience that one of my friends, dowser Harald Karlsson, now unfortunately deceased, once told to me.

The event occurred many years ago at a time when dowsers were in high demand to search for water veins in the countryside. Harald was asked to perform a search for water in a meadow and while he methodically crossed the meadow with the dowsing rod in his hands he felt it give a powerful response in an area of about a meter in length. He understood that it must be something other than a water vein that had caused the reaction, because of its extensive length. The man that had requested Harald's services was eager to dig in the area. At roughly 10 centimeters deep they discovered an old rusty iron bar that had mistakenly been left in the meadow, only to be plowed into the ground by agricultural machinery. I have also questioned the man who requested Harald's services who verified his account. Naturally there had been no clues to reveal that an iron bar was hidden in the ground. An iron bar can cause a deviation in the earth's magnetic field, and therefore the theory that a sensitive dowser could be susceptible to an anomaly of this kind is probable. A few hundred years ago, dowsing men were employed by mining organizations to trace veins of ore, veins that also cause changes in the earth's magnetic field.

There is good reason to take the dowsing phenomenon seriously, and I shall give examples of how my own investigations further prove it to be genuine. It can also be used for purposes other than searching for water.

The Discovery of the Psi-track

As I've already mentioned it was 1987 when I started researching the psi-track, but prior to that I had read an interesting book by the late German psychologist and professor Hans Bender. The title of the book is *Telepathy, Clairvoyance and Psychokinesis*.[2]

The book gives numerous examples of the phenomenon called "psychokinesis" which entails a person being able to unintentionally influence material objects in close proximity without physical contact. This phenomenon is extremely rare, but does occur in a few cases, and notably, in younger people who are experiencing puberty. My own spontaneous idea when I read about this, was that it could be caused by a kind of energy field given out from certain people. Around this time I had also read how skilled dowsers could experience a reaction from "the aura" that surrounds people. The aura is a type of energy field surrounding the bodies of living beings.

During a visit to my parents I recalled what I had read, and immediately asked my father Arthur to walk towards me holding his dowsing instrument, this to test if he felt any reaction from my aura. To our delight, it resulted in a strong reaction about 50 centimeters from my body. My next step was to test if it was possible to increase my aura through thought concentration. This didn't result in an increase of my aura. So I then had a spontaneous impulse to quite simply concentrate on a chair roughly 4 meters away from me, this to see if some sort of energy field was emanated from my aura.

My earlier idea that psychokinesis could have something to do with a kind of energy field stayed with me more or less deliberately. I wasn't trying to make the chair move from a distance, rather to ascertain whether an energy field emanated from me and if so one that would cause the dowsing to react. Impulses and ideas seldom, if ever, come from nowhere. After I'd concentrated on the chair, I asked my father if he had felt any reaction to the chair from the dowsing rod. He wasn't too keen as it seemed he felt that my whim was a little crazy, but to our great surprise the dowsing rod reacted strongly when held over the chair. After this I asked him to pass, dowsing rod at the ready, at right angles through the gap between the chair and I, now the dowsing rod reacted strongly, showing there to be some kind of energy flowing from myself to the chair. After we had found that there seemed to be an energy emanating from me I moved away from where I'd been standing to see what would happen.

My father again used the dowsing tool to check for a reaction, to our surprise the energy field (psi-track) remained between where I'd been standing and the chair. This seemed to show that the track was no longer tied to me after stopping the concentration exercise, yet it appeared that an impression had been formed after the exercise. We were both similarly amazed by this discovery, and I personally have never read or heard about a field similar to this that got a reaction from a dowsing rod. Naturally this very first experiment was not carried out under scientific conditions and a skeptic may suggest that my father, through suggestion, caused the dowsing rod to react, as he knew which object I was concentrating on. For the remainder of the essay I shall use the term "send" when I mean that I shall concentrate on somebody or something.

Naturally I was fully aware of the necessity of conducting the experiment in a more scientific fashion. It was necessary to perform tests where the dowser had no idea as to the object of attention of the sender's (myself) concentration.

Apart from my father, I had come in contact with many other experienced and assured dowsers. One of these, Karin Eriksson, was particularly competent at detecting my psi-track, as we found out. The tests were performed outdoors, thereby giving us large areas to work with. Small meadows and clearings in the woods were suitable places, and there is an abundance of them in the countryside where my colleagues and I live.

The very first trials can be said to be a blind test and were carried out together with Karin. We ventured out to small clearings in the woods where we were surrounded by a great number of trees. To start, Karin moved away from me to a distance of around 10 to 15 meters, blindfolded and with her back turned towards me. My task was to then concentrate on one of the many trees with the purpose of establishing a track to it, Karin of course having no prior indication as to which tree I was going to choose. The concentration needed to be carried out with great feeling while visualizing that I was holding on to the tree's trunk.

When I was finished concentrating, I marked the sending point with a stick in the ground. I asked Karin to come over to the place where I'd been concentrating (now on called the "sending point"). Then she took off the blindfold and circled the stick while carrying her dowsing rod. As I briefly mentioned above, there were remains of the field (psi-track) between the sending point and targeted object for some time after I had moved away. That was the advantage with this type of experiment, as I could leave the area, therefore not giving Karin any unintentional clues or signals through body language. The ground was free of snow when the test was performed, and therefore there were no footprints giving away my position while concentrating on the tree. It was important that Karin walk in circles around the sending point as the probability was equal that I could have chosen any of the trees around us.

When Karin felt the first reaction from the dowsing rod while walking the circular path she immediately changed direction, meaning she walked both clockwise and counter-clockwise while dowsing. Circling now in the opposite direction, the next reaction from the dowsing rod in the same area on her path gave the direction of where the track exited the circle. Then she just needed to cross the track at right angles in numerous places along its length until she reached the targeted tree.

One afternoon we were carrying out experiments using this method, and after 6 tests, 5 were completely successful as Karin followed the psi-track right to the targeted object. As mentioned earlier, traces of the track from the sending point to the object remain thus giving us cause to change area after every experiment. Moving area eliminates the risk of later experiments being spoiled by traces of previous tests potentially leading the dowser onto the wrong track.

These first experiments at the beginning of my research were not carried out randomly in scientific terms, as I felt that the simple, close-to-nature experiments were more inspirational to my dowsing colleagues. Later the experiments were developed to carry out under double-blind conditions.

The work evolved to even include more advanced experiments. People (target persons) had the task of hiding out in the terrain so that neither the sender nor the dowser had any clue as to the hiding place. The task for the sender and the dowser was to work out the exact direction to the target persons and then find them. All possible kinds of clues, e.g., footprints or other marks in the ground, were eliminated. To our delight the phenomenon and the method functioned to our full satisfaction. The accounts of many such experiments are to be found in my two books: *Psi-track* (1994) and *Psi-track II* (2010). Hundreds of experiments were carried out together with dowsers, achieving such good results that it is highly unlikely that chance was a factor.

This gave cause for me to believe that this phenomenon should be brought to the attention of professional researchers having an open attitude toward the Psi-area.

The first person I contacted was the physicist Jens A. Tellefsen. Later I contacted Dr. Nils-Olof Jacobson, a psychiatrist who has written books and articles on parapsychology. Both are members of the committee of the society of research in parapsychology (in Swedish, SPF, Sällskapet för Parapsykologisk Forskning) in Stockholm.

In 1991 the committee of the SPF decided that Psi-track was worthy of closer examination, and a research project was started with support from John Björhems memorial fund. The experiments were carried out under strict scientific conditions, always double-blind, on different occasions, and with the researchers present in my home district of Värmland, Sweden. Out of a total of 40 double-blind experiments 27 were a complete success, a few were partially successful, and a few experiments failed.

The test areas were, as a rule, the outer edges of grass meadows or areas of woodland. This was how we performed the experiments: A person (one of the two test leaders) was given the task of hiding an object along one of the 4 side edges of the grassy meadows, which measured 100 × 100 meters and 70 × 100 meters respectively. Sometimes the areas could be bigger or smaller. The object used was, among other things, a little rock crystal or other small article that belonged to the sender (I usually was the sender) which eased the visualizing process. If you consider the fact that the objects could be hidden anywhere along the 4 edges (all in all 400 meters on the larger fields), making you realize just how advanced the experiments actually were. The person responsible for hiding the object vacated the area after completion of the task so as not to unintentionally give any clues as to the object's location. Naturally, the concealing of the object was carried out in such a way as not to leave marks in the ground. When this was done it was time for the sender and dowser, under the control of the experiment leader, to start their task. The sender concentrated intensively on the hidden object after which the dowser, with dowsing rod ready, circled the sender. When the dowsing rod gave a strong reaction this was carefully noted after which the detecting continued at right angles to the direction the dowsing man had registered. A Psi-track has a certain width, between 0.5 and 1 meter, and it is imperative that the dowser gets a reaction in the middle of this area if they are to be led directly to the hidden object. If the edges of the track are registered then this will give cause to end up a half meter from the object, which must be acceptable given the search area's vastness.

A question that is often asked is whether the object's hiding place actually feels like a natural hiding place and because of this, able to guide those of us taking part. This was avoided in all experiments and furthermore I can refer to an experiment method which had a more random approach, in which the object's hiding place was chosen by chance with a lottery draw, in a more limited area about 150 meters in length. The experience of this showed that even a more random method didn't lead to a poorer result. On one occasion another random method was employed, using a clay pigeon trap that launched a little ceramic disc (10 centimeters in diameter).

For our experiments the small target object was taped to the little disc with the intention that it should be hurled away out onto the grassy meadow in an area of 70 × 100 meters. One of the experiment leaders, Jens Tellefsen, was given the task of activating the clay pigeon trap while dowser Leif Andersson, myself and the other experiment leader, Jacobsson, were in a cordoned-off area. The reason for this was so not to receive any sensory cues concerning Tellefsen's activities with the clay trap. Just prior to the hurling of the disc Tellefsen would close his eyes and keep them shut so not to see where the object fell, and afterwards he removed himself from the meadow.

From a total of 3 attempts all were successful as Leif was able to detect the track leading directly to the target object, while I myself was sender. The method must be able to be called random as no person could possibly know where the object landed out in the meadow; these experiments were therefore triple-blind.

On another occasion, when the above mentioned researchers weren't present, I carried out a slightly different test with the clay trap. I wanted to compare how easy or difficult it was to find a route leading straight to the hurled object without the help of the psi-track and dowsing rod. A person had to randomly guess where the object had landed and thereafter walk in that direction out into the meadow. Out of 10 attempts, all failed, and the object was not found. This test area was the same as the one described above.

The 10 tests without the aid of psi-track can be compared to the 3 successful tests in sequence where the psi-track was found with the dowsing rod and led straight to the object.

There is not enough space in this essay to provide a more in-depth account of all experiments and testing included in the research project. Jacobsson and Tellefsen became convinced that the phenomenon of psi-track was real, and together these academic researchers wrote a report to the *Journal of the Society for Psychical Research* in 1994. "Dowsing Along the Psi-track."[3] The article received first prize in a competition arranged by the journal, for the purpose of highlighting interesting discoveries in the psi-area (Imich Project Prize).

To Use the Psi-track Method in Practical Context

The experiments with the psi-track mentioned above were arranged for the purpose of research. Below I will give a couple of examples of how psi-track method can also be used practically to search for lost objects, domestic pets and in certain cases even people. Leif Andersson has had his dowsing talents enlisted, on occasion, in the search for people's hunting dogs when they disappear. He too is himself a hunter, and therefore naturally willing to help.

At the beginning of the 1990s I first came into contact with Leif. At that moment in time he knew nothing of my research into the psi-track and his experience, up until then, was in detecting water veins and even buried electric cables with his dowsing instrument. After I'd taught him how to send and detect a psi-track he soon showed he could perform both tasks with ease, to send and detect his own tracks and the tracks of others.

Here is an example of how a hunting dog, unfortunately drowned, could be found by Leif using the method. On December 13, 1992, Anders Lindgren and his wife, Berith, together with some friends, were out hunting in the forest. During the hunt their dog disappeared, and they searched for it until dark when they had to stop. They searched for the next two days without success. On December 16 Leif was called and he accompanied the couple to a clearing high up in the forest. This place was chosen as the sending point. Both Anders and Berith acted as senders because of them having fresh pictures of the dog in their mind. Leif circled them and got a reaction with his dowsing stick. The heading of both psi-tracks corresponded with each other, with both tracks pointing in a northeasterly direction, which according to the map headed towards a little lake. After the first attempt it was necessary to find a new sending point so they went back to the car and drove to a new position a few kilometers north. This time only Berith was sender and while Leif circled her with the dowsing stick he received a strong reaction in a westerly direction. When both headings were plotted with map and compass it turned out that the respective headings crossed at a point on the eastern edge of the small lake. A third point was found where another sending and dowsing were carried out, and findings duly plotted showing all three tracks crossed at exactly the same spot. Unfortunately the search had to be called off through failing light this winter's afternoon. The next day Berith and her uncle went through the forest to the small lake where the tracks had crossed. There they found the dead dog near to the water's edge; the dog had gone through the thin ice. A document concerning this incident has been written up by Berith and Anders Lindgren.

Searching for Missing Persons Using the Psi-track Method

On numerous occasions I have been asked if I together with my colleagues would help in the search for a missing person. Unfortunately the length of this essay doesn't allow for a thorough account here, but a more detailed explanation of this is found in my latest book, *Psi-track II*. Here follows short re-cap of such a mission, a tragic case that took place in the county of Dalsland, Sweden, where an elderly gent disappeared and was later found dead. The 84-year-old man disappeared from his home on October 3, 2005, and according to relatives was going to cycle to an acquaintance who lived 10 kilometers north of his home. Reliable dowser Knut Torstenson and I traveled to Dalsland and met with his relatives.

I received a telephone call in the afternoon of October 5 and was duly asked to assist, the fact it was due to get dark at around 7:00 meant we were pressed for time. It was decided that Lisbeth, daughter of the missing man, should act as sender. We used 4 different places from where the sending took place; Lisbeth concentrated while Knut and I detected with dowsing rods around her. The heading of the tracks we had picked up were plotted where they all crossed at exactly the same spot, which according to the map, was in a small paddock surrounded by woodland. The light was failing so we had to stop the search. Our map with plotted psi-tracks and was shown to military persons involved in the search, they assured us our target area unlikely as they'd covered the exact area by foot without result. This information made us a little low-spirited, as we believed our efforts were in vain.

The following days I kept in contact with the man's relatives regarding the search's progress, but no new leads developed, despite intensive searches. October 8 I decided to travel to Dalsland again to try psi-tracking one more time, but unfortunately this time Knut was otherwise engaged. I had arranged with the missing man's son-in-law, Vincent, that he and I would make another attempt with psi-tracking as he had some experience of dowsing. We carried out sending again from various places and plotted the bearings and the courses crossed each other in exactly the same spot, the same place we had plotted during our first attempt. Again the lack of light forced us to break off the search. Vincent was not convinced by our results, especially as military persons said the area had previously been searched. A few days later I received a phone call from Vincent who explained that a hunter had found his father-in-law's body, with bicycle nearby, hidden by grass in a ditch. The spot where he had been found was only a very short distance from where our psi-tracks had crossed when plotted. I can honestly say that we succeeded in finding the correct area where the body lay. The actions of police, military, relations, volunteers and our psi-track searches were all documented by Vincent. Also in the document he states that "if the psi-track had been taken more seriously with all resources (relatives, police, military) mobilised to an area with a maximum radius of 350 meters, and starting point at the middle of the psi-tracks can I say, hand on heart, that the result would have been different." This document is presented in my book *Psi-track II*.[4]

The Lost Kitten

My neighbor called by and explained that they'd lost a kitten a few days ago and could I help. I asked the very reliable dowser Gertrud Holm to assist us. I'd often seen the kitten, and therefore acted as sender from a suitable position in the garden while Gertrud slowly circled me equipped with dowsing rod. Straight away we got a strong reaction marking a track that led to an earth cellar. As I entered the cellar the kitten came cautiously towards me. A skeptic may say that the person who collected potatoes from the cellar had acknowledged the cat's presence subconsciously, which led to clues being available.

Psychological research acknowledges perceptions of a certain kind can occur so the skeptic's theory, therefore, is not unbelievable except that in our case Gertrud (the dowser) was not aware that an earth cellar existed.

A Strange Event—To Search After a Hidden Spade

At times, we experience totally unexpected events in connection with our experiments. Dowser Leif Andersson has often had practical use of psi-tracking which he uses to search for lost items. Leif was, at first, very skeptical to the method until such time that I showed him how it worked, after which he became totally convinced.

Leif has his own construction company and works together with other joiners repairing old houses in the countryside. On such an occasion, working together with others, Leif spoke of the unusual psi-tracking tests he and I had carried out together. His work colleagues were very skeptical, and so one of them suggested they carry out a test to discover just how unrealistic it actually was.

They agreed to hide an object, a spade, in the area that Leif would perform a sending on, then try to detect the track with dowsing rod. He broke off a small supple branch from a nearby tree and then went into the house while the others hid the spade. He returned, decided on a sending point from which to concentrate on the spade and after he was finished sending he methodically circled the place where he'd stood. Immediately he got a reaction that pointed in a direction out onto a grassy meadow, yet this was to his colleague's great pleasure as they knew the track he suggested went in completely the wrong direction. Leif was a stubborn chap and continued with his tracking further out into the paddock. When he'd gotten a way out into the meadow he bent down and picked up, to the enormous surprise of the others, a completely different old ragged spade to the one they'd hidden. It should be noted that none of the men had previously been out into the meadow.

The spade they'd used for the test had actually been hidden under a heavy tarpaulin that was covering a stack of planks, but no psi-track to this was established. The heavy tarpaulin had possibly had a blocking effect of the psi-signal, and from my earlier experiences where this has happened it seems that plastic stops the signal from leading to the psi-track, instead seeking out a similar object. I was not present on this occasion, but I know Leif to be a completely trustworthy person and I have also questioned one of his work colleagues who verified Leif's account. Similar experiences have been described in my first book.

Historic Perspective: Was Psi-tracking Known of Earlier?

Are there signs that the psi-tracking phenomenon was known about before my colleagues and I started our research into it? It was not until a few years after my discovery that I gained knowledge of more anecdotal tales that it was possible to find lost objects with dowsing. It was after the release of my first book, *The Psi-track*, that a reader contacted me explaining that dowsing rods had been used earlier as a means to find lost items. From what I understood from this was that the approach used did not remind me of our method.

Carl von Linné's Experience of the Dowsing Rod

In 1994, I read an article by psychiatrist Nils-Olof Jacobson in the journal *Sökaren* nr.3 1994, in which he related the dowsing experiences of the researcher and botanist, Carl von Linné (Linnaeus).[5]

At first Carl Linnaeus was skeptical to dowsing and reasoned that it couldn't possibly give a reaction to metals or other objects. His secretary was more enthusiastic and broke off a Y-shaped small branch to use as a dowsing rod.

To prove the doubt in dowsing for metal objects, he went out into a large meadow and hid a purse full of metal coins under a grass tuft. As a marker he had a Ranunculus plant next to the purse for the purpose of finding it again when the test failed. Of all the people present, only Linnaeus knew where the purse lay hidden.

The secretary was brought to the field equipped with dowsing rod, and after much time spent walking over the meadow, no purse was recovered. Linnaeus, tired of this, went to reclaim his purse of coins, only to find the marking Ranunculus gone, trodden on and thus made unrecognizable during the secretary's searching.

Linnaeus now had to try to guess where he'd hidden the purse after which they tried again with the dowsing rod, yet it showed the purse to be in a completely different location. Eventually, the purse was found in an area that the last dowsing experiment had pointed to.

This was the only example of literature, known to me, telling of dowsing being used to find lost objects. Jacobson's article came out in some years after my discovery of the psi-track in 1987. From the retold version of Linnaeus's writings it is not possible to conclude that the psi-track was actually used in the search, no sending was done from one specific place to hopefully establish a specific path. It is clearly evident that the secretary has moved back and forth over the meadow, while at the same time trampling on the plant placed as a marker.

It seems clear that the age-old knowledge of a dowsing rod reacting when passed over metal played a big part in the above experiment, as the money in the hidden purse was metal. It can be said the conventional method of dowsing mattered here in the same way in dowsing for water or ore veins, an approach which is noticeably different from the psi-tracking method.

I had never previously read anything about dowsing before I discovered the psi-track, though later I found there to be some literature on the subject. All that I had read on the subject was a short paragraph about the fact that an aura can be detected by dowsing. Readers of my first book had written to me telling of earlier uses of dowsing to find lost items, and explaining that the idea of the earlier methods involved the seeker asking their inner self the question, their subconscious, where the item lay. If the "right question" is asked then the person gets a reaction from their dowsing instrument, according to the letters I'd received. The stated method didn't bear resemblance to the psi-tracking method, which is a concrete energy phenomenon that is established by a sender. The stated method, to find objects by questioning one's inner self, should be treated as anecdotal as no real scientific studies have been carried out to confirm the statements.

Unexplained Energy Fields on Living Beings, Observed by Extraordinary Perception

One beautiful summer's day in 1989 I paid a visit to dowsing man Karl-Ejnar Jansson for the purpose of carrying out some experiments in psi-tracking. His wife, Goldith, hid different objects, under blind conditions, which we then proceeded to trace using psi. Our attempts were very successful. Just when we'd finished our experiment three teenage boys came cycling past and stopped. They were curious as to what we were doing as they saw Karl-Ejnar holding the dowsing rod.

Karl-Ejnar walked towards them, holding the dowsing rod at the ready, and said jokingly to the boys that he was going to test to see if any of them had an aura.

He guided the rod around each of the boys and got a reaction from it, the test was meant as a bit of fun and by no means scientific. Suddenly one of the boys, 16-year-old Pontus, said that what we called aura he could actually see. Straightaway I was interested in what he'd said; for a long time I'd had this theory that the aura phenomenon was in some way associated with the psi-track.

I asked him to tell me about this aura he claimed to see, and he told me that people, animals and plants were surrounded with aura similar to a rainbow. He further explained that the aura which surrounded all living things had the same sort of colors, but that the size could vary between different individuals. Regarding people, some individuals had a rather large aura while others had much less. As time ran out as the lads wanted to move on, but I asked Pontus if he'd be interested in talking more about aura at a later date, which he was happy to do.

I couldn't stop thinking about meeting with a person who claimed to be able to see auras; for a long time now I'd dearly wanted to get into contact with a person with such ability, and therefore possibly be able to see a psi-track. After a short while I telephoned Pontus, and asked if it was possible for me to pay him a visit to which both he and his parents agreed. I started by asking Pontus to observe my aura, he said I was surrounded by a kind of rainbow. Closest to my body was a red ring followed by rings of green, blue, red again, yellow, orange and purple (see illustration) which was the outermost color, while the number and order of colors was not exactly the same as a rainbow. According to Pontus, my aura's periphery was roughly 50 centimeters from my body.

I found it a little strange that his parents knew nothing of this ability, while he'd not mentioned it to them or anyone else because he assumed that everyone else could also see this marvelous thing. He had no particular interest in his ability, rather, he looked upon it as a trivial natural occurrence, and was actually quite surprised by my interest in the subject.

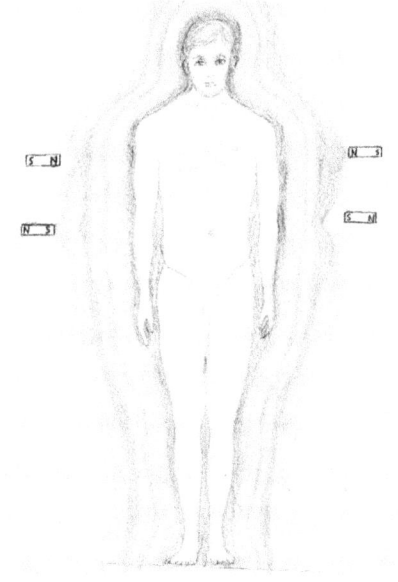

Schematic coloring of the aura. The left side is attracted to the north pole of the bar magnet, but is repelled by the magnet's south pole. The right side of the aura is repelled by the north pole of the magnet, but is attracted to its south pole.

Please note: The proportions of the bar magnet are, for practical reasons, oversized in the illustration in order to more easily show the position of the south pole and the north pole.

Experiment with a Magnet

I had also taken a small bar magnet (4.7 × 1.3 cm) to Pontus' home, as I had a plan to see if the aura would be affected by it in some way. I had a feeling auras could be some kind of electromagnetism.

I stood facing Pontus and asked him to observe what happened when I pointed the magnet at right angles towards the left side of my aura. Pontus had already shown me where the aura's periphery was, to allow me to be able to hold one of the magnet's ends to it. When I held the magnet's north pole towards the left side of the aura he announced that the aura was "sucked" towards it; in physics terms, attracted to it. I turned the magnet so that the south pole was pointing to the same side of the aura, and Pontus now observed how the aura was repelled. His observations were fascinating, but to avoid any suggestions of unintentional aid I felt it necessary to perform the experiment under strict double-blind conditions.

I decided to put the magnet in an empty match box, hiding it completely and thereby making it completely impossible for Pontus to tell which of the magnet's poles was pointed towards the aura. Additionally I decided to toss a coin to determine which pole of the magnet should be pointed towards me. We decided to perform the tests in a series of 50 attempts and during my preparation for coin tossing or putting the magnet into the matchbox, Pontus would stand a few meters away with his back turned. To simplify the experiment all testing was done on my aura's left side.

When the whole series was completed, we found that Pontus' 50 observations on the repelling or attracting of the aura, depending upon which pole was pointing towards the aura, were all totally correct. We didn't perform a series of tests on the right side as I didn't wish to bore Pontus. It was sufficient that we established the fact that the aura's right side reacted to the magnet in the opposite way than the left, i.e., that the north pole repels, while the south pole attracts the aura. This seems to

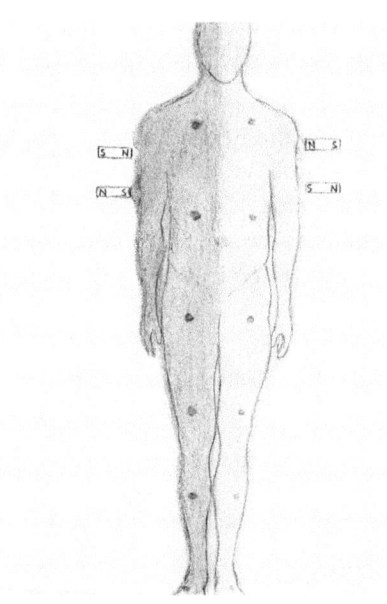

Schematic coloring of both energy fields. Within the left side of the body there is a blue field, which is attracted to the north pole of the bar magnet and is repelled by its south pole.

Within the right side of the body there is a red energy field, which is repelled by the north pole of the magnet and is attracted to its south pole.

At the body's plumb line there is a green flow of energy.

The different points at varying levels within the two fields, together with the flow of energy at the plumb line, represent the "vortex systems" wherefrom energy spirals emanate during a transmission.

Please note: The proportions of the illustrated bar magnet in relation to the proportions of the illustrated human body are, for practical reasons, oversized in this illustration in order to clearly show the position of the north pole and the south pole. In reality the magnet measures 4.7 cm × 1.3 cm.

show that the phenomenon is polarized. After the first experiment we carried out, I was convinced that Pontus' extraordinary ability was real and not fantasy.

It is quite common that skeptics characterize the aura phenomenon as purely an illusion, but I find this to be absurd to say that an illusion can be repelled or attracted by a magnet. The explanation that the aura could actually be body heat (infrared light) can with good reason be excluded because this type of radiation from the body cannot be affected in such way by a magnet.

Polar Energy Fields Associated with the Body

During our first meeting, Pontus mentioned something that I wished to study closer, namely that besides auras there are two other energy fields associated with the body. A few weeks after our testing of a magnet's polar field, we met again to carry out tests on the other fields he claimed to see, and for these tests I would again be the test object. Pontus' description of what he saw is as follows: If you take a vertical line from the crown of one's head to the crotch, the body is split in two halves, the left side of the body and the right side of the body. On my body's right side was a red energy field, on the left was a blue and on the vertical line (in the middle) was a green energy flow (see illustration). Pontus said he perceived that both energy fields moved in two separate circles, also that the field's periphery stretched only 1.5 to 2 centimeters above the skin compared to my aura's periphery, which extended 50 centimeters. The red and blue energy fields were situated within the aura, yet Pontus was able to see the fields straight through the aura, which he described as being transparent.

It seemed pertinent to perform the same magnet test on these fields too, again testing a total of 50 times. Firstly we performed trail tests without hiding the magnet to control whether the field would actually be affected by the magnet. When the north pole of the bar magnet was moved towards the blue field Pontus described an attracting effect, and the south pole caused a repelling effect; in other words the blue field on the left side reacted in the same as the aura's left side. We started the sequence of tests performed in our now "usual" way with tossing a coin and hiding the magnet in the matchbox. When all tests were completed, we could establish that all Pontus' observations on whether attracting or repelling had taken place, and which pole of the magnet was moved towards the field's left, all corresponded. A skeptic to these field's existence may have the theory that Pontus is clairvoyant, and through which he knew the position of the magnet, or perhaps that I telepathically passed over the information. Both of these theories are unlikely for the simple reason that he couldn't see the phenomenon while blindfolded.

Double-Blind Experiment

It was a convincing experience to be able to conclude that our experiments did not depend on chance and that these energy fields were a reality, even if the field of science hadn't discovered (or wanted to admit) that these types of fields existed. I wanted to be convinced that there could be no other degree of error, but the earlier test had been single-blind and so I wanted to carry out the tests under double-blind conditions.

During the single-blind tests I myself knew which way the magnet was placed inside the matchbox, and to eliminate the chance that Pontus could get clues from my unintentional body language, I needed an assistant for the experiments. An acquaintance of mine offered his services and we decided on carrying out a slightly smaller series of tests limited to just 30, given the amount of time needed for 50. The proceedings were arranged in such a way that my acquaintance should toss the coin, as well as place the magnet in the matchbox, in a separate area, during which time Pontus stood away from me with his back turned. When the assistant was finished with his preparations, he passed me the matchbox which I then moved, one end first, towards the blue energy field at right angles, at which point Pontus turned to face me ready to make his observation.

When the entire program of 30 tests was completed, we could see that all 30 were correct, giving us a complete correlation between Pontus' answers regarding attracting or repelling, as well as answering which of the magnet's poles was pointing towards the blue energy field on my left. After this series of double-blind experiments, I was now totally convinced that no body language signals from me could have guided Pontus' decisions in any way. The magnet was placed in the matchbox, by my assistant, in an area separate from us.

Additional Magnet Experiments

Professor and physicist Erik Karlsson and his wife Maj-Britt would come to spend their summers at a place not far from my home town. During the summer of 1989 he was employed by Uppsala University and it was at this time that Pontus and I carried out our many experiments. It was my intention to contact Professor Karlsson to ask if he cared to witness, and preferably, take part in a magnet experiment as mentioned above. He was interested in my suggestion so Pontus and I went to see them.

We arranged the proceedings this time so that Professor Karlsson would toss the coin and place the magnet in the matchbox, with Pontus turned away. His wife Maj-Britt would be the guinea pig in this these experiments and have the matchbox pointed towards her, while I kept at a distance from the professor placing the magnet in the box so as not to risk giving clues to Pontus.

We decided to do a series of 50 tests and when the entire series had been completed 47 were correct, the 3 that were incorrect were possibly human error due to Pontus' nervousness at meeting with unfamiliar people. It was necessary for him to be as relaxed as possible so as to be able to focus on the task in hand which also was the case for all types of experiment.

In my book *Psi-track II* there is the protocol from this series of tests, signed by Professor Erik Karlsson and his wife Maj-Britt.[6] It ought to be mentioned that Professor Karlsson is skeptical to parapsychology in general, but he believed this series of tests could not be explained as being chance or cheating.

Pontus' First Impression of the Psi-track

The first experiments that Pontus and I did together concentrated entirely on aura and the energy fields connected with the body. Research into these phenomenon requires a great deal of time and energy, but it was inspirational and a joy to be involved with these phenomenon unknown to "normal" science. On one occasion when I was at Pontus' house I decided to perform a test to see if Pontus could see the psi-track.

We were outdoors when I saw Pontus' horse peacefully grazing in a meadow. Without mentioning it beforehand, I started to concentrate (sending) on the horse with the aim of forming a psi-track between myself and the animal.

After a short while I asked Pontus if he noticed anything strange about my aura, he focused, then called out excitedly that there was a rainbow-like energy field between the horse and I. He'd used the term "rainbow" in the meaning of the colors, not that the track between the horse and I had a bow shape, he'd also used the term "rainbow" previously too when describing my aura. This very first test was not actually a blind test as Pontus very well could have received a body language signal from me if I had unwittingly looked towards the horse.

An interesting fact was that I'd never once mentioned anything to Pontus concerning the psi-tracking phenomenon it was apparent too that, at this moment in time, he had no knowledge at all of psi-tracking. That he had no earlier experience of psi-tracking can be due to the fact that no one in his home environment, not even himself, had had the bizarre idea that someone could transmit a psi-track. That may seem strange because a person must have, at sometime, thought intensively about him, one of his parents for example, but that he most likely was not focused at the time and being focused on the task is a prerequisite for psi-tracking.

When I told him of how it was possible to seek out people or animals that were hidden or lost with psi-tracking, he immediately became very interested. He rushed into the house and returned bringing with him his younger brother Lucas, with the intention that Lucas should hide somewhere around their home. Pontus and I went indoors while Lucas was left to find a hiding place anywhere around the whole house; there were many hiding places for Lucas to choose from as they lived in the countryside.

After the agreed amount of time had passed, Pontus and I went outdoors again to start the experiment. I stood in one particular spot and visualized Lucas for a short time, Pontus stood beside me, completely focused on trying to visualize the psi-track as I was sending. Almost straight away he pointed in the direction that he saw the psi-track had taken and then proceeded to walk in that direction which led him to a wooden area and one fir tree in particular. When he reached the tree he shouted out that he'd found Lucas. It wasn't a great distance to the hiding place and I could see both of them from my position. Pontus was quite taken by this experiment and thought that we should carry out more. We carried on and performed a couple of more tests, and these also were a complete success. He also felt that tracking his brother's hiding place was by far more exciting than carrying out boring tests with a magnet. After these experiments with psi-tracking I realized that I had found an assistant who, thanks to his exceptional ability, could visualize the psi-track. Earlier I had been totally dependent on using a dowsing rod to detect the track, which had been proven to be reliable but I found it incredibly satisfying when two different methods can be used to verify the same miracle.

At a later date we planned to repeat the experiment of searching for Lucas but this time we chose a sending point indoors from where I would visualize (sending) him. Lucas went outside and I started visualizing, Pontus was stood next to me and saw immediately the psi-track that went to the wall. A wall is by no means a hinder for the track which travels straight through. Pontus laughed, and said he understood that his brother was having difficulty in deciding where to hide as the psi-track moved a little, changing the direction out through the wall. When the amount of time we'd agreed on had passed, we went outside and Pontus went to the outer wall to check where the track passed out through it. He then followed the track to an outhouse where the track also passed through that wall. Pontus went into the outhouse, and shortly after came back out accompanied by his brother.

Afterwards I asked Lucas about the path he had taken while searching for a hiding place, he showed us the exact path he had taken from which we could recognize the psi-track's movements on the inside wall. The experiment is very interesting, and shows that the psi-track is linked to the person being searched for as it follows them if they change their position. The same occurrence has happened to me before, when carrying out experiments together with a dowser.

On one occasion, when I was paying Pontus a visit, I happened to see a newspaper lying open on the table and in the newspaper was an article and a photograph of an inmate who had just escaped from prison. The convict's surname was Ursut, he was of foreign origin and was guilty of shooting two policemen, both of whom were seriously injured. In the press were rumors of the wanted man having been spotted on the Swedish west coast, but also in the south too.

Straight away I asked Pontus to help me perform an experiment to test in which direction the psi-track took as I concentrated on the photograph of Ursut. We went outside to find a good sending spot, and we chose one out in a large field where we also had a long line of sight. For a short while I concentrated on the photograph of the wanted man, while Pontus stood beside me ready to observe a possible track; immediately he saw the psi-track and showed the precise direction to get the heading with a compass. According to the map and compass we could determine that the psi-track had taken an east northeasterly heading, and when plotted on the map a continuation of the track's heading led directly to Uppsala, roughly 300 kilometers from our position.

We, of course would have needed another sending point to see if we would possibly get a spot where they crossed each other. Unfortunately at this point in time, it wasn't possible to travel away as Pontus had made previous arrangements to take part in another day trip. We also realized that we would need to travel a fair distance in order to establish a meaningful crossing point, and plus the fact that this experiment wasn't actually planned, it was rather an impulse from my side. It was a question of a test for our own personal research and not a private investigation, and in any case probably wouldn't lead anywhere as the police would surely be rather skeptical of our unusual experiment.

A few days after our experiment I read in a newspaper that Ursut had been recaptured in a place southwest of Stockholm. The part that I found very interesting was the fact that Ursut had actually been in Uppsala on the day we carried out the experiment;

the newspaper told of how he had stolen a car and driven from Uppsala to the place southwest of Stockholm.

That the wanted man could have been in Uppsala that particular day was something we wouldn't have expected. Especially as there had previously been rumors in the mass media of him being sighted in the opposite direction, either on the west coast or in the south of Sweden. It is a common occurrence in similar cases when someone has escaped or disappears that there are false witness reports.

Observation of How the Psi-track Is Created

I was naturally very curious to know how the psi-track was formed during the actual "sending." I had an intuition that the aura was in some way related to the psi-track even before I first met Pontus, but I held no more detailed knowledge. I had the idea of performing a test to see if Pontus could get an impression of how exactly it worked.

On one occasion Pontus' father, Edvard, was able to join us in an experiment. I asked him to stand 15 meters away facing me with this all taking place outside of course. Pontus stood facing me off to the side a little, his task being to observe what happened when I concentrated on Edvard.

According to Pontus' account of the proceedings, immediately when I started to send and concentrate on Edvard, he saw the formation of "swirls" at 7 different levels in the blue energy field on the left side of my body. Simultaneously another 7 "swirls," also at different levels, formed in the red energy field on the right side of my body. The seven levels (on the red and the blue field) were (1) the area of the forehead/temple, (2) at the collarbone, (3) just above the waist, (4) at the groin, (5) just above the knees, (6) at the lower shin, and finally, (7) down at the foot. Pontus also seemed to observe that the two energy fields that split the body in two halves "moved" in two separate circuits.

On the green energy flow on the vertical centerline one "swirl" formed at the same height as the solar plexus. In total 15 "swirl" formations had been formed (see illustration). From these swirl formations came spiral like energy flows shaped as a thin band, these consequently became 15 energy spirals, with the spirals joining together further forward towards the sender. In more detail, the 7 blue spirals from the blue field merged together to make one thicker spiral. The red spirals from the red field also merged to make the one thick spiral. These two thicker spirals interlaced and in the middle of this ran the green spiral from the solar plexus.

This system of energy spirals formed the center of the psi-track, what happen next was that the spirals joined together with Edvard's own two energy fields on the same level where they left me.

Around these spirals in the center of the psi-track was an aura with the same qualities and color hues as the body aura, it was in fact this aura that Pontus described as a rainbow field when concentrated on his horse. A possible theory is that the central energy spirals generate the immediately surrounding aura. It should be mentioned that all of the 15 spirals leading from my body disappeared immediately when I stopped concentrating/sending.

The puzzling fact was that the aura between the sending spot and the object

(Edvard) remained for long period of time after the sending ceased. After sending I'd removed myself from the sending spot the psi-track was no longer attached to me, rather it was attached to the spot where I'd stood while sending. It seems as though it remains as an impression from the sending activity, in connection to this is the fact that dowsers also still get a reaction after sending has stopped. With this being the case then it ought to be the aura field encasing the psi-track which is registered, this because the energy spirals disappear immediately when the sending stops.

Experiments at a Distance with the Projection of Thought-forms

In my book *The Psi-track II* I have explained about a certain kind of experiment where I create (focus on) a figure in my thoughts, which in certain respects has similarities to myself according to observations made by Pontus.[7] Here I will recount for one experiment to demonstrate how the experiments were carried out.

On one occasion I made a phone call to Pontus, and we agreed to carry out the psi-track to a position close to a small building which was roughly 30 meters from Pontus' house. The distance between Pontus and I was around 15 kilometers as the crow flies. Just before we finished our conversation I asked Pontus to go outside to the position we had agreed on, and then I would project the image of my psi-track there. Pontus' task was to focus and ready himself to observe the appearance of the image and to follow it when it moved.

I immediately began to visualize the distant position and intensively began to visualize myself being there, then I visualized that I slowly started walking towards Pontus' house, up the stairs and in through the front door, into a hallway then to a certain room to the right where I walked diagonally across the floor to a corner where I knew that there was a copper bowl ornament. In this corner my journey via my thoughts ended.

After a while Pontus rang me and described calmly in a matter of fact way how he'd followed a "figure," from the position outdoors, up the stairs and into the house, to the correct room where it moved diagonally across the floor to the corner with the copper bowl. A detail in particular he found strangely peculiar, was the fact that the figure had passed straight through the front door that was closed.

For the entire time the image was linked with the end of my psi-track. Pontus claimed that the image seemed to float as it moved, as opposed to physically walking across the ground.

During many similar experiments with projection over distance I've been visualizing the image performing certain movements, Pontus has had no clues in advance to my doing so. These experiments were also a success, even at a distance, this distance between Pontus and I was absolute proof to the impossibility of him receiving clues by my body language giving away my intentions. I was interested to know whether the figure had my features, so on one occasion I asked Pontus to check, he later told me the figure was diffuse and surrounded by a faint aura but he'd been unable to clearly see any features. After I'd concentrated that my face should be clearer he called excitedly to say that the image now actually had my features.

In my latest book I explain, amongst others things, about the blind-test with the bar magnet on the figure and these were a great success, the figure's aura reacted to the bar magnet in exactly the same way as the body's aura had done too.

A person who is skeptical of figures generated by thought may have a theory that Pontus received telepathic impressions from me, but a theory of this type is not a strong one. For the simple reason, also mentioned earlier, he couldn't possibly have received impressions from any of the phenomenon when he was blindfolded.

Here is another example of how Pontus can see the images that I created. On an earlier occasion I was paying a visit to the dowser, mentioned earlier, Karl-Ejnar, who lives near Pontus. Pontus and a friend came cycling past and stopped to talk with us. I'd been telling Karl-Ejnar about the experiments Pontus and I had performed with the images before they came cycling towards us.

Karl-Ejnar thought that it was a perfect opportunity for us to carry out a test, since Pontus was, after all, with us. In reality I believe that Karl-Ejnar found it hard to swallow all that I'd told him about, and he wanted to see for himself. He asked Pontus and his friend to move away enough so not to be able to see or hear anything from us, thereby avoiding the chance of accidentally receiving any clues.

After this Karl-Ejnar whispered into my ear that I should project a figure into the old forge, roughly 75 meters away. He wanted that I should have the figure stand with arms outstretched to the side. For a short while I concentrated on my task, after this we called Pontus back, still not knowing what the test had involved as we'd not mentioned it. To start with he was asked to tell us in which direction my psi-track had formed; directly he focused on this and hurried away to the old forge, where he went inside. He came out directly again, and told us that he could see an image in there, and an interesting detail was the fact that the figure was stood in the middle of the floor with its arms outstretched to the sides as though crucified. Pontus was always able to see too that the images had a faint aura around them.

Shape-Forming Thoughts and Energy Structure

The phenomenon that I have described above reminds one of the manifestations in parapsychology that are labeled "apparitions." Personally, I don't believe that the other phenomenon are identical to the ones that I created, and that Pontus could see. The difference lies, for the most part, in the fact that the apparitions described in literature are often clothed in some way. This never occurred during any of our experiments. Apparitions in a classical parapsychologic context can perhaps be explained by the fact the receiver of the impressions gets telepathic impulses from the sender which causes the receiver, in their inner vision, to create apparitions that are clothed to some extent. This all takes place on a subconscious level.

In our experiments I prefer to refer to the manifestations as thought-forms or "figures."

A question I asked myself in the beginning was whether Pontus could possibly have received involuntary telepathic impulses from me enabling him to see how the shape I had formed acted or whether the shape actually existed in the outer world. Pontus had announced that the shape had a weak aura around it; this seemed promising as it gave me the chance to carry out tests, using a bar magnet, in the same way I had on my own body's aura.

At a suitable opportunity we decided to carry out a series of experiments at Pontus' house with he and I in the same room. I asked Pontus to focus on what happened when I concentrated on creating a figure close to us in a position in the room which we had both agreed upon beforehand. As per usual, when I transmitted, Pontus could see how the energy spirals emanated from both the red and the blue fields that were associated with my body. These spirals made up a part of the psi-track which has already been mentioned. Pontus observed that in the predetermined position in the room a figure appeared and it had an identical energy field to those connected to my body. On the figure's left side was the blue field, and on the right side was the red. To our surprise the figure's energy field was like a copy of my own! It must also be pointed out that my energy field stayed with me throughout the entire experiment and at no time moved over to the figure.

Furthermore, Pontus announced that the figure had a faint aura that I've just mentioned; Pontus thought that the figure also had the same body form as I. While the shape was present it was time to perform the experiments with the bar magnet on its aura. Naturally, Pontus needed to show me where the figure's aura was, enabling me to hold the magnet at right angles to it. We found that the figure's aura on the left side was attracted to the magnet's north pole, and repelled by it south pole; the results for the aura on the right hand side were exactly opposite to those from the left.

As mentioned earlier, my own aura had exactly the same response.

After this observation by Pontus, I realized there may be a way to decide whether shape actually existed in the outer world. This prompted us to carry out another series of identical experiments, but that now they would be performed on the figure's aura.

We performed these experiments as follows: I placed the bar magnet in a box which allowed ample space for the magnet. I shook the box, magnet enclosed, which resulted in total randomness as to which of the magnet's poles would be pointing towards the figure's aura. When I picked the magnet out of the box I had my eyes tightly closed so I had no idea which way round the magnet lay in my fist. The advantage of my not looking at the magnet was that I had no idea which pole was pointing towards the shape and therefore could not possibly guide Pontus with body signals or telepathic impulses.

It may be of importance to mention that when I stopped concentrating (the transmission process) on creating the figure ended, the energy spirals that had emitted from myself disappeared, but the figure with its aura stayed a short while before its aura faded.

We were able to perform 10 experiments with the magnet before the figure's aura became too weak. When this occurred I had to re-transmit again to make the shape's aura clear and bold. After numerous experiments, the aura became faint, thus requiring that I re-transmit. Our work needed to be carried out in these intervals which proved to be rather awkward.

When 50 experiments had been carried out, we found that 45 were totally correct, which must be seen as a good result. It showed a high correlation between Pontus' task regarding repelling or attracting, and how the magnet's poles were oriented during each experiment. That we encountered 5 misses can with high probability be put down to

Pontus having difficulty on occasion when the aura was weak and therefore not clear. Pontus made no mistakes in the many experiments carried out mentioned earlier in this paper.

After all these experiments I was convinced that the figures that I had created through my concentrating actually existed in the outer world for a limited period of time. They were not some kind of hypothetical hallucination vision that Pontus experienced based upon telepathic signals from me.

The normal phenomenon called a premonition could quite possibly be explained by the shapes that I have described above. According to anecdotes, premonitions were a very common occurrence in times gone by. This phenomenon meant that a person would seemingly go to a place they were planning to visit before the actual visit, during which time they can hear the person they're meeting, hear footsteps, hear how somebody turns a door handle etc. Most probably there is a certain amount of psychokinesis involved. You look for who came, but no one is in sight, then after a while the person actually arrives.

A feasible explanation for this is the person that hears this kind of premonition is quite simply expecting someone to arrive (hallucination) but that this type of hypothesis cannot always be probable as numerous people also experience hearing voices, and of course, it happens when the person is not expected to come.

Here I would like to mention another type of image creation which is rather interesting. Pontus and I were visiting my parents when I suddenly had an idea. My father, Arthur, had unfortunately been involved in an accident, which led to him having his leg amputated from the knee down. I asked my father to take off his artificial limb so Pontus could determine if the red magnet field on his right side stopped where the amputation had taken place, or whether it carried on further down.

Arthur took off the artificial limb and Pontus focused himself, ready to observe. Pontus explained that the red field of the right of the body continued only down as far as the knee joint, stopping where the rest of the leg and foot had been amputated. I then asked Pontus to go in to another room where my mother, Inga-Lisa, was, so there would be no chance of inadvertent clues affecting him.

I whispered to my father that he should visualize he had a lower leg and foot. My father had a good strong concentration, which he had shown in numerous contexts, not the least being that he was a very able dowser.

We called in Pontus and he was asked to check my father's knee joint once again. In a state of amazement, Pontus told us he could now see that the red energy field had formed a kind of a lower leg limb and foot! Through visualizing and concentration my father had momentarily formed an image, an energy field–shaped leg with matching foot. The trial was very interesting and seems to show that consciousness has a great influence over such energy phenomenon.

Plants, Unknown Energy Fields and Their Connections

Pontus had mentioned at one time that even plants had energy fields and auras, yet he'd not been so interested in this, instead taking it for granted. Animals and people had the same kind of energy fields, blue on the left side of the body, and red on the right. Plants and trees also had these fields, but with a different layout. For them the blue field took on a cylinder shape furthest out, then came the green field and the inner layer was the red field. Pontus could actually see the inner field straight through the outer one as it was transparent. He also explained that animals, people and plants all had similar auras, which had the same color spectrum.

During a visit to Pontus' house I had an idea that I dearly wanted to test. Close to his abode was a large fir tree, which we went to. From one of the branches I broke off a little twig that was roughly 10 centimeters long; I then asked Pontus to focus himself on whether he noticed anything peculiar between the branch and the twig. To his great surprise, he could see that a small thread was connecting the branch and the twig. I myself was curious to find out if the thread would break if I were to move or draw it away from the branch, but according to Pontus it remained in one piece. After this I arranged for a blind test so as to verify his statement in a more scientific manner. He removed himself from me and kept his back turned in our direction while also wearing a blindfold, during this time I quietly hid the twig in a certain place, being careful not to leave any tracks as possible clues to the hiding place. Then Pontus took off the blindfold and approached the fir tree that I had removed the twig from. It was important that he stood exactly by the large tree from which I'd taken the twig as the thread was so thin that he may have had difficulty seeing it in the distance. When he could actually see the thread, it was easy for him to follow it all the way to the hidden twig, which he found with ease.

We performed similar experiments on other trees and had equal success with these tests. It was, evidently the first time that Pontus had ever observed the green thread as no one had organized similar experiments with him before.

We also carried out similar experiments with house plants; in these tests I broke off a leaf and there was a green thread between the plant and leaf similar to the tests before. Again, as before, I hid the leaves of the house plants in different places, which Pontus proceeded to find with ease when he positioned himself close to the plant from which the leaf had been picked. He quite simply followed the thread to the hidden leaf. During Pontus' observations I kept myself scarce to avoid the possibility of giving him unintentional signals as to the hiding place. An interesting fact is that Pontus says that all of the threads were exactly the same shade of green as that of the energy flow present in the vertical midline of animals and people. The greatest probability is that the same sort of energy flows through all living things.

Searching for an Explanative Model

Is there a possibility of a scientific model that explains the energy fields, the aura and the psi-track? The tests I carried out together with Pontus revealed quite simply that the aura, both the energy fields (the red and the blue) which part the body in two halves and the spirals in the psi-track all reacted to the bar magnet. The experiments seemed to show that these energy fields can be of an electric/electromagnetic nature, or at least closely related to such. As I mentioned earlier Pontus could see both of these fields, seemingly in circular rotation in their respective body halves, reminding one of a closed circuit.

As mentioned earlier, during my sending and concentration exercises, spirals and swirl formations formed in these circulating energy fields and when I ceased sending, they also stopped. Also mentioned earlier, was the fact that these spirals were found in the center of the psi-track and for a while after sending, parts of the track remained in the shape of its "rainbow" aura.

The psi-track did not actually form on the same level as the brain, rather it formed from different areas in both of the energy fields and also in and around the body. The sender's brain is, of course, a participant in the formation of the psi-track, as visualization, concentration and other mental qualities are prerequisites for a successful experiment.

We perhaps may need to assume that the brain's impulses integrate, in some unknown way, with the energy fields.

The most difficult question remains: Is it the organism that creates the energy fields, or is the energy's source located outside the body? It is naturally too early to give a plausible answer to that question, but the researchers of the future can perhaps solve the problem. If anyway I were to dare present a hypothesis now, my idea is that there exists an unknown energy field that surrounds and flows through all living things, nature in its entirety. The aura and the energy fields (the blue and the red) exists, according to Pontus, around all living beings in nature, and this includes plants of all kinds.

For a long time now man has known that an organism is electrochemical by nature. The brain's electrical activity is measured with EEG and the electrical pulses in the heart are measured with EKG. That known electrochemical entities in the body can cause psi-tracks does not seem likely, therefore maybe the source is outside of the organism. It seems very mysterious that the inner, mental visualizing by the sender can reach the object, animal or human being, that is the subject of the visualizing. To be able to present a hypothesis of how this happens would necessitate leaving normal paths of thought and venturing into unmarked territory.

Is the Psi-track the Energetic Factor in Telepathy and Clairvoyance?

Ever since I started investigating the psi-track I have wondered whether or not it is likely that this phenomenon can explain telepathy. The psi-track can, perhaps, be the information channel that facilitates telepathic impulses.

In my first book, *The Psi-track*, I have included a number of experiments that are thought to prove that this can actually be the case. The experiments are thought to show that a psi-track is formed between two people that concentrate on the same object. The results from the experiments will not be accounted for here because the low number of experiments carried out makes it impossible for a reliable conclusion to be drawn.

As I've mentioned earlier in this essay, Pontus could describe exactly the movements that I visualized the imaginary figure would perform even though no clues could possibly have influenced him. The experiments were executed over a distance of about 15 kilometers which is the distance from my home when my sending took place to Pontus' home. As mentioned the test resulted in the formation of the imaginary figure at the end of the psi-track.

It must be of great interest that I could have the imaginary figure, with similarities to myself, carry out the movements that I visualized in my mind. Among other things, I could make the figure swing its right arm five times as described by Pontus. Impulses of information, of course, must have been transferred between myself and the imaginary figure 15 kilometers away. One may also assume that the same principle takes place during pure telepathy, that a transmitting of information takes place.

In real life there are countless examples demonstrating that telepathy is a genuine phenomenon that often appears in connection with traumatic events. Such telepathic manifestations are very convincing, and therefore it is surprising that there are still skeptics that find them absurd and unreasonable. This seems to point towards a certain amount of blindness to reality.

A good friend, Ingegerd Hebbe, who I feel to be a credible person and who is completely unfamiliar with mystical fantasies, told me about the following experience she had:

> It occurred while I was studying in Gothenburg in 1950 that I awoke one night at 2.00 a.m. with a feeling of anxiety and a sobbing in me. I knew, inside, that my father had just passed away however strange that may sound. I can't remember whether I was dreaming but unexplainably I somehow knew my father had passed away. It was then impossible to fall back to sleep so I lay awake for the rest of the night. Early the next morning the telephone rang, before I answered I knew what the call was about. As I'd dreaded the call was from a relative who'd rung to tell me that my father had passed away at 2:00 a.m. in the morning. I had actually spoken to my father some days before and at that time he was alert and well, showing no signs that he should become ill. My father died of a heart attack.

Ingegerd's experience is not unusual and telepathy often occurs in connection with deaths or near-accidents. Ingegerd was most probably a telepathic receiver while her dying father most likely was the sender. It is probable that his conscious or subconscious thoughts went to his dear daughter in the moment of death, and it is very likely that the psi-track played a large role as the information channel of the telepathic signals.

Research in parapsychology has carried out many experiments in an attempt to prove the existence of telepathy. There is not the room necessary in this paper to explain how such experiments are performed in a laboratory environment, often using rigorous statistical treatment. Be this as it may, there are still large differences between laboratory experiments and experiences of telepathy in real life, yet Ingegerd's experience stands out in such a powerful and convincing way that it is quite impossible to believe that chance was involved.

It is highly probable that telepathy is a true phenomenon, which means that a kind of communication is possible between two people's consciousness, usually relations, perhaps even between their subconscious psychic levels.

Another phenomenon that belongs in the psi-area is clairvoyance, which doesn't occur between two persons' psyches, but rather occurs between a person and a hidden or lost object. While telepathy may be easier to understand, clairvoyance is more complicated as there is thought to be a psi connection between a person and an object. Clairvoyance has certain similarities with our psi-track experiments, even if the phenomenon becomes evident in different ways.

As I've written earlier, it is possible to establish a psi-track that seeks the object, animal or person that the sender visualizes. With the help of either of the two methods of detection—the dowsing rod and Pontus' extraordinary perception—the track can be picked up and in successful experiments discover the sought item. These experiments are, as I've mentioned previously, repeatable.

On the other hand, a clairvoyant does not "send" in the way I have described, rather it's thought that they receive a feeling of the object, whether it be lost or hidden, situated near or far. Despite certain differences between the two, it seems likely that the psi-track actually has some type of background function in clairvoyance, even if the sensitive person is not aware that this is the case. My hypothesis is that the psi-track passes on information to the clairvoyant, so he or she senses where the lost objects are.

It may be possible to go a step further and imagine that a clairvoyant unconsciously transmits their imaginary figure via the psi-track, which then unexplainably passes on the information. During my own experiments with the imaginary figures I created, which Pontus could see, was a figure that in some respects was similar to me. Can an image of thought (thought-form) at the end of a psi-track pass on information to the clairvoyant? During the experiments where I concentrated on imaginary figures Pontus told of how he'd seen that my thought image actually shared facial similarities with me. Quite possibly my accounts of these findings may sound like pure science fiction, but is it so remarkable for a figure of thought in some way to mediate visual impressions to the clairvoyant? This idea is not completely absurd and I shall elaborate on it further below in connection with another variation of the phenomenon that is known as "traveling clairvoyance."

Traveling Clairvoyance

The name suggests that the clairvoyant feels as though they are in another place than they physically are. He, or she, seems to be able to correctly describe the events taking place and objects at the distant spot; the impressions visual in a living way. The Swedish doctor and psychologist John Björkhem (1910–1963) performed successful tests with traveling clairvoyance. He used a method that, by hypnosis, managed to enable a couple of his more susceptible test subjects to "leave the body" and make their way to a distant place and describe events and objects there. These places were unknown to the persons being tested beforehand and were chosen by Björkhem himself, or by one of his assistants. Just such an experiment, among others, showing astounding accuracy, are described in John Björkhem's book *The Occult Problem*.[8]

In the said book by Björkhem is an account of the following experiment which is also about traveling clairvoyance: The French researcher Pierre Janet was in his time a pioneer in this area, he worked together with a person by the name of Léonie who was susceptible to hypnosis. An experiment was carried out in Le Havre; the test subject was hypnotized and then instructed to "leave" her body, and to take herself to physiologist and Nobel prize winner Charles Richet at his laboratory in Paris. Léonie called out in terror that she could see that fire had broken out in Richet's laboratory, but was unable to see any people there. It turned out that a fire had actually broken out at the same time as the experiment took place![9] The experiment seems to show that a susceptible person received visual impressions of what happened, in which case my idea about a test person's figure (energy body) image transmitting impressions is perhaps not so unrealistic.

Test personnel feel as though they are in some kind of a body at the distant spot from where they are making their observations. It's not too unrealistic to believe that the thought-form (figure) I myself created and Pontus could see, were the same type of phenomenon as the bodies that the clairvoyant test persons believed themselves to have during the hypnotic experiment.

Acknowledgments

I discovered the psi-track phenomenon, as I mentioned earlier, a few years prior to my first meeting with Pontus. Even before our meeting had taken place, I had been hoping to meet a person who had the ability to perceive impressions on the senses. This would further confirm the psi-tracks existence, before this time I had only worked together with reliable dowsers that could detect the phenomenon, which in itself was good and realistic.

Following the meeting with Pontus I was convinced that I now had the advantage of a skillful partner to work with, and one who truly was gifted with a true talent. There are, in brackets, many people involved in "new age" and "spiritualistic" connections who, according to themselves, can see auras and much more. It is unfortunately my experience that the vast majority of these cases are pure fantasy, while the real talent is very rare.

Thanks to Pontus' extraordinary capability it was not only possible to get a satisfying verification for the psi-track as such, but also to gain further knowledge about auras, polar energy fields, images of thought and the energy connections between trees and other plants. Sadly Pontus was involved in a serious traffic accident which resulted in him being left paralyzed. This has led to his ability to "see" the phenomenon being reduced, but it is difficult to prove whether it was the accident itself which caused this. It can't be ruled out that this ability may diminish with age after reaching its peak during the teenage years.

The most important thing of all though is that Pontus recuperates well, one step at a time, so he can enjoy a good as possible quality of life despite this. There is an intense research ongoing which hopefully can give hope to those that are paralyzed.

Naturally I am greatly thankful also to my other assistants, the dowsers. It is thanks to their patient cooperation that there existed the possibility to start the studies of the psi-track. A number of these assistants, including my father Arthur, have now passed away, being a great loss to me.

I would also like to thank Professor Jens A. Tellefsen and Dr. Nils-Olof Jacobson for their taking part in the research project, which I have mentioned earlier, which resulted in a scientific article that was published in the English journal *JSPR*.

I am grateful that Professor Erik Karlsson and his wife Maj-Britt cared to take part in and witness a series of magnet experiments performed when Pontus and I visited them.

Finally it is my immovable conviction that the phenomena I have attempted to describe in this paper are not something mystic or supernatural; rather they are a hidden but nonetheless real side of our existence that is possible to research if one has an open mind. Reality seems to be so much larger than we can imagine.

NOTES

1. Leif Engh, "Detection of Underground Water-course by Geophysical and Biophysical (Dowsing) Methods," *Reports och Notices* 5, 1983. Lunds Universitet, Nature Geographical Institute.

2. Hans Bender, "Telepathie, hellesehen und psychokinese." *Aufsätze zur parapsychologie 1972*. (Munchen: R. Piper & Co. verlag, 1972).

3. Jens Tellefsen and Nils-Olof Jacobson, *Journal of the Society for Psychical Research 1994*.

4. Göte Andersson, *Psi-track II*. (Stockholm: Författarnas Bokmaskin, 2010). Document av Vincent Johansson.

5. Carl von Linné, *Journey in Skåne* (Stockholm, 1751).

6. Andersson, *Psi-track II* (Stockholm: Författarnas bokmaskin, 2010).

7. Ibid.

8. John Björkhem, *The Occult Problem*. (Stockholm: Lindblads Publishing House, 1939).

9. Charles Richet, *Traitè de mètapsychique sid* (Paris, 1922), 153.

PART II. FROM THE EVOLUTION OF LIFE TO DNA:
THE UNIVERSE WE CAN'T SEE WITH OUR EYES

The Role of Consciousness in the Origin and Evolution of Life

ALLAN EMRÉN

Abstract

During the origin and evolution of life, there were a number of essential large steps that had to take place in addition to a more or less steady evolution. Common to those steps is that no known mechanism is efficient enough to make them happen. In the present paper a "Super Darwinian" approach will be taken in an attempt to make it plausible that life and evolution towards a conscious species is possible.

An example of the obstacles is that a self replicating peptide has to be smaller than 37 units for life to be probable on earth, or less than 111 for the entire universe. This could be compared to the smallest known RNA sequence able to copy another molecule, being 165 units long.

Furthermore, the initial genetic code had to switch into the present DNA based one. As the original code probably was very different, switching from one to the other was extremely difficult, similar to an evolution of Chinese written language into English.

Thus, intelligent life should not be able to appear anywhere in merely 14 billion years. As we are here, however, there has to be some mechanism that makes intelligent life possible, unless we are created and developed in a supernatural way.

In the Super Darwinian theory presented here, life has been able to overcome the evolutionary obstacles by taking advantage of the fact that consciousness coupled to matter appears to be required for the quantum mechanical wave function to collapse.

When energy is converted to matter, the particles form entangled states. Such states persist until a measurement forces collapse of the wave function. Consequently, one could expect that the entire universe was in a state describing all possibilities simultaneously. Among all those possibilities, there should have been a huge number in which life was initiated at different locations in the universe.

Then, the potential instances of life have undergone evolution. Each of the successful evolutionary routes would lead towards a particular kind of intelligent species, humans being one of them. Other routes would possibly have been developing towards very different kinds, like intelligent insects, or stranger species, like Donald Ducks, trolls, or even an intelligent species built from interstellar gas clouds.

84   Part II. From the Evolution of Life to DNA

The parallel processing would make evolution fast enough to overcome the difficulties mentioned above. Different branches of evolution would proceed at different rates. Finally there would appear a species with a brain intelligent and efficient enough to handle consciousness. The universe would have produced a conscious observer and its wave function had to collapse.

Instantaneously, all other branches disappeared. This Super Darwinian mechanism would cause extinction on a far greater scale than any other known. Actually, there would be no fossils left from erased branches. They were erased not only from continued existence, but even from history itself.

There are at least three ways in which this Super Darwinian theory could be disproved, one of them being that if intelligent life is found anywhere else in the universe, the theory is probably wrong.

Introduction

As noted earlier during the origin and evolution of life, there were a number of essential large steps that had to take place in addition to a more or less steady evolution; common to those steps is that no known mechanism is efficient enough to make them happen.

First of all there is the fine-tuning of physical properties of the universe. The most reasonable explanation for that is that the universe has been created with the purpose of being inhabited by living organisms. There have been several attempts to find alternatives,[1] but they all appear to fail in some way. Some of those theories require the constants of nature to be able to have a huge number of possible values (if not infinite). Furthermore, they would require a multitude of universes with different sets of constants and properties. There is no evidence whatsoever for the requirements to be fulfilled. There is also no mechanism proposed that would prevent one of the universes to have a set of constants that would cause it to "break free" and destroy all the others. One could also state that none of the theories include a kind of physics that gives rise to consciousness as we observe it.

Secondly, life started somewhere in the universe, and probably upon the earth. Current theories on the origin of life could at best be considered as suggestions. There is a lack of evidence, and most of them make use of steps that makes them very unlikely. An example of such problems is that most of the theories ignore the fact that peptide bonds are not stable in aqueous solutions, and as a consequence, peptides do not form spontaneously in a solution of amino acids.

Further problems are the large information content in even simple living organisms, the rapid establishment of the DNA based genetic code, and the rapid evolution of life to form increasingly complex and efficient species, culminating with mankind.

In the present work, a "Super Darwinian" approach will be taken in an attempt to make it plausible that life and evolution is possible. In this theory, it is assumed that the universe developed according to the quantum mechanical laws with wave function dispersion going on where interactions did not occur, and the output channels staying open during creation/annihilation events as well as collision events and other kinds of interaction events. This caused evolution to proceed at rates orders of magnitudes faster than would be possible according to classical mechanics. When evolution had resulted in a brain complex enough, a filtering of the universal wave function occurred and the less successful forms of life were extinguished.

Origin of Life

There is no agreement on how life actually started on earth. Some authors[2] even find the probability for this to happen so low that they assume that life has started somewhere else, and have spread in some way across interstellar, or even intergalactic space.

Most hypotheses, however, assume that life has started by simple organic molecules being dissolved in water. It could be the ocean, some lake, or a pond. In this environment, the molecules have reacted to form chains, like peptides, RNA sequences, etc. By chance, one chain thus formed would be able to replicate, and life would be running. Once such a chain was present, it would undergo Darwinian evolution, increasing the level of complexity. Finally, billions of years later, the present biosphere would have formed.

Prebiotic Life

As mentioned above, it has been proposed that life actually did not start on the earth, but at some place in the universe where the conditions were more favorable. After life had formed there, it would spread as spores or tiny seeds across the galaxy. It has even been proposed that seeds or entire organisms have been transported by purpose in space ships, and planted into other worlds, the earth being one of them.

There are several arguments against this kind of hypothesis. First, it is difficult to imagine an environment more favorable than the early earth for formation of primitive life. The temperatures were in a range where chemical reactions could proceed at reasonable rates, while not high enough to prevent formation of complex molecules. Furthermore, the reducing atmosphere protected organic molecules from being oxidized to water and carbon dioxide.

Secondly, life could not form in a very young universe, as the elements available during the first billions of years were merely hydrogen, helium and lithium. No carbon, no nitrogen, no oxygen, no sulphur, etc. Such elements are formed in the centers of stars when their fuel has been consumed. If a star is large enough, it will explode violently, and the elements in its interior will be spread into space. From there, it is able to serve as raw material for high density planets, like the earth.

Thirdly, once life had originated, there should be a mechanism that makes seeds in huge quantities leave the planet and the solar system in which they were formed. When they had entered interstellar space, they had to survive a very long journey without being destroyed by radiation. The radiation doses collected during millions of years in space are huge, and it looks more or less impossible for the genetic information to survive, even in a dry and frozen state.

Considering such facts results in the conclusion that the most probable place for life to have started would be on earth itself, some 3.5 or 4.0 billion years ago. The building materials, simple organic molecules like amino acids, may have formed in the reducing atmosphere through reactions driven by electrical discharges or UV light. They may also form in space, where the reactions may be driven by UV and gamma radiation. Then they could have reached the Earth via comets and dust from space.

Most of the simple organic molecules would fall into the oceans, where they would be diluted to very low concentrations. This makes it highly unlikely that the life started in the oceans. As will be discussed below, there are other, and even more serious obstacles preventing life from starting in the sea. Some of the organic material, however, would fall to the solid ground, like volcanic islands. There, no dilution would take place. Rather, accumulation during extended periods of time would cause concentrations that were thousands of times higher than in the oceans.

Thermodynamic Obstacles

The theories of life starting in water usually neglect one very important fact: The bonds tying monomers together, e.g., peptide bonds, cannot form spontaneously in an aqueous solution. In a cell, such bonds form by a condensation reaction, like

$$HNH-R1-CH-OCOH + HNN-R2-CH-OCOH \rightarrow$$
$$HNH-R1-CH-OC-NH-R2-CH-OCOH + H2O \qquad (1)$$

The symbol Ri is used to denote an unspecified organic group. The peptide bond, -OC-NH-, is not stable in aqueous solutions. The change in enthalpy of reaction (1), ΔH, is positive,[3] while the change in entropy, ΔS, is slightly negative, as can be seen from the reaction scheme. The change in free enthalpy, ΔG, is given by

$$\Delta G = \Delta H - T\Delta S \qquad (2)$$

Due to the signs of changes in enthalpy and entropy, ΔG is positive. This means that reaction (1) cannot happen spontaneously. Rather, if a peptide bond is formed by chance, it will break spontaneously by hydrolysis. So the natural reaction is

$$HNH-R1-CH-OC-NH-R2-CH-OCOH + H2O \rightarrow$$
$$HNH-R1-CH-OCOH + HNN-R2-CH-OCOH \qquad (3)$$

Raising the temperature does not improve the situation. As ΔS is negative, an increase in temperature causes ΔG to become even larger. Principally, one could move in the direction of spontaneity by a decrease in temperature, but if proper values of thermodynamic parameters are used, one finds that negative absolute temperatures would be required for the reaction to become spontaneous.

In living cells, the reaction is driven in a direction opposite to the natural, by coupling it to other reactions, rich in free energy. Such schemes are complicated, and could not be considered as plausible for the origin of life.

Dew Drop Cell

There exists a possibility for reaction (1) to become spontaneous. To see this, one has to write ΔG in terms of chemical potentials. Denoting them by μ, one will get[4]

$$\Delta G = \Sigma\, n_{products}\mu_{products} - \Sigma\, n_{reactants}\mu_{reactants} \tag{4}$$

The symbol n denotes mole numbers of the species. Chemical potentials may be expressed in terms of activities.[5] We will use the pure solid or liquid substances as standard states. Then

$$\mu_i = \mu^*_i + RT \ln a_i \tag{5}$$

Here, a_i is a notation for the activity of a substance i, R is the gas constant, and T is the absolute temperature. For practical purposes, one may consider the activity to be approximately the same as concentration (mole fraction). Using (5) in (4) and (1) gives

$$\Delta G = \Sigma\, n_{products}\,(\mu^*_{products} + RT \ln a_{products}) - \Sigma\, n_{reactants}\,(\mu^*_{reactants} + RT \ln a_{reactants}) \tag{6}$$

Rearranging (6) gives

$$\Delta G = \Sigma\, n_{products}\,\mu^*_{products} - \Sigma\, n_{reactants}\,\mu^*_{reactants} + \Sigma\, n_{products}\, RT \ln a - \Sigma\, n_{reactants}\, RT \ln a_{reactants} \tag{7}$$

The first two sums in (7) are constants, and are usually denoted by ΔG^*, the change in free enthalpy if the reaction takes place in such a way that both reactants and products are pure solids or liquids. So (7) can be rewritten as

$$\Delta G = \Delta G^* + RT\,(\Sigma\, n_{products} \ln a_{products} - \Sigma\, n_{reactants} \ln a_{reactants}) \tag{8}$$

The products term has two components, the peptide and water. Writing that explicitly gives

$$\Delta G = \Delta G^* + RT\,(n_{peptide} \ln a_{peptide} + n_{H2O} \ln a_{H2O} - \Sigma\, n_{reactants} \ln a_{reactants}) \tag{9}$$

The reaction will become spontaneous if either of the product terms becomes small enough. Making the peptide activity very small, of course is a possibility, but then, the point is missing, as no peptides are formed. The other possibility is making the water activity very small. Then one has to realize that even in a saturated solution of NaCl (approximately Dead Sea water), the activity of water is still about 0.75.[6] This is far too high to turn ΔG into a negative number.

If the monomers are dissolved in a small quantity of water, e.g., a dew drop, the situation may change. It is well known that clay minerals, like montmorillonite, are weathering products of volcanic ash. Typically, clay minerals are composed of poly anions built from aluminum silicates, and more or less free cat ions. The anions form networks, filled with pore water inside the clay. Thus, a dew drop upon such a substrate will be in contact with the pore water. When the dew evaporates during day time, the water activity at the surface will decrease, and it is able to reach extremely low values, far below the point at which ΔG becomes negative. Then, the reaction (1) changes to become spontaneous, and peptides may form. One should also remember that the temperature generally is higher during daytime than during nights. So the formation of chains tend to be more rapid than the hydrolysis. In this way, the chains are able to survive, and to grow in length.

During night time, dew precipitates, the peptides will be dissolved in the drop.

Without a catalyst, the hydrolysis reaction (3) is slow enough that most peptides will remain through the night.

Next day, the drop will evaporate again. Clay that has been dissolved will precipitate. Initially, it will bind to the peptides that fitted into clay structure. The aggregates formed will serve as nucleation seeds when more clay precipitates to form colloidal clay particles. The clay colloids will serve as sorption centers for amino acid monomers, that then will tend to form a pattern similar to the peptide that functioned as nucleation seed. When the evaporation is completed, the dissolved species do not form a dry circular disk on the substrate. Instead, there remains a ring of peptides, peptides to be, and almost dry clay, as seen in figure 1.

Figure 1. Three stages during the evaporation of a liquid drop. Due to surface tension, dissolved substances tend to form a ring after the liquid has disappeared. The shape is caused by the fact that the angle between substrate and liquid remains approximately constant during the process.

The reason is that when a drop of water on a surface evaporates, the shape of the drop changes. Initially, the drop may look like a part of a sphere. As the liquid evaporates, the contact angle between liquid and substrate remains approximately constant (the wetting angle). The surface tension causes the free surface to be as small as possible with a given volume and given contact angle. The result is that the surface initially becomes flatter, and eventually concave in the central parts. Finally, the center of the surface gets in contact with the substrate. Then the angle there too has to be equal to the contact angle, and a ring is formed. In this ring, most dissolved substances are concentrated.

The quantities of earlier dissolved substances at different parts of the ring will depend upon inhomogeneous properties of the substrate. Next night, the local irregularities will serve as nucleation centers. In this way, the contents of a certain drop will be distributed among several drops next night. This will cause a spread of the peptides. One has got a cell division mechanism that does not require any membranes or other complex structures to work.

One unsolved mystery in connection with peptides is that of chirality. Each amino acid is able to exist in two shapes, L and D, being each others mirror images. It is well known that all life on Earth is built exclusively from the L variant. This could be explained by the montmorillionite hypothesis. An amino acid of type L, sorbed upon the clay will not be able to couple to an acid of D-type, as the resulting peptide does not fit into the clay structure. With all bonds being of type L-L, or D-D, a good fit will occur. If this hypothesis is correct, it is merely by chance that we have L acids, rather than D acids in living cells.

One should keep in mind that the scheme suggested above, is merely one out of several ways in which prebiotic life could have started. The advantage is that it avoids several of the obstacles found in other suggested prebiotic life schemes, and it also offers an explanation to the fact that all amino acids in life are the L-form. According to this model, the common chirality amino acids in living cells suggests that all life on earth originates from one single molecule in one single drop of water.

Limitations of Probabilistic Nature

Rather soon after the first occurrence of prebiotic life, several mechanisms had to evolve. Most important perhaps is the formation of multi component life. As an example, one may mention that with a protein like pepsin, that is able to break the peptide bond, a large stock of raw material would become available for building new auto replication systems. Other components that would be of great advantage during early stages were some mechanism for building cell membranes to keep the parts together, and a mechanism for splitting the membrane into two separate "cells."

Although there are peptides in the body that consist of merely a few amino acids, such small peptides do not have the properties required to actually perform enzymatic catalysis. The small peptides, 5 to 40 units in length rather function as signal substances triggering more complex systems to start or stop working. Modern enzymes being able to break the peptide bond are far larger. Typically, pepsin consists of some 325 amino acids. So although, the presence of such an enzyme would be of great advantage, it is not easy to see how it could form by random, or primitive evolutionary processes.

Another obvious obstacle is the formation of a molecule or a set of molecules that is self replicating without assistance from clay minerals. It is easily seen that if the first system of that kind was a peptide, the chain length had to be less than 35 units for its occurrence to be probable on earth, and less than 94 for it to occur at any place in the entire universe.

Similarly, if one imagines an RNA based prebiotic life system, one would not be able to have chains larger than some 37 for it to be probable on earth, or 111 for it to be probable anywhere in the universe. This is far smaller than the smallest RNA sequence (165 units long) known to be able to copy another molecule. Although it has such a considerable length, the fidelity of the copying process is rather poor, and it is not able to copy itself.[7]

Except for the Super Darwinian mechanism to be presented below, there does not appear to exist obvious ways to overcome such probabilistic obstacles. The alternatives are either, an entirely unknown evolutionary mechanism, or an almost impossible chance, or a direct Divine intervention.

RNA-DNA Code for Amino Acid Sequences

Next, the present (DNA based) genetic code had to be established. It is obvious that the code is very old, and it is also obvious that it appeared in one place, perhaps even in one single line of prebiotic cells. Once a code was established, there does exist theories on how the modern code came into being. Even there, however, the number of theories show that the question still is not answered. Also, all the theories suffer from difficulties.[8]

Apparently, there is a lack of theories for establishment of the first, perhaps incomplete, DNA-RNA based code. In the first primitive code making prebiotic life able to copy itself, there would have been either peptides, or chains of nucleic acids making copies of themselves. In some way, an entirely new mechanism would have to be created, in which peptide chains and nucleic acid chains interacted making replication of the other kind of chain more efficient.

This happened while life was still rather new upon earth, probably at least three billion years ago. At that time, life could not have existed on earth more than about one billion years. As the two kinds of coding are very different, entirely new mechanisms had to be established. How to do that in small evolutionary steps is unknown, if it is even possible. The problem is similar to the (hypothetic) problem of finding a process causing a gradual evolution of Chinese written language into the Western kind.

Evolution

As soon as the prebiotic life had been initiated, it probably also started its evolution. The dominant theory at present is that of Darwinian evolution. Other theories have been around, but they have not been as widely accepted. A problem common to all such theories, including the Darwinian, is that none have been proven, and ways for falsification have not been proposed. To take Darwinian evolution as an example: Whenever it has been found that some property is of advantage, this has been looked upon as a support for the Darwinian mechanism. When, on the other hand, some finding appears to contradict the theory, it is supposed that the problem will be resolved in the future, or by some minor modification of the theory. This is a phenomenon that has occurred many times during the history of science when a paradigm shift is about to happen.

Darwinian Mechanism

The evolutionary theory of Darwin has been modified gradually, as new facts have been found. Possibly, the most dramatic change took place when the mutations were discovered. This meant that rather than a continual change of properties of individuals, the properties were found to change in discrete steps. The steps, however could be small enough for the evolution to proceed in almost smooth ways. With mutations, however, there was also the introduction of possibilities for huge steps to be taken at once. So in the evolutionary process, not only the direction of change was found to be random, but also the step length. Later, it was found that entire genes could be transferred from one kind of organism to another, and also that in some cases the environment could cause the genetic properties to change in nonrandom ways, beneficial for the species.

One could summarize the Darwinian process in the following steps:

1. A random number of mutations take place in the genome of an individual in a certain population.
2. The mutation(s) take place at random locations in the genome.
3. The mutated genome is transferred to the next generation.
4. As a result, the new individuals will differ in their ability to mature and give rise to a new generation in the present environment. The differences in that ability may be extremely large, but generally, the effect is small, or almost negligible.

5. In the next generation, there will be a slight increase in the number of individuals with favorable genomes as compared to those with less favorable.

6. After a large number of generations, the population becomes more efficient than originally.

To this scheme, one could add that when two populations of the same origin are separated from each other, they might develop in different directions causing different species to occur.

Evolutionary Algorithms

The Darwinian mechanism has been used to solve difficult problems in physics numerically. Computer programs are then written, that take random steps in the variable space. When a step leads away from the desired solution according to some criterion, it is rejected. If, on the other hand, it is closer, it is used as a starting point for the next random step.

It has been found that the genetic algorithms are very efficient for solving some kinds of problems, like finding extreme values of multi variable functions. There is a limitation, however. Generally, the algorithm cannot get closer to the true solution than about half the step length. So to get accurate solutions, one has to take very small steps. But this makes the program inefficient in terms of number of steps required to find the solution.

In living systems, a high degree of optimization often is found. This means that with small step lengths, the evolutionary process could be expected to be extremely slow. In genetic algorithms, one common way to handle the problem is to use large steps while far from the solution, and then gradually decrease the step length as the solution is approached. Similar mechanisms might be at play in living populations due to the differences in importance of different codons in the genome.

Problems in Evolution

The success of genetic algorithms suggests that the Darwinian mechanism could easily explain most of the properties of life today, as well as giving a possible route leading to it from the first biotic life appearing on earth. In other words, from the first primitive cell up to humans and all our surrounding biosphere. This might, however, not be the case, due to the obstacles mentioned, and that have to be overcome in the evolutionary process.

Local Traps

An evolutionary algorithm is granted to find the solution if the problem can be described in terms of a monotonous function. In many physical systems, this is not the case. Rather, there are local extremes, establishing traps for many kinds of algorithms, and the genetic ones are no exception. In the case of evolution this is the case whenever two or more kinds of properties have to co-develop. There may be other cases too. To overcome that kind of obstacles, there is a need for a variable step length in genetic algorithms. In evolution, there has to exist cases in which the natural selection does not work. To overcome such traps, it has to be possible for less favorable mutations to survive long time enough. It is also necessary that the mutation rate varies by orders of magnitude.

Simulating Evolution

Several evolution simulations have been developed.[9] Typically, they express Darwin's mechanism in terms of differential equations, in some cases combined with stochastic variations of population size. At best, such simulations can tell that if a population is large enough, and if the mutation rate is small enough, the best possible mutation becomes dominant. Generally, they do not take spatial variability into account, and the results apparently contradict the fact that in most cases, evolutionary progress takes place during short periods of time, while no evolution at all takes place during most of the time while the populations are large and environments rather constant (punctuated equilibrium).[10]

To get an idea of the efficiency of the Darwinian mechanism, a program has been written to examine the rate at which optimization takes place. In the program[11] an individual is built, with a genome consisting of bit strings. In the simulations so far, there are two genes, each 24 bits long. The genes are chosen by setting each bit randomly to one or zero. The individual is put into a square grid, where it is able to multiply. Each time seeds are formed, they may undergo mutation at a random location in the genome. A mutation turns a one bit to zero and vice versa.

After a rather small number of generations, about 90 percent of the available space is filled with individuals. This coverage remains essentially constant during the simulations. The system sizes has varied from 50 up to 40,000 locations.

The simulation results indicate that optimization of the population occurs only if the mutation rate is small enough. Also, the number of generations required for the population to be optimized is more or less independent of the size of maximum possible population (system size). If a population has reached optimal properties (as defined by a fitness value of at least 99 percent of what is theoretically possible), and the mutation rate is allowed to increase considerably, the Darwinian mechanism switches to cause degeneration rather than optimization.

This has two important implications. First, there has to be some mechanism in living systems that regulates the mutation rate. Secondly, there is a limit to the rate at which life has been able to optimize using Darwinian evolution. Typically, 30 generations per bit are required for optimization of a population if the mutation rate is as favorable as possible. If the mutation rate deviates by one order of magnitude from the best value, the number of generations required increases by a factor of three to ten.

It is also found that most favorable mutations are extinguished. Only in rare cases, a favorable mutation is able to survive for a considerable number of generations. As an example, it may be mentioned that if the population size is around 2,000, more than 1.2 million mutations are required to optimize the 48 bits of the genome. So about 25,000 mutations per bit are required for optimization. The rate of favorable mutations is between 30 and 50 percent. Thus, in a population of about 2,000 individuals, something like 10,000 favorable mutations of a certain bit are extinguished before one of them is able to grow throughout the population.

Seen from another point of view, one may consider that the human genome consists of some three billion DNA units. As the information content of a DNA unit is 1.46 bits, the total human genome has an information content of 4.38 billion bits. In a random sequence, half of the bits will have optimal values from the start. Consequently, for optimization, of a random sequence of 3 billion DNA units, at least 65 billion generations are required to reach the present state by random mutations and natural selection if the mutation rate is optimized for fastest possible evolution. This would require a time period orders of magnitude larger than the age of the earth. If the mutation rate is not optimal, the time required could be even larger than that by orders of magnitude.

In the simulations so far, it has been assumed that different properties of individuals may evolve independently. This is generally not the case. Getting a mutation for a bigger brain is of no use if it is not accompanied by a mutation causing the skull to get bigger, which requires the birth channel to increase in width etc. The program mentioned above has the capacity to simulate co evolution, but no such simulations have been performed yet. One could expect, however, that such constraints will cause the evolution to proceed significantly slower.

There are several examples of processes in which co evolution has been necessary. Among those, one may mention development of multicellular organisms, development of two sexes. During some periods, the evolution has proceeded at incredibly high rates, the Cambrian explosion being one of the well known examples.[12] Also, the human brain appears to have required a high degree of co-evolution, even if one does not consider its ability to be conscious.

The conclusion to draw from the preliminary results, is that the Darwinian mechanism is far too inefficient to explain our presence here. One could not expect this mechanism to bring forth humans in a time that is less than 100 billion years. On the other hand, on such time scales, one could not expect the universe to be as good to support life, as it is today.

We should simply not be here. On the other hand, we are, and this tells us that something else than Darwin's theory is required. Other processes of radically different kinds have to go along with Darwinian evolution to explain our presence.

Just Lucky, or Perhaps Divine Intervention?

Taking such facts into account, intelligent life appears to be almost impossible in a universe that is merely 14 billion years old. Nevertheless, we are here, so unless we are created and developed in supernatural ways, there has to be some mechanism that makes intelligent life possible.

One possibility is that extraordinarily good luck has made evolution proceed at a rate far greater than random processes could be expected to give. One could have a huge number of cases in which combinations of favorable mutations and other processes with low probability made the evolution proceed at an unnatural rate. After all, there is no physical law preventing a dice to give the number six one thousand times in one thousand throws. This possibility cannot be ruled out, but if one is forced to accept such an explanation, one will have to give up the idea of a universe that is ruled by laws, and therefore intelligible.

Another possibility would be a direct intervention by God to direct the evolution and speed it up, perhaps by deciding which mutations were to happen, and when. If no other possibility, except an incredible chance, is available, this could be a footprint that God has placed in the creation to make it possible for us to see that He is the ultimate source of everything. If, on the other hand, it is found that there exists another solution, that can explain the evolution without direct intervention, God would be silly to put such a mechanism into the universe, and then avoid making use of it. Such a mechanism is the Super Darwinian mechanism proposed below.

Quantum Mechanical Wave Function

Observable States

During the first half of the 20th century, it was found that all measurable properties of material systems can be described in terms of wave functions. The functions generally are very complicated, and the values of a function are complex numbers except possibly at certain locations in space and time. The wave function, Ψ, of an object does not have any physical significance, but together with its complex conjugate, Ψ^*, and possibly one or more operators, it is able to tell the results that may be found if a property described by the wave function is measured. Wave functions may describe properties like position or momentum in ordinary spaces, but in addition to that, also any other property that one is able to observe, like spin or charge. To calculate the actual value, or the possible values, one has to let an operator work upon the wave function. As an example, to find the energy of a system, one has to apply the Hamiltonian operator (H). If the property in question has a specific value, the operator acting upon the wave function gives the same wave function back, multiplied by a number.

$$H\Psi = E\Psi \tag{10}$$

In this case, E is the energy of the system. Generally, the operator changes the wave function to a different one, so that rather than (10) one would get

$$H\Psi = \Psi' \tag{11}$$

Here, the system described by the wave function does not have one specific energy, but could be said to have several energies at the same time. Similar interpretations of results are valid for other operators.

In many cases (here if the operator H is not time dependent), equations like (11) can be written as sums

$$H\Psi = \Sigma\, c_i\, \psi_i \tag{12}$$

in which the ψ_i functions fulfill equations like

$$H\psi_i = E_i\, \psi_i \tag{13}$$

In this case (12) describes a situation in which the system can be said to simultaneously carry all the energies E_i that are given by (13) for any of the i values in (12). One should note that the energy of the system is NOT something like the sum of all the individual E_i values, or their weighted mean value. There simply does not exist a value for the energy of that system. If the energy of the system is actually observed (measured), the value found will be ONE of the Ei values.

Wave functions describing different objects may be combined to form global functions of the shape

$$\Psi = \Psi_A \Psi_B \tag{14}$$

if the objects do not interact. In the case that they do interact, the interaction operators will force the overall wave function to be a linear expression (a sum) of such terms, so that

$$\Psi = \Sigma\, c_i\, \psi_{Ai}\, \psi_{Bi} \tag{15}$$

Here, ψ_{Ai} and ψ_{Bi} are the i:th function fulfilling equations similar to (13) for the corresponding interaction operator. Such functions are named eigenfunctions of the operator, and the corresponding numerical values are named eigenvalues.

Collapse of the Wave Function

In the common case that the wave function is not an eigenfunction of the operator that describes properties thereof, that property, could be determined by a measurement. Before the measurement takes place, all eigenvalues are possible results of a measurement. When the measurement has been completed, only one of the possible values remains.

One possibility, of course, would be that the coefficients of the wave function, c_i in (12), are not constants, but vary with time, so that all of them except one approach zero, while one approaches one. This possible explanation suffers from two problems. First, it violates conservation properties, e.g., energy conservation. The problem is avoided if energy conservation is merely a statistical law. But there is another problem with the explanation: Experiment.

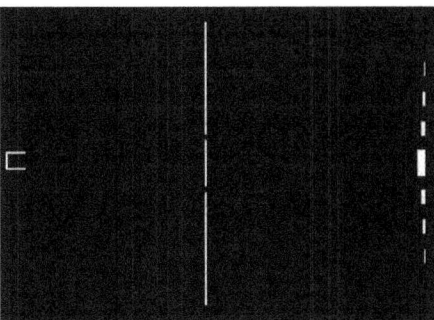

Figure 2. Double slit and the pattern that results from interference of the wave function. The pattern is a result from additive interference where the distances to the two slits is close to a number of whole wavelengths so that wave tops meet, while at the dark areas a wave top from one slit meets a bottom from the other, so that they cancel each other.

In a double slit experiment, one has a source of particles, e.g., photons or electrons directed towards a wall with two holes or parallel slits. Behind the wall, there is an array of detectors. This could be a white wall, or a device that gives off light when it is hit by a particle. If the system is undisturbed, one finds a pattern with light and dark areas (see figure 2). The explanation is that waves traveling through the two slits, have different distances along their paths to points at the detector array. In some locations, the waves interfere to extinguish each other (dark areas), while they add to each other at other locations (light areas). In such an experiment, the interference pattern appears in the detector array only if it is not known through which slit a particular particle (e.g., photon) passes. So if the wave function can be written as

$$\Psi = \text{const} (\psi_{\text{upper slit}} + \psi_{\text{lower slit}}) \tag{16}$$

an interference pattern is seen, but if the experiment is modified, so that one is able to find the route of the photon (which slit it actually went through), the interference pattern disappears. Then only one of the terms in (16) is present, and no interference is able to occur. The outcome depends upon which knowledge the observer is able to have.

An even more strange kind of observation can take place if some kind of quantum eraser is involved. This is a device that is able to undo a measurement. In a way to take an event that has already happened away from the history of the universe, so that it never happened. One simple example of that is a set of experiments that can be performed upon photons.

Figure 3. When light that is not plane polarized enters a plane polarizer (PP), half of the photons will exit each of the two channels. The same happens when light that is not circularly polarized enters a circular polarizer (CP). Light cannot be both plane polarized and circularly polarized.

A photon may be polarized in two ways. Either, the polarization may be linear or it may be circular. It cannot be both at the same time. If photons in arbitrary states are allowed to enter a plane polarizer (PP), the result will be plane polarized photons leaving the device via one out of two channels. Either via the channel for vertical (upper) or the one for horizontal (lower) polarization as indicated in figure 3. Half of the photons will exit via each channel. A similar result applies if the photons are sent into a circular polarizer (CP). Half of them will leave via the channel for clockwise polarization, and the rest will be polarized counterclockwise.

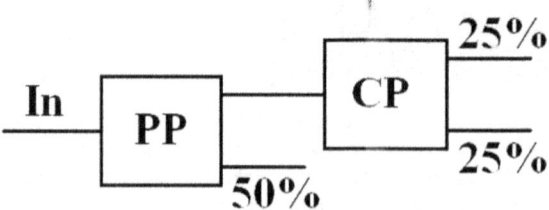

Figure 4. The output of a plane polarizer cannot carry any circular polarization. So when the output of a plane polarizer is fed as input to a circular polarizer, half of the photons will appear in each exit channel.

If the two kinds of polarizers are put in cascade, so that a circular polarizer (CP) get its input from one output of a plane polarizer (PP), 25 percent of the photons entering PP will exit through each output channel of CP, as indicated in figure 4. The reason is that the plane polarizer destroys any kind of information on circular polarization that the photon might have had earlier.

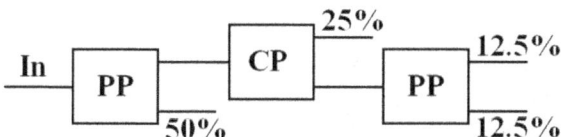

Figure 5. Any information on plane polarization is destroyed by a circular polarizer, so if one of its output channels is fed into a plane polarizer, half of the entering photons will use each of the output channels.

Now, let us put a second plane polarizer at the output of the circular polarizer. Then, 12.5 percent of the original photons will exit through each of the last polarizer's output channels, as seen in figure 5. All this is exactly what to expect. Measuring circular polarization destroys all information about plane polarization and vice versa.

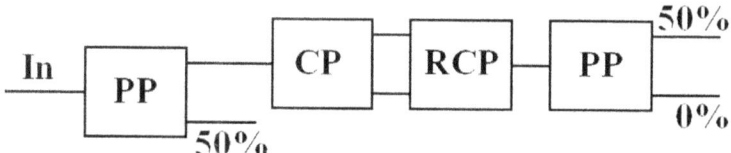

Figure 6. If a reverse circular polarizer (RCP) is placed between CP and PP of figure 5, all photons entering CP will exit through the upper exit channel. The information that was destroyed has been restored. Although each photon passes merely one output channel of CP, both channels have to be fed into RCP for the information to be restored. When nobody observes, each photon will pass through both channels.

In figure 6, we have a sequence of four devices. After the circular polarizer, we have put a reverse circular polarizer (RCP), and after that a plane polarizer. Then strange things start to happen. Although the circular polarizer (CP) destroyed all information about plane polarization, this has been restored. It is like the RCP is able to undo what the CP did, a quantum eraser. The distance between CP and RCP does not matter. We could place a mirror at one of Jupiter's moons, send the output of CP there, have it reflected back to earth to enter the second PP. The result would be the same. The RCP acts like it could go back in time, even several hours, to undo an event that happened then.

One could decide to break one of the channels between CP and RCP, *after* the photon has passed CP. So although the photon will use only one output channel of CP, the information that RCP is in place, or not in place, has to proceed backwards in time to influence the photon when it passed CP.

Even stranger results will appear if we create the photons by letting an electron and a positron form an atom consisting of the two particles. Such an atom may exist during a few milliseconds, and is named Positronium. If it is prepared in a state with zero angular momentum (the 1s state), two photons are created when the atom annihilates. They move in opposite directions, and when sent through some kind of polarizer, they will exit through separate output channels. If one is found to be polarized clockwise, the other is found to have counterclockwise polarization. On the other hand, if one is found to be polarized horizontally, the other will carry vertical polarization. A photon cannot carry both circular and planar polarization. So this is strange enough, as measurement upon one will tell something about the other, even about properties that it did not have when it left the location of its creation. That kind of state is given the name entangled.

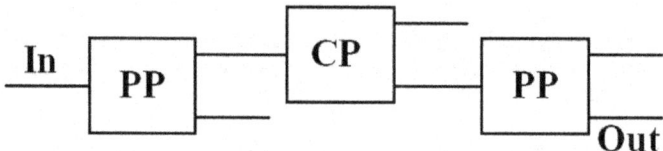

Figure 7. Let one photon in an entangled pair pass through a sequence of polarizers (PP+CP) that destroys any information on polarization before the photon entered the first plane polarizer. Then use a second PP to analyze the output of the sequence. The photon will exit through one of the outputs, e.g., the lower.

The really strange things happen if we allow one of the particles to enter an array of the kind shown in figure 7. In this figure, merely parts of the polarizers are drawn. The actual array should have one CP at each output of the first PP, and one PP at each of the outputs of the two CP:s. So in all, there should be eight possible output channels, but the photon can exit through only one of them. Assume that it exits as indicated in figure 7. Then, if we let the other photon enter a similar array, perhaps after traveling for years away from earth, we will know in advance that it will exit through the channel indicated in figure 8. How can the photon know how its twin reacted to such an array?

Information should not be able to travel faster than the photon itself (speed of light). Or could there be hidden variables telling it how to react? But how could it store information about all kinds of possible experiments that could be done with its twin photon? The most reasonable explanation appears to be that all parts of the wave function are in instantaneous contact.

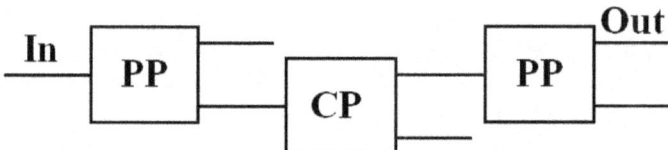

Figure 8. The partner of the photon studied in figure 7, will follow a predicted path through a similar set of information destroying polarizers. In some way, the two photons are able to communicate instantaneously in violation to the theory of relativity. They behave as one single very large object.

Building Wave Functions

Now, let us have a closer look upon measurement processes. To make a measurement, one has to use some kind of device, and that device also is an object following the laws of quantum physics. While the measurement takes place, this gives rise to an extremely complicated expression, in which the wave function has to contain all kinds of cross terms.

$$\Psi = \Sigma \Sigma\, c_{ij}\, \psi_{Ai} \psi_{Mj} \qquad (17)$$

Before and after the measurement process, the interaction between the object (A) and the measuring device (M) is negligible. Then all the cross coefficients cij, where i differs from j, become zero and (17) reduces to the much simpler

$$\Psi = \Sigma\, c_i\, \psi_{Ai} \psi_{Mi} \qquad (18)$$

So the measuring device (M) should show all the different possible values simultaneously. Or it could also be in a totally undefined state. As this is not what we usually observe, it is obvious that (18) does not give the full description of what happens during the measurement. One possibility could be that measuring devices are not bound by the laws of quantum physics. But why should they not? A measuring device can consist of merely one elementary particle. So how could it know that most interactions are ordinary, and should follow quantum rules, but that some are measurements, and should result in a different behavior? From the point of view of the interacting particles, there is no difference.

To get around this, one has to introduce an observer (O) as well. If the observer too is a quantum object, the total wave function includes that of the observer too. After the end of interaction between object A, the measuring device M, and the observer O, the overall wave function has to be

$$\Psi = \Sigma\, c_i\, \psi_{Ai} \psi_{Mi} \psi_{Oi} \qquad (19)$$

The interpretation is that when an observer (O) reads the measuring device (M), all possible values are seen at the same time. This too is contradictory to our experience. We see merely one value.

This means that there is something in the human observer that goes beyond quantum physics. Or alternatively, that quantum physics includes a term that goes into action when an observation takes place and a human observer is involved. The only known property that differs between a human observer and any other kind of measuring equipment is the presence of consciousness in the observer.

Consciousness and Collapse

The experience is that when we observe an event, we see merely one out of the multiple realities that exist simultaneously according to (19). So the observation causes (19) to change giving

$$\Psi = \Sigma\, c_i\, \psi_{Ai} \psi_{Mi} \psi_{Oi} \rightarrow \Psi = \psi_{Aj} \psi_{Mj} \psi_{Oj} \qquad (20)$$

All possibilities except one, possibility j, have been filtered away. The phenomenon is given the name "collapse of the wave function," and obviously, it is caused by the consciousness, or at least coupled to it. Possibly, our consciousness is actually located in the brain, although it looks more probable that it extends well outside our bodies, as will be discussed below.

The collapse happens instantly, and as wave functions in principle extend across the entire universe, this causes interactions propagating at infinite speed as seen in our universe of three (or four) dimensions. Generally, wave functions are located essentially to small regions of space, but in some cases (e.g., entangled particles), the wave function is able to give high probabilities in several locations separated by huge distances. In spite of that, the collapse happens everywhere in the same instant (whatever that may mean relativistically).

This contradicts the theory of relativity, as according to that, nothing carrying information is able to proceed at a speed faster than the speed of light. Strictly speaking this is not exactly true. Relativity tells that it is impossible for matter to accelerate to the speed of light. In case some kind of matter is created in a state faster than light, or if it makes a quantum jump to a speed exceeding the speed of light, it is able to reach any higher speed, but not the speed of light or lower.

One consequence of the instantaneous nature of the wave function collapse, is that causality is not absolute. As far as nothing happens faster than the speed of light (inside the light cone), the order in which events occur is unique. But outside the light cone, there does not exist unique definitions of "before" and "after." Rather, the order in which events happen depends upon the frame of reference in which the event is observed. This means that the cause of an event may happen at a time later than the event itself. Consequently, the collapse of the wave function has the potential to change history. Or to be more accurate, to choose one out of several possible histories. This is exactly what happens in the polarizer experiments described above.

Brain and Wave Function Collapse

Obviously, consciousness is tied to the brain in some way. If the brain of a person is caused to be out of function, consciousness disappears as well, at least as seen from an external observer. This suggests that consciousness is a process going on inside the brain. Walker suggested[13] that consciousness is caused by quantum mechanical phenomena, like tunneling among the synapses. This could be a possibility.

Another possibility is that parts of the brain rather are kinds of receivers and transmitters that are able to connect an immaterial consciousness to ordinary matter. If so, consciousness itself dwells outside the body, perhaps even outside the physical universe, something that is not impossible in Walker's model either.

Whatever the connection is between consciousness and brain, this connection gives us the possibility to interact with objects far from ourselves, and with past times as well. Once, however, the collapse has taken place, the process is irreversible as far as we know. Possibly, this is the true arrow of time. Before the collapse, time might be able to proceed in any direction, but when the collapse takes place, it is impossible to move back to an earlier event to change it. It could even be that the photons in the double slit experiment move forwards and backwards in time to actually pass through both slits. When the photon is observed at the detector array, it thus has passed through both slits. This interpretation would be consistent with Feynman's results, in which he showed that the wave function can be described in terms of a collection of all possible paths between starting point and end point.[14]

The role of consciousness in the collapse of the wave function gives rise to the well known paradox of Wigner.[15] This paradox deals with two persons, Wigner and Wigner's friend. In the original version of that paradox, Wigner's friend observes an event, and then tells Wigner the outcome. We could modify the paradox slightly, to let both Wigner and his friend observe the same event. The distance between them may be large, as well as the distance between each of them and the location of the event, and they may be moving with respect to each other, and to the object that undergoes the event. Each of them observes the event, and will cause collapse of the wave function. When they meet later, we know that they will both have caused collapse of the wave function in the same way. Out of all possibilities described by the uncollapsed wave function, both have observed the same kind of collapse. Of course, if one of them was first to do the observation, the other one would see a collapsed wave function, and is bound to do the same observation.

From their own point of view, however, it might be impossible to tell who was first to make the observation. Both may be the first one in his own frame of reference, so who caused the wave function to collapse, and who did simply observe a collapsed wave function?

This question could be resolved if the frame of reference of the observed event is taken as preferred frame (for this purpose). Information on the event cannot move faster than the speed of light, so the observer that is closest in this frame should be the one that causes the wave function to collapse.

But what if both are at the same distance in that frame of reference? One possibility is that some random mechanism makes a choice on who will cause the collapse, and who will just view the result. It could also be that the minds are connected in some way via a global pool of consciousness that causes Wigner and his friend to collapse the wave function in the same way. A third possibility is that the minds simply trigger the collapse to take place, but that the outcome is determined by some mechanism that is not at all connected to consciousness. The three possibilities mentioned here would give slightly different outcomes, so there exist in principle a possibility to find out which is the correct one. This, however, is outside the scope of the present work.

Theory of Super Darwinian Evolution

As has been discussed above, the universe appears to be far too young for the traditional Darwinian evolution to explain our presence. The laws of quantum mechanics offer a solution to that problem.

The initial state of the universe is unknown, but eventually, when the age was tiny fractions of a second, there was a violent evolution, with all kinds of particle pairs popping into existence and then rapidly disintegrating and also annihilating again whenever an anti particle was met. The temperatures were extremely high. As the universe cooled down, stable and metastable particles formed. Protons, neutrons, and electrons being the most important. Still the universe was hot enough for all reactions to be able to maintain their equilibrium states. Macroscopically, the universe could look in merely one way. Any deviation from this state by random fluctuations was quickly cancelled by the rapid equilibration processes. The universe was in a state of heat death. Macroscopically, all possible states were identical. The wave functions of individual particles were combined to a global wave function consisting of a huge number of products of the kind shown in equation (15), but now extended to one factor for each particle in the universe.

$$\Psi = \Sigma\, c_i\, \psi_{Ai}\, \psi_{Bi}\, \psi_{Ci}\, \psi_{Di}\, \psi_{Ei}\, \psi_{Fi}\ldots\ldots \tag{21}$$

At an age of a few minutes this situation changed dramatically, as the low temperature (still hundreds of million degrees) caused the universe to freeze in a non-equilibrium state. Equation (21) is complicated beyond any imagination, but from the time when the universe woke up from the state of heat death, the complexity of the situation increased dramatically. As each of the factors in (21) is a linear combination of possible eigenvalues of operators that are able to work upon the wave function, each factor has to be written as

$$\psi_{Ai} = c_{Ai1}\, \psi_{Ai1} + c_{Ai2}\, \psi_{Ai2} + c_{Ai3}\, \psi_{Ai3} + \ldots = \Sigma\, c_{Aij}\, \psi_{Aij} \tag{22}$$

From this time, terms in the wave function could cause different macroscopic results depending upon what events are described by that term. As an example, ψ_{Ai1} could describe the situation that particle A collides with an anti particle and annihilates. From that moment, the coefficient c_{A1} becomes zero. That term then describes a situation in which particle A does not exist any more. The partial wave ψ_{Ai2} and all the other could perhaps avoid the collision, so in their descriptions of reality, particle A still exists, and interacts with other particles.

Consequently, a huge number of different histories of the universe started to develop. As time went on, the complexity of the universal wave function continued to grow at a exponential rate or faster. As mentioned above, it is not even clear that the time proceeded in any particular direction then. But the result does not depend upon the local direction of time, as the wave function describes the states of the universe at specified times. So how time was able to reach a certain value is irrelevant for the result.

When the age of the universe was some 300,000 years, it had cooled to a few thousand degrees, and became transparent, and the space between atoms was filled with free photons, so in addition to being filled with hydrogen and helium, the universe was also filled with visible light. There was also dark matter present, at least that is the most common explanation to the structure of the universe as we see it today. The continued expansion of the universe had two effects. The gases became thinner and the light waves were stretched by the expansion. After a few million years, the light was no longer visible. The universe became a dark place filled with thinning gas.

Irregularities in the gas and in the dark matter caused collapse of the dark and cold gas. Initially, clouds were formed, and some parts of them collapsed to form galaxies and stars. Some 100 million years after Big Bang, the stars were ignited and started the processes eventually leading to formation of heavy elements that were sent out to form dust clouds when heavy stars exploded.

The locations and properties of individual galaxies and stars, depended upon details of the partial wave functions. Such processes are highly nonlinear, and very small differences in initial states have huge influences upon the final result.

Parallel Evolutions

About five billion years ago, one specific out of an innumerable number of terms in the global wave function had caused formation of the earth. In even much larger numbers of terms, the earth did not exist at all, but other similar planets in other galaxies. Some terms should describe a universe, in which no planets were formed, or even no stars. On could imagine the wave function as describing huge numbers of potential universes, each with individual properties, developing in parallel.

In many of the potential universes containing the earth, life was started, perhaps as described above. Similarly, life also started in other potential universes, in which the earth did or did not exist. Possibly, life also started in potential universes not having any planets at all. This could be like living gas clouds, as imagined by Hoyle in his novel *The Black Cloud*.[16]

All those life forms would undergo evolution at different rates. Most of them too slow to ever being able to go beyond one cellular organisms, or even beyond prebiotic life. The obstacles against evolution described above would cause life to stay in very primitive states. But the exponentially growing number of potential universes would assist Darwinian evolution in many cases. Whenever, the evolution hit an obstacle due to the Darwinian mechanism being too inefficient, the formation of new terms in the global wave function overcame the low probability in each individual potential universe, by supplying a number of branches large enough for the evolution to take place there in spite of low individual probabilities.

Consequently, evolution was able to proceed rapidly in a large number of branching potential universes. Due to the numerous possibilities, the different branches developed in different directions. One could speculate on what would have happened here, if the earth had not collided with an asteroid or comet about 65 million years ago. Would the earth have been inhabited by intelligent dinosaurs, or perhaps intelligent birds rather than humans?

So the branches would aim at very different intelligent species: humans here, dinosaurs in another, trolls, elves, intelligent insects, centaurs, Donald Ducks, or even intelligent trees in some branches. All the branches were developing at different rates according to possibilities for the life in each individual branch.

Super Extinctions

At some time, a brain complex enough to handle consciousness appeared in one of the potential universes. Either powerful consciousness developed inside the brain, or the brain became efficient and intelligent enough, to connect an existing external consciousness to matter. The potential universe in which we live was first to reach that state. Suddenly, the universe had a conscious observer looking out towards the surroundings. Instantly, the global wave function had to collapse, and the universe went into a definite state. Time could not go back again beyond that moment. A unique universe and a specific direction of time became real.

Out of the myriad potential universes, merely one survived. Or to be more accurate, merely one group of potential universes continued to exist. Due to the uncertainty relations, there still remained a huge number of potential universes, but compared to the number immediately before the collapse, the number was negligible, and all of them included a rapid route towards a human observer.

The extinction taking place was far more radical than any extinction found among the fossil records. There, traces remain telling about species that once existed, and then disappeared. But in the case of collapse of the global wave function due to occurrence of a human observer, no kinds of fossils could remain. The erased universes were erased not only from continued existence. They were erased from the history of the universe. No kind of trace remained. They were erased from ever having existed. The universe had chosen its history.

We had not only survival of the fittest, but survival of the fittest and fastest. This is what Super Darwinian evolution is about.

In a way, this resembles many kinds of phenomena found in nature. A female fish produces ten thousands of eggs. Most of them become little fishes, but just two out of the ten thousand survive to become mature individuals. All the other perish in different ways. It is remarkable that nature is able to make just enough survivals to keep the fish population essentially constant.

Similarly, after ejaculation during human intercourse, millions of sperms participate in the race towards the egg. Each of them strive to be fastest. One of them will reach the egg a tiny fraction of a second before anyone else. Within milliseconds, the egg changes its membrane, to become impenetrable for all other sperms. The one successful will give rise to a new human, while the millions of losers will die and hydrolyze into their monomeric components.

So it is nothing unusual or very remarkable with the need for a huge numbers of potential universes to evolve and then disappear in order to produce one real universe inhabited by humans.

Disproving the Theory

When a theory is launched, it is desirable that criteria can be given, that would disprove the theory if one or more of the criteria are found to be fulfilled. If the theory stands one or more falsification tests, this does not grant the theory to be correct. Similarly, if a theory makes predictions that turn out to be correct, this is no evidence for the theory to be correct. The theory of relativity as well as theories on quantum physics have both turned out to correctly predict the results of large numbers of experiments. Nevertheless, one of them or both have to be wrong, as they give contradictory predictions under certain circumstances, e.g., at very small distances.

The theory of Super Darwinian evolution, can be disproved in at least three ways. The first, and conceptually easiest is that if one is able to find an intelligent and conscious species somewhere else in the universe, the theory is probably wrong. Conceptually, this is easy. Meeting one would be an example. And it is easily seen that such species should not be there, as all virtual universes leading to one, would have been erased from history in the moment there existed a human observer. Practically, finding such a species is very difficult. During decades, search for exo planets and extra terrestrial life has been performed. The results are discouraging. Among thousands of planets found, there are a handful that possibly could have environments in which life would be possible. None of them can be said to be even similar to the earth. Similarly all attempts to receive radio signals originated from intelligent species have been failures so far.

The second way to disprove the theory would be to prove that consciousness is not involved in the collapse of the wave function. As this collapse is a cornerstone of the theory, it cannot survive such a finding. There is, however, nothing found so far that makes this plausible.

The third condition would be if it can be proven that no collapse actually happens. There exist theories of that kind. An example is Everett's multiverse theory. According to that theory, the universe splits in several parallel universes each time there is a possibility for more than one outcome. So far, the contents of the theory is similar to that of virtual universes described above. The difference is that in Everett's theory, the universes continue to exist after the observation, but they become isolated from each others. Also, the theory does not clearly state the difference between an observation and other kinds of interactions.

Another theory that does not have collapse of the wave function is Bohm's theory of pilot waves. In this theory, it is assumed that all variables describing a particle are exact. There do not exist any uncertainty relations in the particles themselves, but the values are externally hidden, so viewed from outside, there is an illusion of uncertainty. Such theories avoid one problem by introducing one or more other, and possibly more serious.

If such a theory is found to be correct, the Super Darwinian theory is more or less wrong. In the case that the multiverse theory is correct, all the kinds of evolutions described above would be real, but there would not be more than one intelligent species in each universe. So far, there is no evidence against collapse of the wave function, and all theories without such a collapse have in themselves consequences that are even more strange.

Conclusion

Quantum physics describes the universe and its components in ways that are so far from our everyday experience, that it is far stranger than any earlier imagination, including philosophies, myths, or even fairy tales. To a large extent, it is still unexplored, and more surprising facts could be expected to be found in the future.

The Super Darwinian theory for origin of life, and its evolution, gives a reasonable explanation to the astonishingly rapid rate at which evolution has taken place. Unfortunately, there is no known way to verify the parallel development of the universe along innumerable paths, one of them leading to the universe in which we are living, and to ourselves. As mentioned above, this is impossible, as the past of the universe was chosen when humans appeared on the earth. So the alternative histories do not exist any more, and have never existed. No alternate fossils. They are erased from ever having been along.

As far as is known, there is no direct way to prove correctness of the theory. As mentioned above, there are ways to prove it false. Most promising, probably, is the search for extraterrestrial civilizations. So according to my view, this search is of major importance, as each failure to find one increases the probability for the theory to be correct.

If the theory is correct, new questions arise. The Super Darwinian theory may be interpreted in terms of the universe being a huge quantum super computer programed for finding a way to couple consciousness to matter. It worked at an incredible speed along innumerable parallel processes for 14 billion years until it found the solution of the problem. Then it stopped, to present the result, and here we are.

This raises new questions. If the universe is a kind of computer programed to find us, then, we are the purpose of the universe. This is amazing. For centuries, mankind has been removed from the center of the universe, to a tiny planet in the outer regions of one galaxy among billions. Now, we apparently are back again. Not merely back into the center of the universe. Our role has increased to being the purpose of the entire universe.

So who did the programming? And why? Throughout history, people have felt messages telling that Someone even outside the universe has a purpose with mankind. Could such messages tell us something important? Could future scientific studies of consciousness lead to a better understanding of its source, and its location, if location is a correct word?

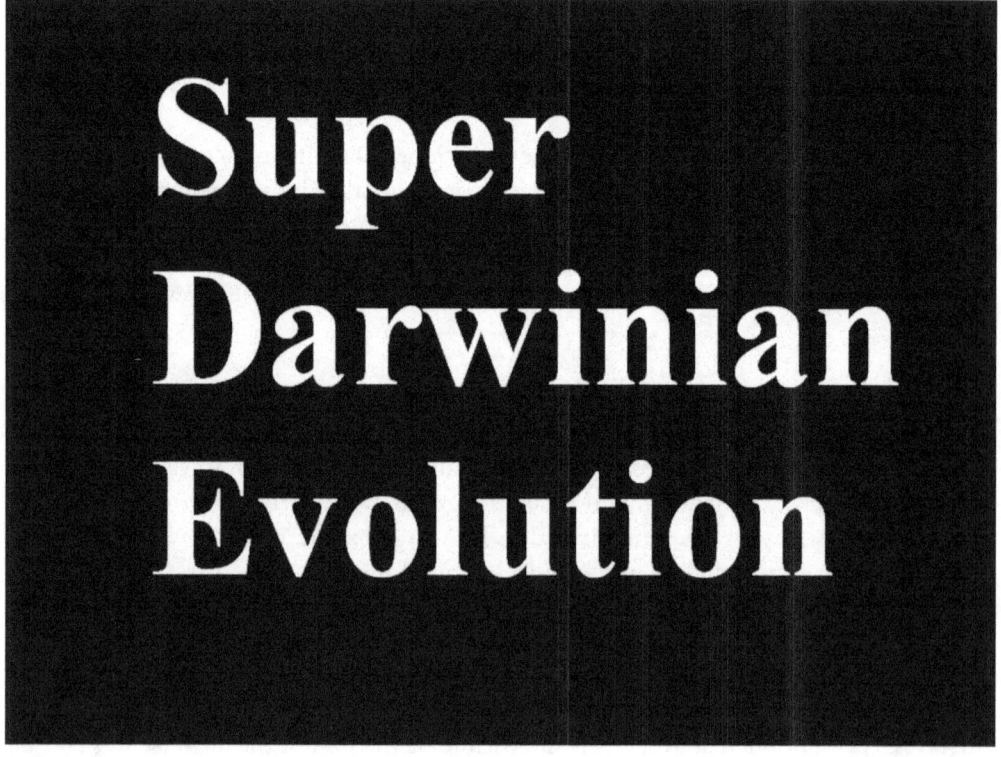

Big Bang

Matter created

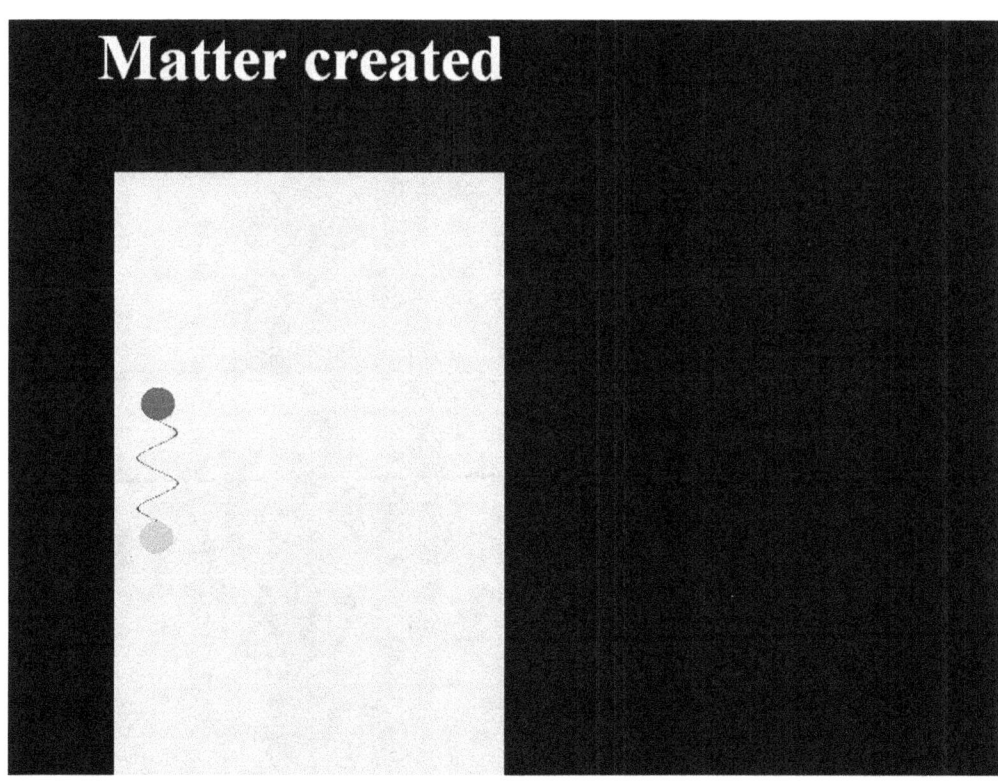

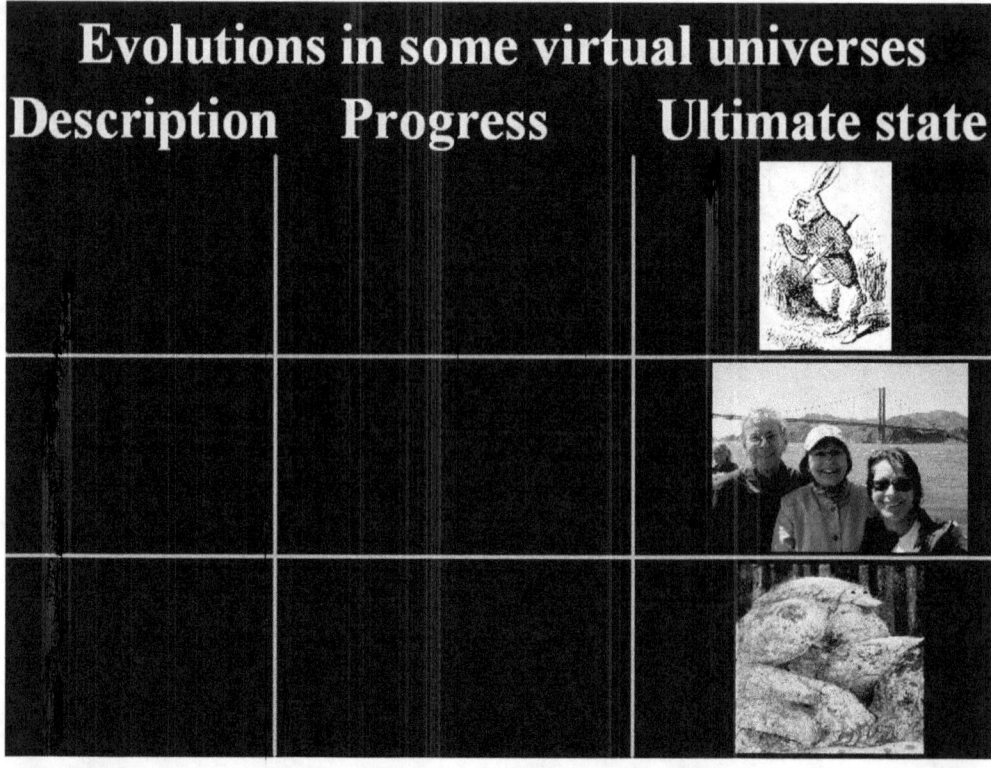
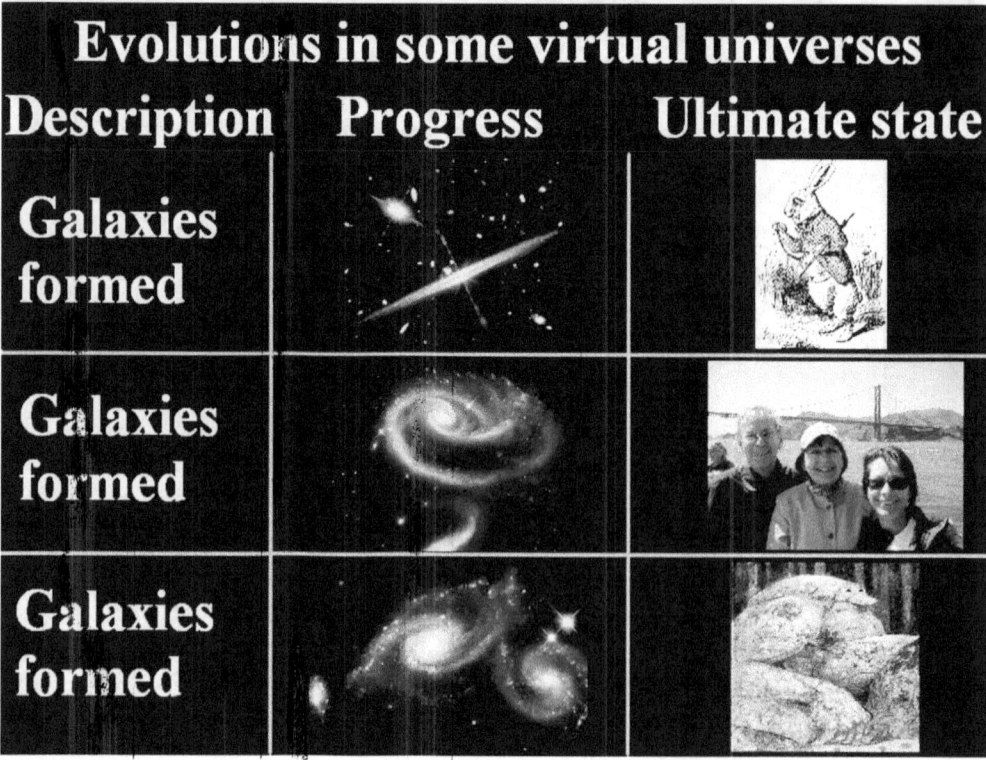

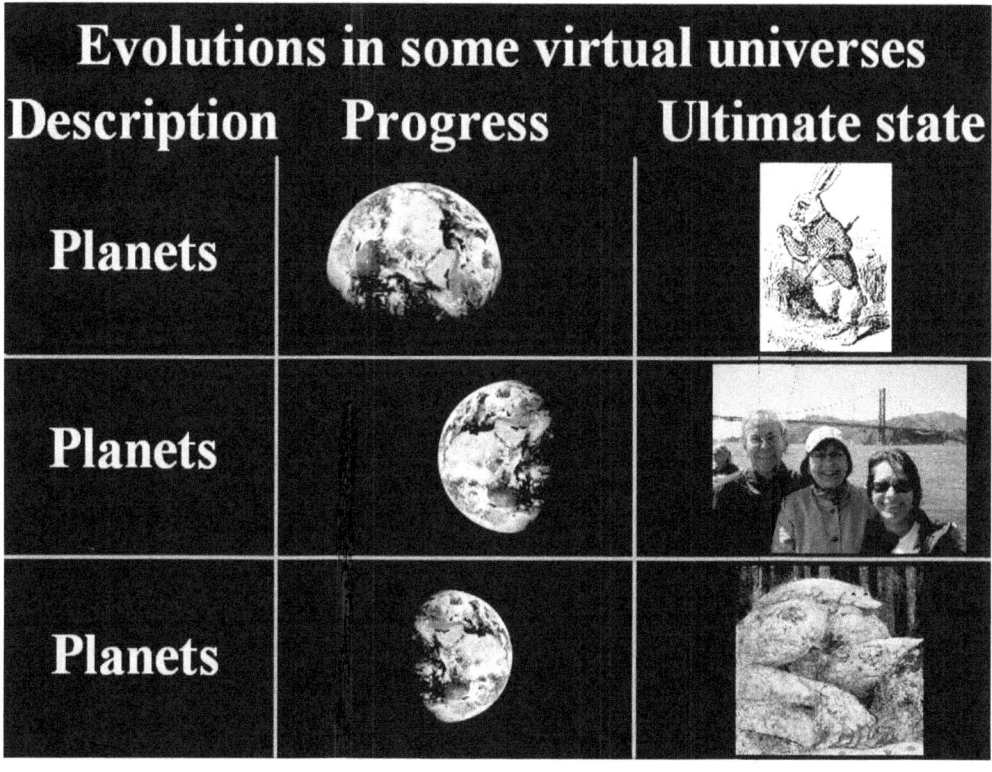

110 Part II. From the Evolution of Life to DNA

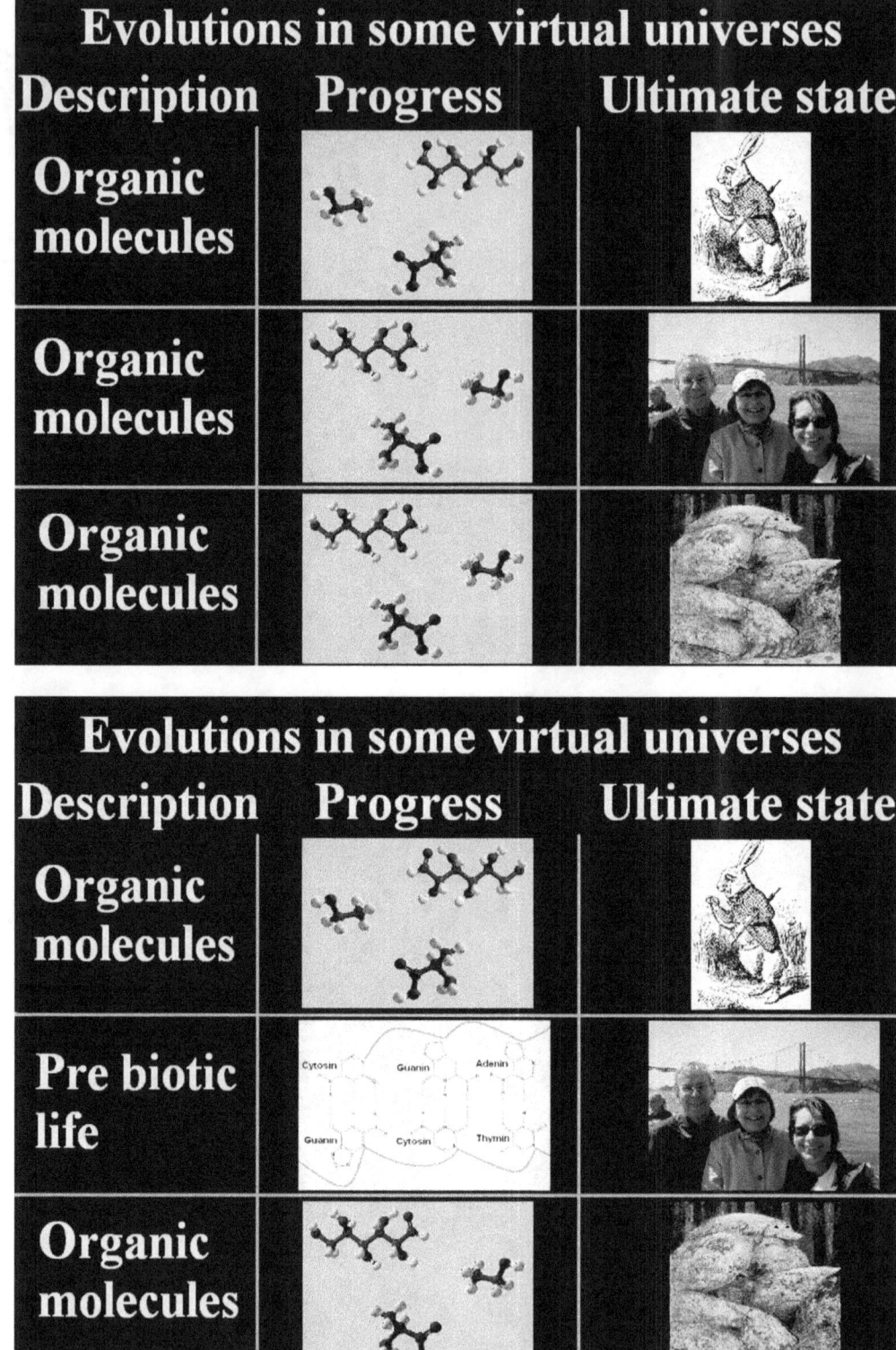

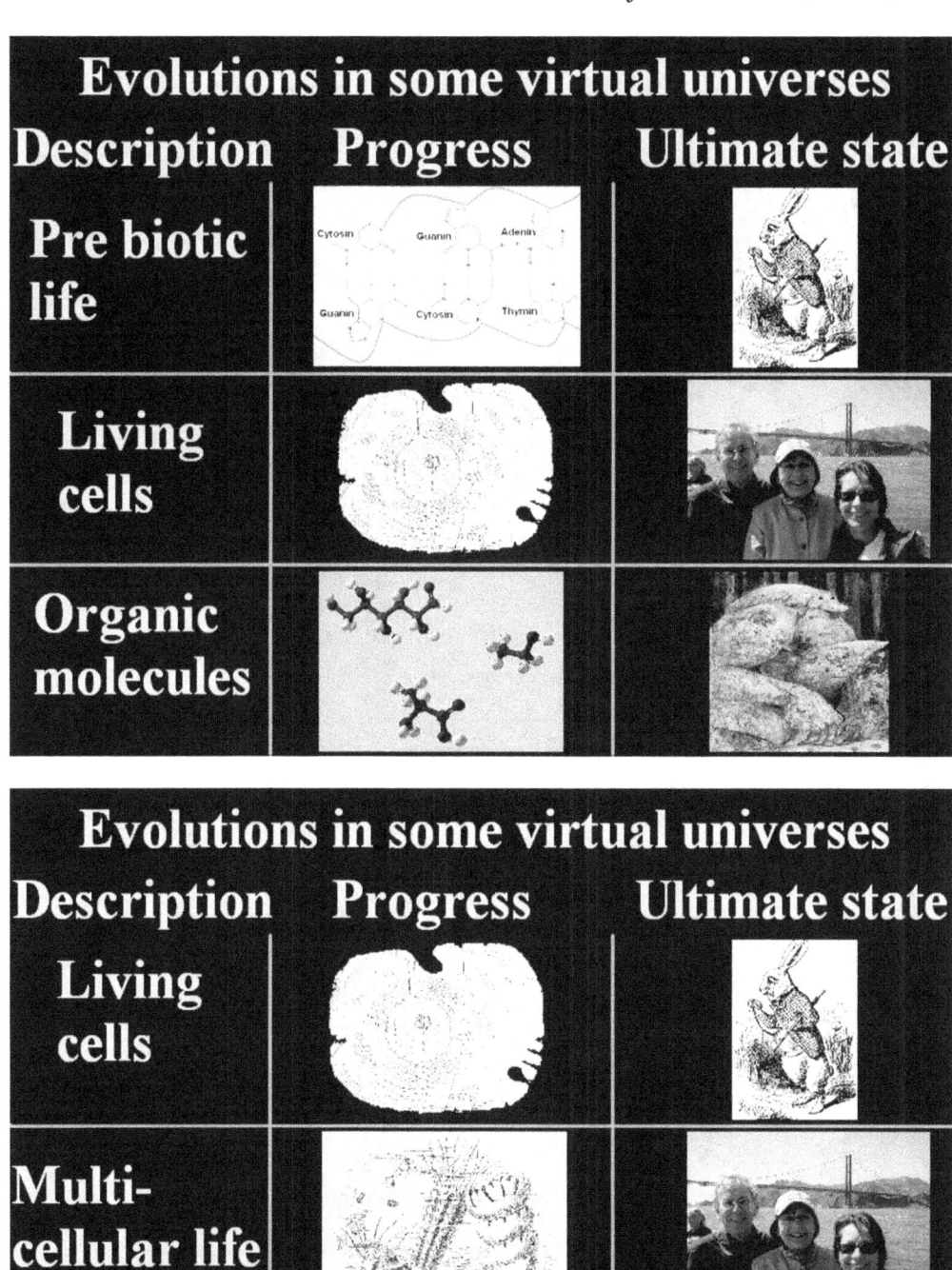

112   Part II. From the Evolution of Life to DNA

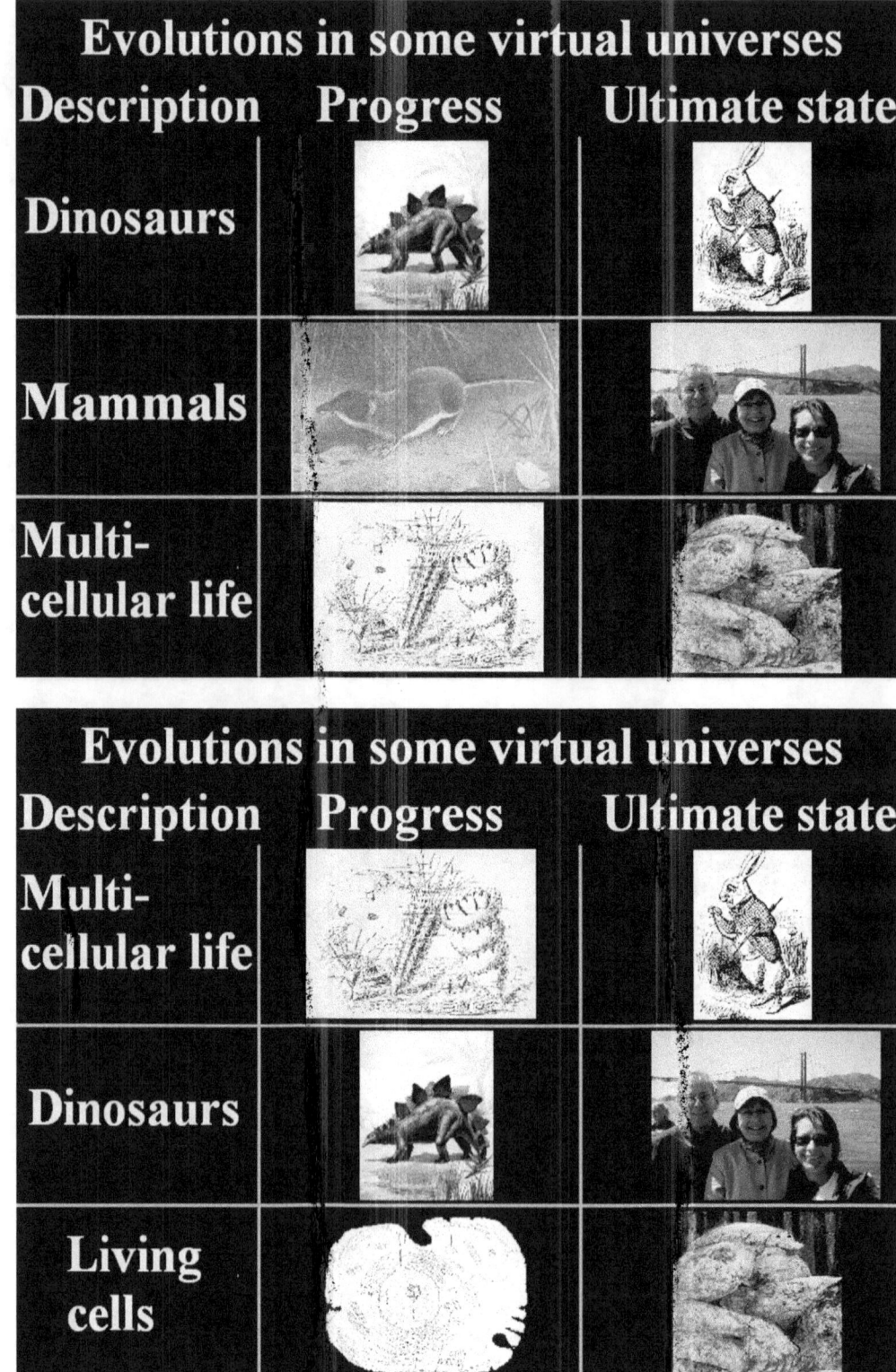

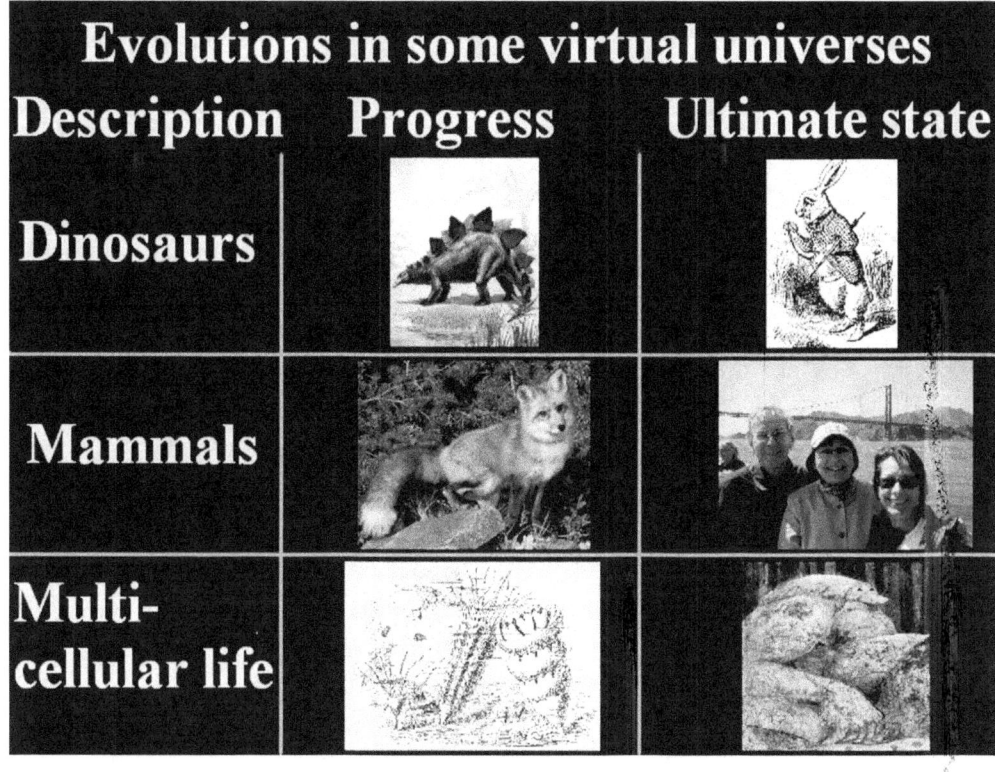
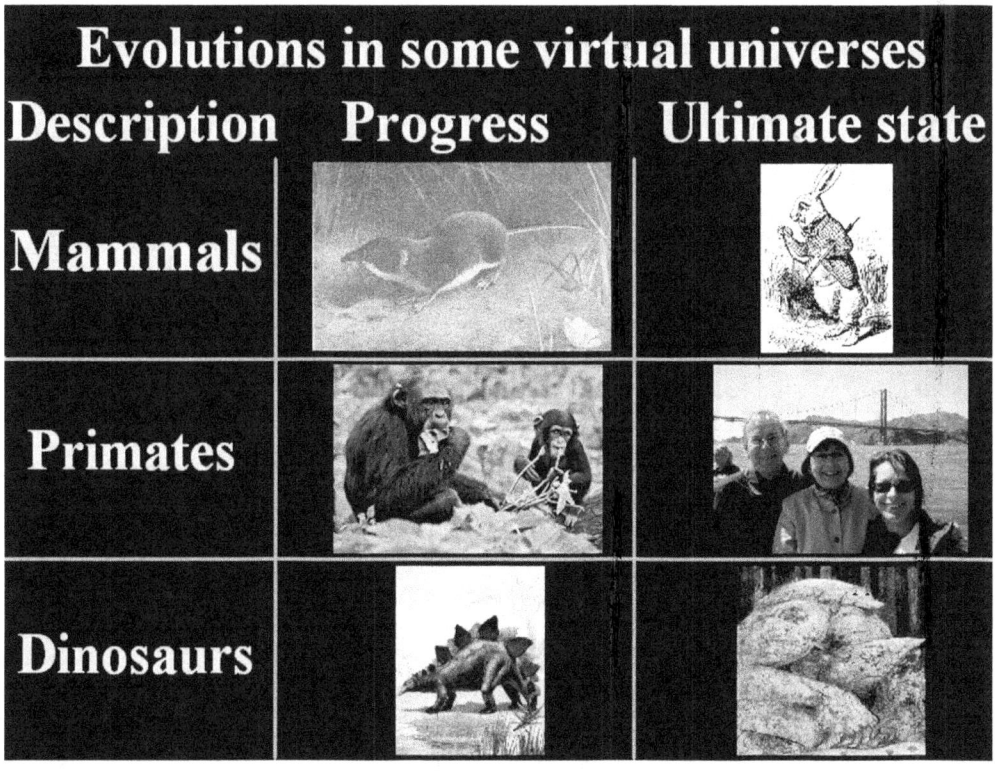

Evolutions in some virtual universes
Description
Progress
Ultimate state
Rabbit
Human
Dinosaurs

Universal collapse of wave function
Description
Progress
Ultimate state
Never able to really exist
Erased from history of the universe
Human is real
Never able to really exist
Erased from history of the universe

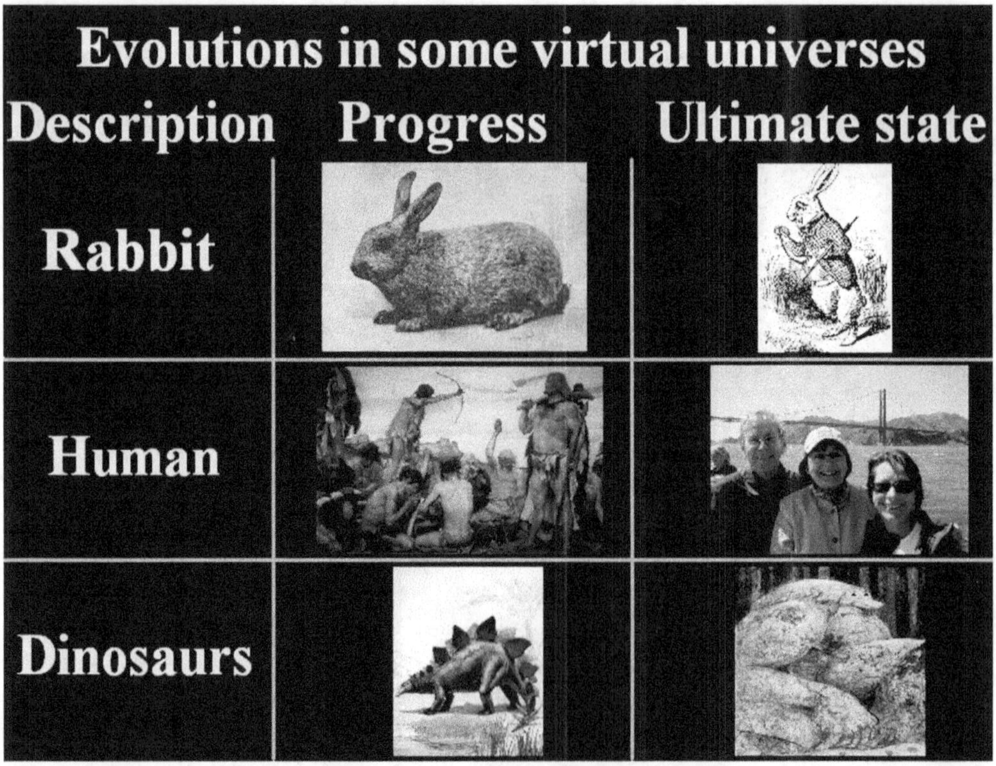

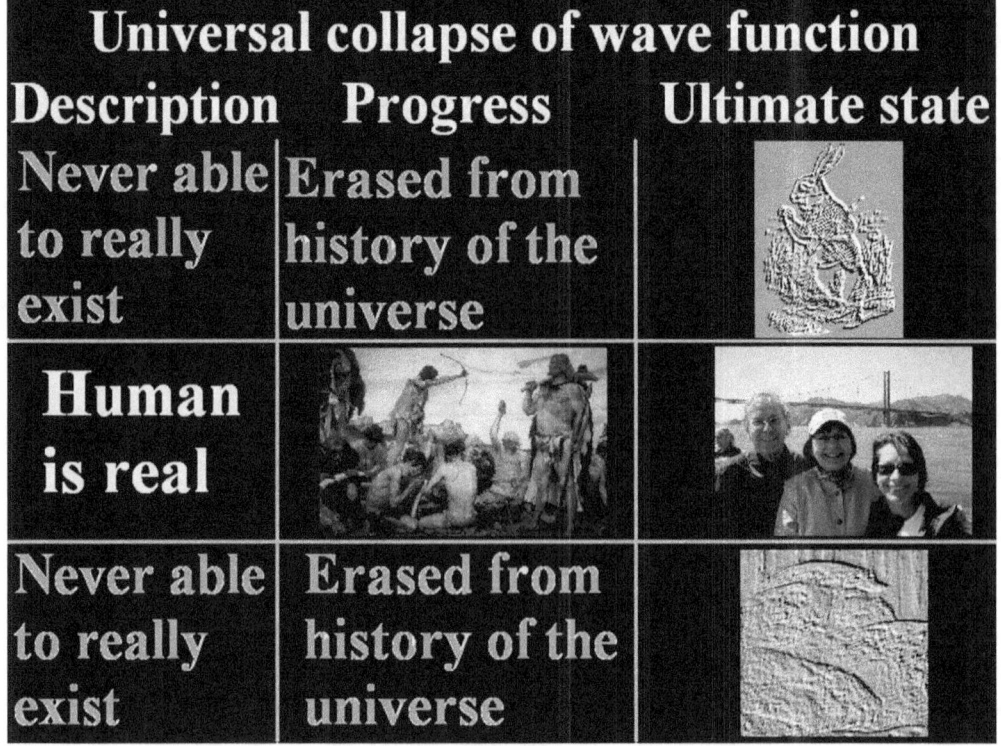

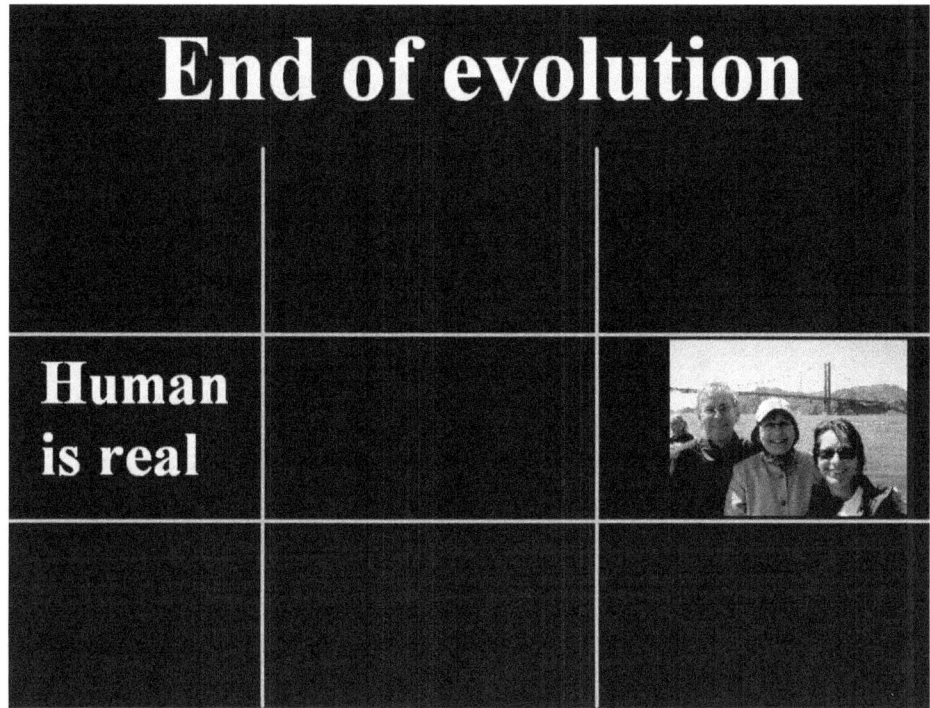

Notes

1. L. Smolin, "Scientific alternatives to the anthropic principle," Perimeter Institute for Theoretical Physics, Waterloo, Ontario N2J 2W9, Canada (2008), http://arxiv.org/pdf/hep-th/0407213v3.pdf

2. P. D. Ward, *Rare Earth*" (New York: Springer-Verlag, 2000).

3. O. Buczek, D. Krowarsch, and J. Otlewski, "Thermodynamics of single peptide bond cleavage in bovine pancreatic trypsin inhibitor (BPTI)," *Protein Science* 11 (2002), p. 924.

4. Any textbook on chemical thermodynamics, e.g., F. Daniels and R.A. Alberty, *Physical Chemistry* (New York: John Wiley & Sons, 1979).

5. Ibid.

6. E.C.W. Clark and D.N. Glew, "Evaluation of the Thermodynamic Functions for Aqueous Sodium Chloride from Equilibrium and Calorimetric Measurements below 154oC," *J. Phys. Chem. Ref. Data*, 14 (1985).

7. W.K. Johnston, P.J. Unrau, M.S. Lawrence, M.E. Glasner and D.P. Bartel, "RNA-Catalyzed RNA Polymerization: Accurate and General RNA-Templated Primer Extension." *Science* 292 (2001), p. 1319.

8. R.D. Knight, S.J. Freeland and L.F. Landweber, "Selection, History and Chemistry: The Three Faces of the Genetic Code." *Trends in Biochemical Science* 24 (1999) p 241.

9. R.A. Cartwright, http://scit.us/redlynx (2009); V.F. Levchenko and V.V. Menshutkin, "Computer Simulation of Evolution: Genetic and 'Memetic' Ways," *International Journal of Computing Anticipatory Systems*, 18 (2007), p. 86.

10. S.J. Gould and N. Eldredge, "Punctuated Equilibria: The Tempo and Mode of Evolution Reconsidered." *Paleobiology* 3 (1977), p. 145.

11. A.T. Emrén, "Darwin simulation version 2012," http://nuchem.se/evolution_en.htm (2012).

12. C.R. Marshall, "Explaining the Cambrian 'Explosion' of Animals," *Annu. Rev. Earth Planet. Sci.* 34 (2006), p. 355.

13. E.H. Walker, *The Physics of Consciousness* (New York: Basic Books, 2000).

14. R.P. Feynman, "Space-Time Approach to Non-Relativistic Quantum Mechanics," in *Quantum Electrodynamics*, ed. J. Schwinger (New York: Dover Publications, 1958).

15. E.P. Wigner, "Symmetries and reflections: Scientific Essays" (Cambridge: MIT Press, 1970).

16. F. Hoyle, "The Black Cloud" (London: William Heinemann, 1957).

DNA Consciousness
From Theory to Science

John K. Grandy

I have often said that consciousness wears a mysterious cloak, but why? For centuries philosophers and later scientists have attempted to lift corners of this cloak in order to gain insights to her well-kept secrets. However, with all the modern knowledge at humankind's fingertips, those same very fingertips go numb when they touch her thigh. Even with a multitude of theories and "scientific explanations" the entire throng of great minds are all staring at the same stop sign and reevaluating the road map that brought them there. They quack and bark at each other and the paper maps flap in the wind. They are all wondering how much further down the road she is? Is she smiling or frowning? Is she angry or waiting to be seduced? Will her lips reveal secrets or freeze you where you stand?

When I first began my journey into the nature of what consciousness *is* I was forced to recognize that consciousness was not merely one thing involving the human brain, but rather that consciousness existed in several forms. If consciousness is not one thing then how is it possible that it can be many things? Are there different forms or different degrees of consciousness? My answer is *yes* and I have proposed in several works in the past that there are unlimited degrees of consciousness in nature.

I first realized this back in 1997 when I was a graduate student starting my master's degree. While I was taking a neurophysiology course, part of the curriculum was to complete a paper on a topic of our choice in this field. I had recently read a book by Noble laureate Gerald Edelman entitled *Bright Air Brilliant Fire* so the topic that I chose was consciousness. At that time there was almost nothing scientific published about the neurophysiology of consciousness. In fact many still were wearing the festering headpiece of dualism and Daniel Dennett's book *Consciousness Explained*, which did not actually explain consciousness, was being lauded for the past six years or so. Incidentally my pit bull, Rogue, had casually chewed the one corner of Dennett's book one evening and perhaps back then she was trying to tell me something—that this book should have instead been entitled *Perception Explained*.

During my research for this project I was rereading the chapter on *consciousness* in Ernst Haeckel's monumental book *The Riddle of the Universe* which I had from a course that I took during my undergrad studies. This chapter was Haeckel's account of the different theories of consciousness of his time and he enumerated six: anthropistic, neurologic, animal, biological, cellular, and atomistic. This chapter made me suspect that there are different *forms* of consciousness and that great thinkers believed this back in the 1890s. But how is it possible to account for this? How can different forms or degrees of consciousness exist? I would spend a great deal of time trying to answer this.

Amusingly, I only received a B– on my paper as the professor did not feel my topic was scientific enough. In retrospect, she was well within her rights. As it turned out, during the course of completing my master's degree I would take courses in biochemistry and cell biology, where I would learn a great deal more about the DNA molecule. The fascinating DNA molecule would inspire me to finally account for the possibility of ascending degrees of consciousness throughout nature.

My first touch of enlightenment occurred in 2004 when I was writing two articles for *The Encyclopedia of Anthropology* (Sage Publications). One article was on "Consciousness" and the other was on "The DNA Molecule." It was during this period that something clicked, something was remembered from my project from seven years ago; that consciousness meant more than human consciousness, rather it was several degrees of consciousness. Intuitively I knew that the answer had to do with the DNA molecule and I coined the phrase "DNA Consciousness," which meant that not only does DNA give rise to consciousness (in neuron-based animals and also the cellular forms of consciousness as discussed by Haeckel) but it also possesses a form of consciousness of its own, i.e., DNA consciousness!

The editor was impressed with this idea and allowed me to publish the phrase *DNA Consciousness* in both of my articles as a theory. That was the beginning of another seven year journey that would bring me to this point where DNA consciousness would ultimately transform from a theory into a science.

I. An Introduction to the Theory of DNA Consciousness

After the phrase DNA Consciousness was first published as a theory simultaneously in the two publications in *The Encyclopedia of Anthropology* by Sage Publications in 2006, I quickly realized that there was something very special about this speculation.[1] However, even though I was very excited and felt that I was on the right road to explaining the nature of consciousness, there still appeared to be something lacking. It seemed that I needed to expound upon this theory and perhaps attempt to provide a novel definition of consciousness.

At that time the theory of DNA consciousness had two themes: (1) that the DNA molecule possesses a degree or form of consciousness of its own and (2) that the DNA molecule is responsible for the emergence of all organic degrees of consciousness. Eventually, I would expand these two nascent themes into the five major themes of DNA consciousness.

The Five Major Themes of DNA Consciousness[2]

1. **The *specialness* theme.** The DNA molecule possess a degree of consciousness of its own but is also a special molecule that presents this degree of consciousness in a

manner that can be observed objectively in what I call the *3 dynamic levels of DNA consciousness*. This means that as DNA molecules exist in various combinations in nature that those combinations are also at the same time projected as various degrees of biological consciousness. These various degrees can be observed on three dynamic levels as DNA molecules interact with: (1) itself (e.g., gene-gene interactions and transcription factors), (2) other nucleotide-based life forms (e.g., other cells), and (3) outside of the cell with the external environment. I have reserved an entire section to further explain these three dynamic levels of DNA consciousness. I should also point out that viewing DNA in this manner is a clear break from the dogma that DNA is merely a cookbook or storage facility that some scientists still cling to.

2. **The *surreptitious* theme.** This theme points out that DNA consciousness is a degree of consciousness that cannot be perceived by humankind's neuron-based consciousness and exist in a clandestine fashion. This is primarily because the human sensorium can only detect a small portion of the electromagnetic spectrum in the macroscopic world and DNA exists in the microscopic world. Consequently, no obvious communication is possible between these two different degrees of consciousness at this time.[3]

3. **The genome-dependent complexity theme.** DNA is directly responsible for all the physical parts of an organism including the brain. In addition, it gives rises to a multitude of degrees of consciousness throughout the process of organic evolution. During this trajectory genetic content dictates those degrees of consciousness as well as the physical parts. This is mainly because the DNA is what codes for the machinery that will be used to experience consciousness. For example, in vertebrates specifically, the Hox and Pax gene families are responsible for giving rise to the brain and nervous system, as well as body patterning. The genes underlying the emergence of the nervous system are one part of a subject that I call *The Neurogenetics of Consciousness*. The second half of this chapter is devoted to this topic.

4. **The extragenomic theme.** Once the genes in the DNA molecule, in collaboration with RNA and other proteins, gives rise to degrees of consciousness in biologic entities, the DNA molecule then provides a continuum of consciousness utilizing the 3 dynamic levels of DNA consciousness. This is done in an extragenomic and epigenetic manner. This is the focus of discussion in the second part of the neurogenetics of consciousness—*The Continuum of DNA Consciousness*.

5. **The transformation theme.** Humankind is just a small phase in the transformation and evolution of DNA consciousness. Through the course of evolution and natural selection the DNA molecule gave rise to a species [humans] that would develop the technological ability to unlock the secrets of the DNA molecule. In other words the DNA molecule discovered itself through the vessel of humankind and now with genetic engineering it can continue to evolve. In the future the process of genetic engineering will replace the much slower mechanism of natural selection. This is what I call *selected genetic destination* (SGD)[4] and it will eventually give rise to the next phase of evolution—*Homo sapiens genomicus* or "the man with the wisdom to alter his genome." This phase of the transformation is a transgenic intermediate that can potentially give rise to many more subspecies and eventually new species, each with the possibility of having higher degrees of consciousness. Natural selection and SGD do represent and display

that the *will* of DNA consciousness has the intention to evolve and transform into higher degrees of consciousness. Obviously these are not the typical characteristics of a cookbook or storage facility.

The five major themes of DNA consciousness were presented for the first time at the International Conference on Humanism and Posthumanism that was held at Belgrade University, Serbia in April 2009. This conference and four additional conferences that I would be invited to over the upcoming two years would have a profound influence on the transformation of DNA consciousness from theory to science.

At this point in the development of the theory of DNA consciousness I felt that I did an adequate job illustrating the five major themes. However, none of the definitions of consciousness that existed at that time could account for DNA consciousness. In fact, most of them were completely incompatible. So here lay an apparently insurmountable hindrance. Consequently, I realized that a new definition of consciousness would need to be derived. Next, I will discuss and explain how I derived a novel definition of consciousness that could account for DNA consciousness and ultimately all ascending degrees of consciousness.

The Interaction-Based Model of Consciousness

In past articles I argued that the focus of consciousness has historically been on human consciousness.[5] However, there was no all-encompassing definition of consciousness which allows the inclusion of other forms or degrees of consciousness. It became obvious during my synthesis of the theory of DNA consciousness that a novel definition needed to be derived that encompassed all degrees of consciousness; from the level of quarks (I don't know enough about string theory to include the substructure of quarks) up to the level of humans.

In order to derive an all-encompassing definition of consciousness many problematic elements that are found in other definitions would need to be eliminated. A superior definition would have to exclude words like *human*, *mind*, *brain*, *awareness*, and *perception*. This would allow the gravitation toward the derivative of what consciousness actually *is*. When these problematic elements were ousted one pure element lay there in front of me like an infant on plush soft white sheets and that infant's name was *interactions*. If everything were to have a degree of consciousness, then what did they all have in common? They all interact! Quarks interact. Cells interact. Brains interact. Consciousness is interactions and these interactions take place on different scales.

I would eventually derive the interaction-based model of consciousness. This proposal states that "consciousness is the interaction of a thing (be it an organism, DNA molecule, or atom) with the external environment and more specifically the interaction of energy with other forms of energy." In 2011 I would modify this definition to "the interaction of things (be it an organism, DNA molecule, or atom) with other things, the external environment, different forms of energy, and forces." This was done to account for what was actually being interacted with in the external environment, i.e., other *things* and forms of energy, ergo the definition of the interaction-based model of consciousness evolved in 2011 from the one proposed in 2009.

The interaction-based model of consciousness allows four specific advantages that no other definitions of consciousness can collectively offer:

1. Transcendence of the limitations that the anthropistic and reductionist models impose.[6] There are some theories of consciousness that attempt to support the anthropistic theory of consciousness. Currently, anthropistic models of consciousness are typically considered outdated by most modern consciousness researchers. However, there are no adequate models to account for the possibility that all things have a degree of consciousness. This is exactly the problem that the interaction-based model of consciousness attempts to solve. The proposal of reductionism is that consciousness is purely a result of the brain and its activity. This would imply that consciousness cannot exist without a brain or neurons, which I will maintain is not true nor is it possible. Ironically, I use to be a reductionist, but after some time I was unwilling to accept that consciousness was not possible below the emergence of neurons. I do recognize that neurons allow consciousness (or interactions) to occur on a much larger scale. Once again, the interaction-based model of consciousness neatly accounts for other degrees of consciousness based on interactions.

2. The eradication of any exclusion criteria as to what does or does not possess consciousness. This allows the graduation from *forms* of consciousness; anthropistic, neurologic, animal, biological, cellular, and atomistic, to *degrees* of consciousness. Antecedent to this point I have occasionally used forms and degrees interchangeably however, in the next section I will discuss the concept of interaction-complexity-consciousness that provides a strong argument and structure for the phenomenon that everything exists as ascending degrees of consciousness.

3. This interaction-based model of consciousness allows consciousness to be viewed within the dynamic framework of evolution. In fact, the evolution of consciousness mirrors the dynamic process of organic evolution and the evolution of matter. Therefore, consciousness can be seen as property inherent in all matter in nature and perhaps the universe. Note that there are theories stating that consciousness is an inherent property of all matter but the notion of interactions or a mechanism to account for this is poorly defined.

4. This definition allows the incorporation of quantum physics into the explanation of consciousness. The involvement of quantum physics in consciousness creates many problematic issues with some of the definitions of consciousness. However, interaction (of an observer) with a system in superposition is proposed to cause decoherence, for example in the Schrodinger's theoretically cat experiment. Therefore, the interaction-based model of consciousness may provide answers to the quantum enigma.[7]

So I have derived a novel definition of consciousness that avoids many of the traps and pitfalls that other definitions typically cede to. I have also enumerated four important advantages that this definition provides. Next, I will discuss how the interaction-based model of consciousness transforms into the concept of interaction-complexity-consciousness, which will ultimately account for all ascending degrees of consciousness from quarks to brains.

The Concept of Interaction-Complexity-Consciousness

In early May of 2011, I attended the Towards a Science of Consciousness Conference: Brains, Mind, and Reality at Stockholm University, Sweden at Aula Magna Hall.[8] While preparing my poster presentation on DNA consciousness I was struggling to justify how the interaction-based model of consciousness could account for a universally underlying consciousness from a scientific point of view.[9] It was at this point that the interaction-based model of consciousness transformed into a physical process that can account for all degrees of consciousness from the level of quarks up to the level of humans. This process is now known as the concept of interaction-complexity-consciousness (ICC).

The concept of ICC states that as *things* interact, these interactions increase the degree of complexity, and as these interactions increase the degree of complexity the consequence is that there is an increase in degrees of consciousness. This takes place from the level of quarks up to the level of the human brain. Simply stated:

↑ interaction ↔ ↑ complexity ↔ ↑ degrees of consciousness

This direct relationship can also be conceptualized as a linear equation, where complexity acts as a mathematical operator that connects the relationship between degrees of interactions to degrees of consciousness:

interaction (complexity) = degrees of consciousness

Now I would like to walk through how this works by starting at one of the lowest levels that are known—quarks. Please note that I am not a quantum physicist so I will not go into the parts of quarks or string theory as it has not been tested experimentally at this point in time. For the purpose of this illustration of the ICC starting with quarks will suffice.

At the initial step quarks interact with each other to form subatomic particles, many consider this *primordial consciousness*. The subatomic particles then give rise to atoms. Now the atoms interact to form molecules that also interact with each other and start to become more complex. Note that at this level as the interactions increase that the levels of complexity increase, and as a result we see ascending degrees of consciousness from primordial consciousness to degrees of atomistic and molecular consciousness.

I would like to draw attention to the fact that something special happens when nucleotides emerge from the realm of molecular degrees of consciousness. As DNA and RNA species begin to interact, complexity explodes! In fact, the ability of these molecules to self-assemble and reliably store a chemical record to produce protein products allows the exponential emergence of billions of life forms and consequently ascending degrees of consciousness. This is where DNA consciousness initially emerges on the ascending scale of ICC. Please note that it is generally accepted the RNA appeared before DNA, but RNA was unable to ignite the explosion of complexity that gave rise to larger degrees of consciousness.

At this stage simple cells emerge and contain repertoires of DNA, which possess genes that define those cells and the biological products within those cells. Through mutations and natural selection these cells can accumulate new genes. This allows them to increase the amount of interactions with the environment, thus increasing complexity and resulting in increases in degrees of consciousness. It is also at this stage where a direct relationship to genome-dependent complexity, which is major theme III of DNA consciousness, becomes obvious.

As cells continue to specialize a second special thing happens in the ascending chain of the ICC. This is when some cells develop electrochemical properties and eventually neurons emerge.[10] These cells are able to develop into neurons because they develop new genes. For example, genes that produce *synapsins*, which are critical of the development of neurons and also the myelin gene regulatory factor that produces the transcriptional regulator that is required for the *myelination of the central nervous system*. The emergence of neurons gives rise to the earliest degrees of neuron-based consciousness which is first seen in the invertebrates. Again, DNA consciousness plays an enormous role in the explosion of increases in new levels of interactions that are manifested in primordial sensory perception. This new level of interactions increases complexity and as a result increases degrees of consciousness in the animal kingdom.

Once invertebrates attain a certain degree of consciousness a third special thing happens in the ascending chain of the ICC—the evolution of the Hox and Pax gene families.[11] At this point in evolution DNA develops novel genes that allow the centralization of the nervous system and cephalization (the appearance of a brain); thus the first vertebrates are born. This birth ushers in a massive explosion of complexity and exponential increases in degrees of consciousness that, through natural selection, will continue to evolve for millions of years.

It is from this process of the ICC that DNA consciousness and then the degree of human consciousness both emerge from. It should be clear now that it is ridiculous to assume that consciousness is a process that involves only the human brain! Further proof of this can be seen in the Cambrian explosion where there is evidence of billions of degrees of consciousness antecedent to human consciousness. It has been proposed and generally accepted that the Hox genes (and perhaps the Pax genes) had a significant role in the Cambrian explosion.

It should be apparent at this point that not only does the ICC concept fit within the dynamic framework of evolution (not just organic evolution, but the evolution of all matter), but it goes hand-in-hand with it! The concept of ICC can be seen in a trajectory beginning with primordial consciousness ascending up to the degree of human consciousness. I have proposed that with genetic engineering (or what I have termed SGD) that these degrees of consciousness can continue to ascend past the stage of the modern human. In previous works I have identified this as the *fourth* special thing that takes place in the ICC. This is mentioned in major theme V of DNA consciousness—the transformation theme, and will be discussed in more detail at the end of this chapter.

Let us summarize the first part of this essay. First, I have derived a novel definition of consciousness—the interaction-based model of consciousness. This definition provides four advantages that no other definition of consciousness provides. Secondly, I have explained how the interaction-based model of consciousness transforms into the concept of ICC, which accounts for all matter and organisms having degrees of consciousness. Finally, I illustrated how DNA consciousness emerges within the ICC and then manifests genome-dependent complexity, which shares a direct relationship to the ascending degrees of consciousness. Including the assembly of nucleotides four special things take place in the ICC involving DNA consciousness. Figure 1 is an artist rendition of the ICC and DNA consciousness that was done in 2009 by Morris Tucker.

Next I would like to focus on the three dynamic levels of DNA consciousness, which I also call genomic dynamics. This is important because it allows the scientific observation of DNA consciousness from three different aspects that are grounded solely on interactions.

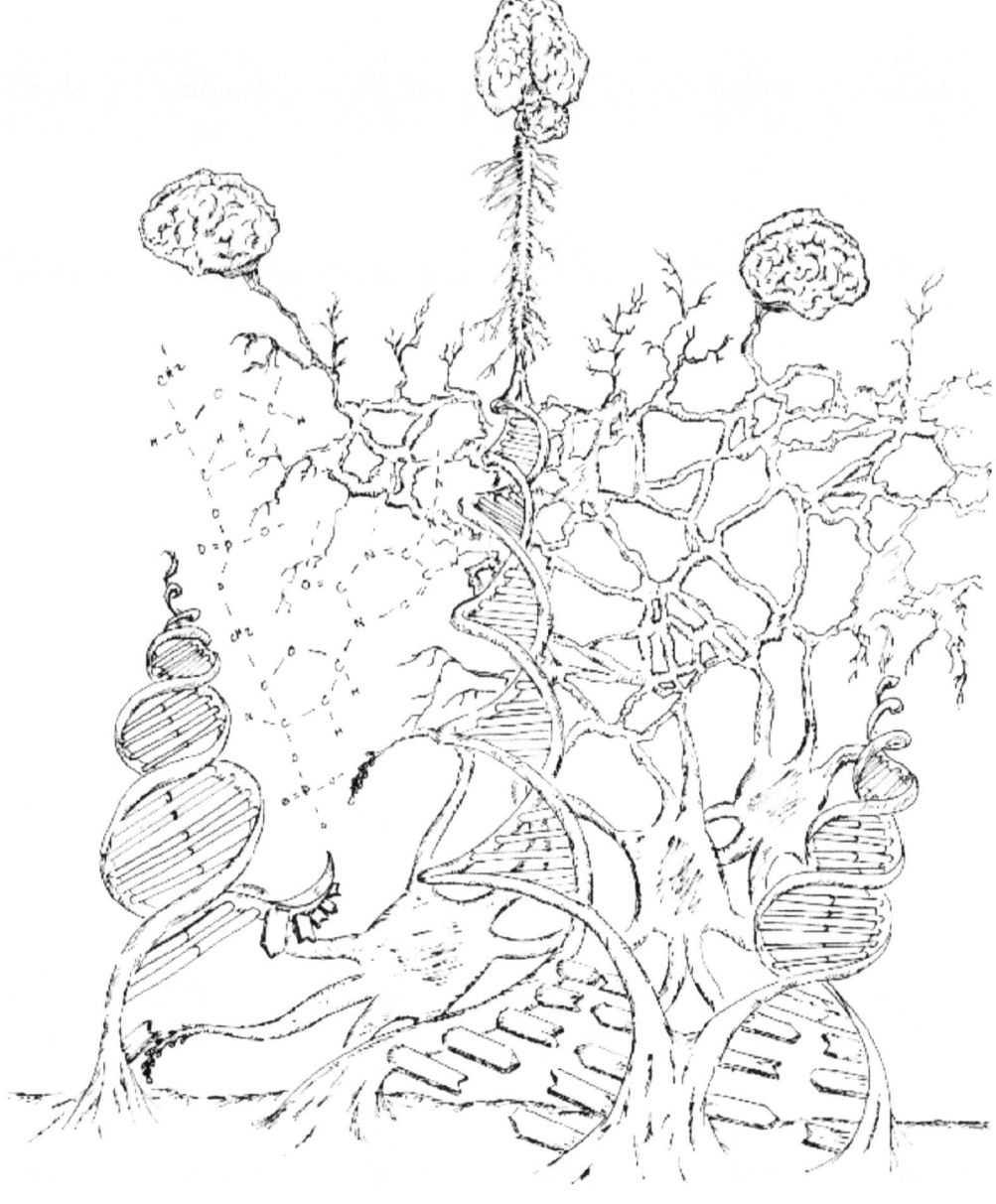

Figure 1: This is an artistic visualization of the ICC and DNA Consciousness. The artwork here was done by Morris Tucker in 2009 after John K. Grandy's return from the Belgrade conference.

II. Genomic Dynamics: The Three Dynamic Levels of DNA Consciousness

The term *genomic dynamics* refers to the changing processes of the DNA molecule that can be observed on three levels. These processes include but are not exclusive to genomic inheritance, extragenomic inheritance, and genomic symbiotics.

A process is considered dynamic if it is energetic and continuously changing. Human consciousness, for example, is considered a dynamic process as it is energetic, there is interaction between components with exchanges of energy, and it is continuously changing through psychological states.[12] The DNA molecule is also dynamic for similar reasons; it uses energy, there are interactions between components, and it is always changing. The 3 dynamic levels of DNA consciousness are:

- Level one—the interactions between DNA and itself. These interactions include genomic inheritance and DNA replication. There are also thousands of gene-gene interactions that begin as early as fertilization and continue throughout the lifespan of the organism.
- Level two—the interactions of DNA and other nucleic entities e.g., RNA, viruses, the mitochondria, and other cells. The interaction between the genome of the host DNA and the DNA (or RNA) of other cellular organelles is known as genomic symbiotics or genetic symbiosis.
- Level three—the interaction between DNA and the external environment beyond the cell or body of the organism. DNA is capable of doing this because it is an autopoietic system which by definition mandates that it is mechanistic or subject to cause and effect. The third dynamic level of DNA consciousness is significant in that it illustrates that the DNA molecule is not a closed system and can be affected by interactions with the environment.

These three dynamic levels will now be discussed as they pertain to the emerging science of DNA consciousness. This is important as many of these biological processes that will be discussed here are already established themes in the scientific literature. However, they have not yet been applied to the interaction-based model of consciousness, the ICC, or DNA consciousness. Next I will discuss each of the three levels and how they apply to the interaction-based model of consciousness, the ICC, and DNA consciousness.

The First Dynamic Level of DNA Consciousness

Genomic inheritance is considered the type of inheritance based on the nucleic acid content of the genome. This is what is inherited from the parent cell in asexual reproduction and what is inherited from both the parents in sexual reproduction.

The storage and replication of genetic information is believed to have originated with the RNA molecule. However, the DNA molecule offers more thermal stability, reliability of replication by a semi-conservative model, transmissibility of protein products after replication, and the ability to produce RNA products that maintain vital housekeeping roles in the cell. In addition to these attributes, the DNA molecule displays two other phenomena. The first is the ability to reproduce an identical copy of it's self (mitosis). The second is the ability to split in half (what is known as a haploid) while allowing genetic rearrangement of some alleles (meiosis) and then recombine with another different strand of haploid DNA to form a new but slightly different DNA molecule—essentially a variation of the two original strands. This is what takes place during fertilization. This new DNA molecule will go on to self-perpetuate. Mitosis and meiosis gives the DNA molecule the ability to self-perpetuate itself uniformly and uniformly with just minor changes; known as asexual and sexual reproduction of the genome, respectively.

But how does the DNA molecule do these things? How does it *know* when and when not to do it? Do these actions of self-perpetuation of a *fixed genetic arrangement* or the perpetuation with minor genetic modifications imply consciousness or random chance? In order to attempt to answer this question let us look at two important biological processes: DNA methylation and genomic imprinting.

DNA Methylation and Genomic Imprinting

First let me address some basic concepts about DNA and how it is stored in the nucleus of the cell. Chromosomes are made up of strands of DNA wound around balls of proteins called histones.[13] A group of 8 histones converge to form a *nucleosome*, which are bound to each other with histone H1 to form chromatin fiber. Chromatin can undergo methylation,[14] which occurs on C-residues (regions high in the cytosine nucleotide) in promoter genes. This methylation causes the impedance of transcription by RNA polymerase, which is needed to form template DNA for transcription. Therefore, methylating portions of the DNA molecule can prevent the expression of certain genes.

Oddly enough the process of DNA methylation becomes less active during DNA replication and gametogenesis. After these processes are complete DNA methylation becomes more active in determining the final state of the genome and the determination of what genes will and will not be expressed is made. When the final genetic state of the DNA is complete it is known as a *genomic imprint* or *chromatin signal*. I have often referred to this determined state of genetic expression as a fixed genetic arrangement in that this state will remain somewhat consistent as to what is expressed, minus damage or mutations of course. So now that we understand in a very general sense how a fixed genetic arrangement is obtained by the DNA molecule through DNA methylation we must now establish how this pertains to the first dynamic level of DNA consciousness.

DNA methylation appears to be an important component to the first dynamic level of DNA consciousness.[15] How does DNA methylation undergo the dramatic reprogramming required during gametogenesis and fertilization (or a decrease of DNA methylation) but then afterwards shift gears into having profound effects on the entire genome (with an increase in DNA methylation)? Interestingly, it has been well established by the investigation of genome-wide patterns of DNA methylation on promoters of the *Hells* gene that this gene encodes for lymphoid-specific helicase (LSH), which is a member of the SNF2 family of chromatin remodeling ATPase. LSH has been shown to be very important for DNA methylation during the establishment and differentiation of embryonic lineage cells.[16]

So if we stop to think about it, a gene, the *Hells* gene, is responsible for producing a product (LSH) that has a profound effect (through DNA methylation) on the fixed genetic arrangement of the genome (or genomic imprint). This clearly illustrates the first dynamic level of DNA consciousness. That a gene affecting the state of other genes, which increases interactions allowing higher degrees of complexity in various genomes to emerge. These are gene-gene interactions and contributed significantly to all degrees of DNA consciousness.

Thus far, I have illustrated a few of the biological factors that regulate genomic inheritance patterns; mainly DNA methylation and genomic imprints, and how they pertain to the first dynamic level of DNA consciousness. I also provided an example of how one gene, the *Hells* gene, can have a profound effect on other genes in the genome. The gene-gene interactions are what define the first dynamic level of DNA consciousness. Next, I will illustrate how quantum theory is involved by explaining the following scenario involving two haploid gametes call gamete one and gamete two. Don't worry there will be no confusing quantum equations or tedious calculations. This will illustrate that a degree of consciousness, DNA consciousness, is involved at the first dynamic level.

First we start with gamete one which has x number of genes. Of those x genes, only a certain percent, which we will call i, of them will be expressed because DNA methylation will later prevent the rest from being expressed.[17] This will then exist as the genetically fixed state of *gamete one ix*. Now we must factor in some basic concepts from quantum theory.

Before gamete one's state *ix* underwent genetic rearrangement, determined which genes will be express or not expressed, and then selected a fixed genetic state (that is now thermodynamically irreversible) many possible genetic states could have existed before the x number of genes became *ix*. That is to say that gamete one was in a state of superposition prior to DNA methylation determining the specific fixed genetic state *ix*. Therefore, gamete one was in a state of superposition and then wave function collapse (decoherence)[18] took place and a determined genetic state emerged—gamete one ix.

Now that we have dragged quantum theory into the picture (hopefully not kicking and screaming) allow us to reevaluate what is implied here in terms of consciousness. It is largely agreed upon, in quantum theory, that when a state of superposition undergoes decoherence that this happens secondary to observation or measurement. That is to say that the electrons in orbit of an atom's nucleus do not exist in one place at any one time until they are measured by an external observer or measurement device. In fact those electrons exist in thousands of positions simultaneously until consciousness intervenes and caused decoherence. This measurement problem is also referred to as the "quantum enigma" or where physics meets consciousness.[19] By association, I will insist that the same process of decoherence applies to gamete one ix.

With this illustration I propose that it is possible that a degree of consciousness, DNA consciousness, causes wave function collapse of all the possible genetic states of gamete one which resulted in the fixed determined genetic state of gamete one ix. It is implicit that a degree of consciousness that is not observable to us, which is major theme II of DNA consciousness—the surreptitious theme is at work here otherwise gamete one would continue to exist in a state of superposition and the commitment of a thermodynamically irreversible and determined genetic state would never be obtained. If the determination of the genetic state of gamete one ix was merely random (and not a degree of consciousness), then there would also be billions of other random states of gamete one ix in existence. However, this is not the case because only a small percent of the variations (compared to the billions of possibilities) of gamete one ix are ultimately manifested. Consequently, this does not qualify as a random event; it involved DNA consciousness on the first dynamic level.

There is now a second part to this illustration. Let us now say that gamete two undergoes the same quantum process that gamete one underwent, i.e., a state of superposition and then decoherence into a fixed genetic state = *gamete two ix*. Afterwards the two gametes unite and undergo fertilization. Once again we arrive at a scene were many genetic states or combinations are possible when the two haploids become one diploid DNA molecule. The new DNA molecule will express some genes from gamete one and some genes from gamete two as determined by the genomic imprint. Again many potential states could exist from the combination of these two strands, but then this particular DNA molecule commits to one fixed genetic arrangement, which involves decoherence. It is also worth noting that decoherence takes place three different times; once with gamete one, once with gamete two, and again in the formation of the diploid DNA molecule. Are we to accept that this is random chance at all three points of this illustration?

It is unlikely that these are random events at the level of the genome. Otherwise the DNA molecule could not consistently give rise to cells and organisms with any degree of consistent reproducibility. If these were completely random events then there would be completely random results, but this is not what happens. These determined genetic states are in large part ordained by a gene(s) that is important to the process of DNA methylation. Thus, it is possible that the *Hells* gene, LSH, and DNA methylation are all involved in the decoherence of the DNA molecule's final fixed genetic state. This is also where DNA may serve as an intermediate between the primordial consciousness and larger scale consciousness in the macro-world. This is all part of a degree of consciousness that we can observe to only a very small degree scientifically. In the future, when the technology grows we may be able to observe more.

I have proposed a few biological and scientific examples of how DNA is able to have a degree of consciousness of its own, which is major theme I—the specialness theme. Secondly, I have pointed out in the first dynamic level of DNA consciousness that the human sensorium cannot directly observe DNA consciousness, which is major theme II—the surreptitious theme. However, through some molecular processes that can be seen experimentally, and theoretical extrapolations made with quantum theory we can begin to appreciate that there is a degree of consciousness at work here. Next, we will now look at the second dynamic level of DNA Consciousness.

The Second Dynamic Level of DNA Consciousness

The second dynamic level of DNA consciousness involves the interaction of the genomic DNA with other nucleotide-based entities, epigenetic processes, extragenomic inheritance, and symbiotics. *Symbiotics* is sometimes classified as extragenomic inheritance; however the term *genomic symbiotics* refers to not only the interactions of nuclear DNA with symbiotic eubacteria (mitochondria) and retroviruses involved in *horizontal gene transfer*[20] but also the interactions between DNA and all the forms of RNA in the cell. We will now look at two important biological processes—extragenomic inheritance and genomic symbiotics—and how they are vital to the second dynamic level of DNA consciousness.

EXTRAGENOMIC INHERITANCE

Extragenomic inheritance is the epigenetic inheritance that covers the range of self-perpetuating states of gene regulation to the self-perpetuating states based on preexisting cell structures. Note that even though DNA methylation was mentioned in determining genomic inheritance, it is also involved in extragenomic inheritance as well. *Epigenetic* refers to changes in phenotype (gene expression) that is caused by factors other than the underlying DNA sequences in the host genome, i.e., factors outside the genome.[21]

Structural inheritance is the manner in which the structure of the cell and the structures with in the cytoplasm of the cell descend from preexisting cell structures in a manner that intrinsic molecular DNA is not needed.[22] This is important to our topic because it indicates that there is another symbiotic coexisting relationship between DNA consciousness and other molecular/chemical degrees of consciousness which underlies the collective cellular degree of consciousness. A relationship based on interactions is implicit because there must be interactions between the DNA and the molecular structure of the cell because they both *know* when to divide at the same time during cell division.

Although it is beyond the scope of this chapter to evaluate and illustrate the molecular and biological mechanisms that underlay extragenomic inheritance I will make the following generalizations. The cellular structures and organelles do not randomly replicate in an incorrigible fashion. There is communication based on interactions with the genomic DNA and this implies a degree of consciousness on the second dynamic level. Next, allow me to discuss genomic symbiotics which will provide an example of these types of interactions.

GENOMIC SYMBIOTICS

There are two very important interactions that are significant to the second dynamic level of DNA consciousness, the interactions between the genomic DNA with intracellular symbiotic bacteria (in particular mitochondria) and RNA species. We will now examine the relationships between the intracellular symbiotic bacteria using the mitochondria as a primary example and then discuss RNA species.

It has long been established that several organelles in eukaryotic cells have eubacterial origins. These symbiotic organisms were incorporated into primitive host cells about 1.5 billion years ago, when substantial amounts of oxygen entered the Earth's atmosphere. This is seen today as chloroplast that evolved from cyanobacteria that are found in plant cells and mitochondria that evolved from alpha-proteobacteria that are in eukaryotes.[23] There is also some speculation that the peroxisomes in eukaryotic cells arose from aerobic bacteria.

So how does the symbiotic relationship between genomic DNA and mitochondrial DNA (mtDNA) work? In general mitochondrion possesses around 37–50 genes (this varies from specie to specie), however the mitochondrion genome does not produce all of its proteins and enzyme subunits; e.g., NADH-dehydrogenase is produced by the nuclear genome of the host cell. During the course of evolution some genes from the mtDNA were translocated into the nuclear genome, which provided a benefit to the mitochondria. It is well established that there is a high rate of mutation frequency as the mitochondria produces free oxygen radicals and lacks proof-reading DNA repair systems. So some mitochondrial genes where incorporated into the nuclear genome which now produces some very important products for the mitochondria because it possesses some of its genes. In order for this system to function properly there must be some communication between the two genomes. This communication and interaction implies a degree of consciousness otherwise the products required for the mitochondria would be transcribed from the nuclear host DNA randomly, and this would be extremely ineffective and unbeneficial to the survival of the cell.

Another line of proof that communication must exist between nuclear DNA and mtDNA that implies a degree of consciousness is the fact that during mitosis the mitochondria *know* when the nuclear DNA is preparing to divide. This is supported by the fact that the mitochondria start replicating during the S-phase of the cell replication cycle. S-phase is the phase in where the host cell begins producing cellular products that the two dividing cells will ultimately need. Once again, accepting this occurrence as a completely random act is not possible. Otherwise there would be dividing cells with out enough mitochondrion in them and non-dividing cells with too much mitochondrion however these types of cells do not exist in nature. This is because there is a degree of consciousness at work on the second dynamic level of DNA consciousness and this allows the mitochondria to know when to make copies of themselves while the nuclear genome is copying its self.

Is this symbiotic relationship between genomic DNA and mtDNA something that can affect human consciousness? Yes. In fact there are several mitochondrial disorders; also called mitochondrial cytopathies, that affect the human nervous system. Some examples of neurological disorders that are related to primary defects in the mitochondrial genome are:

- MELAS—mitochondrial encephalomyopathy, lactic acidosis, and stroke-like episodes[24]
- Myoclonic epilepsy and ragged red fibers
- Retinitis pigmentosa
- Some forms of ataxia and neuropathy

These are four examples of mitochondrial cytopathies that affect human consciousness. I will mention these again in the second part of the neurogenetics of consciousness as these cytopathies affect the continuum of human consciousness. However, the fact that it affects the continuum of consciousness makes it significant to major theme IV— the extragenomic theme. At this point I have illustrated one of the important interactions involving genomic symbiosis that involves mtDNA. Next, let us look at interactions with RNA species.

RNA

I have mentioned earlier that DNA-RNA interactions contributed to the explosion in complexity and consequently in degrees of consciousness. In fact this is involved in the first special thing that occurs in the ICC. Now I will briefly explain the involvement of RNA in the second dynamic level of DNA consciousness.

It is generally accepted that RNA existed prior to DNA. However, it is hard to imagine that RNA existed too much longer with out the appearance of DNA, and in fact they in all likelihood evolved together utilizing the symbiotic relationship that is currently in place. This proposal is based on the following facts: the similarity in structure of DNA and RNA, the interchangeability of uracil and thymine, the existence of single-stranded DNA (ssDNA) and double-stranded RNA (dsRNA), and the effortless manner in which two species of molecules interact. There are many species of RNA that have been discovered (see figure two) and most likely many more unstable intermediates that will be discovered.

DNA-RNA interactions are vital in the ascending complexity of consciousness in the ICC. In fact, from a biological perspective, RNA is directly involved in the transcription of gene from the DNA and the translation to protein production.[25] I will not review these processes step by step because that has been done in other works. The point is that this DNA-RNA relationship works exceedingly we to produce the building blocks of all organisms—proteins.

As I have already stated in regards to the interactions between nuclear DNA of the host cell and mtDNA, it is unacceptable to view these complex interactions of DNA and RNA as merely random. I will apply the same point of view in regards to DNA-RNA interactions. They are not random. Otherwise the process of transcription and translation would not work effectively all of the time. This of course is not the case because the DNA-RNA system works exceedingly well.

It can be seen in figure 2 that RNA species perform many important functions for the cell. All of those species work in accordance to a biological feedback system in where RNA is produced by the genomic DNA. Therefore, DNA-RNA interactions are not only significant for the increase of complexity but they highlight a form of communication, a degree of consciousness that is based on these interactions. Therefore, DNA-RNA and DNA-mtDNA interactions cannot be condoned as thousands of random processes taking place in the cytoplasm and nucleus of a cell. In the future, as more scientific breakthroughs occur in biology, we may see this second dynamic level of DNA consciousness solidify into reproducible experiments. I will now discuss the interactions that take place between DNA and the external environment.

The Third Dynamic Level of DNA Consciousness

The third dynamic level of DNA consciousness consists of the interactions between DNA and the external environment. This is readily seen as DNA interacts with various forms of radiation, e.g., UV and gamma radiation. In fact, it is these various forms of radiation that can cause mutations to the DNA molecule. This is already well established and has been verified in decades of experimentation. Another entity that can alter DNA is mutagens, which are chemicals or agents that interact with and produce changes in the DNA. These interactions can damage the p53 gene which can be manifested by cancer.[26]

Besides radiation and mutagens, there are other biological phenomena that can affect the DNA in the genome, e.g., horizontal gene transfer. This was mentioned briefly in our discussion about genomic symbiotics in the second dynamic level of DNA con-

1. **Heterogeneous nuclear RNA** (hnRNA) is transcribed directly from DNA by an enzyme called **RNA polymerase**. This form of RNA contains all the coding regions (exons) and non-coding regions (introns). hnRNA is then processed to yield mRNA for protein synthesis.
2. **Messenger RNA** (mRNA) is the modified version of hnRNA, which has had all of the introns removed. mRNA possesses only the coding regions, which contain a code (the triplet code or codons) that is used for transcribing proteins.
3. **Transfer RNA** (tRNA) is transcribed from coding sequences on the DNA molecule by **RNA polymerase III**. This type of RNA possesses an "anti-codon" on one of its ends, which matches a particular section of mRNA. On the other end tRNA has an amino acid attached. In a basic sense, tRNA serves as an adaptor between mRNA and amino acids during protein synthesis.
4. **Ribosomal RNA** (rRNA) exists as several species of rRNA, which are categorized by their sedimentation coefficents that is recorded in Svedberg units (S). A ribosome is composed of two subunits; a large subunit (5S, 5.8S, and 28S) and a small subunit (18S). The ribosome's function involves holding mRNA in place while the corresponding tRNA attaches amino acids together during protein synthesis.
5. **Small nuclear RNA** (snRNA) is found in RNA-protein complexes called spliceosomes. There function is to remove introns from hnRNA to produce mRNA. In the disease systemic lupus erythematous the body produces anti-bodies to snRNA molecules.
6. **Small nucleolar RNA** (snoRNA) functions in site-specific base modifications in rRNA and snRNA. These modifications include methylation and pseudouridylation.
7. **Signal recognition particle RNA** functions by recognizing particular signal sequences on some proteins and assist in transporting them outside the cell, a process known as exocytosis.
8. **Micro-RNA** (miRNA) is believed to control the translation of structural genes. They are proposed to do this by binding to the complementary sequences in the 3 prime untranslated regions of the mRNA.
9. **Mitochondrial RNA** replicates and transcribes independently of the other nuclear DNA and RNA. However, mitochondrial DNA exists as a double stranded loop (or circle) with an outer heavy strand and an inner light strand. Both strands are transcribed by mitochondrial-specific RNA polymerase to produce 37 separate mitochondrial RNA species (mitochondrial rRNA, mitochondrial tRNA, and mitochondrial mRNA).
10. **Large intergenic non-coding RNAs** (lincRNA) poorly understood but one example is HOTAIR that is encoded antisense to the human Hox C cluster and has a global epigenetic state of the Hox D cluster on a separate chromosome.

Figure 2: This is a list of different RNA species and their various functions.

sciousness (also see endnote 21). I will now discuss horizontal gene transfer and how it applies to the third dynamic level of DNA consciousness.

HORIZONTAL GENE TRANSFER

The basic biology is that viruses cannot produce the raw materials needed to replicate themselves. They are considered obligate cellular parasites and require a host cell to produce the parts necessary to produce progeny. Viruses do this by first attaching to a receptor site on the host cell and then inserting the viral DNA into the host cell. After this step the viral DNA incorporates itself into the DNA of the host genome and uses the host materials to produce viral components.

During this process of the viral life cycle, in some rare cases, the viral DNA will copy one or more genes of the host DNA and these gene(s) will be transferred to the genome of the new generation of viruses. These new viruses will ultimately infect a second organism and can then add the genes from the first host into the genome of the new host. This is how horizontal gene transfer operates.

We now have three examples of the third dynamic level of DNA consciousness—radiation, mutagens, and horizontal gene transfer. This is a third dynamic level of interactions with the external environment that can affect the interactions and complexity of the DNA molecule, and consequently ascending degrees of consciousness. Therefore, DNA can interact with the external environment and it can also be modified by these interactions. This allows DNA the opportunity to evolve and change. This is also allows the ICC to ascend. In the future genetic engineering will allow this to take place under more controlled conditions which is significant to major theme V of DNA consciousness—the transformation theme.

I have reviewed the three dynamic levels of DNA consciousness and how they are important to the interaction-based model of consciousness, the ICC, and DNA consciousness. However, these three levels are not isolated, there is some overlap. One example is that the first and second level both involves DNA methylation at some point. A second example is that the second and third levels are connected by intercellular cascades that affect the nuclear genome and the production of proteins, which affect the other end of the cascade—positive and negative biofeedback (see figure 3).

If you look at the three dynamic levels of DNA consciousness you can see how DNA operates as a conscious entity. These three levels also interact to form a continuous cycle of consciousness. In addition, I have provided many scientific examples to validate these statements. The three dynamic levels of DNA consciousness also validate that DNA is not merely a cookbook or a molecular storage unit! Now that I have completed our discussion of the three dynamic levels of DNA consciousness I will illustrate how this all applies to human consciousness in the next part of this chapter—the neurogenetics of consciousness.

First Dynamic Level of DNA Consciousness

Third Dynamic Level of DNA Consciousness

Second Dynamic Level of DNA Consciousness

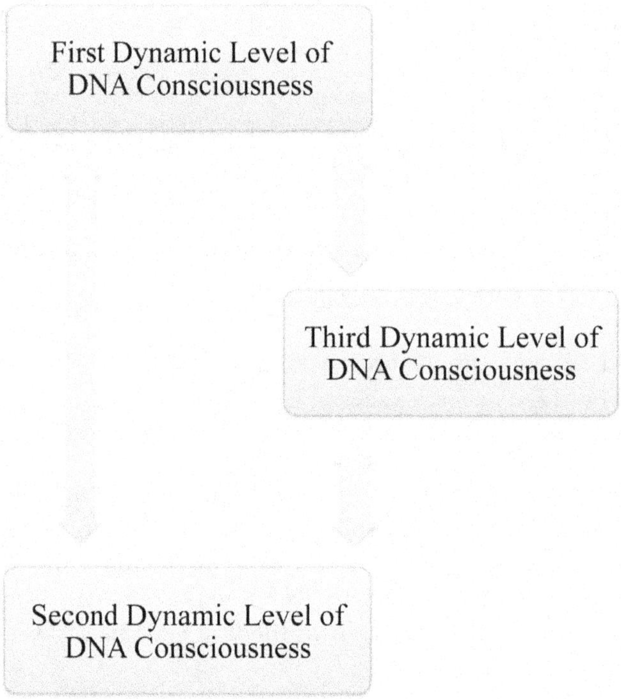

Figure 3: The first dynamic level and the second dynamic level are connected by processes, e.g., DNA methylation and interactions between RNA species. The second dynamic level and third dynamic level are connected by process, e.g., intercellular cascades, second messengers, and RNA species. The third dynamic level and the first dynamic level are connected by processes, e.g., mutations and horizontal gene transfer.

III. The Neurogenetics of Consciousness

Before I begin our discussion on the topic of the neurogenetics of consciousness, allow me at this juncture to summarize what I have addressed so far in the first half of this essay. First, I have explained the interaction-based model of consciousness and how this transforms into the ICC. Second, I have demonstrated how DNA consciousness emerges with in the ICC. Third, I have enumerated four special things that happen involving the assembly of nucleotides and DNA consciousness in the ascending chain of consciousness. Fourth, I demonstrated how DNA consciousness can be observed scientifically on three dynamic levels. Now I shall discuss how this all translates to the neurogenetics of consciousness.[27]

The neurogenetics of consciousness is a term that I have applied to describe the involvement of DNA consciousness with human consciousness. I have organized this topic into three distinct phases. The first phase is neurogenesis, which is were DNA initially gives rise to the brain and the central nervous system, both of which will be the machinery that interacts with the external environment and makes the degree of human neuron-based consciousness possible. The second phase is the continuum of neuron-based consciousness. Here I demonstrate how DNA is involved in human consciousness and how mutations have pathological consequences that decrease degrees of human consciousness. The third phase is the process of deterioration of the brain and nervous system. In this phase there are genes that can cause neurodegeneration earlier and more aggressively than that which is normal for age-related decline. Neurodegeneration contributes to the decrease in interactions resulting in decreased degrees of consciousness.

Phase One: The Emergence of Neuron-Based Consciousness

I have mentioned several times that the Hox genes are responsible not only for body segment patterning, but also for initiating brain morphogenesis, and ultimately neuron-based consciousness in all vertebrates, including humans. In addition to Hox genes, the Pax genes are responsible for the initial patterning of some sensory organs, mainly the eyes and ears. Much of the information regarding these two families of genes is extrapolated from animal studies. However, these genes are highly conserved in most vertebrates or equivalent ancestor versions are present, in some cases as far back as the invertebrates. Consequently a reasonable amount of accuracy may be ascertained with these genetic extrapolations.

In this section I will give a general description of the Hox and Pax gene families, which I will use in order to illustrate the science behind major theme III of DNA consciousness—the genome-dependent complexity theme and display the role that these genes play in the ICC.

The Hox Genes

The Hox genes (or *Homeobox* genes) have been defined as the groups of genes found in highly conserved sequences in all vertebrates and some invertebrates. They are involved in early embryonic development of the brain and central nervous system. They initiate this by forming an anterior-posterior (AP) axis that is also known to directly specify and identify the spatial arrangements of the body segments in the developing embryo. Some of the first experiments involving the Hox genes and the proteins that they produce (Hox proteins) were performed on *Drosophila melanogaster*, more commonly known as the fruit fly.

Characteristic of the Hox genes is the presence of a 180 nucleotide DNA sequence (the homeobox gene) that encodes for a 60 amino acid domain that is known as the *homeodomain protein*. This homeodomain is a Hox protein, which is also called a homeotic selector gene that acts as a DNA binding domain[28] and can either activate or repress other Hox genes as well as non–Hox genes that are important for development.[29]

The proteins encoded by these homeotic selector genes are related to other Homeodomains at the structural level by their conservation of similar versions of the homeodomain motif throughout the vertebrate subphylum. This motif allowed scientists to make molecular comparisons across large phylogenetic distances, which was first recognized by William McGinnis and colleagues in 1984.

These proteins have such a high degree of sequence similarity and functional similarity that this functional equivalence has been demonstrated experimentally. One famous experiment illustrates that a fly can develop normally by replacing certain fly Hox proteins with the corresponding chicken Hox protein.[30] This proved that the fly developed normally using chicken Hox proteins, which validated that these proteins are highly conserved phylogenetically.

The number of Hox genes differs from specie to specie. In more complicated vertebrates (e.g., the amniotes taxi mice and humans) there are 13 genes that form four clusters A, B, C, and D. Whereas in simpler organisms, like *C. elegans*, there are only 6 genes and one cluster of them. Additional clusters emerged during evolution by duplication of the original genome. These are also known as prologue genes (or Paradox), which by definition are genes in one species that have arisen by the duplication of an ancestral gene.[31]

I have briefly explained what Hox genes are. I will now discuss three key features of the Hox gene clusters: colinearity, some important Hox proteins, and the three phases of Hox gene expression.

1. COLINEARITY

Colinearity is the parallel between the physical position of Hox genes along the chromosome and the pattern of their expression in the developing embryo along the AP axis. For example, the most anterior group of genes code for the head, the middle group of genes codes for the thorax, and the most posterior genes code for the tail. For example, *C. elegans* possesses six Hox genes: 1 anterior, 2 central, and 3 posterior group genes. This phenomenon was first discovered in fruit flies by Ed Lewis in 1978. This type of anterior-posterior colinearity is also known as *spatial colinearity*.

Temporal colinearity is the correspondence between the spatial ordering of the Hox genes and the timing of their first expression during embryonic development. The temporal colinearity was first appreciated in the vertebrates during embryogenesis by Denis Duboule in 1994.

Spatial and temporal are the two components of colinearity in the Hox genes. However, temporal colinearity appears to be less significant (or absent entirely) in simpler animals, like fruit flies, but more profoundly noticed in more complex animals like mice. Conversely, spatial colinearity is more pronounced in flies but appears to lose some consistency in more complicated animals with larger genomes. In fact, there are a few experiments that showing that the Hox genes are not always spatially colinear.

2. Hox Proteins—Some Examples

Interaction exists between Hox proteins and other genes. One Hox gene may produce a Hox protein that affects the transcription or silencing of other Hox genes such as gap proteins, pair-rule proteins, and segment polarity proteins. For example, Hoxb2 and Hoxd2 are both neural
enhancers involved in the enforcement of the anterior brain border and also rhombomeres 6 and 7 in the hind brain.[32] In addition, the Holcomb (also called Polycomb) and Trithorax proteins, which are chromatin associated proteins, function to maintain Hox boundaries along the AP axis. This is achieved by the association of both proteins with chromatin, which is how DNA is stored. The manner in which DNA is stored was explained briefly in the first section of DNA methylation and genomic imprinting.

DNA methylation and polycomb-mediated repression are well established epigenetic mechanisms of gene silencing during development. LSH, which was mentioned in the first dynamic level of DNA consciousness, acts as a regulator of DNA methylation and is involved in polycomb repressive complex-mediated silencing of various Hox genes. So as we can see a very complex system exist that scientist are still attempting to figure out.

Otx1 and Otx2 genes: I would like to quickly mention two other Hox genes that have recently been shown to be important in brain development, the Otx1 and Otx2 genes. These genes are considered a subfamily of homeodomain-containing transcription factors. The human Otx genes are orthologs to Drosophila orthodenticle homeobox genes, which is how they get their name.

Otx1 proteins are involved in the neocortical and hippocampal formation. Otx2 proteins are involved in the forebrain and midbrain formation. These results were discovered first in studies using knock-out mice and later confirmed with the immunohistochemical staining of these proteins in human fetal brains.[33]

In the knock out mice (KOM) studies the corresponding brain regions developed abnormally. For example, the homozygous Otx1 KOM where shown not to form neocortical or hippocampal regions properly and the homozygous Otx2 KOM where shown not to form forebrain and midbrain regions properly. These two genes, Otx1 and Otx2, have identical functions in human brain development. This was illustrated in the Larsen 2010 study using immunohistochemical staining in human fetal brains (weeks 7–9 weeks). Therefore, these two genes are important for the process of corticogenesis, which is the formation of the cortex.

3. The Three Phases of Hox Gene Expression

Now that I have discussed some of the Hox genes and their importance to the AP axis and brain development I will now begin to summarize the three phases in which they operate.

1. Initial phase—During this phase the posterior primitive streak forms and extends anterior to complete the AP axis. This is the core from which the embryo is formed.

2. Somitogenesis—This phase involves the refinement of the anterior border of expression and establishes a segmentation clock. This is also when the somites are formed, which are the nascent forms of the body segments.

3. Final phase—This phase consists of maintaining the expression of borders. This maintenance is orchestrated by hundreds of genes.

Now that we have explored some of the basics about the Hox genes let us look at another gene family involved in the development of the brain and central nervous system.

The Pax Genes

The Pax genes (also called paired domain genes) are known to contain *conserved bipartite DNA binding motifs*.[34] The Pax families also possess a Pax homeodomains similar to the one that Hox genes have. Pax genes are also known to code for proteins that activate and repress the transcription of target genes, which is done by attaching to critical parts of the DNA molecule. Some Pax genes e.g., Pax 6 have been proven to exert control over the actions of some Hox genes. In addition, several Pax genes have been shown to be involved in the development of brain regions and sensory organs. Therefore, Pax genes have functions similar to Hox genes, however one main difference is that Hox genes express in an anterior-posterior direction the Pax genes express in a dorsal-ventral direction.

The Pax genes family is divided into four groups of genes:

Group I—Pax 1, Pax 9
Group II—Pax 2, Pax 5, Pax 8
Group III—Pax 3, Pax 7
Group IV—Pax 4, Pax 6

I will now discuss a few of these Pax genes and illustrate their importance in giving rise to sensory organs that contribute to neuron-based consciousness. The most extensive research has been done on Pax 2, Pax 3, Pax 6, and Pax 8.

Pax 3

This gene codes for proteins that are active early in development and are found in the neural crest cells. These cells ultimately give rise to a prodigious number of different cells; among those important to our topic are the neurons and glial cells of the sensory, sympathetic, and parasympathetic nervous system. Mutations to the Pax 3 gene have been shown to cause Waardenburg syndrome, which involves pigment abnormalities and hearing loss. In addition, other studies have proved that Pax 3 is required for the development of hearing.

Pax 2 and Pax 8

Pax 2 proteins have been shown to be involved in the development of the eye, brain, spinal cord, kidneys, and genital tract. Pax 8 proteins have been shown to be involved in the formation of the kidneys and thyroid gland. Both Pax 2 and Pax 8 proteins are both known to be involved in the development of the inner ear. This is significant as the ear is the primary organ used in detecting sound waves.

Pax 6

The Pax 6 gene is well conserved in the invertebrates and vertebrates. It is important for eye development and functions high in the regulatory hierarchy of development. The protein that Pax 6 encodes for functions to mediate the commitment of ectoderm above the optic vesicle and into the lens ectoderm that promotes the formation of the lens vesicle. In addition to the importance of Pax 6 proteins to eye development, they also activate other genes that are involved in brain and spinal cord development, the olfactory nerve, and the pancreas. Pax 6 has also been shown to be a "master gene" that controls the activation of Hoxb4 and Hoxd4 genes, which were both mentioned previously.

The Pax genes, in general, appear to be involved in the development of brain regions and sensory organs e.g., the eyes and ears; in addition to the spinal cord. The significance of this should not be underestimated because these sensory pathways will be the means by which brains throughout the animal kingdom obtain sensory information. It is this information which allows increases in those interactions that ultimately give rise to higher degrees of consciousness.

In addition to the Hox and Pax genes there are many other genes that are involved in the emergence of neuron-based consciousness. However, I will discuss only one more gene at this point before moving on to the continuum of neuron-based consciousness (phase two) section of the neurogenetics of consciousness.

Brain Derived Neurotrophic Factor

Brain derived neurotrophic factor (BDNF) gene produces BDNF protein. This protein is very important for brain development. Studies on BDNF have shown that it is involved in the development of the prefrontal cortex and the hippocampus. BDNF is also integrated in a particular cascade of genetic effects that are involved in a specific single nucleotide polymorphism (SNP). For example, SNP rs6265 in BDNF genes result in decreased hippocampal and prefrontal cortex volume. I will discuss BDNF in the next section as it is not only important for early brain development, but it is also involved in the ongoing continuum of neuron-based consciousness. At this point it is important to note that, like Hox and Pax genes, that BDNF gene plays a role in brain development.

There are many more genes involved in the development of the human brain (e.g., EMX genes) and many more genes that will be discovered in the future. I have mentioned a few genes to illustrate how DNA gives rise to neuron-based consciousness. In addition, it is clearly demonstrated that there is a genome-dependent complexity, which is major theme III of DNA consciousness and this is directly related to degrees of consciousness. This phenomenon is seen with the Hox genes. For example, in simpler animals like a fruit fly there is only one group of 6 Hox genes and as a result the fruit fly has a lower degree of consciousness. However, if you look at more complicated animals, like mice and humans, they both have four copies of the original group of 13 Hox genes. It can clearly be seen that both of these animals have a higher degree of consciousness than that of the fruit fly. This is primarily because more Hox genes allow more interactions resulting in more complexity, which ultimately translates into higher degrees of consciousness.[35] Consequently, the effect of genome-dependent complexity and its result on degrees of consciousness should be evident at this juncture.

Phase Two: The Continuum of Neuron-Based Consciousness

Major theme IV of DNA consciousness—the extragenomic theme—states that after genes in the genome give rise to the machinery (mainly the brain, neurons, and neurotransmitters) that allows neuron-based consciousness to materialize, it then continuously generates RNA and proteins that unfurl extragenomic and epigenetic pathways. These pathways allow the continuum of neuron-based consciousness and they are directed by genes in the DNA molecule. In this section I will first illustrate how BDNF serves this function. I will then point out some genetic abnormalities and mutations that affect the normal functioning of the continuum of human consciousness and cognitive processes.

It was discussed previously that BDNF is involved in the development of the prefrontal cortex and hippocampus. BDNF has also been shown to function in hippocampal learning mechanisms after the development of the human brain. This is supported by some genetic abnormality studies. The SNP in rs6265 results in improper regulation of BDNF which produces abnormalities in episodic memory performance. This, then is a perfect example of a gene which produces a product; in this example BDNF, that is involved in one of the many neurological processes that manifest human neuron-based consciousness; and when that gene is abnormal (SNP in rs6265) a small component of the continuum of consciousness is adversely affected.

I will briefly mention a few other genetic abnormalities that affect the continuum of human consciousness:

- PTCHD1 locus disruptions—linked to Autism spectrum disorders and intellectually disabilities.
- PDE4B gene deletions—cause abnormalities in phosphodiesterase 4B and have demonstrated an association in certain populations of schizophrenics.
- Slitrks gene family (1–6)—genetic abnormalities in these transmembrane proteins have been shown to have an involvement in obsessive compulsive disorders and schizophrenia.
- Mutations of the EMX2 gene—result in Schizencephaly which involves developmental delays, delays in speech and language skills, ataxias, and mental retardation.
- Mutations in the PAK3 gene—result in X-linked mental retardation which involves mental retardation, behavioral and motor abnormalities, and dysmorphic features.
- Mitochondrial cytopathies mentioned in our discussion of the second dynamic level of DNA consciousness have been shown to affect (among other systems in the body) degrees of human consciousness.

So now we have a handful of examples that clearly display that an abnormality in a gene—or sequence of genes—can affect the continuum of human consciousness. These abnormalities are manifested as disturbances in the sensorium of human consciousness and drastically change the interactions in the ICC formula. For example, some of the signs and symptoms of schizophrenia are auditory and visual hallucinations, which is the patient actually seeing or hearing stimuli that is not actually in the external environment. Another example is autism, which is believed to be on the same diagnostic spectrum as schizophrenia. Here there is an abnormal, or lack of, perception to external stimuli. With these two examples it can be seen that changes in certain genes can translate into different degrees of the continuum of human neuron-based consciousness. Now that I have provided a few good examples to illustrate the second phase of the neurogenetics of consciousness, I will now discuss the third phase—neurodegeneration.

Phase Three: Neurodegeneration

Neurodegeneration represents the age-related deterioration of the nervous system and brain. During this process neurons can decrease in size and number, resulting in loss of function and decline in cognitive processes. Neurodegeneration happens gradually during a normal age-related process. However, some diseases can accelerate this process. As a first example I will look at Alzheimer's Disease (AD) and the genetic factors which are known to be involved in this type of neurodegeneration.

AD is a well established cause for over 50 percent of all patients diagnosed with dementia. It is typically a slow progressive disease that is marked by a decline in cognitive and behavioral attributes with the predominant symptom initially being the inability to retain new memories or "forgetfulness," but later in the disease progression there may be severe loss of remote memories. In my years of practicing medicine this is one of the most devastating diseases, not just to the patient, but also to the family members. One of the most frequent comments is "they are just not the same person anymore."

During the process of neurodegeneration that is caused by AD specific regions of the brain undergo atrophy, mainly the cortex and limbic system, which has been illustrated in several clinical studies using MRI. As these portions of the brain, as well as other regions, change the patient begins to lose a sense of self and the interactions with the external environment begin to decrease or at the very least are impaired, i.e., AD causes a decrease in the degree of neuron-based consciousness. Now that I have given a general description of AD from a medical and personal perspective I will now discuss how some genes are involved in this process.

Genes Known to Be Involved with AD

The main pathological finding in AD is neuritic plaques with beta-amyloid deposits and neural fibrillary tangles that have accumulations of hyperphosphorylated tau protein. The process that causes this pathology is still being disputed and new discoveries continue to surface. There are many genes being researched, but at the time this section was written, there are four main genes proposed to be involved in AD:

1. Amyloid Precursor Protein (APP) Gene—This gene produces a cellular membrane protein on neurons that is concentrated in the synapse. The APP regulates synapse formation, neural plasticity, and iron export. Proteolysis of APP generates many forms of beta-amyloid (39–42), some of which are normal products of cellular metabolism. However, some to the forms, specifically beta-amyloid 42 is neurotoxic and believed to initiate the AD pathology.

2. Presenilin–1 (PSEN1) Gene—This gene produces PSEN1 protein which is pro-

posed to perform proteolysis on APP through its effect (cleavage) on gamma-secretase. This produces beta-amyloid 39–42.

3. Presenilin–2 (PSEN2) Gene—This gene produces PSEN2 protein which has been proposed to have similar actions to PSEN1.

4. APOE ε4 Phenotype—This phenotype produces APOE ε4 protein, which is technically an apolipoprotein. APOE ε4 has been shown to influence brain structure and functions by affecting synaptic generation via restorative mechanism involving cholesterol transport and metabolism.

It has been established that the presence of APP, PSEN1, and PSEN2 genes or mutations in these genes are associated with a strong incidence of AD.[36] The APOE ε4 phenotype shows an increase in the prevalence of AD but there have been some studies disputing this. However, APOE ε4 phenotype does show a clear association for the early onset form of AD and has also been seen to have a gene-dose dependent affect.

So when we talk about neurodegeneration in context of the ICC we must go in reverse in that neurodegeneration causes a decrease in the interactions (via less neurons and atrophy), which causes a noticeable decrease in complexity (in terms of the nervous system and brain), and consequently a decrease in neuron-based consciousness. At the derivative of some of these processes are genes and thus a facet of DNA consciousness. Therefore, DNA consciousness can give rise to neuron-based consciousness, provide a continuum, and then cause the deterioration of that system. This represents the three phases of the neurogenetics of consciousness.

Up to this point, I have discussed some genes that give rise to neuron-based consciousness, some genes that are involved in the continuum of human neuron-based consciousness, and some genes that can cause the degeneration of degrees in human consciousness. This brings us to ask the question "What can humankind do in the future regarding the deterioration of human neuron-based consciousness?" We have now approached the final topic of this chapter—SGD.

Selected Genetic Destination and DNA Consciousness

During my discussion of the ICC earlier in this chapter I mentioned SGD as being the *fourth* special thing that takes place with the emergence of DNA consciousness. First allow me to give a brief history of the proposal of SGD and then discuss how it is represented as major theme V of DNA consciousness—the transformation theme. Finally, I will discuss the future evolution of DNA consciousness through the process of SGD.

In 2010, I included a brief section on DNA consciousness at the end of my chapter "DNA and Genetic Engineering" which was published in the two-volume reference handbook *21st Century Anthropology*. In this work I proposed that there was a phenomenon called DNA consciousness. I also speculated how DNA was involved in the emergence of neurological consciousness and was based on the fact that gene clusters known as the Hox and Pax genes are responsible for giving rise to the basic plan of the nervous system and brain in humans. More importantly I proposed that in the future genetic engineering may enable scientists to further explore how DNA is able to interact with itself, with other molecules and cells, and with the external environment—the three dynamic levels of DNA consciousness, which were already discussed earlier. Most importantly, genetic engineering may enable humankind to enhance its very own degree of consciousness.

In a subsequent 2010 publication in the *International Journal of Arts and Sciences*, "Selected Genetic Destination: The Rise of Homo sapiens genomicus" I had addressed two important implications central to the evolution of DNA consciousness. The first was that with the advent of genetic engineering significant improvements could be made in humankind's degree of neuron-based consciousness. This could be accomplished by creating *aggressive human enhancements*[37] that would improve elements of neuron-based consciousness such as better memory, the ability to perceive more regions of the electromagnetic spectrum, increase neuron density, increase neuron-neuron interconnections, and enhance neuroplasticity. These types of aggressive human enhancements could give rise to a new subspecies *Homo sapiens genomicus* or ultimately, new species with a higher and superior degrees of neuron-based consciousness.

The second important theme discussed in the 2010 article was the supposition that perhaps the degree of DNA consciousness has a *will* of its own. If, in fact, DNA consciousness is the driving force behind all biological evolution and responsible for the emergence of neuron-based consciousness then perhaps humankind was only meant to be transient. That is to say that DNA consciousness, through natural selection, gave rise to the emergence of *Homo sapiens sapiens* and their higher degree of neuron-based consciousness for the sole purpose of discovering the DNA molecule and unlocking its secrets. The implication, then, is that DNA discovered itself through the vessel of humankind. This knowledge of DNA will eventually provide a new means of evolving DNA consciousness, i.e., SGD to replace the much slower process of natural selection.

Allow me briefly to review the four special things that take place with the emergence of DNA consciousness in the ICC. This is an attempt to illustrate the future course that DNA consciousness may take. These four special things are:

1. Nucleotides emerge from molecular degrees of consciousness and cause an explosion in complexity and degrees of consciousness by allowing exponentially larger amounts of interactions.

2. Eukaryotic cells develop the ability to conduct electrochemical signals over long distances, giving rise to early degrees of neuron-based consciousness. This is possible when cells developed genes that distinguish themselves as neurons. Two examples of these genes were discussed in our discussion of the ICC.

3. The development of Hox and Pax gene families allow the emergence of vertebrates with cephalization and a centralized nervous system. Antecedent to these genes there were ancestral versions or orthologs that existed in the invertebrates.

4. SGD—the ability to select a genetic destination and make it happen utilizing genetic engineering. By refining this technology humankind's current degree of consciousness can be enhanced and new degrees can emerge as well.

It is very important to note that all four of these special things that take place in the ICC involve DNA consciousness. The fact that all four of these special things can be studied scientifically should make a compelling case to substantiate the science of DNA consciousness as it is involved in several key moments in the evolution leading up to the development of human consciousness. Scientists will some day be able to enhance human consciousness by enhancing DNA consciousness with SGD. An example of this is the research currently being conducted on gene therapy involving fibroblast growth factor 2 (FGF2) to potentially reverse the memory decline in AD. At this point this has only worked in KOM mice with AD, but even at that degree of consciousness we can see a reversal of neurodegeneration utilizing SGD. Therefore, a gene that is underactive in one region of the brain contributes to AD, but when genetic therapy adds this gene to that region of the brain there is improvement in AD symptoms and an increase in neuron-based consciousness. This perfectly displays DNA consciousness and its relationship to neuron-based consciousness. There is also the potential to use this genetic therapy in normal brains to markedly increase memory!

I will mention one last example of SGD being used to reverse neurodegeneration. The focus of this research is on a gene that produces an antibody (anti-amyloid-antibody). In the pathophysiology of AD beta-amyloid plagues accumulate in the brain; therefore the strategy is that this antibody will combat the accumulation. There have been successful trials in mice so far. But even at the level of the mouse we have yet another example of the reversal of a neurodegenerative disorder and an increase in the degree of consciousness which was provided by SGD.

I had already mentioned in the 2010 *selected genetic destination* article that implementing SGD would give rise to a new transgenic subspecies *Homo sapiens genomicus*. However, I also pointed out that *Homo sapiens genomicus* was not an end, but rather a new point in evolution that could lead to more future subspecies and species.[38] Therefore, it is important to realize that the will of DNA consciousness can manifest itself through SGD. This would be proven if genetic therapies, like the example with FGF2, emerged in the future that can improve modalities of human consciousness or the attainment of abilities beyond that of the *subjective medium of functioning* of the subspecies of *Homo sapiens sapiens*.[39] Again, this is major theme V of DNA consciousness—the transformation theme.

When it comes to the future there is no limit as to where speculation may take you. However, I would like to refocus the direction of this conversation back to DNA consciousness. The concept of SGD displays that humankind in the future may be able to control or at the very least manipulate DNA consciousness, but what does that actually mean? It means that DNA consciousness is a dynamic and potentially tangible process!

Conclusion

In my 2011 article "The DNA Molecule Is Autopoietic, Dynamic, Evolving, and a Form of Consciousness," I made a compelling case to justify the theory of DNA consciousness as an emerging science. I had also provided enough credible scientific evidence to validate the degree of DNA consciousness. This is a significant leap since my early speculations in 2004 and my published theories in 2006.

The five major themes of DNA consciousness have also been revised and improved. To reflect this I have made a list of these five major themes and indicated parts of this chapter where they were mentioned in providing scientific proof to validate them (see figure 4). This should make it easier to focus on any one of the major themes of DNA consciousness in future discussions.

The 5 Major Themes	Sections mentioned or discussed
I- DNA has a degree of consciousness	This was mentioned in all three dynamic levels of DNA consciousness, specifically in the first. How DNA consciousness gives rise to neuron-based consciousness was addressed in detail in the section on the Hox and Pax genes.
II- Human consciousness cannot perceive DNA consciousness directly.	This is exemplified in the first dynamic level of DNA consciousness. The point was also made that scientific observation is not the same as communication.
III- Genome-dependent complexity	This is exemplified in the four special things that happen in the ascending chain of the ICC. In addition, the section on the Hox and Pax genes address this.
IV- DNA consciousness provides a continuum for neuron-based consciousness.	This is exemplified in the second dynamic level of DNA consciousness. In addition, it is addressed again with specific regards to human consciousness in the continuum of neuron-based consciousness section.
V- The transformation theme	SGD is mentioned as the fourth special thing that will take place in the ICC and also in the third dynamic level of DNA consciousness. In addition the entire section called selected genetic destination and DNA consciousness discusses this theme.

Figure 4: These are the five major themes of DNA Consciousness and the parts of the chapter that they addressed.

In this chapter I believe that I have provided enough evidence to show beyond a reasonable doubt that DNA is a degree of consciousness and gives rise to all other degrees of consciousness that is found in all nucleotide-based organisms. Other scientific proof was demonstrated in my 2011 article, "The DNA molecule is autopoietic, dynamic, evolving, and a form of consciousness," published in *The International Journal of Arts and Sciences*, of which most of that was mentioned in this chapter. I have also presented proof on the three dynamic levels of DNA consciousness and in the three phases of the neurogenetics of human consciousness. In addition, I have illustrated how SGD will provide a tool to continue to increase degrees of DNA consciousness in the future.

In closing, consciousness is the interactions of things interacting with other things. These things can be quarks, molecules, organisms, or forms of energy. This trajectory of evolving interactions can be expressed in the ICC schematic. Within the ICC DNA consciousness emerges and four special events take place. Oddly enough, I arrived at this conclusion in reverse. I first proposed DNA consciousness, then the interaction-based model of consciousness, and then finally linked them together with the ICC. DNA consciousness can now be regarded as a science that possesses five major themes, can be objectified on three dynamic levels, and ultimately gives rise to the neurogenetics of human consciousness, which has three phases—the emergence of human consciousness, the continuum of human consciousness, and the neurodegeneration of human consciousness. Lastly, humankind is not the teleological end point. DNA consciousness is poised to continue to evolve slowly through the process of natural selection or more rapidly with the advent of SGD in the future.

Notes

1. Recently it has been brought to my attention the phrase "12-stranded DNA consciousness" was published in a self-motivational book by Anne Brewer. Upon review, this phrase has more of a metaphysical meaning in which a process of "DNA recordings" is performed. Evidently, the recordings gradually increase telepathy, remove fear and guilt from the mental body, and improve the ability to "manifest." According to Brewer, she received this information "telepathically from a group of friendly, non-physical beings sent to help raise the consciousness of earth." As it can be clearly seen my definition of DNA consciousness is not the same thing as Brewer's, who does not actually define what her DNA consciousness means.

2. The five major themes of DNA consciousness have undergone some revisions over the years as they were reevaluated, but I tried to present them in this work as close to the original proposals as I could. In addition, this is the first work in where I gave names to the five themes.

3. I mention degrees of consciousness in the explanation of the concept of interaction-complexity-consciousness. However, when the original five major themes were synthesized I had not yet conceptualized this idea. Also note that observing the degree of DNA consciousness on three dynamic levels is not the same as communicating with it.

4. SGD is defined as the ability to control the evolution of a species with the technology of genetic engineering. This is discussed in great detail in the "Selected Genetic Destination: The Rise of Homo Sapiens Genomicus" article. This topic will be addressed later in this chapter as it pertains to DNA consciousness.

5. For further reference please consult my consciousness articles in the *Encyclopedia of Anthropology 2006* and the *Encyclopedia of Time 2009*.

6. The anthropistic theory of consciousness maintains that only humans possess consciousness, because only humans possess a soul, which is where this theory proposes that consciousness comes from. This is extremely similar to dualism and conversely dualism is a form of the anthropistic theory of consciousness, which I have discussed in previous works. I also highlight the problems with reductionism in the 2011 article "The DNA Molecule Is Autopoietic, Dynamic, Evolving, and a Form of Consciousness."

7. This is a term conceived by Rosenblum and Kuttner in their book *The Quantum Enigma*. It addresses the phenomenon of decoherence and proposes that this is where physics encounters consciousness.

8. It was at this conference where I met Ingrid Fredriksson, who is the editor of this book.

9. Links to the abstract are provided: http://www.consciousness.arizona.edu/documents/CCS_2011_Program_pg2-13-1.pdf and http://sbs.arizona.edu/project/consciousness/report_poster_detail.php?abs=745. These can also be found in the Wikipedia article "DNA Consciousness."

10. All cells intrinsically have electrochemical properties. However, neurons can conduct electrochemical signals over longer distances and this is the property that distinguishes them from other cells. These novel properties evolved as a result of new genes that are expressed in neurons but not other types of cells. This is further evidence to support that genome-dependent complexity ultimately affects degrees of consciousness in the ICC after the assembly of nucleotides.

11. It was once thought that Hox genes were only found in the vertebrate genome. However, newer

evidence shows that some invertebrates have a Hox gene cluster or families of genes that resemble precursors to these genes, which are also called orthologs. There is still some debate in this area as more and more is being discovered about these gene families.

   12. This concept was originated by Allan Comb and was discussed in my comparison of the dynamics of human consciousness and DNA consciousness as autopoietic processes. For more information please consult "The DNA Molecule Is Autopoietic, Dynamic, Evolving, and a Form of Consciousness" and/or Combs' two articles listed in the references.

   13. Of interest is that the genes that code for histone proteins are highly conserved throughout all eukaryotic cells. For more information about the basics of DNA please consult my 2006 article on the DNA molecule or the 2010 chapter for more in-depth detail.

   14. Methylation is the addition of the hydrophobic chemical group CH_3, which is derived from methane (CH_4).

   15. Keeping in mind that DNA methylation is vital to other processes, e.g., x chromosome activation in females.

   16. It is also important to mention that LSH has been shown to silence Hox genes. This has been shown in Xi's 2007 article. Hox genes will be discussed in the first section of the neurogenetics of consciousness section.

   17. We could take introns and exons into consideration but this can be ignored for the sake of this example.

   18. This is a theme central to quantum physics. In a basic sense, all systems exist in a state of superposition or a very large number of wave functions. When observation occurs, it is proposed that the system collapses into one wave function or what is measured. This is also referred to as decoherence.

   19. Please consult the Rosenblum and Kuttner book *The Quantum Enigma* for more detail.

   20. This is also called lateral gene transfer. This is a process in which an organism acquires genetic material from another organism. I will discuss this further in the third dynamic level of DNA consciousness. Interestingly, genomic research has shown that about 1 percent the human genome contains genes acquired in this fashion from human endogenous retroviruses (HERVs). See the 1996 review article by Lower, et al.

   21. These factors can include methylation, chromatin remodeling-dynamic structural changes, and processes that occur during embryonic development, e.g., X-inactivation and gene silencing. In addition, there are other epigenetic phenomena, e.g., histone post-translational modifications, protein-protein interactions, and RNA-mediated gene silencing, however this is beyond to scope of the goals of this chapter.

   22. Intrinsic DNA (genomic DNA) may not be required directly, but frequently enzymes or catalysts are. Those are of course produced by genes in the intrinsic DNA. There are structures that do arise from molecular self-assembly, e.g., microtubules, and consequently require no intrinsic DNA.

   23. This has been illustrated by researchers such as Gray in 1999, as well as Kurland and Anderson in 2000. Please consult the references for further information.

   24. MELAS is a syndrome comprised of mitochondrial encephalomyopathy, lactic acidosis, and stroke-like episodes. This is caused by a microdeletion mutation in the mtDNA and is a complicated multisystem disease that affects, among other things, degrees of human consciousness.

   25. The basics of transcription and translation are explained in my 2006 "DNA Molecule" article and in more detail in the 2010 chapter, "DNA and Genetic Engineering." Please consult the references for more detail.

   26. The TP53 gene produces a protein known as p53 which is involved in the G1-phase of the cell cycle. This causes a delay between the cell phases that allows time for defects in the DNA molecule to be detected and repaired before the cell enters into G0-phase where mitosis suppressor proteins activate tissue-specific proteins to be synthesized.

   27. The topic "The Neurogenetics of Consciousness" was first presented on November 8, 2011, at The U.S. Psychiatric and Mental Health Congress Conference. Link: http://www.cmellc.com/psychcongress/2011/abstracts/134.html

   28. Homeodomains typically bind to a core TAAT sequence with additional binding specificity that is contributed by base-specific interactions with two of the nucleotides 3-prime of the TAAT motif.

   29. An example of non–Hox genes that are important to development is the switch genes, which are activated or deactivated by Hox genes. Switch genes are a family of genes that cause epigenotype to switch to a different developmental pathway.

   30. These experimental results were published by Lutz Beat, et al. in the 1995 article "Rescue of

Drosophila labial Null Mutant by the Chicken Ortholog Hoxb–1 Demonstrates That the Function of Hox Genes Is Phylogenetically Conserved." Please consult this article for these fascinating results.

31. The manner in which the Hox gene clusters evolved and their phylogenetic history are discussed in the 2003 Ferrier and Minguillon article and the 2007 Abbasi and Grzeschik articles.

32. Rhombomeres 1–9 become the rhombencephalon during embryological development. Some rhombomeres give rise to some of the cranial nerves.

33. These results were discussed in detail in the Larsen 2010 article. I also incorporated these finding into my presentation on the neurogenetics of consciousness at the 2011 U.S. Psychiatric Congress Conference.

34. A DNA binding motif involves an independently folded protein domain that contains at least one motif that recognizes DNA. With the PAX proteins this is bipartite in that there are two parts that recognize DNA.

35. Genome-wide analysis and comparative studies have shown that humans have fewer genes, as a whole, than some other animals and plants. This was very surprising to many scientists. However, humans have more copies of the same genes or some genes may have streamlined to become more efficient during the course of evolution. In addition, there have been some conflicting studies as to how many genes are active or inactive, which genes are introns or exons, and no current methods of determining how some genes are more or less efficient; for example able to control other genes.

36. Currently some of these genes are being researched to accompany the early diagnosis of AD. For more information please consult my 2011 "What's New in Alzheimer's Disease" article.

37. In the article "Selected Genetic Destination: The Rise of Homo sapiens genomicus" I made the distinction between passive human enhancements and aggressive human enhancements. Simply stated, passive human enhancements are genetic therapies to correct an underlying medical defect whereas aggressive human enhancements are genetic therapies aimed at enhancing certain attributes, i.e., height or memory, beyond the subjective median of [genetic] functioning. This was to defend the notion that any gene therapy is a form of enhancement established on what I called the genetic baseline. For more information please consult the article.

38. In that paper I go into a long discussion as to what the difference between a subspecies and species is and propose how this would be affected by SGD. I also propose several subspecies that could emerge.

39. The term *subjective median of functioning of a subspecies* was originated in my 2010 "Selected Genetic Destination: The Rise of Homo sapiens genomicus" article to establish parameters that determine the cutoff between passive and aggressive human enhancements. Please consult this article for more information.

REFERENCES AND FURTHER READINGS

Abbasi, Amir Ali, and Karl-Heinz Grzeschik (2007). An insight into the phylogenetic history of *HOX* linked gene families in vertebrates. *BMC Evolutionary Biology* 7: 239.

Balczarek, K., et al. (1997). Evolution and Functional Diversification of the Paired Box (Pax) DNA-Binding Domains. *Mol. Biol. Evol.* 14 (8): pp. 829–842.

Bouchard, Maxime, et al. (2010). Pax2 and Pax8 cooperate in mouse inner ear morphogenesis and innervations. BMC Developmental Biology 10:89.

Combs, Allan, and Sally Goerner (1998). Consciousness as a self-organizing process: an ecological perspective. *Biosystems* 46 pp. 123–127.

Combs, Allan, and Stanley Krippner (2003). Process, structure, and form: An evolutionary transpersonal psychology of consciousness. *The International Journal of Transpersonal Studies* Vol. 22 pp. 47–60.

Duboule D (1994). Temporal colinearity and the phylotypic progression: a basis for the stability of a vertebrate Bauplan and the evolution of morphologies through heterochrony. *Dev Suppl.* 1994: pp. 135–142.

Edelman, Gerald (2005). *Wider Than the Sky: The Phenomenal Gift of Consciousness.* New Haven, CT: Yale University Press.

Emery, Ben, et al. (2009). Myelin Gene Regulatory Factor Is a Critical Transcriptional Regulator Required for CNS Myelination. *Cell* 138, pp. 172–185.

Ferrier, David, and Carolina Minguillon (2003). Evolution of the *Hox/ParaHox* gene clusters. *Int. J. Dev. Biol.* 47: pp. 605–611.

Fornasiero, E.F., et al. (2010). The role of synapsins in neuronal development. *Cell Mol Life Sci* May, 67(9) 1383–96.

Gaunt, S.J., and Strachan L. (1996). Temporal colinearity in expression of anterior Hox genes in developing chick embryos. *Dev Dyn.* 207 (3): pp. 270–280.
Grandy, John (2012). 2011 Updates for Diagnosis Alzheimers Disease. *JAAPA* April 2012.
Grandy, John (2012). Grandy, J.K. (2012). International experience presenting my theory of DNA consciousness. *Journal of International Students, 2* (1). Ed.
Grandy, John (2011). What's New in Alzheimer's disease: Biomarkers and gene mutations as aids for detecting AD early. *JAAPA*, June 2011 24(6) 56–57.
Grandy, John (2011). The DNA molecule is autopoietic, dynamic, evolving, and a form of consciousness. *The International Journal of Arts and Sciences* 4(20): 7–28.
Grandy, John (2011). DNA Consciousness. Belgrade University, Serbia. The proceedings from the international conference on "Humanism and Post-humanism" 6–9 April 2009. In: Deretic, I., and Sorgner, S.L.: Humanism and Posthumanism. The original is available as a PDF on the Wikipedia article "DNA Consciousness."
Grandy, John (2010). DNA and Genetic Engineering. *21st Century Anthropology* pp. 76–90. Thousand Oaks, CA: Sage Publications.
Grandy, John (2010). Selected Genetic Destination and the Rise of *Homo Sapiens Genomicus*. *The International Journal of Arts and Sciences* 3(9): 166–190.
Grandy, John (2009). Consciousness. *Encyclopedia of Time.* Vol. 1 (pp. 212–216). Thousand Oaks, CA: Sage Publications.
Grandy, John (2009). DNA Molecule. *Encyclopedia of Time.* Vol. 1 (pp. 333–335). Thousand Oaks, CA: Sage Publications.
Grandy, John (2009). Dying and Death. *Encyclopedia of Time.* Vol. 1 (pp. 352–355). Thousand Oaks, CA: Sage Publications.
Grandy, John (2009). History of Medicine. *Encyclopedia of Time.* Vol. 2 (pp. 842–845). Thousand Oaks, CA: Sage Publications.
Grandy, John (2009). Memory. *Encyclopedia of Time.* Vol. 2 (pp. 849–853). Thousand Oaks, CA: Sage Publications.
Grandy, John (2006). Bioinformatics. *Encyclopedia of Anthropology.* Vol. 1 (pp. 362–363). Thousand Oaks, CA: Sage Publications.
Grandy, John (2006). Biometrics. *Encyclopedia of Anthropology.* Vol. 1 (pp. 371–372). Thousand Oaks, CA: Sage Publications.
Grandy, John (2006). Consciousness. *Encyclopedia of Anthropology.* Vol. 2 (pp. 563–566). Thousand Oaks, CA: Sage Publications.
Grandy, John (2006). DNA Molecule. *Encyclopedia of Anthropology.* Vol. 2 (pp. 753–756). Thousand Oaks, CA: Sage Publications.
Grandy, John (2006). Euthenics. *Encyclopedia of Anthropology.* Vol. 2 (pp. 873–875). Thousand Oaks, CA: Sage Publications.
Grandy, John (2006). Freud, Sigmund. *Encyclopedia of Anthropology.* Vol. 3 (pp. 1005–1007). Thousand Oaks, CA: Sage Publications.
Grandy, John (2006). Human Genome Project. *Encyclopedia of Anthropology.* Vol. 3 (pp. 1223–1226). Thousand Oaks, CA: Sage Publications.
Grandy, John (2006). RNA Molecule. *Encyclopedia of Anthropology.* Vol. 5 (pp. 2026–2027). Thousand Oaks, CA: Sage Publications.
Gray, M., G. Burger, and F. Lang. (1999). Mitochondrial Evolution. *Science* 283: 1476–1481.
Hall, Brian, and Wendy Olson (2003). *Keywords and Concepts in Evolutionary Developmental Biology.* Cambridge MA: Harvard University Press.
Kurland, C.G., and S.G.E. Anderson (2000). Origin and evolution of the mitochondrial proteome. *Microbiology and Molecular Biology Reviews* 64:786–820.
Larsen, K., et al. (2010). Expression of the Homeobox Genes *OTX2* and *OTX1* in the Early Developing Human Brain. *J. Histochem & Cytochem* 58(7): pp. 669–678.
Lewis, E.B. (1978). A gene complex controlling segmentation in *Drosophila*. *Nature* 276:565–570.
Lower, Roswitha, et al. (1996). The viruses in all of us: Characteristics and biological significance of human endogenous retrovirus sequences. *Proc. Natl. Acad. Sci. USA* Vol. 93, pp. 5177–5184, May 1996.
Lutz, Beat, et al. (1996). Rescue of *Drosophila labial* null mutant by the chicken ortholog *Hoxb-1* demonstrates that the function of *Hox* genes is phylogenetically conserved. *Genes & Development* 10: 176–184.

McGinnis, W., M.S. Levine, E. Hafen, A. Kuroiwa, and W.J. Gehring (1984). A conserved DNA sequence in homeotic genes of the *Drosophila* Antennapedia and bithorax complexes. *Nature* 308:428–433.

McGinnis, W., and R. Krumlauf (1992). Homeobox genes and axial patterning. *Cell* 68:283–302.

Moore, Keith, and T.V.N. Persaud (2008). *The Developing Human: Clinically Oriented Embryology*, 8th edition. Philadelphia, PA: Saunders Elsevier.

Myant Kevin, et al. (2011). LSH and G9a/GLP complex are required for developmentally programed DNA methylation. *Genome Res* 21: 83–94.

Pritchard, Dorian, and Bruce Korf (2008). *Medical Genetics at a Glance*. Second edition. Malden, MA: Blackwell.

Rosenblum, Bruce, and Fred Kuttner (2006). *Quantum Enigma: Physics Encounters Consciousness*. New York: Oxford University Press. Second edition (2011) available.

Van Auken, K., D.C. Weaver, L.G. Edgar, and W.B. Wood (2000). *Caenorhabditis elegans* embryonic axial patterning requires two recently discovered posterior-group Hox genes. *Proceedings of the National Academy of Sciences, USA* 97:4499–4503.

Xi, Sichuan, et al. (2007). LSH controls Hox gene silencing during development. *PNAS* 104 (36) pp. 14366–14371.

Yan, Qin, et al. (2010). Sumoylation activates the transcriptional activity of Pax-6, an important transcription factor for eye and brain development. *PNAS* 107 (43) pp. 21034–21039.

Do Consciousness and Electrons Exist in Water?

INGRID FREDRIKSSON

Abstract

Every one of your cells are conscious, together they make up you and your consciousness. Does consciousness and electrons exist in water? In every living being and organism there is an entire world as amazing as the one we see around us. In our body there are 100 trillion cells (10^{12}), and DNA that extends 10,000 kilometers. The base pairs in our DNA are held together by hydrogen. Maybe the hydrogen bonds in DNA's base pairs constitute our immune system and our consciousness! There is water in the cells, and between them, and while large molecules have to go through membrane proteins to enter the cells, small molecules like H_2O and O_2 can pass through the cell membrane without difficulty. In the spaces between the brain cells, at the end of every neuron, the basic unit of a brain cell, are synapses, where chemical charges build up. In the same space dendrites—tiny filaments of nerve endings—communicate with other neurons, sending out and receiving their own electrical wave impulses. This, together with the quantum hologram and non-local consciousness, provides an explanation and an exciting developmental phase in the illusion in which we live. Consciousness appears to exist in everything that has DNA. If we conceive a non-local consciousness, as it is demonstrated by the EPR paradox, Alain Aspect, or modern information technology, we gain a number of explanations for what had previously been unexplained, as when consciousness leaves the body in out-of-body or near-death experiences when people describe having seen their body from above, or—why not?—when a loved one dies and knowledge of this reaches us instantaneously on another continent. "I have my body and I am consciousness" says Pim van Lommel.

The Cell Is Able to Perceive and Convey Information

There are more than two hundred different kinds of cells in our body, all of which communicate with one another via chemical, physical, and electrical systems. The shapes of cells depend on their function. In the same way, the internal parts of the cell are also dependent on the function of the cell.

In the 1970s the polygraph expert Cleve Backster discovered that plants and even cells possess a basic form of consciousness that he subsequently named primary perception. Plants and cells exhibited a number of reactions on polygraph tests that could only be explained by their own independent consciousness, including functions like their own memory, communication, and, to a certain degree, their own will. All this despite the fact that plants or individual cells have no neurological network whatsoever, something that, according to the view of traditional science, is a basic criterion for any consciousness at all.[1]

There are principally two kinds of cells: eukaryotes and prokaryotes. The crucial difference between them is that the prokaryotes, unlike the eukaryotes, have no nucleus (thus no DNA, etc.) and therefore seldom develop into multicellular organisms. Bacteria are prokaryotes, while all other living organisms like human beings have cell nuclei and therefore belong to the eukaryotic group.[2]

It is clear that a cell is able to perceive; it is like a whole society within society and a life within life. In the cell there are mitochondria, power-plants that produce energy for the whole cell. The mitochondria contain enzymes that convert nutrients into energy. The cell puts a lot of time into manufacturing proteins as well. The way it works is that first, twenty basic building-blocks called amino acids are manufactured. These parts are sent on to the ribosomes,[3] which link the amino acids together in exactly the right order to form a certain protein. Fully computerized, in other words! The functions of the cell are governed by DNA, which delivers a set of detailed instructions to the individual ribosomes. Which protein is to be built and how is it do be done?[4]

Professor of molecular biology Leonard M. Adelman has noted that "one gram of DNA, which when dry would occupy a volume of approximately one cubic centimeter, can store as much information as approximately one trillion CDs."[5] DNA contains the genes, the instructions for constructing a unique human body, and every cell has a complete set of instructions.

What happens when a protein is manufactured is more or less a miracle. Every protein folds itself into a unique three-dimensional structure.[6] It is this structure that determines which particular task the protein is going to have. An enzyme, for example, is a protein that is manufactured in cells. Each enzyme is folded in a particular way for the purpose of catalyzing a certain chemical reaction. Hundreds of enzymes collaborate to regulate the activities of the cell.

But how does the protein end up in the right place after it has been produced? Well, each protein has a built-in "address label" which guarantees that it will be delivered to the place where it is needed. Despite the fact that thousands of proteins are being constructed and sent on every minute, they all come from the Golgi apparatus and go to their proper destination.

The cell is not only able to perceive but also conveys information. Inside the cell there is another membrane surrounding the nucleus, which contains the chromosomes. These are arranged in identical pairs of varying size. Our genetic material is located in our twenty-three pairs of chromosomes in the form of DNA. The twenty-third pair determines our sex. In the chromosome pairs that look like a sloppy x our DNA is very tightly wound in a helical structure. It looks fairly modest, but fully extended, the DNA of a single cell would go halfway round the globe.

The last piece of a chromosome is called a telomere. Its length decreases a little with each cell division until the telomere reaches a certain length at which division is no longer possible, whereupon the cell ages and dies. This is a normal course of events. A cancer cell, however, triggers a gene that instructs the cell to create an enzyme, telomerase, which prevents the telomeres from getting too short in the course of cell division. The discovery of telomerase provides new possibilities for stopping cancer growth. If the gene that shuts off the production of telomerase is found, cancer cells could be prevented from continuing to divide. It was feared at first that ordinary cells would be converted into cancer cells if they were exposed to telomerase. But that is not the case.[7]

The Micro and Macro World

The universe can be divided into two equal parts, one that we can see and one, equally significant, that we cannot see with our eyes. I call it the quantum world, as in the world of the atoms where the unpredictable quantum world is in force. And why not earlier than that, in somewhat larger things which are so small that we still cannot see them with the naked eye? And, by the way, a cell can be quite large; just think about an unfertilized hen's egg or, even bigger, an ostrich egg.

Consider the fact that there are 100 trillion cells in our body, most with forty-six chromosomes, having DNA that extends for 10,000 kilometers! In every living being and organism there is an entire world as amazing as the one we see around us.

Human beings have between 20,000 and 25,000 genes, each of which codes for completely specific traits. A gene is a piece of the DNA spiral, and every gene functions as a code for a specific protein and as such determines what this protein is to do. Some genes have a major influence on our external appearance, while others determine how the body functions.

The complete set of genes is called a genome. The length of the genome depends to some extent on the complexity of the organism; despite that, we have "merely" 3.2 billion base pairs while a single-celled amoeba has more than 670 billion.

A gene always begins and ends with a triplet. The order of the bases between the different triplets determines what function the gene has in the body. The DNA helix is constructed of the four bases: guanine, cytosine, adenine, and thymine.

It is in the genes that our cellular memory is held for many decades, despite the fact that no cell in our body becomes more than seven years old. Our lifestyle switches genes on and off. We have one example of epigenetic inheritance through the fruit fly whose eggs were heated to 37°C. At that point, its eyes suddenly became red, and the next generation of fruit flies had red eyes, and the next.[8]

DNA and Centrioles

DNA is an abbreviation for deoxyribonucleic acid. The DNA molecule is formed as a double helix, and all the information needed to construct the body, keep the system running, and guarantee uniformity between the generations is here.

When the cells divide into two, new DNA must be produced as well. The process is possible only by means of the four bases that constitute the steps of the DNA strand, attached to one another in fixed pairs.

The DNA strand divides into two separate strands within a small, delimited area. Loose bases attach themselves to both of the strands in the order that their bases indicate. The process continues along the entire DNA strand, which opens up as the process progresses, and presto, two identical DNA spirals have now been formed from the first. This takes place at the rate of 44,000 base pairs per second.

For the cell to be able to divide, centrioles are necessary. These are a specialized organelle, also called the cell body, which exists in us humans and most animals. The centriole, despite its smallness (it cannot be seen without an electron microscope), plays a critical role in cell division. Its shape is quite fascinating and beautiful, consisting of nine triplets of microtubules arranged in a pinwheel around a central cylinder. A pair of centrioles together, with one centriole perpendicular to the other, forms a structure in the cell that is called the centrosome. When a cell divides, two centrosomes are formed, and these move to opposite sides of the cell. Each centrosome then sends out spindles that will split the cell, its nucleus with its chromosomes and DNA, dividing the cell into two copies of itself.[9]

The DNA is doubled, such that two identical sets of genetic material are formed. In the cell what are called centrioles are formed of fibers. The chromosomes divide and place themselves in the equatorial plane of the fibers. The fibers, or spindles, draw the chromosomes to both poles of the cell. A ring forms around both groups of chromosomes, and the two halves start becoming two separate cells. Two independent but identical cells have been formed.[10]

Micro-RNA and the Effects It Has on the Health of Plants, Animals and Humans

Soon, 20 years will have passed since the discovery of micro–RNA, minute RNA sequences of around 20 nucleotides (the founding building blocks of our genes), which influence the gene's behavior.

Chinese researchers have recently been able to show an interesting relationship between these short sequences of nucleotides and what we eat, and in time possibly even our health.

An interesting fact of micro–DNA, of which there are thousands of different kinds, is that it has great significance for behavior of the gene—in other words, which genes are active and can therefore affect us in regard to both sickness and our health. This covers a wide spectrum, from the early stages of cancer to how our nerve cells function. The majority of eukaryote cells (i.e., those that have a cell nucleus) can generate micro–RNA, except for fungus, algae and certain marine plants. Bacteria lacking a cell nucleus doesn't contain micro–RNA.

The majority of research is performed using raised levels of certain kinds of micro–RNA from tumors caused by disease. Researchers have also carried out experiments to block the micro–RNA in the hope of preventing the spread of the tumor, thus providing a new method of cancer therapy.

Previously, many people have believed that we are only affected by that which we produce through our own genes, i.e., parts of genes that aren't coded for proteins. These were originally thought not to have any importance in the biological processes. What is interesting is the discovery that micro–RNA from, amongst other things, rice and corn can be found in human cells. This means that micro–RNA from the food we eat can be absorbed through the membrane of the intestine into the blood stream, thus transporting it to other cells in the body.

Another interesting fact is that all of the higher cultures on the earth during the last 10,000 years have had cereal products, e.g., corn, wheat and rice, as their base fodder. This was during a time when human beings took the biggest steps forward in development. Can part of this development be the reason for the micro–DNA we gain from these foodstuffs? Can it be the case that the micro–DNA from these plants influence the gene's behavior in a way that creates people with higher intelligence?[11]

Micro-RNA is a very small yet powerful molecule that is believed to play an important role in the controlling of genes. So far there are around 1,000 different micro-RNAs reported to be found in a human. Researchers in Lund, Sweden, have studied the specific molecule micro–RNA-124 which has been seen to play an important role in controlling neurogenesis in mice.

For a long time it has been believed that the nerve cells of the brain couldn't reproduce. In other words, the brain cells a person was born with would be those they had for life. Now researchers know that new nerve cells are produced even in the fully matured brain. The production of new cells has significance for memory and learning abilities.

The results from tests carried out on animals indicate that neurogenesis is involved in both psychiatric (trepidation, depression) and neurogenerative illnesses (e.g., Parkinsons, Alzheimer's). The understanding, in detail, of how neurogenesis occurs increases our understanding of the different illnesses of the brain. This may, in time, lead to better treatment and possibly even a cure for the illnesses.

A stem cell is a cell that has the ability not only to create exact copies of itself but one that can also develop into the different specialized cells in the body. Nerve stem cells can be found in a few specific places in the brain, during the development process from stem cell to being a functioning nerve cell they move to another pre-decided area of the brain. The fact that microRNA is such a small molecule enables it to leak out from the brain thus allowing it to be studied in the spine marrow fluid. Research is already underway with the main aim being to find out whether differing concentrations and/or patterns of microRNA can be linked to different illnesses in the brain. It is hoped that analyzing a specific microRNA will lead to an early diagnosis, this having great bearing upon the illness' continued course.[12]

The Nobel Prize in physiology or medicine 2012 was given to John B. Gurdon and Shinya Yamanaka for discovering the fact that mature cells can be reprogramed to pluripotent stem cells, immature cells that can develop into any of the bodies different tissues. This has revolutionized our view on the development of cells and organisms:

> A key question in developmental biology is how cells exchange positional information for proper patterning during organ development. In plant roots the radial tissue organization is

highly conserved with a central vascular cylinder in which two water conducting cell types, protoxylem and metaxylem, are patterned centripetally. We show that this patterning occurs through crosstalk between the vascular cylinder and the surrounding endodermis mediated by cell-to-cell movement of a transcription factor in one direction and microRNAs in the other. SHORT ROOT, produced in the vascular cylinder, moves into the endodermis to activate SCARECROW. Together these transcription factors activate *MIR165a* and *MIR166b*. Endodermally produced microRNA165/6 then acts to degrade its target mRNAs encoding class III homeodomain-leucine zipper transcription factors in the endodermis and stele periphery. The resulting differential distribution of target mRNA in the vascular cylinder determines xylem cell types in a dosage-dependent manner.[13]

Stuart Hameroff

Stuart Hameroff's work with microtubules has shown that they can function as information transmitters through the agency of different patterns to create adapted changes in the tubulin.[14] This can be an important aspect of how halographic information—which is emitted by the halo on an organismic level and which is received by the centriole—can be transferred to other cells. Hameroff, who is an anesthesiologist, has shown that unconsciousness comes about when narcotic gases block the flow of information in microtubuli. From the perspective of the theory that has been developed here, unconsciousness could then be explained as a blockage of the organism's resonance with the Cosmic Tree of Life—the source of consciousness.[15]

Cells that are able to communicate with one another and help one another; cells that are protected by amazing defenses that rescue us from intruders—sometimes it is a life-and-death struggle. There is so little that science actually knows about this fascinating connection. We can medicate and help a part of the body when something goes wrong, but we cannot do very much about the desire for life and life itself. From the very first heartbeat when we are three-week-old fetuses, to three billion heartbeats later when we come to leave this life, we are a part of life on earth.

People who have been resuscitated after being near death are able to tell of a special experience of light, or that they saw a white light at the end of a tunnel; met deceased family members; observed their lifeless body as they floated above it; or had other extraordinary experiences. This is called a near-death or out-of-body experience. The cause is unknown, though one possible explanation is said to be that the person is hallucinations because the brain is getting too little oxygen.[16] But this is not consistent with lack of oxygen to the brain, not if one is to believe what the cardiologist Pim van Lommel writes in his book, *Consciousness Beyond Life*. Many authors and doctors have the same understanding as van Lommel.

Eben Alexander states in *Newsweek*:

> I am not the first person to have discovered evidence that consciousness exists beyond the body. Brief, wonderful glimpses of this realm are as old as human dimension (a) while their cortex was completely shut down, and (b) while their body was under minute medical observation, as mine was for the full seven days of my coma.
>
> All their chief arguments against near-death experiences suggest that these experiences are the results of a minimal, transient or partial malfunctioning of the cortex. My near-death experience, however, took place not while my cortex was malfunctioning, but while it was

simply off. This is clear from the severity and duration of my meningitis, and from the global cortical involvement documented by CT scans and neurological examinations. According to current medical understanding of the brain and mind, there is absolutely no way that I could have experienced even a dim and limited consciousness during my time in coma, much less the hyper-vivid and completely coherent odyssey I underwent [Oct. 8, 2012].

Out-of-body, OBE, or Near Death Experiences are similar transpersonal experiences. Those who have had them experienced peace, joy and harmony and had no sense of the body. They also experienced their senses as being more acute. Some of them saw a bright light, experienced a different dimension or saw deceased family members.

Following an NDE people know of the continuity of their consciousness, retaining all thoughts and memories of past events. And this insight causes their process of transformation and the loss of fear of death. Man appears to be more than just a body.

The conclusion that consciousness can be experienced independently of brain function might well induce a huge change in the scientific paradigm in Western medicine, and could have practical implications in actual medical and ethical problems such as the care of comatose or dying patients, euthanasia, abortion, and the removal of organs for transplantation from someone with a beating heart but with a diagnosis of brain death.

"There are still more questions than answers, but, based on the aforementioned theoretical aspects of the obviously experienced continuity of our consciousness, we finally should consider the possibility that death, like birth, may well be a mere passing from one state of consciousness to another," says Pim von Lommel, one of the pioneers within this research. Other pioneers are the British doctors Sam Parnia and Peter Fenwick, and Prof. Stuart Hameroff in Arizona.

"I have my body and I am consciousness ... endless consciousness," says Pim van Lommel.[17] Pim van Lommel, Elisabeth and Peter Fenwick and Ornella Corazza give a lot of examples in their books.

Psychologist Kenneth Ring proposed that near-death experiences could be explained by the holographic model. Ring believes such experiences, as well as death itself, are really nothing more than the shifting of a person's consciousness from one level of the hologram of reality to another (in *The Holographic Universe*, by Michel Talbot).

Or do we move into another dimension? In the string theory there are 11 dimensions according to professors of theoretical physics Edward Witten and Stephen Hawking, while others propose models with even more dimensions.

Water and Our Genetic Code

Water is able to dissolve the majority of chemical elements and carry them with it. Iron, calcium, and nitrogen compounds are but a few examples of the substances that can be dissolved in water. Chemically pure water does not exist in nature, and water's solvent capacity is a precondition for life itself. The water that rises in plants conveys dissolved nutrients to all parts of the plant. The human body is likewise sustained by nutrients that have been dissolved in the water of the blood.

What of oils and non-polarized substances which are not water soluble? It is this very circumstance—the fact that some substances seem to love spending their time in water while others abhor it—which is the key to how water helps life's most important building blocks—genes and proteins—achieve the specific, three-dimensional shapes that determine the function of the large bio-molecules. When proteins react with one another or with the genes it is crucial, of course, that the molecules fit one another.

Newly constructed proteins emerge from the cell's protein factories like a long necklace whose beads are amino acids, and only in the cellular fluid does the protein fold itself up into its compact three-dimensional form. Some of the amino acids are water-shunning, and these are folded naturally into the center of the proteins, where they avoid all contact with water, while other amino acids are water-loving, and these end up on the outside of the protein instead. In the 1980s Robert J. Lefkowits and Brian K. Kobilka managed to find the gene that encrypts for the benefit of the adrenaline receptor, the molecule to which the adrenaline hormone actually attaches itself.

The receptor consisted of seven long strings and their construction indicated that they were not fond of water, but instead preferred an environment rich in fat. The strings twisted back and forth through the cell wall seven times. Rhodopsin is another receptor that twists seven times. It is located in the retina of the eye and catches light. Similar receptors are located on the surface of the cell and they take care of the communication between what is outside of the cell and what is inside. Without these receptors we would not be able to see any light, smell any scents or experience any flavors. For this discovery Lefkowitz and Kobilka were awarded the Nobel Prize in Chemistry in 2012.

Computer simulations have shown that the double helix of DNA breaks apart if there is an attempt to model it without the presence of water. This is due to the fact that the water molecules create hydrogen bonds between the phosphate groups of the DNA strands, which would otherwise repel each other.

Water molecules can also be captured in water-loving pockets inside proteins. An experiment by biophysicists in Bochum, Germany, has shown how water plays a central role for the function of these proteins. Measurements of the protein bacteriorhodopsin provide one example. This protein is stored in the cell membrane of photosynthetic bacteria and handles the first step in the bacteria's photosynthesis. When the protein absorbs a light particle, it uses a network of water molecules in an interior channel to transfer a proton from the inside of the cell to the outside of the membrane, where a different protein snaps up the proton and puts energy into producing biological fuel. The researchers established that the process is possible only because the hydrogen bonds in water are formed and broken very easily.

New research indicates that water participates actively in the communication between genes and proteins. Without this interaction, life as we know it would simply be inconceivable.[18]

Our body as a whole consists of at least two-thirds water—and the brain is 80 percent water. As the brain tissue converts glucose from the blood into oxygen and energy, which are consumed in the brain cells' communication, it produces water. A human brain contains about one liter of water and produces fifty milliliters of water every twenty-four hours. Thus the brain's water is entirely replaced in about three weeks. Our body contains the most water in the fetal stage and somewhat less when we are children. As we age, the water content of our body decreases.

What Exactly Is Water?

What is water? It is a chemical union between hydrogen and oxygen. The atoms are attached to each other in an asymmetrical fashion which means that one end has a surplus of positive electrical energy while the other has a surplus of negative electrical energy. Water, then, is a dipole. Water molecules have a tendency to adhere firmly to each other so that a positive end attracts a negative end and vice versa. This is called hydrogen bonding and is the basis of water's totally unique characteristics.

Its outstanding solvent capacity has already been mentioned, and it has other remarkable properties as well, including its peculiar density ratio. Water is heaviest at 4°C, not at 0°C, the freezing point. The density of a substance depends on how tightly atoms and molecules are packed. Ordinarily, a solid substance has greater density than the same substance in liquid form. Water is an exception: ice has a lower density than water. It is due to the more spacious construction of ice that ice floats on water. If water were heaviest at 0°C, ice would form at the bottom of lakes and rivers, freezing from the bottom up; fish would die and the ice would never have time to melt in the spring. The question is whether life would have been able to arise on earth at all if that had been the case.

It has a great ability to store heat. In hot weather, the water in oceans and big lakes absorbs heat, which it radiates when the air is cold. This tempers the climate.

The boiling point of water is about 160°C above the boiling point of comparable substances. This is the reason liquid water exists on our planet—and without it, no life would exist on Earth. Water also has a high fusion coefficient; it takes eighty times more energy to melt one gram of ice compared to similar substances.

It has high surface tension and capillary action. Surface tension makes it possible for objects to be carried by the hydrogen bonds on the surface of water, even if the material is heavier than water. This gives insects the possibility to stand on water, and all of us have probably seen mosquito larvae in a puddle of water. Capillary force means that water can climb upwards in fine tubes despite the power of gravity. Thanks to capillary force a tree is able to "lift" water high up into its foliage.

Solutions Are More Complex Than Expected

Water is not just H_2O molecules. It contains a number of molecular species including *ortho* and *para* water molecules, water molecules with different isotopic compositions such as HDO and $H_2^{18}O$, such water molecules as part of weakly bound but partially covalently linked molecular clusters containing one, two, three or four hydrogen bonds, and hydrogen ion and hydroxide ion species. Apart from such molecules there are always adventitious and self-created solutes in liquid water. Distilled and de-ionized water contain significant and varying quantities of contaminating ions. Often the criteria for "purity" is the conductivity, but this will not show ionic contaminants at nanomolar, or even somewhat higher, concentrations due to the relatively high conductivity of the H+ and OH− naturally present.[19]

Electrochemistry

In every eukaryotic cell there are organelles, i.e., mitochondria, that supply our body with energy.

Through food we receive; amino acids and proteins, carbohydrates and fats. Amino acids are used to build proteins, which—amongst other things—work as building material. Larger carbohydrates, such as starch, have to be separated into glucose, in order to then be transported into the cells with the help of the blood. From glucose the body can also build glycogen, a kind of animal starch, which can then be stored in the liver as an energy reserve. We also need to breathe, which is a way of transporting oxygen to the cells. One of the most important link in the energy conversion of the cells is exactly that—the cellular respiration—our equivalent to the photosynthesis of the plants.

Carbohydrates (sugar) and oxygen are consequently the two raw materials that the cell works with to be able to extract energy. Finally, glucose is what is converted into usable energy and oxygen is needed as fuel for the actual conversion process. In the cellular respiration process these two raw materials are converted into two waste products (carbon dioxide and water) and energy.

Adenosine triphosphate, ATP, is the end goal for the mitochondria's process of cellular respiration. ATP is the most useful form of energy, not just for the human being, but for everything living. ATP has been called the body's "energy currency," the form of energy that is used as fuel in practically all organisms. Inside the membrane of the mitochondrion glucose is converted into different substances, to then finally end up as ATP. Please see below for the different steps in the conversion process:

1. Glycolysis
2. Link/chain reaction
3. Citric acid cycle
4. Electron transport chain
5. Oxidative phosphorylation

In the electron transport chain energy is transferred through the transport of electrons; an electrical current has therefore sort of occurred.

The electron transport chain takes place in the membrane of the mitochondria. There are extremely unique electron transport proteins containing metal atoms able to participate in such a redox-reaction. These pass on electrons that have been freed during the energy conversion, in many step, until it finally reaches the electron accepting oxygen, which is oxidized to water. The proteins are therefore reduced/oxidized and they move the electrons further forward in the chain. But what is the point of transporting all these electrons just for them to be picked up by an oxygen atom and turn into water?

This "electric current" is not the whole electrochemical aspect within ATP-production and the energy conversion of the cell. No, there are three magic words: *ATP, electron transport* and *the proton motive force.*

The proton motive force is by far the most thought provoking and impressive of all electrochemical processes within the body. The point of the whole electron transport chain is to transport protons. One hydrogen ion, H+, is a proton. These exist inside the mitochondrion and the movement of the electrons brings these protons, which cannot actually pass through the membrane of their own accord, through to the other side. This type of transportation is called osmosis.

To the person who is searching for electrochemical processes inside human cells, the implications of this fact cannot be highlighted enough. What it means is that an electrochemical potential is formed when one part of the membrane is presented with a surplus of protons. The tension that occurs is called membrane potential.

The protons are used as the last step in the energy conversion process in order to fuel the protein machine that synthesizes ATP. The whole process with the conservation of the tension in the membrane potential is known as the chemical osmosis coupling mechanism. This is the theory behind the ATP-production process, but we have also discovered something very exciting about the nature of the energy conversion—it is actually electrochemical.

There is not just one form of electric current occurring in every human cell due to the electron transport chain. Every mitochondrion is actually a little proton motive battery and the tension that occurs is used to drive the energy conversion process—the ATP-production.[20]

Adenosine Triphosphate, ATP, and Krebs Cycle

Our cells are 70 percent water. Thus a voltage begins to drop in ourselves, oxygen leaves the cells. This has a serious consequences. Our cells contain a process for turning fatty acids into glucose. They are processed trough a series of chemical reactions called the Krebs cycle. The end result is a rechargeable battery called ATP. As ATP provides electrons to keep the cell functioning, it becomes a discharged, rechargeable battery called ADP.

When oxygen is available, for every unit of fatty acids run through the Krebs cycle, we create 38 molecules of ATP. However, if oxygen is unavailable, only two molecules of ATP is created for every units fatty acids. Thus as voltage drops, and oxygen levels drop, our metabolism goes from "38 miles per gallon to 2 miles per gallon." Thus it is very difficult for cells to have enough energy to function with such inefficient metabolism.

Another problem of decreased oxygen is infections. Our bodies contain perhaps 1 trillion microorganisms. However, most of these are inactive as long as oxygen is present. However, when oxygen levels drop, these bugs wake up. The first thing they want is to have lunch. And they want you for lunch.[21]

This is what Dr. Jerry Tenant writes in his book *Healing Is Voltage*, a book that also describes the photoelectric effect, Schrödinger and quantum mechanics. He further states:

Every cell in the body is designed to run at -20 to -25 millivolts. To heal, we must make new cells. To make a new cell requires -50 millivolts. Chronic disease occurs when voltage drops below -20 and/or cannot achieve -50 millivolts to make new cells. Thus chronic disease is always defined by having low voltage. This book tells you how to measure your voltage in each organ, how to correct it, and how to determine why your voltage dropped enough to allow you to get sick.

The Body's Third Circulatory System

Professor Björn Nordenström at the Karolinska Institute in Stockholm developed a hypothesis of a third cycle within the body. Apart from the earlier circulatory systems, blood vessels and lymphatic system, this new system should consist of several closed electrochemical systems. The walls of the blood vessels have two hundred times higher resistance than the plasma. Therefore these could work as electroconductive cables using the plasma as the conductor. An example of this type of closed electrochemical system within the human body is the acidic gastric juices that are connected to the alkaline bile through the intestines and gut. Between the gastric juices and the bile there is a potential due to an excess of electrons within the bile and deficit within the gastric juices. The intestine and its contents are the equivalent of electrolytes.

The Water Crystal

We know that no two snowflakes are alike. When water freezes, ice crystals are formed. Masaru Emoto is a Japanese businessman who has become known as a researcher into water's inner forces and is most known for his photographs of water crystals. He has developed a method of photographing water during deep-freezing in a standardized manner, so that separate water tests can be compared. No one else, however, has replicated his work with photographing ice crystals; as a result, it cannot be evaluated from a scientific standpoint.

What makes Emoto's work a bit controversial is that he ascribes to water the ability to hear and to read.[22] If the label on the water bottle says "idiot," for example, there will be a totally different crystal image than when it says "truth and happiness." Tap water also changed after a prayer, and after "love and thanks" the water formed beautiful crystals. When the SARS epidemic was raging, Emoto showed the water the abbreviated term in both English and Japanese, but there was not much difference between them and the crystals that are normally found in ordinary distilled water. When the whole name, Severe Acute Respiratory Syndrome, was written out there were no well-formed crystals in this water at all. Then the "Severe Acute Respiratory Syndrome" labels were removed and replaced with "love and thanks." These words, according to Emoto, then created beautiful crystals, regardless of language.

For Emoto, this bears out his theories on water: water captures the vibrations of words and reflects them in the form of crystals. As long as a word is used in the right way, the water's reaction is the same, regardless of language.

It is good to be as concrete as possible, since the water is sensitive to vibrations. (This means, for example, writing "Severe Acute Respiratory Syndrome" instead of the abbreviation "SARS," so that the water can really take in the import of the words.)

The words "love and thanks" have strong positive energy. Even if the water's energy is damaged, it can be restored again.

Although Masaru Emoto's work cannot be evaluated from a scientific standpoint, he is not alone in ascribing great significance to water. In healing and homeopathy as well, the same thing is being done. What if Emoto is right, and the water in our body is not only able to listen but also reads thoughts?

What if it is the hydrogen bonds in DNA's base pairs that constitute our immune system and all our consciousness?

Water Is Crucial

"It all depends on water," said the Italian researcher Guiseppe Vitiello, whom I met first at a conference on Quantum Mind in Salzburg, Austria, in the summer of 2007 and later on at several similar conferences. And the issue, of course, had to do with our brain and our consciousness.

Vitiello speaks of a strange "time-reversed mirror" mode *in the environment* that pairs off as a non-locally quantum-connected *Einstein-Rosen-Podolsky* (EPR) *twin* or *doppelganger* to a DWQ quantum. In other words, he has a non-locally correlated pair of quanta, one in the dipole wave and its time-reversed twin in the "environment." He claims that this non-local quantum connection or entanglement between the two quanta, one in the Fröhlich wave and the other in the external environment, "can be seen as a self-interaction term" of the Fröhlich mode in which the environmental twin is part of the "self-recognition" process.

Vitiello has produced a detailed mathematical model of dissipative damped quantum oscillators, in which the coupling to the environment undergoes the "superconducting."[23]

Perhaps our thoughts consist of electromagnetic wave motions, energy we emit when we think. Nobel Laureate Luc Montagnier told *Science* in a discussion of the phenomenon of electromagnet waves produced by DNA in water.

> What we have found is that DNA produces structural changes in water, which persist at very high dilutions, and which lead to resonant electromagnetic signals that we can measure. Not all DNA produces signals that we can detect with our device. The high-intensity signals come from bacterial and viral DNA.
> I have found these signals coming from bacterial DNA in the plasma of many patients with autism, and also in most, if not all, patients with Alzheimer, Parkinson's disease, and multiple sclerosis.
> It seems that the bacteria we are detecting are coming from the gut. So it is quite possible that products from gut bacteria end up in the plasma and cause damage to the brain.[24]

The base pairs in our DNA are held together by hydrogen. Essential water, the precondition for all life! I recall how, at a Toward a Science of Consciousness conference, I asked Nobel laureate Luc Montagnier and Guiseppe Vitiello if it could be said, a bit simplified, that our entire immune system was dependent on water. The answer was yes. And that is how it is, then (Vitiello 2001).

Electromagnetism

An extraordinary paper by Luc Montagnier and several co-authors has described memory effects in aqueous DNA solutions that the authors propose depend on interactions with the background electromagnetic field. These effects, if real, require the prior processing and dilution of the solutions and are explained by Montagnier as resonance phenomena with nanostructures derived from the DNA and water.[25]

Jacques Benveniste proposed water memory in the 1980s, and famously managed to publish some of his results in the journal *Nature*.[26] Lacking any objective grounds to reject the seemingly impossible paper through the process of peer review (so the many claims that established science merely rejects quack ideas with a closed mind are patently false), the paper was sent to press. The journal's editor, John Maddox, however, remained skeptical and allowed the results to be published, accompanied by a small editorial on the subject by himself, stating in the piece the number of laws of physics and chemistry such a result would violate and that "There are good and particular reasons why prudent people should, for the time being, suspend judgment."[27] The only other remaining condition was that the research mentioned was independently replicated following publication and the controversy created a small media storm in 1988. The team sent to investigate Benveniste's claims included James Randi—whose expertise on sleight of hand and fraud detection were put to use in the lab. The report from the team concluded that although Benveniste was innocent of academic misconduct and fraud, he had been misled by flawed experiments. Thus, one of homeopathy's most shining moments was tarnished, and even John Maddox was almost disappointed, concluding "I'm sorry we didn't find something more interesting."[28]

The studies of the memory of water spurred Benveniste on to investigate how the molecules communicate within living cells. During all the stages of life the molecules have to talk to each other. In a transparent cell, containing one protein molecule to 10,000 water molecules, the molecules are jostling and pushing each other inside the cell. But if every molecule instead had its own signature frequency, its receptor or the molecule with matching spectrum of properties could tune to this frequency. They can tune in to the same resonance as each other—a body's vibration is amplified by another body's vibration at the same or almost the same frequency. This creates a cascade of electromagnetic impulses that travel at the speed of light, as Benveniste expressed it (McTaggart 2001).

On the subject of frequency, Penny Peirce writes, "Because science has long taught us to rely what we can see and touch, we often don't notice that our spirit, thoughts, emotions, and body are made of energy—that everything is vibrating. As we move out of the age of technology and into the age of intuition, we need tools to understand what it means to be a vibrational being and how natural frequency affect us" (*Frequency: The Power of Personal Vibration*, 2009).

Entrainment is a term in physics which means that two oscillating systems fall into synchrony. It was coined in 1665 by the Dutch mathematician Christiaan Huygens, after he discovered that two of his clocks with pendulums standing in close proximity to each other had begun to swing in unison. He had been toying with the two pendulums and found that even if, we he started one pendulum swinging at the one end, and the other at the opposite end, eventually the two would swing in unison.

Two waves peaking and troughing at the same time are considered "in phase," or operating in sync. Those peaking at opposite times are "out of phase." Physicists believe that the entrainment results from tiny exchanges of energy between two systems that are out of phase, causing one to slow down and the other to accelerate until the two are in phase. It is also related to resonance or the ability of any system to absorb more energy than normal at a particular frequency (the number of peaks and troughs in one second). Any vibrating thing, including an electromagnetic wave, has its own preferential frequencies, called "resonant frequencies," where it finds vibrating the easiest. When it "listens" or receives a vibration from somewhere else, it tune out all pretenders and only tunes into its own resonant frequency.[29]

Benveniste's experiment showed that the cells don't rely on random collisions, but instead on electromagnetic signals with low frequency waves. Water is like a tape recorder that carries the information regardless of whether the original molecule still exists or not. Water is so important for the transmission of energy and information, that Benveniste's own studies shows that molecular signals cannot be transmitted inside the body apart from through water.[30] Through a vast range of trials and experiments Benveniste obtained evidence proving that the electromagnetic waves from living creatures affect their surroundings, the same result as the biophysicist Fritz-Albert Popp and predecessors had come to.

My reflection: Water is a prerequisite for life to exist, but does it have to be inside a living cell in order for the water to tune in to the right frequency and carry the information forward? It is likely that life (a living cell) is a prerequisite for the water "to remember."

Also to be considered is bioresonance therapy which is also is based on the memory of water. Bioresonance therapy is a holistic medical technique that is based on the old learnings of acupuncture as well as biophysics; it originates from Germany. In Germany this method is used within the ordinary health service and has helped many people through the years to get rid of their allergies, stomach troubles, etc.[31]

By simply using the allergen the patient's hypersensitivity can be "erased." The method of treatment was founded by the German biophysicist Fritz-Albert Popp, who has conducted research within cell communication. According to Popp one could clearly see that our cells are surrounded by electromagnetic vibration areas. He also came to the conclusion that the body communicates with the help of cell vibrations. Popp has proven that it is possible to steer biochemical processes in the cells by influencing their vibration areas. The research and discoveries of other scientists confirm Popp's result.

Robert O. Becker, M.D., is a pioneer in the field of regeneration and its relationship to electrical currents in living things, and challenges the established mechanistic understanding of the body. He is the author of a book about the electromagnetism and the foundation of life, *The Body Electric*, which explores new pathways in our understanding of evolution, acupuncture, psychic phenomena, and healing (Becker 1985). He has also written a book, *Cross Currents*, about the perils of electropollution and the promise of electromedicine (Becker 1990). Professor Becker has twice been nominated for the Nobel Prize.

Consciousness is a phenomenon that cannot be explained inside the frame work for today's natural science.[32] Maybe it is not so strange that science of consciousness brings together various fields approaching the issue of consciousness from different perspectives, orientations and methodologies. These include neuroscience, philosophy, medicine, quantum physics, biology, psychology, anthropology, artificial intelligence, contemplative and experimental traditions, arts, culture, humanities and others. Cutting edge, controversial issues are emphasized.

In order to try to understand life quantum mechanics is needed, parallel to classical physics and a broad interdisciplinary studies, where physics get on with other sciences. We also have to try to understand that atoms and molecules have—in the same way as bacteria—become visible to us humans. First of all many truths are revealed with the help of the electron microscope. With an electron microscope you can actually see an atom, but not its components. Before we completely understand what life *is*, there will be a lot of denying of what is not convincing today because it hasn't been "scientifically proven."

Ignaz Semmelweis (1818–1865) was a Hungarian doctor who came to the conclusion that the number of cases of puerperal fever could be reduced if doctors just washed their hands before an autopsy of a pregnant woman. During 1848 Semmelweis widened this cleaning to incorporate all the medical instruments that came in contact with the patients during labor. He statistically documented that this almost completely eradicated puerperal fever from the hospital ward. However the other doctors felt it was hard work to wash their hands and that Semmelweis' ideas didn't have solid scientific evidence! Only after the death of Semmelweis was the bacteria theory developed and Semmelweis was eventually recognized as a pioneer in his field and in the prevention of hospital infections. That the establishment hadn't recognized what wasn't visible to the naked eye did lead to thousands of young mothers' deaths. How many similar cases are there today that, seen through the eyes of the science of today, don't have solid scientific evidence?

What was first assumed to be complex but natural neurological and chemical reactions in the dying brain has had to give way to a new view, as more and more unexplainable cases have been discovered. In many cases, patients have been able to accurately recount verifiable aspects of the experience that they could not possibly have been able to perceive through their ordinary senses: blind patients have reported visual impressions and patients without any brain activity at all have been able to describe medical procedures that had been performed on them in this state.

Our Thoughts

The mystery of what happens when we die and the nature of the human mind has fascinated humankind from antiquity to the present day. Although traditionally considered a matter for philosophical debate, advancements in modern science and in particular the science of resuscitation have now enabled an objective, scientific approach to seek answers to these compelling questions, which bear widespread implications not only for science, but also for all of humanity.

The body's cells remember. This is the reason we react reflexively before the brain has had time to send its signals. Our brains are computers that are programed, and every thought is a program. The brain does not distinguish between fantasy and reality. Perhaps our thoughts consist of electromagnetic wave motions, energy we emit when we think. We have certainly noticed that with negative stress we attract what we are afraid of, and the reverse—with positive thoughts we come closer to what we wish. All thoughts we think have power and affect our lives. Perhaps the power of thought is the greatest of all the forces that exist. It may be here that we have the solution to the effects of acupuncture, yoga, healing, telepathy and homeopathic medicine via the function of memory and energy, the sunlight, and feelings that exist even though they are not seen.

Action from a distance is well known in quantum physics and may be capable of explaining distance healing. To explain the phenomenon, physicists have invented the concept of non-locality, as it is described in Bell's theorem. Non-locality is one of the primary concepts in quantum mechanics and signifies that the matter in the universe is connected through non-localized forces like the strong and weak atomic forces, gravitation and electromagnetic force.

Is there some connection between burnout and the combination of over-stimulated left brains with starved right brains? There is clearly a connection between energy deficiency and a brain that has been receiving too many impulses. But what is the relationship between the two halves of the brain? We already know that someone who normally stammers does not stammer when he or she sings, because then the right brain comes into play. We also know that expressing power-words works well for a person who normally cannot to talk.

Concerning injuries to the right brain Blakeslee writes: "This emotional flatness is often accompanied by a flat, non-musical tone of voice while speaking and an insensitivity to the meaning communicated by other people's tone of voice. Musical discrimination and sense of pitch are often lost after right-brain damage—a contributing factor. However, there is also a definite pattern of reduced emotional capability."[33]

We Can Actually Manipulate Our Brains

The brain works on four known wavelengths that correspond to different states of consciousness. Alpha waves, 7–14 Hz, are dominant in a person who is awake with closed eyes, while beta waves, 14–28 Hz, appear if the person opens his or her eyes and concentrates on something. When the person sinks down toward a meditative state, the picture is dominated by delta, 0.3–3.5 Hz, and theta, 3.5–7 Hz. In the meditative state, one has the possibility of having experiences that lie outside the normal perception of physical reality (which happens, for example, in a dream). Here the difference is that the subject of the experiment has his or her waking consciousness along in the dream world. (Some people think they have had what is called an out-of-body experience, which is a phenomenon known from people who have been exposed to life-threatening situations.) Very high levels of brain activity—exceeding 28 Hz—are called gamma waves and indicate pathological stages of tension, excitement, and a high degree of stress or anxiety. If we feel this, it is high time to meditate or at least think loving thoughts so that the body relaxes. The discovery of this fascinating science has led to the creation of the Silva Method. José Silva, its founder, says, "The discovery that Human intelligence can learn to function with awareness and self control at Alpha and Theta frequencies of the brain will go down in history as the greatest discovery of man. This discovery is sure to change our concepts of Mind, Psychology, Psychiatry, Hypnoanalysis and of the Subconscious."[34]

Low Frequencies

Remote Viewing (RV), like the Silva Method,[35] presumes that we work with low brain frequencies. The precondition for being able to carry out remote viewing is to be capable of working at the right frequency for a relatively long period, 30 to 70 minutes. The "right frequency" for Coordinate or Controlled Remote Viewing (CRV) is the alpha level, 7–14 Hz. That is, a state of very relaxed alertness.

The Right Temporal Lobe

The right temporal lobe and the adjacent associated limbic lobe structure are clearly linked to all types of human religious experiences, including conversion experiences and near-death experiences. Just because the religious experiences are brain-based does not automatically diminish or devalue their spiritual significance. Rather, these discoveries of the role of the neurological substrata for the religious experiences may supply the proofs for their objective reality.

The right temporal lobe allows the human being to integrate with a timeless, spaceless, "non-local" reality. The clinical experience of accessing that reality is an important component in the religious experience. The existence of that such a reality has been predicted by modern quantum theory physics. A theory of this kind has a value through supplying a theoretical explanation for many well-documented phenomena which for the time being exist outside our present scientific model.

Spiritual experiences like premonitions or death or near-death experiences often include precognition of future events or remote viewing. This makes the experiments impossible to understand according to the present medical model. And there is still no coherent theory of how precognition or remote viewing works, seen from a perspective of brain biology. This lack of a theoretical model allowing interaction with an interconnected universe has led to a century-long debate between "skeptics" and "believers" that has not led to any understanding of human consciousness. This debate is primarily philosophical between "atheists" and "believers." It has dominated all areas of paranormal and near-death research and is often framed in a scientific terminology [Hansen 1992].

The debate between both "skeptics" and "believers" fulfills Carl Sagan's definitions of a pseudo-science in that there is extremely little data that comes out of it and it is full of references to various experts as authorities [Sagan 1996].

Clinical studies could be made of paranormal abilities like remote viewing after simulation of the temporal lobe. There is some evidence for electromagnetic activity being able to change paranormal abilities [E. Haraldsson 1987]. Studies of this kind could also be applied to chi gong and spiritual healing.

This new model of an interactive universe, with our right temporal lobe as mediator, explains more than existing models do. They have specific areas that can be proved or disproved through replicable experiments. Morse prophesies that even if the suggested model does not ultimately pass the test of time, a completely new understanding of human consciousness will be the result of these investigations.[36]

Albert Einstein, David Bohm and Karl Pribram

One of Einstein's discussion partners was the physicist from the University of London, David Bohm. Einstein had never before had quantum theory so clearly presented. Bohm's textbook *Quantum Theory* was published in 1951 and soon became a classic. But Bohm was looking for a deeper explanation of reality, dissatisfied as he was with the possibility of the standard theories to explain the phenomena of quantum physics.

For his part, Karl Pribram, neurophysiologist at Stanford University, was seeking something other than the explanation provided by the standard models to solve neurophysiological puzzles. Thus they approached the problem from different directions, and both agreed that the brain—the entire universe—is a hologram. Here was the solution to many problems. And more than that, the holographic model was also capable of explaining problems that had been "inexplicable" (and therefore denied by scientists), among which are telepathy, precognition, near death experiences (NDEs), out-of-body experiences (OBEs) and psychokinesis.

Karl H. Pribram was born in Vienna, Austria, and was a professor at Georgetown University and an emeritus professor of psychology and psychiatry at Stanford University and Radford University. Board-certified as a neurosurgeon, Pribram did pioneering work on the definition of the limbic system, the relationship of the frontal cortex to the limbic system, the sensory-specific "association" cortex of the parietal and temporal lobes, and the classical motor cortex of the human brain. To the general public, Pribram is best known for his development of the holonomic brain model of cognitive function and his contribution to ongoing neurological research into memory, emotion, motivation and consciousness.

Pribram understood that the one area of the brain where wave-interference patterns might be created was not in any particular cell, but in the spaces between them. At the end of every neuron, the basic unit of a brain cell, are synapses, where chemical charges build up, eventually triggering electrical firing across these spaces to the other neurons. In the same spaces, dendrites—tiny filaments of nerve endings wafting back and forth, like shafts of wheat in a slow breeze—communicate with other neurons, sending out and receiving their own electrical wave impulses. These "slow-wave potentials," as they are called, flow through the glia, or glue, surrounding neurons, to gently touch or even collide with other waves. It is at this busy juncture, a place of a ceaseless scramble of electromagnetic communications between synapses and dendrites, where it was most likely that wave frequencies could be picked up and analyzed, and holographic images formed, since these wave patterns criss-crossing all the time are creating hundreds and thousands of wave-interference patterns.

Pribram conjectured that these wave collisions must create the pictorial images in our brain. When we perceive something, it's not due to the activity of neurons themselves but certain patches of dendrites distributed around the brain, which, like a radio station, are set to resonate only at certain frequencies. It is like having a vast number of piano strings all over your head, only some of which would vibrate as a particular note is played.[37]

> The concept of the quantum hologram is based on quantum emissions from all physical objects, you, me, the camera. Any physical object of macroscopic size, molecular and above, emits quanta of energy and absorbs quanta of energy. The quanta emitted from every object we've discovered carries information about the physical. The quantum hologram is this informational structure about a physical object and it is non-local, which means it is not space-time restricted. It appears to be a proper mechanism for explaining virtually all of these types of psychic manifestation that we humans know. We are now beginning to understand what consciousness is, and what we understand so far is that the quantum holographic record survives. It is our history, it records our passage, it records what we do, and it's available to the future. It appears to be nature's way of preserving our experience; that's the non-local part. It's the informational part of us, so that everything we do as physical beings is recorded in the ephemeral quantum holographic record, the giant hard disc in the sky, if you will. Because we are brought up not to trust inexplicable perceptions, these thoughts are a bit difficult for laypeople as well as scientists to believe" [Edgar Mitchell, *Nature's Mind*].

Are we moving towards a scientific paradigm shift? A paradigm shift where the foundations have in fact been laid by Albert Einstein and the quantum physicists Niels Bohr, Max Planck, Werner Heisenberg, Erwin Schrödinger, David Bohm, Edward Witten and professor of neurophysiology Karl Pribram? It is very likely so. The Large Hadron Collider, the particle accelerator in CERN, Switzerland, will yield many new answers, such as that the Higgs particle does exist.

The Mathematical Language of the Hologram[38]

While the theories that enabled the development of the hologram were first formulated in 1947 by Dennis Gabor (who later won the Nobel Prize), in the late 1960s and early 1970s Pribram's theory received even more persuasive experimental support. When Gabor first conceived the idea of holography he wasn't thinking about lasers. His goal was to improve the electron microscope, then a primitive and imperfect device. His approach was a mathematical one, and the mathematics he used was a type of calculus invented by an eighteenth-century Frenchman named Jean B.J. Fourier.

Roughly speaking what Fourier developed was a mathematical way of converting any pattern, no matter how complex, into a language of simple waves. He also showed how these wave forms could be converted back into the original pattern. In other words, just a television camera converts an image into electromagnetic frequencies and a television set converts those frequencies back into the original image, Fourier showed how similar process could be achieved mathematically. The equations he developed to convert images into wave forms and back again are known as *Fourier transforms*.

Fourier transforms enabled Gabor to convert a picture of an object into the blur of

Henry P. Stapp, Karl Pribram and Patrik Heelan at Red Bulls restaurant in Salzburg the summer 2007. Photograph by Ingrid Fredriksson.

interference patterns on a piece of holographic film. They also enabled him to devise a way of converting those interference patterns back to an image of the original object. In fact the special whole in every part of a hologram is one of the by-products that occurs when an image pattern is translated into the Fourier language of wave forms.

The brain has many characteristics that can be associated with holograms. The interference between (perceptual and memory) waves results in oscillations at their points of interference. All perception can be analyzed through Fourier analysis. The brain's microprocesses and physical microprocesses can be described according to principles of quantum theory.

Throughout the late 1960s and early 1970s various researchers contacted Pribram and told him they had uncovered evidence that the visual system worked as a kind of frequency analyzer. Since frequency is a measure of the number of oscillations a wave undergoes per second, this strongly suggested that the brain might be functioning as a hologram does.

Pribram and Bohm Together

Considered together, Bohm and Pribram's theories provide a profound new way of looking at the world: Our brains mathematically construct objective reality by interpreting frequencies that are ultimately projections from another dimension, a deeper order of existence that is beyond space and time: The brain is a hologram enfolded in a holographic universe.

For Pribram, this synthesis made him realize that the objective world does not exist, at least not in the way we are accustomed to believing. What is "out there" is a vast ocean of waves and frequencies, and reality looks concrete to us only because our brains are able to take this holographic blur and convert it into sticks and stones and the other familiar objects that make up our world. How is the brain (which itself is composed of frequencies of matter) able to take something as insubstantial as a blur of frequencies and make it seem solid to the touch? "The kind of mathematical process that Beksey simulated with his vibrators is basic to how our brains construct our image of a world out there," Pribram states. In other words, the smoothness of a piece of fine china and the feel of beach sand beneath our feet are really just elaborate versions of the phantom limb syndrome.

According to Pribram this does not mean there aren't china cups and grains of beach sand out there. It simply means that a china cup has two very different aspects to its reality. When it is filtered through the lens of our brain it manifests as a cup. But if we could get rid of our lenses, we'd experience it as an interference pattern. Which one is real and which is illusion? "Both are real to me," says Pribram, "or, if you want to say, neither of them are real."[39]

This state of affairs is not limited to china cups. We, too, have two very different aspects to our reality. We can view ourselves as physical bodies moving through space. Or we can view ourselves as a blur of interference patterns enfolded throughout the cosmic hologram. Bohm believes this second point of view might even be more correct, for to think of ourselves as a holographic mind/brain *looking* at a holographic universe is again an abstraction, an attempt to separate two things that ultimately cannot be separated.

Do not be troubled if this is difficult to grasp. It is relatively easy to understand the idea of holism in something that is external to us, like an apple in a hologram. What makes it difficult is that in this case we are not looking at the hologram. We are a part of the hologram.

The difficulty is also another indication of how radical a revision Bohm and Pribram are trying to make in our way of thinking. But it is not the only radical revision. Pribram's assertion that our brains construct objects pales beside another of Bohm's conclusions: *that we even construct space and time.* The implications of this view are just one of the subjects that will be examined as we explore the effect Bohm and Pribram's ideas have had on the work of researchers in other fields.[40]

"Neither Dennis Gabor, David Bohm or I think (thought) of the universe as a hologram. The holographic arrangement is an enfolded (implicate) background for the space-time universe we navigate. It is a potential reality rather than the experienced reality that we navigate," says Karl Pribram.[41]

Simulations Supporting the Hologram Theory

A team of physicists has provided some of the clearest evidence yet that our universe could be just one big projection. In 1997, theoretical physicist Juan Maldacena proposed[42] that an audacious model of the universe in which gravity arises from infinitesimally thin, vibrating strings could be reinterpreted in terms of well-established physics. The mathematically intricate world of strings, which exist in nine dimensions of space plus one of time, would be merely a hologram: the real action would play out in a simpler, flatter cosmos where there is no gravity.

Maldacena's idea thrilled physicists because it offered a way to put the popular but still unproven string theory on solid footing—and because it solved apparent inconsistencies between quantum physics and Einstein's theory of gravity. It provided physicists with a mathematical Rosetta stone, a "duality" that allowed them to translate back and forth between the two languages, and solve problems in one model that seemed intractable in the other and vice versa. But although the validity of Maldacena's ideas has pretty much been taken for granted ever since, a rigorous proof has been elusive.

In two papers posted on the arXiv repository, Yoshifumi Hyakutake of Ibaraki University in Japan and his colleagues now provide, if not an actual proof, at least compelling evidence that Maldacena's conjecture is true. In one paper,[43] Hyakutake computes the internal energy of a black hole, the position of its event horizon (the boundary between the black hole and the rest of the universe), its entropy and other properties based on the predictions of string theory as well as the effects of so-called virtual particles that continuously pop into and out of existence. In the other,[44] he and his collaborators calculate the internal energy of the corresponding lower-dimensional cosmos with no gravity. The two computer calculations match.

"It seems to be a correct computation," says Maldacena, who is now at the Institute for Advanced Study in Princeton, New Jersey, and who did not contribute to the team's work. The findings "are an interesting way to test many ideas in quantum gravity and string theory," Maldacena adds. The two papers, he notes, are the culmination of a series of articles contributed by the Japanese team over the past few years. "The whole sequence of papers is very nice because it tests the dual [nature of the universes] in regimes where there are no analytic tests."

"They have numerically confirmed, perhaps for the first time, something we were fairly sure had to be true, but was still a conjecture—namely that the thermodynamics of certain black holes can be reproduced from a lower-dimensional universe," says Leonard Susskind, a theoretical physicist at Stanford University in California who was among the first theoreticians to explore the idea of holographic universes.

Neither of the model universes explored by the Japanese team resembles our own, Maldacena notes. The cosmos with a black hole has ten dimensions, with eight of them forming an eight-dimensional sphere. The lower-dimensional, gravity-free one has but a single dimension, and its menagerie of quantum particles resembles a group of idealized springs, or harmonic oscillators, attached to one another. Nevertheless, says Maldacena, the numerical proof that these two seemingly disparate worlds are actually identical gives hope that the gravitational properties of our Universe can one day be explained by a simpler cosmos purely in terms of quantum theory.[45]

Edgar Mitchell

What strikes me about the attempt of astronaut Edgar Mitchell to send messages telepathically was that the recipient received the information immediately when it was sent, that is, independent of time and space, if you will. We know that a delay normally occurs, that it takes eight minutes for light to travel here from the sun. The speed of light, then, is just over 1 billion kilometers per hour. Sound travels significantly more slowly—1,200 kilometers per hour. But here the information was instantaneous. Olof Jönsson, a Swedish engineer who lived for many years in the United States, became best known for the successful telepathy experiment with Edgar Mitchell from the moon during NASA's *Apollo 14* voyage.

We can read an interview with Edgar Mitchell on the Internet.[46] To the question of what his most important current project was, Mitchell replied:

> My biggest work is developing further the understanding of the quantum hologram and how it works in relation to the brain. The real enigma we don't have a handle on yet is the psychokinetic effect. It has to do with intentionality and the quantum hologram, but exactly how that functions physically is not obvious to us. The perception of non-local information like ESP is easy to explain through the quantum hologram; you are just picking up the information from another person. Telepathy is just information coming in; psychokinesis, just information going out. But the material deformation of things is a little more mysterious. It takes energy to bend a ring. We can understand healing; you are a sick person, and I give you the information and your body heals itself. But how to move a ring is a different problem. The universe and the experiences within it arise from natural causes. The remainder of the problem, of consciousness, that is, is to look for the evidence from modern science that points the way to reality. Eventually we will be able to explain it all, because it is natural, not supernatural. It's just our ignorance that causes it to seem supernatural.

Kaivarainen and Water[47]

The Finnish researcher Alex Kaivarainen is fully convinced of the significance of water. He is the author of 5 books and more than 110 scientific publications. Kaivarainen has developed theories on bivacuum, duality, electromagnetism, gravitation, and time. One of his computer programs deals with condensed matter like water and ice in the hierarchic theory. A great deal has to do with water's being a dipole.

A water molecule consists of one oxygen atom and two hydrogen atoms. The two hydrogen atoms stick out from the oxygen atom at a 105° angle. The water molecule as a whole is not electrically charged, but it has two poles. The electrons which oxygen and hydrogen share are in lower periods around the oxygen atom than they are around the hydrogen atom. The two remaining electron pairs in the outer shell of the oxygen atom stick out from the oxygen atom like two electron clouds with a mildly negative charge. Conversely, there are two mildly positive charges around the two hydrogen atoms, which lack their electron. The mutual attraction between the positive and the negative charges in water molecules creates what are called hydrogen bonds. They function as handles between the water molecules, and in liquid water they are constantly being formed and broken. It is the hydrogen bonds that give water its unique characteristics. Water molecules prefer to have four bonds with other water molecules, and they therefore arrange themselves so that the surface where they turn one side out towards the air is as small as possible.

The water molecule looks like a fat little figure whose body corresponds to the oxygen atom. The figure has two outstretched arms corresponding to the electron clouds around the oxygen atom and two outstretched legs corresponding to the two hydrogen atoms. When several water molecules are gathered, each water molecule tries to take hold of four other water molecules. The negatively charged arms catch their neighbors' positively charged legs, and vice versa.

Water becomes more difficult to describe the lower the temperature gets, since more and more phenomena and structures are able to occur then. There are eighteen different crystal forms, for example, and complicated links between the electrons in the water molecules.

Non-locality and the EPR Paradox[48]

Albert Einstein, along with Boris Podolsky and Nathan Rosen, demonstrated a baffling feature of quantum mechanics. If two particles have a common origin, and a measurement of a characteristic of one of the particles is performed, in certain cases the same characteristic could be affected in the other particle, even if the measurements were arranged in such a way that not even a signal at the speed of light would have time to transmit the result from the first particle to the second. This goes against common sense, and the contradiction goes by the name of the EPR paradox, after its discoverers.

In 1965 the British physicist John Bell came up with a way to determine whether the EPR paradox is compatible with reality. Using this test, and with measurements having a precision of several billionths of a second, the French physicist Alain Aspect succeeded in experimentally demonstrating in 1982 that the EPR paradox does in fact exist. This is the Aspect experiment, which proves a non-local reality, something that has been asserted by many writers of books on theoretical physics.

Scientifically Proven

Bill Moyers' book *Healing and the Mind* contains an interview with David Felten, M.D., Ph.D., professor of neurobiology and anatomy at the University of Rochester School of Medicine. He and his wife, Suzanne Felten, Ph.D., discovered nerve fibers that physically link the nervous system with the immune system.[49]

It started when they were examining a spleen and to their surprise found a bundle of nerve fibers in the large fields of cells that form part of the immune system. The practical significance was that the many stress factors in our life that affect the autonomous nervous system could also affect the immune system. A constant stream of information goes back and forth between the brain and the immune system. And we know with certainty that hormones are constantly being produced and released, and signal substances are constantly speaking with receiver cells all around in the body. Extremely fine changes and shifts in activity can arise in a person as a consequence of a sequence of thoughts. A study at UCLA used male and female actors who were challenged to think of a scenario and put themselves in the frame of mind, feel the feelings that went with it. While the research subjects were doing this, the hormones in their blood were studied, and certain changes in the immune system could be seen depending on what they were feeling.

One area where these small changes in the immune system can play an especially important role is in individuals who find themselves on the very edge of no longer being capable of reacting—the very old, for instance, or people who have viral illnesses or who must take medications that put the immune system out of operation. In such cases the extra pressure from a stress factor or some psychosocial factor or some feeling or some mood may break them, Felten says.

Clearly, consciousness is, or at least can be, non-local. What we experience and how we experience it depends in large part on our culture and our beliefs. Some people have gifts beyond the ordinary. Before they know that they are different, they think everyone has the same skills.

Water, Science and Life

Cells that are able to communicate with one another and help one another. Cells that are protected by amazing defenses that protect us from intruders; sometimes it is a struggle between life-and-death. It is the hydrogen bonds in DNA's base pairs that constitute our immune system and all our consciousness, but consciousness, which is in the DNA's hydrogen bonds, can't see, hear or feel. It congregates in the brain together with the senses and it is this that is consciousness.

All over the world new science is discussed. Scientists like Nobel laureate Luc Montagnier, Jacques Beneviste (1935–2004) et al. are rebuked but not to the same extent as Ignaz Semmelweis (1818–1865); their methods are not accepted by all.

The Semmelweis Reflex is the dismissing or rejecting out of hand any information, automatically, without thought, inspection, or experiment. The phrase stems from a number of people's personal experiences with the phenomenon, and denotes the reactions of anyone who engages in such behavior.

Can life be reduced to nothing more than an interesting arrangement of atoms and molecules? No! LPAC Basement research team member Oyang Teng and *21st Century Science & Technology* editor Laurence Hecht discuss the implications of Luc Montagnier's recent experiments demonstrating water-mediated, low-frequency electromagnetic emission from bacterial and viral DNA.

> By demonstrating the interaction of living organisms with electromagnetic waves, perhaps including the low-frequency Schumann resonance waves in the Earth's atmosphere, the work has revolutionary implications for biology and our whole understanding of the universe extending the work begun in the 1920s by such figures as Alexander Gurwitsch, who detected ultraviolet radiations from growing plant cells. The Schumann resonance refers to the waves of base frequency 7.83 Hz and its higher harmonics which propagate in the waveguide formed between the surface of the Earth and the ionosphere. In 1952, German atmospheric physicist Winfried Schumann hypothesized that lightning activity would produce such low-frequency waves, and by dividing the circumference of the Earth by the velocity of light, he predicted the approximate frequency later detected.
>
> A remarkable feature of the results with bacteria and viruses is that many of the emitting filtrates are so highly diluted as to have almost no likelihood of containing the original infectious agent or its complete DNA. In order to account for this, as well as the appearance of signals from pure water, Montagnier adopted a hypothesis developed by researchers into the anomalous properties of water, namely, that coherent, polymeric nanostructures are formed in the water. A number of physical studies have reported the formation of long polymers of hydrogen-bonded dipoles in water.
>
> The attempt to reduce the principle of life to something derivable from the laws of chemistry and physics was never very satisfactory. The argument of the vitalists, that an animating principle must be superimposed upon the presumably self evident material substance of living matter, also had its limitations. With the results of Montagnier, we recognize that the principle, *omne vivum ex vivo*, still holds, but only on the condition that we adopt a non-particle conception of life [Hecht, 2011].

"Every person, our consciousness, and our cells live in order to learn. One thing I have noticed—and for which I feel deep gratitude—is synchronicity. Everything I have been part of, all the courses and experiences, are the kind of thing that I have benefitted from later in life. Chance is no accident!"[50]

I think we will enter the nano-era where we can discover a whole new universe—which we wouldn't be able to see without an electron microscope. Not only are our hearts powered by electricity, but actually so is every living cell. Maybe it is not so strange that the Nobel laureate Luc Montagnier found low frequency electromagnetic waves from bacterial DNA sequences.

Our bodies consist of 70 percent water and all body fluids contain water, water that is conductive and that is a solvent in which nourishment can be ionized. Our 100 trillion cells are two thirds water. What is more natural than the idea that our immune system, our memory and our whole consciousness all operate and function with the help of water?

Perhaps life ends (transfers into another dimension) when the electric current has run out within our cells—when the electrons stop moving.

NOTES

1. T. Owe, *Beyond Death*.
2. L.J. Nielsen (ed.), *Livets utveckling* (The Evolution of Life), p. 25.
3. H.P. Yockey, *Information Theory, Evolution and the Origin of Life* (Cambridge: Cambridge University Press, 2005), p. 182.
4. S. Schultz, "Nuts, Bolts of Who We Are," *Princeton Weekly Bulletin*, 1 May 2000 <http://www.princeton.edu/pr/pwb/00/0501/p/brain.shtml> accessed 27 March 2009.
5. M. Adelman, "Computing with DNA," *Scientific American*, August 1998, pp. 54–61.
6. The Nobel Prize in Physiology or Medicine 2002, 7 October 2002 <http://www.nobelprize.org/nobel_prizes/medicine/laureates/2002/press.html>.
7. P. Wilhelmsson, *Lev ung längre* (Live Young Longer), pp. 33, 82. See also L. Hayflick, *How and Why We Age* (New York: Ballantine, 1994), p. xxix.
8. SVT Kunskapskanalen (Swedish Television Knowledge Channel), 21 Jan. 2011.
9. <http://www.nimade.info/vetenskap/2011/01/Vad-ar-en Centriole.html> accessed 22 Nov. 2011.
10. L.J. Nielsen (ed.), *Livets utveckling* (Evolution of Life), p. 27.
11. http://www.halsobygget.se/pjblogg_entry.php?blogg_id=101.
12. http://www.vetenskaphalsa.se/liten-molekyl-med-stor-makt-over-hjarncellernas-ode/.
13. http://www.nature.com/nature/journal/v465/n7296/full/nature08977.html.
14. S. Hameroff, *Ultimate Computing: Biomolecular Consciousness and Nanotechnology* (Amsterdam: Elsevier, 1987).
15. Calleman, *Vårt intelligenta universum* (The Purposeful Universe—How Quantum Theory and Mayan Cosmology Explain the Origin and Evolution of Life), p. 229.
16. L.J. Nielsen (ed.), *Hjärnans Mysterier* (Mysteries of the Brain), p. 109.
17. Private communication with Pim van Lommel, May 2009.
18. Nielsen, "Livets vatten" (Water of Life), *Illustrerad Vetenskap* (*Science Illustrated*), 4/2007.
19. http://www.lsbuac.uk/water/memory.html accessed 30 July 2012.
20. http://olle.reinhammar.org/litteratur/prosa/bioelektronikens_roll_i_mansklig_metabolism (accessed 22 Oct. 2012)
21. J. Tennant, *Healing Is Voltage*. Second edition, p. 60.
22. M. Emoto, *Love Thyself*.
23. <http://www.qedcorp.com/pcr/pcr/vitiello.html> accessed 14 Sept. 2008.
24. M. Enserink, "French Nobelist Escapes 'Intellectual Terror' to Pursue Radical Ideas in China," *Science*, 330, 6012 (24 December 2010), p. 1732 (quoting Luc Montagnier).
25. L. Montagnier, J. Aïssa, S. Ferris, J.-L. Montagnier, C. Lavallée, "Electromagnetic signals are produced by aqueous nanostructures derived from bacterial DNA sequences," *Interdiscip. Sci. Comput. Life Sci.*, 1, 2009, pp. 81–90. L. Montagnier, J. Aissa, E. Del Giudice, C. Lavallee, A. Tedeschi, G. Vitiello, "DNA waves and water," *Journal of Physics Conference Series*, 306, 1 (2011), pp. 12007–12016, arXiv:1012.5166v1 [q-bio.OT].
26. J. Benveniste, et al., "Human basophil degranulation triggered by very dilute antiserum against IgE," *Nature*, 333, 6176 (1988), pp. 816–818.
27. "When to believe the unbelievable," *Nature* 333, 6176 (1988), p. 787.
28. J. Langone, A. Constable, and W. Dowell, "The Water That Lost Its Memory," *Time*, <http://www.time.com/time/magazine/article/0,9171,968080,00html>.
29. Lynne McTaggart, *The Intention Experiment*, p. 52.
30. J. Benveniste o.a., "The molecular signal is not functioning in the absence of 'informed' water," *FASEB Journal*, 1999; 1313:A163.
31. http://www.brt.nu/index.php?option=com_content&task=view&id=1&Itemid=2 (accessed 10 June 2012).
32. I. Ernberg, *Vad är liv i kosmos, i cellen, i människan?* (What is life?) p. 149.
33. Thomas R. Blakeslee, *The Right Brain* (Garden City, NY: Anchor Press/Doubleday, 1980), p. 141.
34. The Silva Method, http//:www.silvametoden.nu (accessed 12 Feb. 2008).

35. For more information on the Silva Method, see http://www.silvaultramind.se/Default.aspx?tabid=86.
36. Bo Kindstrand, Compendium for course in Extended Remote Viewing, Kinnekulle, Sweden, 20–23 November 2003.
37. Lynne McTaggard, *The Field*, p. 88.
38. The Mathematical Language of the Hologram http://www.bibliotecapleyades.net/ciensia/holographicuniverse/holographicuniverse0… (accessed 22 Oct. 2009).
39. Michael Talbot, *The Holographic Universe*, pp. 54–55.
40. Michael Talbot, *The Holographic Universe*, p. 55.
41. Private communication with Karl Pribram, Jan. 2009.
42. J.M. Maldacena, Adv. Theor. Math. Phys. 2, 231–252 (1998).
43. Y. Hyakutake. Preprint available at http://arxiv.org/abs/1311.7526 (2013).
44. M. Hanada, Y. Hyakutake, G. Ishiki, and J. Nishimura. Preprint available at http://arxiv.org/abs/1311.5607 (2013).
45. doi:10.1038/nature.2013.14328
46. F. Backström, "Private Lunar ESP: An Interview with Edgar Mitchell," *Cabinet Magazine*, 5, Winter 2001/02 <http://www.cabinetmagazine.org/issues/5/esp.php> accessed 16 Nov. 2008.
47. A. Kaivararainen <http://web.petrsu.ru/~alexk/> accessed 10 Aug. 2007.
48. <http://sv.wikipedia.org/wiki/EPR-paradoxen> accessed 22 Nov. 2011.
49. B. Moyers, "The Brain and the Immune System," interview with D. Felten in *Healing and the Mind*.
50. J. Cederquist, *Slumpen är ingen tillfällighet* (Chance Is No Accident). See also C.G. Jung, *Mitt liv* (My Life).

REFERENCES

Ader, R., D.L. Felten, N. Cohen, eds. *Psychoneuroimmunology, Part IV: Psychosocial Factors, Stress, Disease and Immunity* (847–931). New York: Academic Press, 1991.
Barret, E.A.M., M.B. Doyle, V.M. Malinski, et al. The relationship among the experience of dying, the experience of paranormal events, and creativity in adults. In E. A. M. Barret (ed.), *Visions of Rogers Science Based Nursing*. New York: National League for Nursing Publication No. 15–2285, 1990.
Becker, R.O. *The Body Electric: Electromagnetism and the Foundation of Life*. New York: Quill, 1985.
Becker, R.O. *Cross Currents: The Perils of Electropollution, the Promise of Electromedicine*. Los Angeles: Jeremy Tarcher, 1990.
Benson, H., and E.M. Stuart. *The Wellness Book*. New York: Simon and Schuster, 1992.
Blackmore, S. "Near-death experiences." In G. Stein, ed. *The Encyclopedia of the Paranormal* (pp. 425–441). Amherst, NY: Prometheus, 1996.
Blakeslee, T.R. *The Right Brain*. Garden City, NY: Anchor Press, 1980.
Bohm, D., and B. Hiley. "The Causal Interpretation of Quantum Theory," in *Science, Order and Creativity*, by D. Bohm and D. Peat. New York: Bantam Books, 1987.
Chapra, F. *The Tao of Physics*. New York: Bantam, 1976.
Corazza, O. *Near-Death Experiences: Exploring the Mind-Body Connection*. London and New York: Routledge, 2008.
Davies, P. *The Mind of God: The Scientific Basis of a Rational World*. New York: Touchstone, 1992.
de Duve, C. *Vital Dust: Life as a Cosmic Imperative*. New York: Basic Books, 1995.
Fenwick, P., and E. Fenwick. *The Art of Dying: A Journey to Elsewhere*. London and New York: Continuum, 2008.
Gleick, J. *Making a New Science*. New York: Penguin, 1987.
Hameroff, S.R. "Fundamentality: Is the conscious mind subtly linked to a basic level of the universe?" *Trends in Cognitive Sciences* 2 (4) (1988):119–127.
Hameroff, S.R. "Quantum computing in microtubules: an intraneural correlate of consciousness?" *Cognitive Studies: Bulletin of the Japanese Cognitive Science Society* 4 (3) 67–92.
Hansen, G.P. "CSICOP and the Skeptics: An Overview." *J Am Soc Psych Res* 86 (1) (1992):19–63.
Hennesley, J.A., P.J. Christenson, R.A. Hardoin, et al. "Premonitions of sudden infant death syndrome: a retrospective case control study." *Pediatr Pulmonol* 16 (1993):393 (abstract).
Henschen. *Klinische und anatomische Beitrage zur Pathologie des Gehirns*. Uppsala: Almquist and Wiksell, 1890, i–vii *Arch f Psychiat* (1925) lxxv: 630.

Hirshberg, C., and M.I. Barasch. *Remarkable Recovery.* New York: Riverhead, 1995.
Hufford, D.J. *The Terror That Comes in the Night.* Pittsburgh: University of Pennsylvania Press, 1982.
Makarec, K., and M.A. Persinger. "Electroencephaleographic validation of temporal lobe signs inventory in a normal population." *J Research in Personality* 24 (1990):323–337.
McMoneagle, J. *Mind Trek: Exploring Consciousness, Time and Space through Remote Viewing.* Charlottesville, VA: Hampton Roads, 1993.
Morgan, H. "Doestoyevsky's epilepsy: A case report and comparison." *Surg Neurol* 33 (1990): 413–416.
Morse, M.L. "Near Death Experiences and Death Related Visions: Implications for the Clinician." *Current Problems in Pediatrics* (Feb. 1994): 55–83.
Morse, M.L., and P. Perry. *Closer to the Light.* New York: Villard, 1990.
Morse, M.L., and V. Neppe. "Near Death Experiences" (letter). *Lancet* (1991) 337–386.
Mullin, S., and W. Penfield. "Illusions of Comparative Interpretation and Emotion." *Archives of Neurology and Psych* 81 (March 1959): 269–285.
Nelson, G.K. "Preliminary study of the EEG of mediums." *Parapsychologica* 4 (1970): 20–45.
Neppe, V.M. "PSI, genetics, and the temporal lobes." *Parapsychological Journal of South Africa* 2 (1981): 35–55.
Neppe, V.M. "The Temporal Lobe and Anomalous Experience." *Parapsychological Journal of South Africa* 5 (1984):1 36–47.
Peirce, P. *Frequency the Power of Personal Vibration.* New York: Simon & Schuster, 2009.
Persinger, M. *The Neuropsychological Bases of God Beliefs.* New York: Praeger, 1987.
Persinger, M.A. "Near-death experiences and ecstasy: A product of the organization of the human brain?" In S. Della Sala, ed., *Mind Myths: Exploring Popular Assumptions About the Mind and Brain* (pp. 85–99). Chichester, England: Wiley, 1999.
Persinger, M.A., and K. Makarec. "Complex partial epileptic signs as continuum from normal epileptics: normative data and clinical populations." *J Clin Psychol* 49 (1993): 33–45.
Peat, D. *Synchronicity: The Bridge Between Mind and Matter.* New York: Bantam, 1987.
Remote viewing. <http://www.fjarrsyn.info/hist.html>.
Sagan, C. *The Demon Haunted World: Science as a Candle in the Darkness.* New York: Ballantine, 1996.
Saver, J.L., and J. Rabin. "The Neural Substrates of Religious Experience." *Journal of Neuropsychiatry* 1977: 498–510.
Schrodinger, E. *What Is Life.* Cambridge: Cambridge University Press, 1994.
Sheldrake, R. *A New Science of Life.* Los Angeles: Tarcher, 1987.
Talbot, M. *The Holographic Universe.* New York: HarperCollins, 1992.
Targ, R., and J. Katra. *Miracles of Mind: Exploring Nonlocal Consciousness and Spiritual Healing.* Novato, CA: New World Library, 1998.
Tiller, W. *Science and Human Transformation.* Walnut Creek, CA: Pavior, 1997.
Tippler, F.J. *The Physics of Immortality.* New York: Anchor, 1994.
van Lommel, P. *Endless Consciousness.* New York: Harper Collins, 2010.
Whinnery, J.E. "Psychophysiological correlates of unconsciousness and near-death experiences." *Journal of Near-Death Studies*, 15 (1997), 231–258.
Whinnery, J.E., and A.M. Whinnery. "Acceleration Induced Loss of Consciousness." *Arch Neurol* 47 (1990): 764–766.
Williams, D. "The structure of emotions reflecting in epileptic experiences." *Brain* 79 (1956): 29–67.
Zukav, G. *The Dancing Wu Li Masters.* New York: Bantam, 1979.

The Non-Local Universe Is the Conscious Universe

MENAS C. KAFATOS, HYEJUNG LEE
and KEUN-HANG SUSAN YANG

Introduction

Today we realize that quantum theory has many profound implications for understanding the nature of consciousness. Consciousness continues to challenge all of science and it is fair to say that, although much progress has been made in the understanding of the brain as a physical object of incredible complexity, not much progress has been achieved in understanding or even accounting for the most elementary subjective experiences. Today, scientists in many polls about what are the two most important and unsolved topics facing science, they respond the nature of the universe and the nature of conscious experience. It turns out that these two profound issues are closely related to each other. As such, what used to be in the domain of philosophy and metaphysics, the origin of the mind and in more general terms the nature of consciousness and how consciousness arises, can now be approached by science. Here we look at these issues and specifically the connection between quantum theory from the microcosm to cosmological scales and consciousness. We rely heavily on previous and forthcoming publications such as Kafatos and Nadeau (2000), Kafatos (2002), and Kafatos (2014).

The issue of consciousness presents a clear embarrassment to modern science. Despite the great successes of theoretical physics, cosmology and quantum field theory, despite the advances of molecular biology, and brain science (cf. Bernroider, 2003; Bernroider and Roy, 2005; Pribram, 1991) to just mention a few of the most successful scientific fields, we still don't have a comprehensive theory of consciousness. It is even worse than that; we seem not to agree on a common framework of terms. Yet, any theoretical advance will have to involve an understanding and development of a suitable set of mathematical languages (Kato, 2001; Kafatos, 2014).

It is now an accepted construct from quantum measurement theory that observational choices in the laboratory determine the context of what is to be observed, we may even state (as Richard Feynman and John A. Wheeler would hold) that without observation, particles don't even have any properties. In the participatory quantum universe, as Wheeler (1981) would say, "no phenomenon is a phenomenon until it is an observed phenomenon" and as such, the observer's choices play a fundamental role. The observer is an integral part of the process of what is to be observed. Quantum theory opened the door to consciousness but did not provide a solution, except hints of what the next steps might be (Kafatos and Nadeau, 2000; Kafatos, Tanzi, and Chopra, 2011).

The Cosmological Realm

Cosmology, like quantum theory, was developed starting in the 20th century. Cosmology is based on Einstein's General Theory of Relativity. Today, there are great efforts to unify these two most successful theories, quantum mechanics and general relativity, basically theories about the world of the very small and the world of the very large but without success. Here we explore how cosmology is tied to large-scale relationships and structures that may be hinting at unifying relationships at deeper levels.

Great progress in ground-based and space-based telescopic observations has revealed a dynamic, evolving universe that fits general relativistic equations. Today, the most accepted theory of the large-scale structure of the universe is Big Bang general relativistic cosmology, having achieved impressive results (Silk, 1989). There are however, problems with Big Bang cosmology as it was originally developed and today more and more adjustments have to be made, first with inflation (Guth, 1981) and more recently with dark matter and dark energy, which appear to contain more than 95 percent of the mass-energy of the universe. As such, one needs to critically examine not only some apparent difficulties in the overall framework but also its underlying assumptions. At the very early stages of such an expanding universe, quantum effects become paramount. Therefore, by studying the very early universe, *both* general relativity and quantum theory have to be brought together. At the Planck time and Planck space, they become one. As the universe evolves, any general relativistic Friedmann-Robertson-Walker Big Bang model, as well as any other non–Big Bang cosmological model, needs to be closely coupled to cosmological observations, and is, therefore, ultimately intricately interwoven with limits imposed by the process of observation itself (Kafatos 1989, 1996, 1998).

These limits in our knowledge, what we may term *horizons of knowledge*, always involve complementary constructs which displace each other in actual applications but *both* are needed to provide a complete picture of the system studied. Complementarity, which forms the cornerstone of the Copenhagen Interpretation (Bohr, 1961) is the first and foremost foundational principle in science (Kafatos, 1999, 2000, 2014). The reason is that, as Bohr first noted, it also applies to biology (Theise and Kafatos, 2013a).

As such, also in cosmology any theoretical model of the universe ultimately involves some horizons of knowledge at some ultimate, faint observational limit (Kafatos and Nadeau, 2000). For example, for the Big Bang theory, as one looks further into space, one is also looking further back into time. And at some point, light (or even neutrinos) cannot be used to observe further back than a certain limit of very large redshifts (where redshift is defined as the relative difference of observed from the emitted light, and consists a surrogate for distance, at least in Big Bang cosmology) to test the Big Bang theory close to the beginning that it predicts.

180 Part II. From the Evolution of Life to DNA

We see that if we follow the paradigm of *non-locality*, we face the paradox that the whole (universe) cannot be studied from its parts, particularly as we approach the "beginning" to an arbitrary limit; to put it in the context of time, the beginning is forever hidden from the pre-sent and our observations carried out in the present. Ultimately, observational limitations themselves prohibit us from verifying cosmological theories to *any prescribed degree of accuracy for any given observational test*. For example, for all practical purposes, galaxy formation under the Big Bang theory runs into verification problems at redshifts z ~ 4–10, close to distances discerned by the Hubble Space Telescope and future space telescopes. There is a simple and obvious, yet often ignored, reason: The nature and evolutionary history of the "standard candles" (such as galaxies) which are used to measure the Hubble expansion flow and the overall structure of the universe cannot be unequivocally determined independently of the cosmology framework itself (Kafatos, 1989).

Cosmological Constraints

In cosmology (Kafatos, 2002), there are a number of observational conclusions about the large scale structure which must be taken into account and, in turn, understand what type of constraints they provide for physical cosmology. Here we provide several known observationally-based truths which have led to some extraordinary theoretical views of the universe.

- It appears that the universe is essentially flat, which is known as the *flatness problem*, where the critical parameter for describing how much the universe deviates from flatness is given by

$$\rho_{crit} = 2 \times 10^{-29} \left(H_0 / 100 \text{km s}^{-1} \text{ Mpc}^{-1} \right)^2 \text{ gr cm}^{-3} \qquad (1)$$

with H_0 being is the present-day value of the Hubble constant (or present rate of expansion). H_0 is defined as $\dot{R}/R$ where R is arbitrarily defined as the scale of the universe. This particular issue is a *problem* because if the universe is close to being flat today, it must have been *exactly* flat close to the time of the Big Bang itself, at least to one part in 10^{50}! The Hubble constant provides an estimate of the *current* expansion rate (current measurements by the Hubble Space Telescope indicate its value is close to 75 km s^{-1} Mpc^{-1}). The usual interpretation of the *flatness problem* proposed in the early '80s is that at some point in the early universe, the universe was in an inflationary state (Guth, 1981), and this state washed away any departures from flatness on time scales of 10^{-35} sec. In more general terms epistemological terms, it would appear that the universe has followed the simplest possible theoretical construct (namely being flat) in its large-scale geometry (Kafatos and Nadeau, 2000). Yet, the flatness issue has not gone away as most of the *observable* matter in the universe fails to provide enough mass-energy to achieve even flatness, requiring unknown forms of *dark matter*, and recently even leading to larger percentages (~ 70 percent or more) of *dark energy*, which provides an accelerating expansion.

- The universe is remarkably homogeneous at large scales as deduced by the so-called microwave background radiation of 2.73 K–T being constant to 1 part in 10^6, and this is known as the *horizon problem*.

In other words, the universe is remarkably homogeneous at large scales as observed by the microwave radiation that fills all space. The inflationary model proposed by Guth and others (cf. Guth, 1981) was developed in its various forms to account for the flatness of the universe and as such it appeared to also solve the horizon problem. This problem is manifesting in terms the apparent homogeneity of the 2.73 K black body radiation seen by NASA's space mission COBE (Smoot, 1996). More recent results by WMAP (Bennett et al., 2012) provide even tighter constraints about the nature of the cosmic microwave background (CMB) radiation.

The observations indicate that although the 2.73 K radiation was, according to theory, emitted $\sim 10^5$ years after the beginning, opposite sides of the sky at that time were out of causal contact, separated by $\sim 10^7$ light years. How could, as observations indicate, the background be so homogeneous if no information could travel over such large distances as the universe was expanding? This makes it rather obvious why it is a *horizon* problem. To make matters worst, other correlations in the large-scale structure of the universe exist such as very large structures in the distribution of matter (Geller and Huchra, 1989), extending in many cases over hundreds of millions of light years. In fact, these structures may be manifesting at all scales, all the way to the universe itself.

- The Cosmological constant "coincidence" with an improbable coincidence of 10^{120}. As it is, recent observations indicate a cosmological constant might be needed in a flat universe framework to account for an accelerating expansion, manifesting as dark energy. This issue is known as the *Cosmological constant problem*.

In taking the above three considerations into account, and although the universe appears to be *close* to a flat, Euclidean, Einstein–de Sitter state as indicated from the fact that the density is close to closure, it is still not beyond doubt that we know what the geometry of the universe is today; *exactly* flat (as inflation requires); open (yielding a forever-expanding, negatively curved space-time); or closed (yielding a maximum expansion, a positively curved space-time and a final *big crunch*); or maybe even open and forever accelerating, which implies a non-zero cosmological constant as recent observations of distant Type I supernova, seem to indicate.

The cosmological constant was first introduced by Einstein to counter gravity and produce a closed, stable or static universe, his preferred model—it essentially acts as negative gravity. It was later abandoned by Einstein himself when observations by Hubble and others indicated an expanding universe, although we note that Hubble himself was careful to point out that the interpretation in terms of Doppler redshifts was not the only possibility for the observed redshifts. The cosmological constant has been recently re-introduced by cosmologists as the present observations of distant Type I supernovae seem to be indicating (if taken at face value ,which really means that the distant supernovae were the same as the ones observed nearby) that the universe not only is expanding, but it is also accelerating in its expansion! Observations indicate that baryons (and luminous matter) contribute at most 0.05 or less of the closure density at present.

As such, if one insists on exact flatness of the universe, one needs to introduce unknown forms of dark matter and dark energy for the other 95 percent, exotic forms that hitherto have evaded observational verification. In other words, the dilemma we face is that if we insist on a flat universe, this forces us to in turn adopt increasingly, complex and unknown physics, literally, the *Big Bang begets unknown physics*. The mathematical model is relatively simple in its assumptions but the underlying physics required to maintain have increasingly become complex and even unknown. And we also note again that the Big Bang itself would be completely unobserved and subject to unknown quantum gravity unification, which *must* at some point be brought in. The current epistemological dilemma does not seem to bother the majority of astrophysicists, as Big Bang is so ingrained as the orthodox view, perhaps because of other metaphysical reasons, that we are ready to accept unknown physics in order to preserve it. In some ways this reminds us of the historical Ptolemaic universe situation: To keep the orbits of the planets circular in a geocentric universe (which was also back then considered as the simplest and most natural, but as it turned out, wrong universe), required an increasing amount of complexity, more and more epicycles.

In going beyond the previous considerations and perhaps even more remarkably, the universe seems extremely fined tuned (cf. Kafatos, 1998). Eddington (1931, 1939) and Dirac (1937, 1938) noticed that certain "coincidences" in dimensionless ratios involving physical quantities can be found. These ratios link microscopic to macroscopic quantities (cf. Kafatos, 1998).

- For example, the ratio of the electric force to gravitational force (presumably a constant), is a large number

$$e^2 / G m_e m_p \sim 10^{40} \qquad (2)$$

- A number that yields the same large ratio is the ratio of the observable size of the universe (presumably changing in an expanding universe) to the size of an elementary particle, and this last ratio is surprisingly close to the first number, or

$$R / (e^2 / m_e c^2) \sim 10^{40} \qquad (3)$$

Dirac argued that it is hard to imagine that two very large and seemingly unrelated numbers would turn out to be so close to each other. The two numbers, he argued, *must* therefore be related. The problem though is that in (3) the numerator is changing as the universe expands while (2) is presumably constant. Why should two such large numbers, one variable and the other not, turn out to be so close to each other? Dirac's (1937) *Large Number Hypothesis* states that the fact that the two ratios in (2) and (3) are equal is not a mere coincidence. He and others (cf. Dyson, 1972) have attempted to account for the apparent equality between (2) and (3) by assuming that constants such as the gravitational constant itself may be varying. We will explore even more generalized scenarios of that flavor in the next section.

- For now, it is worth noting that other ratios such as the ratio of an elementary particle to the Planck length,

$$\frac{e^2 / m_e c^2}{(\hbar G / c^3)^{1/2}} \sim 10^{20} \qquad (4)$$

and even larger numbers such as the "Eddington's number," ~2 × 10,^{79} etc., exist as well as that "harmonic" numbers can be constructed from them (Harrison, 1981), e.g., Eddington's number is approximately equal to the square root of (2) or (3).

These "coincidences" may be indicating the existence of some deep, underlying unity, a *generalized non-locality beyond space and time, perhaps even involving all physical and even biological theories,* manifested in the fundamental constants and linking the microcosm to the macrocosm.

- We have to note that other, less traditional ways, perhaps even more radical views than ours, such as the Anthropic Principle (Barrow and Tipler, 1986) have been proposed to account for the above fine tuning properties of the universe. The recent popularity of the multiverse (Tegmark, 2003) and M-Theory, based on string theory, have not resolved the basic issue of unification of physics with biology and consciousness.

The Universe Is Extremely Fined Tuned

To recapitulate,

- Ratio of the electric force to gravitational force

$$e^2 / G m_e m_p \sim 10^{40}$$

- Ratio of the observable size of the universe (presumably changing) to the size of an elementary particle is also a large number, surprisingly close to the first number, or

$$R/(e^2 / m_e c^2) \sim 10^{40}.$$

These two relations yield what is known as Dirac's *Large Number Hypothesis*

- Ratio of an elementary particle to the Planck length,

$$\frac{e^2 / m_e c^2}{(\hbar G / c^3)^{1/2}} \sim 10^{20}$$

- Large numbers such as "Eddington's number," ~2 × 10^{79}, etc., exist. "Harmonic" numbers can be constructed from them, e.g., Eddington's number is approximately equal to the square root of Dirac's relations.

Although it is possible to search for solution of the above dilemmas in terms of a future physics or even some form of Anthropic Principle or multiverse, we believe they point to an underlying connectedness; in other words, it is possible to invoke a *generalized non-locality*, akin to quantum non-locality, as the underlying principle of the cosmos. However, more on this will follow below.

The Arrow of Time as a Measurement of Change— An Alternate View Involving Scale-Invariance

Kafatos, Roy and Amoroso (2000) and Kafatos, Roy and Roy (2005) have shown that one may use these so called coincidences from a completely different point of view. They can be re-interpreted and generalized in terms of relationships linking the masses of elementary particles as well as the total number of nucleons in the universe (or Eddington's number) to other fundamental "constants" such as the gravitational constant, the charge of the electron, Planck's constant and the speed of light. Kafatos et al. concluded that scale-invariant relationships result, such as all lengths are then proportional to the scale of the universe R, etc. The arrow of time results as these fundamental "constants" change (e.g., Eddington's number varies from $N_p \to 1$ at some initial state which could be suitably identified as the time of Big Bang, but not necessarily, to $\to 10^{80}$, a time suitably identified as the present, but not necessarily, etc.). *In this view, time is not fundamental, change is. Time (perhaps an illusion) arises as change occurs.*

Specifically, one may adopt Weinberg's relationship which in one of its forms is

$$m_e \sim \left(\frac{\hbar e^2 H_0}{(8\pi)^3 G c^2} \right)^{1/3} \quad (5)$$

where m_e is the electron mass, H_0 is the (present) Hubble constant and the other parameters in (5) are the usual physical constants. Weinberg's relation can be shown to be equivalent to Dirac's relationships (2) and (3), when the latter are equated to each other (Kafatos, Roy and Roy, 2005). We can then obtain a relationship linking the speed of light c to the rate of change of the scale of the universe, R, the latter being arbitrary (scale invariance). In fact, the proportionality factor is ~ 1 if one substitutes for values of fundamental quantities like the present number of particles in the universe, etc. The next step is to assume that the relationship linking c and R is an identity, i.e., $c \equiv \dot{R}$ (for example, at the Planck time, or the *beginning*, one observes that this relationship still holds if the ratios of all masses $\to 1$ and the number of particles also $\to 1$). As such, in this picture *all* the fundamental constants are changing and not some, as was assumed in past works. It is interesting that, recently, the possibility that the cosmological constant Λ itself might be changing has been suggested.

As such, what is suggested here as a scale-invariant framework of the cosmos is a natural extension of previous ideas. Therefore, as N_p changes from an initial value of 1 to the present value of 10^{80} ($1 \to 10^{80}$), the universe would *be appearing to be evolving to an observer inside it or the arrow of time can be introduced as an apparent reality.* We note that the outcomes of this prescription are not just that an arrow of time is introduced and the mysterious coincidences of Dirac and Eddington now can be understood as scale-invariant relationships linking the microcosm to the macrocosm; but in addition, all scales are linked to each other and what one calls, e.g., *fundamental length*, etc., is purely a convention.

The existence of *horizons of knowledge* in cosmology (Kafatos and Nadeau, 2000; Theise and Kafatos, 2013a), indicate that as a horizon is approached, ambiguity as to a particular unique view of the universe applying as a complete framework sets in. At the *initial time*, if we set the conditions like c ≡ Ṙ, as proposed by Kafatos, Roy and Roy (2005), we can take as axiomatic the numerical relations connecting the microcosm and the macrocosm. In other words, after setting c ≡ Ṙ, at the initial Planck time, which could be taken to mean some sort of "beginning," this relationship remains invariant even at the present universe. This relation is a type of scaling law at the cosmological scale and connects the microcosm and the macrocosm. Time is not fundamental, change is. And the agent of change is light speed. Or to put it more fundamentally, *light connects everything in the universe*.

This evolutionary universe is totally equivalent to a Big Bang cosmos. In such views, if one wants to insist that there is expansion of the Universe, R itself is changing and more specifically, then the fundamental constants like G, ℏ, and c may also *all* vary with time. Telling the difference between an evolving universe with constant "constants" and a universe that *appears to be evolving* as the "constants" evolve, may prove impossible. *They are complementary views.*

Due to the variation of these fundamental constants, N_p will also be changing from the initial value 1. This implies that more and more particles will be created due to expansion of the universe. So an observer who is inside the universe will instead see an arrow of time and evolutionary universe. As $N_p \to 10^{80}$, which is the present number of nucleons in the observable universe, the fundamental constants achieve their present values. Therefore, the arrow of time can be related to a kind of complementarily between two constructs, i.e., the universal constants are constant, on the one hand; and constants are changing, on the other hand. In the latter case, *the observer is brought in fundamentally*, and as such it is connected to conscious observations. *Time itself derives from consciousness.*

The Non-Local Universe

In the generalized complementarity framework (Kafatos and Nadeau, 1990, 2000; Nadeau and Kafatos 1999; Theise and Kafatos, 2013a), complementary constructs need to be considered to formulate a complete picture of a scientific field under examination (e.g., the large-scale structure of the universe) as a horizon of knowledge is approached. This means that as a horizon is approached, ambiguity as to a unique view of the universe sets in. It was precisely these circumstances that apply at the quantum level, which prompted Bohr to affirm that complementary constructs should be employed (Bohr, 1961). Moreover, the remarkable correlations exhibited at cosmological scales are reminiscent of Bell-type quantum correlations (Bell 1964) that were so abhorrent to Einstein (Einstein, Podolsky and Rosen, 1935—the so-called EPR thought experiment) and yet confirmed by the Aspect, et al. (1982) and similarly by the Gisin and his team (Zbinden, et al., 2001) experiments.

Kafatos (1989) and Roy and Kafatos (1999) proposed that Bell-type correlations would be pervasive in the early universe arising from the common electron-positron annihilations—binary processes involving Compton scattering of the resultant gamma-ray photons with electrons would produce N-type correlations. In these conditions, the outcome of the cascade of processes (even in the absence of observers) would produce

186 Part II. From the Evolution of Life to DNA

space-like correlations among the original entangled photons. Kafatos and Nadeau (1990, 2000) and Kafatos (1998) have in turn proposed three types of non-localities: Spatial or Type I non-locality occurs when 2 quanta (such as photons) remain entangled at all scales across space-like separated regions, even over cosmological scales (fig. 1).

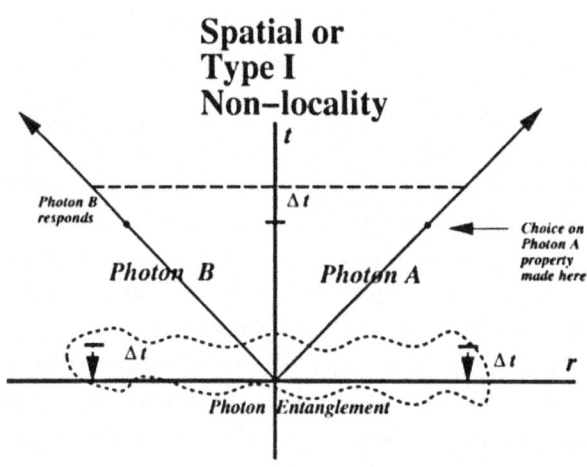

Figure 1, top: Experiment Testing Bell's Inequality. Figure 2, bottom: Delayed-choice Experiment.

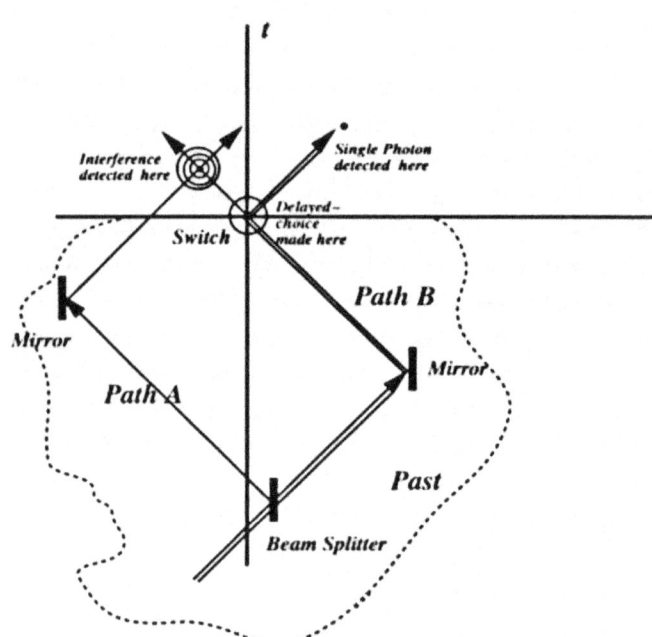

Temporal or Type II non-locality (or Wheeler's *Delayed Choice Experiment*) occurs in situations where the path that a photon follows is not determined until a delayed choice is made. (fig. 2)

In some strange sense, the past is brought together (in the sense that the path is not determined) by the experimental choice. This non-locality confirmed in the laboratory could also occur over cosmological distances (Wheeler 1981). Type III non-locality (Kafatos and Nadeau, 1990, 2000) represents the unified whole of space-time revealed in its complementary aspects as the unity of space (Type I) and the unity of time (Type II non-locality). It exists *outside* the framework of space and time and cannot, therefore, be discerned by the scientific method although its existence is *implied*. Type III non-locality is the real non-locality, unifying Type I and Type II.

Consciousness and Unification

To proceed towards unification, we must ultimately rely on mathematics. We propose that through utilizing the fundamental role of mathematics, we can create a *theoretical framework* of how consciousness operates in the universe. So far we saw that complementarity and recursion apply across vast numbers of scales. The mathematical framework we are searching may become a blueprint to understand consciousness or to at least to begin to develop the right path towards that understanding.

We emphasize that any mathematical framework cannot say anything about the ontology (which means nature of being) of consciousness. This, we believe, is the root of the problem of a lot of confusion in the field of consciousness. What consciousness *is* can only be directly experienced. However, *how* consciousness operates (rather than what is) can be put into a mathematical framework. The hypothesis as emphasized by Kafatos, Tanzi and Chopra (2011) is that *universal Consciousness is the foundation of the Universe and, as such, the Universe itself is steeped in Consciousness* (where the capital C refers to universal, rather than individual—including human, consciousness). This hypothesis not only resolves a host of problems in consciousness studies but may also be the next stage of development of a unified quantum-gravity based physical theory. The alternatives lead to a series of never-ending loops of assumptions and, ultimately, a meaningless, infinite number of parallel universes, most of them devoid of life and conscious awareness. Such views are totally unpalatable and increasingly non-converging and non-consistent, even though attractive because of the imagination they inspire. Imagine almost infinite number of universes with their own physical laws, unknown physical laws we may add. But imagination cannot run afoul and leave science behind.

In our view, the most scientific view may indeed turn out to be the conscious universe. *Non-locality is its hallmark*. It operates under three foundation principles: *Complementarity, recursion, and sentience*. Theise and Kafatos (2013b) have provided reasonable arguments that sentience applies at all scales and for all objects in the universe. The mathematical framework of consciousness proposed here and in Kafatos (2014) must begin from the three foundational principles in a non-local unity of everything. In particular, the framework has to accommodate the qualitative nature of *qualia*, the units of subjective experience (Kafatos, 2014). Qualia, which is Latin for qualities, are the everyday qualities of experience, the sense of color red, a thought in the mind, an experience of feeling (Chopra, Kafatos and Tanzi, 2012, 2013).

Consciousness operates through qualia, by undergoing limitations of its infinite, non-local entangled nature through the operations of the three principles. Now this unified view is not just a challenge for current science. It points to the direction of a need to marvel at the universe as we proceed towards unification. Today, most workers in the consciousness field identify consciousness with neuro processes in the brain, i.e., they presume that consciousness is a derivative of neurophysical processes.

Consciousness operates in living systems and such biological structures are also tied to the quantum vacuum, as elementary particles are (Grandpierre and Kafatos, 2013). Yet, it manifests physical effects and can be put in some ways to information theory (Grandpierre, et al., 2013). We note that there must be two clear choices for consciousness: Either human beings alone are conscious, or there is consciousness everywhere. Unification in an ultimate sense may even combine conscious awareness in the brain, gravity and quantum theory, which would indeed tie brain processes to the fundamental structure of the universe (e.g., Penrose, 1994; Hameroff and Penrose, 1996a, 1996b; Hameroff and Penrose, 2014).

Conventional neuroscience takes it for granted that conscious awareness is an epiphenomenon of brain activity, a product of physical processes (called *physicalism*). However, as Kafatos and Nadeau discussed in the *Conscious Universe* more than 20 years ago, the measurement problem in quantum theory puts the observer (of everything in the physical universe) at the center of reality. If the universe itself is conscious, the dichotomy of human-based versus universal Consciousness is resolved—in fact, it never existed. Equating consciousness with processes in the human brain is just not tenable. We know from experience that higher forms of life, primates, dolphins, whales, to name a few species, have brains similar to humans. Are they conscious? Or are they not? At what point do we stop? With domesticated animals? With birds? With all animals? What about cellular life?

Theise and Kafatos (2013b) follow the more reasonable conjecture, that *sentience is everywhere*. How do newborn mammals know how to be attached to their mother? Perhaps through some sort of entanglement. How do flocks of migratory birds know how to travel thousands of miles and find the exact location where they gather? Perhaps through quantum effects. If we are to have a different theory for each animate behavior, we will not have a coherent picture of what life is. How do electrons in a solid find themselves in the most appropriate configurations? It is much simpler and rational to put forward the view that sentience imbues everything in the universe, and that conscious awareness evolves in higher biological structures but is *implied* everywhere through sentience. Living entities would then connected at some fundamental level and that so-called "inanimate" objects would still have a fundamental way to respond to their environment.

The question where consciousness resides leads to many other questions about defining it, seeing how we can measure it "objectively." Ultimately, *what* is consciousness after all? What are the limits of human consciousness? When and where does it break down? In studying human consciousness, neuronal disorders or the limits of human consciousness, along with computer modeling, can give us important information and hints (cf. Yang, Franaszczuk, and Bergey, 2003, 2005). In neuroscience research, there are many different types of neuronal disorders such as Alzheimer's, Parkinson's disease, epilepsy, autism, etc., which are widely being studied. Neuroscientists know that if you look at those neuronal disorders, there are many phenomenal similarities. What does that tell us? We think perhaps it tells us that they are all related in some fundamental way, or we are talking about one basic issue using many different terms since we are dealing with an extremely complex system like the brain.

Science has struggled but it is clear we have to enlarge science itself to accommodate physics, biology and consciousness itself. Did consciousness arise after billions of years of evolution of the universe on a planet far from the center of the Milky Way galaxy called Earth? The question of what consciousness is forms the most important questions in today's world. In fact, it always was the most important question, but now a plethora of fundamental problems that may spell the end of human civilization require that we seriously take a look at who we are and how we fit in the scheme of existence. We must take a serious look at how our own consciousness may be collectively driving us to a point of no return. Asking one question after another relating to consciousness quickly leads to a host of interrelated questions, all equally hard to grasp within the confines of present-day science. The whole issue was rapidly put into the forefront by the development of quantum theory, examined here. In following its development and moving to the next stage of evolution of science, we will encounter several marvels. *These marvels are the core characteristics of the conscious universe.*

In classical physics and in relativity theory, space and time or four-dimensional space-time are taken as given, as the underlying fabric of the universe. Even in quantum theory this fabric is assumed. Yet quantum theory and its various interpretations (whether the two main schools, the Copenhagen Interpretation [C-I]; the de Broglie–Bohm formalism; or other theoretical models such as the many worlds interpretation, etc.) admit a non-locality that does not exist in classical theories. This non-locality (or to be more exact non-localities, as there are several of them, e.g., Chiao, 2002) is an inescapable consequence as shown by the beautiful experiments of Aspect and co-workers and Gisin and co-workers testing Bell's inequalities (cf. Zbinden et al., 2001), developments that originated with Einstein's objections as revealed in the Einstein-Podolsky-Rosen (1935) thought experiment. Arguments may still continue between physicists about the "reality" of the wave function or the "reality" of the pilot wave or whether, independent of observers, the world is real. Nevertheless, the very nature of wave phenomena, which provide the foundation of quantum theory (whether one in C-I accepts the complementary wave aspect of quanta; or one accepts the reality of pilot-waves in the Bohm theory) make, in some way, the whole issue of reality somewhat secondary and the issue of non-locality primary (cf. Nadeau and Kafatos, 1999). What is implied is a connectivity "beneath" space-time, an underlying reality that physics can say little about be-cause physics operates in space-time, yet physics cannot deny it. In fact, even if one were to continue accepting the fundamental nature of space-time, physics and space-time eventually break down at the Planck scale. *Whatever reality may be, it has to be non-local.* This is the first marvel of the universe.

Quantum theory has also shown that the act of observation is fundamental. Again, whether the wave function is real or not; whether pilot waves exist or not, no one can deny that quantum theory has opened the door to, in the words of John Archibald Wheeler (1981), a "participatory universe." Maybe quanta, as C-I holds, do not possess pre-determined values of physical quantities such as spin until an experimental choice is made; maybe they do, as de Broglie, Einstein, Schrödinger and Bohm would hold (holding on to *local realism*). The very debate illustrates that quantum theory is unlike classical theories. In some way quantum theory has opened the door to the issue of consciousness, without though addressing the issue directly. *Whatever reality may be, it has to be participatory.* This is the second marvel of the universe.

If quantum theory is relevant to consciousness (Kafatos, Tanzi, and Chopra, 2011), quantum theory may then be *very* relevant to brain processes (cf. Pribram, 1991; Stapp, 1993; Penrose, 1994; Roy and Kafatos, 1999; Bernroider and Roy, 2005; Hameroff and Penrose, 2014) and specific sites of the collapse of the wave function may be identified in microtubules (Hameroff and Penrose, 1996a, 1996b, 2014). Roy and Kafatos (2004) have studied the possibility that an anatomical structure of the brain permits one to assign geometrical notions like a distance function as well as a Hilbert space structure.

More specifically, the very anatomical structure of the brain permits one to define a statistical distance between the cluster, or columns of oriented neurons. These oriented neurons act like polarizing filters in optics. Under certain conditions this kind of statistical distance gives rise to Hilbert space structure. These filters can be used to explain the motor functioning as well as the cognitive activities of the cerebellum (Roy and Kafatos, 1999). They proposed a generalized complementarity principle in order to integrate these two types of mutually exclusive behaviors of the cerebellum.

Taking the idea of fundamental principles further, a set of principles like complementarity, non-locality, self-similarity, etc., which can describe all levels of conscious and unconscious activities have been proposed (cf. Kafatos, 1999; Kafatos and Kafatou, 1991; Kafatos and Nadeau, 2000; Drăgănescu and Kafatos, 1999, 2001; Struppa, et al., 2002; Kafatos, Roy, and Drăgănescu, 2003). However tempting it is simulating certain function of the brain, the brain is *not* a computer, and consciousness cannot be reduced to Turing machines (cf. Von Neumann, 1958; Penrose, 1994).

Scientists in general assume that certain inherent principles exist—otherwise the universe would be chaotic and not subject to description. We now can make this assumption more precise: It is possible to utilize the mathematical category theory formalism which is shown (Kato and Struppa, 1999a, 1999b; Kato, 2001; Drăgănescu 2001a, 2001b; Struppa, et al., 2002) to be compatible with the above foundational principles and applicable to all levels of conscious and unconscious activities. Through the most fundamental language of mathematics, category theory, one can identify fundamental principles which may indeed be the "fundamental" underlying reality. The universe does indeed obey a mathematical approach but the mathematics is much more generalized than ordinary mathematics (e.g., second order partial differential equations used in dynamics, etc.). Quantum phenomena, life processes as well as conscious processes may adhere to these fundamental principles: Complementarity, recursion and sentience. For example, complementarity in C-I is a case of a much more general principle of complementarity manifesting in other realms, such as cerebellum processes, etc. As such, the fundamental role of these three principles reminds us of the ancient Hermetic approach and Plato's Ideas. These principles, similarly to Plato's Ideas, *are embedded in the very fabric of the universe* (Drăgănescu and Kafatos, 1999; Kafatos, 2000; Kafatos, 2014). Hameroff and Penrose (2014) hold a similar view.

Consciousness itself may be impossible to define in precise terms, as an object, since consciousness is fundamentally holistic, non-divisible and always referring to the subject. Nevertheless, the generalized principles describe aspects of consciousness. Since the same principles are underlying the physical universe, one may speak of the *universe as conscious* (Kafatos and Kafatou, 1991; Kafatos and Nadeau, 2000; Kafatos 2000; Kafatos, Tanzi and Chopra, 2011; Kafatos, 2014). The principles not being physical objects, point to an underlying sub-stratum that is noetic or composed of fundamental consciousness. By its very nature, it may be indescribable in the ordinary sense of object-subject scientific descriptions. *Whatever reality may be, it is conscious.* Sentience (sensing of itself and the environment) is the hallmark of the conscious universe. This is the third marvel of the universe.

Hints to the underlying generalized non-locality may exist not just in the microcosm and at laboratory scales as shown by the Aspect and Gisin experiments. They may also exist in the large scale structure of the universe. The universe itself also reveals order and amazing coincidences (Dirac, 1935; Kafatos, 1998) as well as structures and relationships that extend over 100 orders of magnitude as revealed in the Universal Diagrams (Kafatos, 1998: Kafatos and Nadeau, 2000). If fundamental principles operate at all levels, if the universe is indeed extremely finely tuned, then an undeniable order and precise design are implicit. *Whatever reality may be, it is by design.* But this design is not an external creation. It is self-design, and guides the self-evolution of the universe, *from the inside*. This is the fourth marvel of the universe.

One can deduce that a more general approach than ordinary mathematical physical theory is needed if we are to go beyond the apparent limits of modern science. The seductiveness that somehow the universe is completely knowable has to give way to a new approach that embraces humility. This humility exists in all perennial philosophies and is an integral part of the human facing the Divine (but unfortunately not the way religion is sometimes practiced). Quantum theory has shown that the indescribable as revealed in the uncertainty theory and the mysterious "waviness" are always present, even though quantum theory *describes* physical process. *Whatever reality may be, it is both describable and indescribable.* Complementarity showed us that the universe is paradoxical. This is the fifth marvel of the universe.

Kafatos and Drăgănescu (2001) proposed an integrative approach for science. This approach will go beyond ordinary structural science. It will include phenomenological approaches. Integrative science has been emerging for some time now, in fact ever since the quantum paradoxes forced us into admitting that new approaches are needed. Integrative science will be the only hope to understand the nature of life, mind and consciousness. It can be shown (cf. Kafatos and Kafatou, 1991) that Eastern perennial philosophies, particularly Vedanta and Shaivism are complete monistic systems dealing with the nature of reality and Fundamental Consciousness. It is proposed that integrative science could be guided by perennial statements in revealed philosophies. In humility, it will accept the five marvels of the universe. The philosophy of science will become the *philosophy of integrative science*, thus returning philosophy to its original primacy as it was in both the East and the West.

As such, the future *society of consciousness*, that we believe will follow the present-day society of information and knowledge, and the new *Science of Consciousness* will be possible only when a well-developed integrative and interdisciplinary science occurs, which will bring new levels of deep knowledge on the nature of life, brain, mind, consciousness and Fundamental Consciousness itself. In approaching the issue of Fundamental Consciousness, the new integrative science will include statements and insights of perennial philosophies, particularly from the East. This very volume is a manifestation of the emergence of integrative science.

This work is dedicated to Mihai Drăgănescu who played such an important role in the development of many ideas presented here. We have listed many of his works here. We will remember him forever.

References and Further Reading

Aspect, A., Grangier, P., and Roger, G. (1982). *Phys. Rev. Lett.* 49, 91.
Beck, F., and Eccles, J.C. (1992). "Quantum aspects of the brain activity and the role of Consciousness." *Proceedings of the National Academy of Science*, 89, 11357–11361.

Bennett, C.L., et al. (2012). "Nine-Year Wilkinson Microwave Anisotropy Probe (WMAP) Observations: Final Maps and Results." arcXiv:1212.5225 [astro-ph.CO].
Bernroider, G. (2003). "Dimensional Analysis of Neurophysical Processes Related to Mentation." http://www.consciousness.arizona.edu/quantum-mind2/.
Bernroider, G., and Roy, S. (2005). "Quantum entanglement of K ions, multiple channel states and the role of noise in the brain," *SPIE* 5841–29, 205–14.
Bohr, N. (1961). *Atomic Theory and the Description of Nature*, 4, 34. London: Cambridge University Press.
Chauvet, G.A. (1993). *J. Math. Biol.* 31, 771–95.
Chopra, D., Kafatos, M.C., and Tanzi, R.E. (2012, 2013). "From Quanta to Qualia: The Mystery of Reality (Part 1, 2, 3, 4)," http://www.sfgate.com/search/?action=search&channel=columnists percent2Fchopra &search=1&fi rstRequest=1&query=opinion percent2Fchopra&x=0&y=0&searchindex=property
Dirac, P.A.M. (1937). *Nature* 139, 323.
Dirac, P.A.M. (1938). *Proc. Royal Soc.*, A165, 199.
Drăgănescu, M. (1979/1979), "The Depths of Existence," published in English, 1997, on the Web: http://www.racai.ro/books/doe (translation of the Romanian edition "Profunzimile lumii materiale," Bucharest, 1979).
Drăgănescu, M. (1990). *Informatia materiei* (Information of matter). Bucharest.
Drăgănescu, M. (1993). "Principes d'une science structurale-phénoménologique." *Bulletin de la Classe des Lettres et des Sciences Morales et Politiques*. Academie Royale de Belgique, 6e série, Tome IV, 7–12, pp. 255–311, 1993.
Drăgănescu, M. (1996). "L'universalité ontologique de l'information," préface et notes par Yves Kodratoff, prof., Université de Paris-Sud, Directeur de recherche au CNRS, Bucharest, Editura Academiei Române.
Drăgănescu, M. (1998a). "Structural-phenomenological theories in Europe and USA." Paper presented at the workshop *Convergences*, 1998.
Drăgănescu, M. (1998b). "Constiinta fundamentala a existentei (The Fundamental Consciouness of Existence)," *Academica*, ianuarie 1998, pp. 20–21 (p. I-a), February 1998, p. 20 (p. II-a), March 1998, p. III-a, pp. 28–29.
Drăgănescu, M. (1998c). "Taylor's Bridge Across the Explanatory Gap and Its Extension." *Consciousness and Cognition* 7, 1998, pp.165–168.
Drăgănescu, M. (1998d). *Noesis* XXIII, 87.
Drăgănescu, M. (2000a). "The Frontiers of Science and Self-Organization." Comm. at the IV-th Conference *Structural-Phenomenological Modeling*, Academia Romana.
Drăgănescu, M. (2001a). "Automorphisms in the phenomenological domains." Published by Proceedings of the Romanian Academy, Series A, 2, No.1. Also at http://www.racai.ro/~dragam.
Drăgănescu, M. (2001b). "Some results in the theory of phenomenological categories." Communication at the Vth Conference on structural-phenomenological modeling; categories and functors for modeling reality; inductive reasoning. Romanian Academy, Bucharest, June 14–15, 2001, *Noesis*, XXVI.
Drăgănescu, M., and Kafatos, M. (1999). "Generalized Foundational Principles in the Philosophy of Science." *The Noetic Journal*, 2, No. 4, October 1999, pp. 341–350; published also in the volume *Science and the Primacy of Consciousness: Intimation of a 21st Century Revolution*, pp. 86–99. Eds. Richard L. Amoroso, et al. Orinda: The Noetic Press (2000).
Drăgănescu, M., and Kafatos, M. (2000a). In *Consciousness in Science and Philosophy*, Charleston, IL.
Drăgănescu M., and Kafatos, M. (2001). *The Philosophy of Integrative Science*. eBook (Microsoft Reader format), Academy of Scientists-Romania.
Dyson, F.J. (1972). In *Aspects of Quantum Theory*. Eds. A. Salam and E.P. Wigner. Cambridge: Cambridge University Press.
Eddington, A.S. (1931). *M.N.R.A.S.* 91, 412.
Eddington, A.S. (1939). *The Philosophy of Physical Science*. Cambridge: Cambridge University Press.
Einstein, A., Podolsky, B., and Rosen, N. (1935). *Phys. Rev.* 47, 777. Geller, M.J., and Huchra, J. (1989). *Science* 246, 897.
Grandpierre, A., and Kafatos, M. (2012), "Biological Autonomy," *Philosophy Study* 2 (9), 631– 649.
Grandpierre, A., and Kafatos, M. (2013). "Genuine Biological Autonomy: How Can the Spooky Finger of Mind Play on the Physical Keyboard of the Brain?" Chapter 9, *An Anthology of Philosophical Studies*, Vol. 7. P. Hanna, editor. Athens Institute for Education and Research 2013, pp. 83–98.
Grandpierre, A., Chopra, D., Murali Doraiswamy, P., Tanzi, R., and Kafatos, M.C. (2013). "A Mutidisciplinary Approach to Mind and Consciousness." *NeuroQuantology* 11, No. 4, 607–617.

Guth, A. (1981). *Phys. Rev. D.*, 23, 347.
Hameroff, S.R., and Penrose, R. (1996a). "Orchestrated reduction of quantum coherence in brain microtubules: A model for consciousness." In *Toward a Science of Consciousness: The First Tucson Discussions and Debates*, S.R. Hameroff and A.C. Scott Kaszniak, eds., 507–540, Cambridge, MA: MIT Press, 507–540. Also published in *Mathematics and Computers in Simulation* 40 (1996) 453–480.
Hameroff, S.R., and Penrose, R. (1996b). "Conscious events as orchestrated spacetime selections." *Journal of Consciousness Studies*, 3(1), 36–53.
Hameroff, S., and Penrose, R. (2014). "Consciousness in the Universe: A Review of the 'Orch OR' Theory" (in press).
Harrison, E.R. (1981). *Cosmology: The Science of the Universe*. Cambridge: Cambridge University Press, 329.
Hubel, D. (1995). *Eye, Brain and Vision*. New York: Scientific American Library.
Kafatos, M. (1986). *Astrophysics of Brown Dwarfs*. Eds. M. Kafatos, R.S. Harrington, and S.P. Maran. Cambridge: Cambridge University Press.
Kafatos, M. (1989). In *Bell's Theorem, Quantum Theory and Conceptions of the Universe*. Ed. M. Kafatos. Dordrecht: Kluwer Academic Publishers, 195.
Kafatos, M. (1996). In *Examining the Big Bang and Diffuse Background Radiations*. Ed. M. Kafatos and Y. Kondo. Dordrecht: Kluwer Academic Publishers, 431.
Kafatos, M. (1998). In *Causality and Locality in Modern Physics*. Ed. G. Hunter, et al. Dordrecht: Kluwer Academic Publishers, 29.
Kafatos, M. (1999). "Non-locality, Foundational Principles and Consciousness." *The Noetic Journal*, 2, 21–27.
Kafatos, M. (2000). "Cosmological, Quantum and Underlying Principles: Clues to the Fundamental Role of Consciousness in the Universe." Communication, the IVth Conference on Structural-phenomenological Modeling, Romanian Academy, Bucharest, 20–21 June 2000, *Noesis*, XXV, 2000.
Kafatos, M. (2002). "Non-locality, Consciousness and the Emerging New Science." The Science of Non-locality and Eastern Approaches to Ultimate Reality, Jongny-sur-Vevey, Switzerland, 21–23 June 2002.
Kafatos, M. (2011). "The Science of Wholeness." In *Analecta Husserliana*. T. Tymieniecka and A. Grandpierre (eds.). Springer Science, Business Media, B.V.
Kafatos, M. (2014). Book chapter in *BRAIN, MIND, COSMOS: The Nature of Our Existence and the Universe*. Ed. D. Chopra. eBook (May, 2014).
Kafatos, M., and Drăgănescu, M. (2001), "Toward an Integrative Science." *Noesis XXVI: Travaux du Comte Roumain d'Histoire et de Philosophie des Sciences* (Book Chapter).
Kafatos, M., Tanzi, R.E., and Chopra, D. (2011). "How Consciousness Becomes the Physical Universe." *Journal of Cosmology* 14, 1318–1328.
Kafatos, M., and Kafatou, Th. (1991). *Looking In, Seeing Out: Consciousness and Cosmos*. Wheaton, IL: Quest Books/The Theosophical Publishing House.
Kafatos, M., and Nadeau, R. (1990, 2000). *The Conscious Universe: Part and Whole in Modern Physical Theory*. New York: Springer-Verlag.
Kafatos, M., Roy, S., and Amoroso, R. (2000). In *Studies on the Structure of Time: From Physics to Psycho(path)logy*. Ed. Buccheri et al. New York: Kluwer Academic/Plenum.
Kafatos, M., Roy, S., and Drăgănescu, M. (2003). "The Nature of Time: Geometry, Physics and Perception," *The Conscious Universe: Physical Processes, Consciousness and the Nature of Time*. R. Buccheri, M. Saniga, and W.M. Stuckey, eds. New York: Kluwer Academic Publishers, 115–127.
Kafatos, M., Roy, S., and Roy, M. (2005). "Variation of Physical Constants, Redshift and the Arrow of Time." *Acta Physica Polonica*, 36, 3139–3161.
Kato, G., and Struppa, D. (1999). "A Sheaf Theoretic Approach to Consciousness." *The Noetic Journal*, 2, No. 1.
Kato, G., and Struppa, D. (1999b). *Category Theory and Consciousness*, Proceedings of the International Conference Tokyo held at the United Nations University, May 1999.
Kato, G. (2001). "Cohomology, Precohomology, Limits and Self-Similarity of Conscious Entity (Sheaf Theoretic and Categorical Formulation of Consciousness)." Communication at the Vth Conference on structural-phenomenological modeling; categories and functors for modeling reality; inductive reasoning, Romanian Academy, Bucharest, June 14–15, 2001. *Noesis*, XXVI.
Masuno, K., and Paton, R.C. (2000). "Quantum mechanics in the present progressive mode and its significance in biological information processing." *Biosystems* 49, 229–37.

Nadeau, R., and Kafatos, M. (1999). *The Non-local Universe: The New Physics and Matters of the Mind*. Oxford: Oxford University Press.

Penrose, R. (1994). *Shadows of the Mind*. Oxford: Oxford, University Press.

Pribram, K. (1991). *Brain and Perception—Holonomy and Structure in Figural Processing*. Hillsdale, NJ: Lawrence Erlbaum.

Rosen, R. (1997), "Are our modelling paradigms non-generic?" Ch.14 in van der Leeuw and McGlade. *Time, Process and Structured Transformation in Archeology*. New York: Routledge.

Roy, S., and Kafatos, M. (1999), "Complementarity Principle and Cognition Process," *Physics Essays*, 12, 662–668.

Roy, S., and Kafatos, M. (2004). "Quantum Processes and Functional Geometry: New Perspectives in Brain Dynamics." *Forma* 19, 69–84.

Silk, J. (1989). *The Big Bang*, New York: W.H. Freeman.

Smoot, G.F. (1996). In *Examining the Big Bang and Diffuse Background Radiations*, eds. M. Kafatos and Y. Kondo. Dordrecht: Kluwer Academic Publishers, 31.

Stapp, H. (1993). *Mind, Matter and Quantum Mechanics*. New York: Springer-Verlag.

Struppa, D.C., Kafatos, M., Roy, S., and Amoroso, R.L. (2002). "Category Theory as the Language of Consciousness." *Noetic Journal* 3 (3), 271–281.

Tegmark, M. (2003), "Parallel universes. Not just a staple of science fiction, other universes are a direct implication of cosmological observations." *Scient. Am.* 288(5), 40–51.

Theise, N.D., and Kafatos, M. (2013a). "Complementarity in biological systems: a complexity view." *Complexity* 18, No. 6, 11–20.

Theise, N.D., and Kafatos, M. (2013b). "Sentience Everywhere: Complexity Theory, Panpsychism & the Role of Sentience in Self-Organization of the Universe." *Journal of Consciousness Exploration & Research*, 4, Issue 4, 378–390.

Tittel, W., Brendel, J., Zbinden, H., and Gisin, N. (1998). *Phys. Rev. Lett.* 81, 3563. Von Neumann, J. (1958). *The Computer and the Brain*. New Haven: Yale University Press.

Wheeler, J.A. (1981). *Some Strangeness in the Proportion*. Ed. H. Woolf. Reading, MA: Addison-Wesley.

Yang, K-H., Franaszczuk, P.J., and Bergey, G.K. (2003). "The Influences of Somatic and Dendritic Inhibition on the Patterns of Bursting in a Neuronal Circuit Model." *Biological Cybernetics* 89, 242–253.

Yang, K-H., Franaszczuk, P.J., and Bergey, G.K. (2005). "Inhibition Modifies the Effects of Slow Calcium-Activated Potassium Channels on Epileptiform Activity in a Neuronal Network Model." *Biological Cybernetics*, 92, 71–81.

Zbinden, H., Brendle, J., Tittel, W., and Gisin, N. (2001). *Phys. Rev. A*, 63, 022111/1–20.

PART III. HOW TO FEEL WELL IN YOUR BRAIN AND HEART

What Is Love?
The Physical Cosmology of Spiritual Union
RICHARD L. AMOROSO

Abstract

Until now descriptions of the nature of love have been left to the muse of poets and inspiration of philosophers. Psychologists usually refer to love as an emotion and biologists as a biochemical condition. Proponents of Artificial Intelligence (AI) suggest love can be described by a computer program even with current computer technology if we only knew the correct algorithm. Cognitive psychologists would profess that love reduces to configurational states in neural networks, microtubules or synapses. These aspects are not denied only that they are the wrapping and not the essence of love itself. Now that the physical cosmology of the mind-body interaction (awareness) has been discovered, it is possible to describe the fundamental basis of love. What is the soul, what is life, what is intelligence, and especially what is love and why it takes a whole cosmology to be adequately described are questions that noetic science begins to formally answer. It will take volumes to completely describe the physical cosmology of love; thus in this work we give basic descriptions as a way of introducing what comes in the near future as new noetic technologies become available to explore Self-Organized Living Systems (SOLS). A unique form of meditation to subjectively experience the soul of another person as if one were them is also introduced.

Introduction—Noetic Parameters of Love

The poet Keats cursed Isaac Newton for scientifically describing the prismatic optics of rainbows; but this author (an award winning poet, LDS [Mormon] High Priest and physicist) hopes the reader will agree that the esoteric beauty and ethereal wonder of love is enhanced by a deeper understanding of the complex cosmological basis for the spiritual nature of love. Noetic cosmology claims to have solved the ancient mind-body problem by discovering an empirically testable comprehensive model for the "life principle" animating self-organized living systems (SOLS) [1–11]. In terms of noetic science this means that the "Spirit of God," Chi, ki, or *prāna* is a physically real action of the unified field of physics [3, 12]. Descartes is criticized for believing his concept *res cogitans*—"mind-stuff" is nonphysical. What he actually meant from the nomenclature of his time is that mind-stuff is spiritual. Contemporary scientists abandon Cartesian dualism as intractable because they believe such a mind-stuff violates the laws of thermodynamics and energy conservation. However unified field propagation in SOLS directly overcomes this problem [2, 4, 5].

To briefly review the tenets of the noetic model of Cartesian interactive dualism, it is sufficient to state that an additional life principle beyond the brain/body not only gives life but supplies the "light of the mind" (qualia) as a physically based noetic unified field cosmology [2–5]. In simplest terms in this context, when two loving people interact over an optimal length of time (which varies per couple) letting their guard down, implying a certain element of trust (this opens nonlocal boundaries of the soul) such that various boundary conditions of their souls coherently align. This alignment entrains the natural flow of the spirit from locally separated individual states into a coupled pair-state producing a nonlocal coherence (soul to soul connection at a level of awareness) causing a "noetic light explosion." This is how a laser operates—perfectly align mirrors (entrained souls), shine a light (spirit) between them and a light explosion (love) occurs! Nonlocal connections always exist interpersonally; but the coupling loci must move into a position where the flow can be perceptually experienced. This is like the "Way of Nonattachment" or opening the "Lotus" in Buddhist meditation; if the spiritual eye is coupled to the stomach one does not "see." This higher-level coupling breaks down the so-called first person–third person barrier.

In scientific parlance and popular literature love is discussed in terms of

- Biology—genetic, sexual, biochemical and neural
- Sociological—cultural, familial, matrimonial
- Psychological—emotion, dependence, attraction, personality type

Here we completely ignore these commonly discussed aspects and concentrate fully on the spiritual basis of love—not from a theological or philosophical context; but by introducing totally new principles of physical cosmology required to complete the task of understanding love as a physically real aspect of the noetic unified field. Now that the cosmology of mind (awareness), which includes an associated physically real "life principle," has been discovered it has become possible to define love fundamentally within the soul of a living system. Think of this as how modulated configurations of the electromagnetic field produce images on a TV or movie theater screen.

Our task would seem so much easier if consciousness was merely a brain property as cognitive scientists believe. If this were so then mere programming structures in a neural network configuration or biochemistry would suffice to explain a particular thought, emotion or experience such as love. But this is not the case; cognitive and AI scientists fail to prove their case for mechanism, a universe populated by programed minds devoid of spirituality. Is it any wonder they classify mind as a "hard problem" too difficult to research [13]. In order to describe awareness, a whole new cosmology is required; not a Darwinian naturalistic or atheistic Big Bang cosmology, but an anthropic multiverse cosmology that includes the spirit of God. Evolution still exists but it is not random. Evolution is "guided" by this anthropic principle or spirit of God synonymous with the unified field of physics. This anthropic reasoning is in opposition to biological mechanism. Biological Mechanism states: The laws of chemistry and physics are sufficient to describe all life; no additional life principle is required. Noetic theory by introducing an anthropic life principle is able to definitively describe awareness and related properties such as love, intelligence and transcendence.

We have claimed that it is easy, meaning we can do it; but it is still not so simple a task. The cosmology of awareness cannot be described in the usual 3D or 4D spacetime dynamics of quantum theory and Big Bang cosmology. To describe awareness requires a minimum twelve dimensional (12D) space with a duality between our limited 3D temporal existence and the higher dimensional (HD) holographic reality of eternity of which we are a subspace. Our purpose is to delineate love in this new context. Although we are now able to define the anthropic cosmology of living systems, thought, emotions and feelings; describing love at this early stage (without telecebroscope technology) is in a sense like putting a cart before the horse because love is a more special (higher) configuration requiring something extraordinary in order to fully describe it. To be perfectly clear we are not claiming to know the essence of the spirit of God which is said to be love; only that noetic science has found empirical methods to access and observe the pathways and geometry of that structure in the living matter of SOLS.

Defining love requires an additional feedback loop causing lasing between interpersonal unified field boundaries. Let's clarify. The stream of thought or awareness (technically called qualia) entails an alignment of spacetime mirrors (boundary conditions gating spirit into living systems) producing the flow of mental content within SOLS; but it is a lesser form of evanescent coherence. The configuration of love requires a duality of "superradiance" interpersonally breaking the first person–third person barrier. These added coherence parameters are required for transpersonal effects—especially love. Whereas love is a form of "constructive interference" (wave summation), it should be noted that there is an obverse telergic "noetic effect" affecting the health of others—a form of destructive interference. This will lead to a new field of noetic medicine relating especially to the hundreds of heretofore incurable autoimmune disorders as in [14].

Anthropic Multiverse Cosmology—Noetic Context for Love

Noetic Science is based on an alternative to Big Bang cosmology called the Holographic Anthropic Multiverse (HAM) [1, 3]. This alternative cosmology is required because the Big Bang has no life principle able to describe consciousness beyond chemistry or an erroneously theorized computer program in the brain (Mind = Brain). Scientifically Hubble discovered a cosmological redshift, not an expansion of the universe as has been concluded by Big Bang cosmologists. A cosmological redshift is however observed. But in HAM cosmology if one assumes that the photon of light has a tiny mass, 10^{-65}g, then redshift occurs instead by a "tired-light" mechanism [1]. Imagine skipping a flat stone across water. Each time the stone hits the water and skips, it loses a little energy and the skips and velocity of the stone get shorter and smaller until the stone stops and sinks into the water. In terms of astrophysics this means light still gets redder and redder with distance but eventually it loses all its energy and disappears from view in our telescopes. This is the limit of observation in cosmology. In physics minute photon mass is created by the periodic internal rotation of the photon's energy that creates a gravitational field (periodic mass) causing the photon to couple to spacetime once per wave cycle and lose energy just like the skipping stone [1]. If the photon had no mass, why wouldn't the speed of light be infinite instead of merely 300 k/s?

In Big Bang cosmology the observational limit in cosmology (as far as telescopes can see) is to the postulated origin of time or initial moment or singularity when the grand explosion called the Big Bang occurred. In HAM cosmology if one traveled to that limit ~ 14.7 billion light years away, one could see out again for another 14.7 billion light years. This as we mentioned is a result of the so-called tired-light phenomena caused by a tiny periodic photon mass [1]. See [1, 3] for details on other alternative cosmological parameters required for cosmology containing a life principle.

Another major property of HAM cosmology is the anthropic principle equated with the unified filed of physics [2, 3]. In the philosophy of science the unified field is the same as the spirit of God that supplies the gravitational force, guides the evolution of living systems (SOLS) mentally and physiologically [2, 12]. As illustrated in fig. 2b reality is perceived as a hologram; the anthropic principle or spirit of God acts as the laser creating the holographic 3D image of the reality of our world as the cube in fig. 2a.

This can also be thought of as an observer sitting in a movie theater. The light at the projector bulb is the unified field or laser, the discrete frames of film are segments of spacetime and the smooth image on the movie screen is our observed 3D virtual reality. While the film in the projector moves at a few centimeters per second, in reality the surface of matter is made of electrons moving at a velocity near the speed of light.

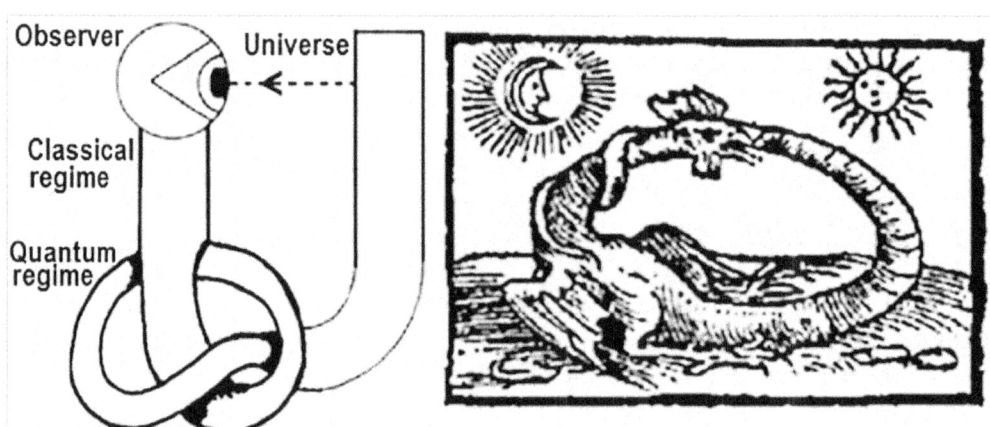

Figure 1. (a) Modified model of L.H. Kauffman's adaptation of J. Wheeler's Uroboros cosmology based on an ancient archetypal universe related to topological surfaces like the Mobius strip or Klein bottle, especially the topology of holographic universe models. In HAM cosmology the observer is embedded in and made out of the anthropic substance of creation where the "knot" (quantum uncertainty principle) limits observation to a limited temporal 3D virtual reality. (b) The Uroboros, among the ancient Gnostics a symbol of the *aeon*, or eternity of life. The image is from Horapollo, *Selecta Hieroglyphica*, 1597.

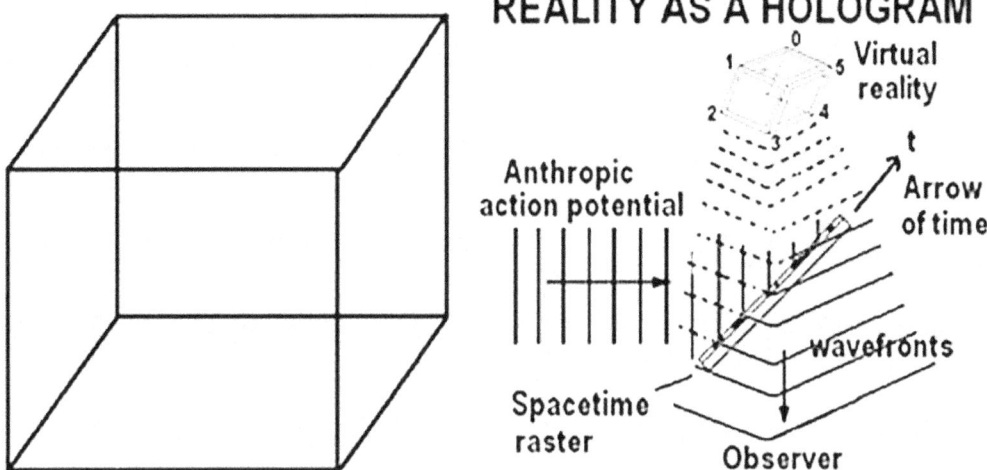

Figure 2. (a) Observed reality depicted as a virtual 3D Euclidean spacetime cube. (b) Actual reality is more like a hyperdimensional hologram in a 12D background of infinite quantum potentia (Schrödinger's dead and alive cat). The "laser" is the teleological unified field anthropic action principle (fig. 3) "piloting" the continuous evolution of observed reality.

Imagine being embedded in the Uroboros cosmology of fig. 1. We only see reality based on the discrete segments of 4D spacetime, not the complete 12D eternal reality of the multiverse. This subtraction by being embedded in the Uroboros, and the propagation of the spacetime segments gives us the perceived arrow of time [3]. There are many other amazing properties of HAM cosmology [1–9].

Noetic Consciousness—A Cartesian Interactive Dualism

Current thinking in the field of consciousness studies or cognitive science asks, "*What processes in the brain give rise to awareness?*" [13]. We know this cognitive model is incorrect because it is an atheistic model with no allowance for an anthropic action principle or spirit of God giving life to the soul or animating the mind. We are not programed robots. Evolution still exists but it is not random/Darwinian; it is guided by the spirit of God—like a super quantum potential in de Broglie-Bohm causal interpretation of quantum theory [15, 36]. Cartesian interactive dualism says mind and body are distinct entities, allowing life of the soul after death and the spirit of God to be the light of SOLS and the mind.

The important understanding to take from figs. 2 and 3 is that in an anthropic cosmology the unified field or spirit of God enters each spacetime point and every atom and molecule after passing through the cosmological least-unit gating mechanism separating the domains of temporal and eternal reality [1, 3]. This is how the life principle enters living systems to give life and also be the light of the mind or awareness. In the HAM cosmology model of living systems, the spirit (life principle) and the body comprise the soul [2, 12], so that there are no disembodied souls. When a person dies his eternal

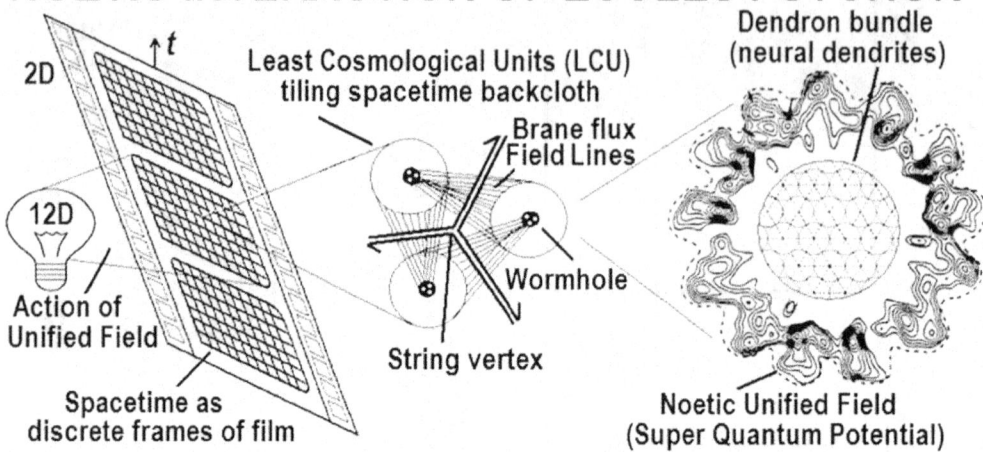

Figure 3. Conceptualization of Interactionist Cosmology embedding a modulated locus of thought (qualia) into the inherent life principle structure of fig. 2. (a) Showing injection of the noetic field (bulb) or *élan vital* into spacetime points (film), (b) Planck scale array of least-units mediating the noetic unified field. Spacetime is virtual in HAM cosmology and the least cosmological units (LCUs) tiling its backcloth are driven by a teleological anthropic action principle. Each "point" is a continuous-discrete wave-particle duality. (c) An Eccles Psychon field coupled to a brain dendron where positive functioning leads to health and transcendence or negative actions deplete the corona of the noetic field in the soul and create autoimmune interactions that may interrupt normal homeostasis and health.

spirit (mind or intelligence) is eventually reunited with a body (resurrection). This is the Cartesian dualist-interactionist model of mind-body. We call the boundary of the soul the psychosphere because there is more to SOLS than the brain and body chemistry; the soul also includes a surrounding spacetime region like the solar corona and additional eternal boundary conditions comprising the limits of individual intelligence.

The Noetic Effect: Psychons and Qualia

The mind-body interaction process between the 12D eternal realm of God and the temporal 3D/4D realm of mankind is defined as the Noetic Effect [2, 9] because it entails a force of coherence with inertial tension related to the quantum uncertainty principle. We will now begin to illustrate how this Noetic Effect mediates the production of qualia. Qualia, the plural of quale, is short for the "qualitative feel" of subjective awareness of a thought or feeling like the experience of the color redness for example [2, 13]. Sir John Eccles, winner of a Nobel Prize for the discovery of the synapse, postulated that a concept he called the "psychon" coupled the spirit or unified field to brain dendrons. A dendron is a bundle ~ 100 of the dendrites of nerve cells [4]. This is the basis of the dualist-interactionist model of the mind-body first proposed by Descartes. Eccles left the concept of the psychon as an empty philosophical construct because at the time he did not know how to develop the model further. Although Eccles was severely criticized for not defining the psychon, we cannot fault him because during his day no way to define this interaction properly had yet been invented [2, 4]. As the reader may have surmised, before we define love, the consciousness that houses it must be described.

With the advent of Noetic Theory we are now in position to define the physical basis for the psychon-dendron interaction, a necessity before defining the physical cosmology of love. We first suggest that psychon energy should be quantified in a similar manner to that of Einstein's, the physical unit defined as a mole or Avogadro's number of photons (10^{23}) used to measure photosynthesis [3]. But instead of photons the tenets of NFT postulates one psychon to be tantamount to a mole of "noeons," the exchange unit of the unified field (recall that the photon is the exchange unit of the electromagnetic field). Furthermore this noeon exchange mechanism is not confined only to the neural synaptic sites of dendron bundles as Eccles surmised. In addition it applies to microtubules, sensory receptors, DNA oligomers and any other pertinent biochemical molecules. This occurs not just in the brain, but anywhere throughout the whole body that plays a role in the bioenergetics of the soul or mind-body psychosphere, which as we stated includes the boundary conditions of the whole physical and spiritual body in both the usual 4D spacetime and associated 12D nonlocal space up to the "footstool of God."

We don't know too much yet about the noeon that is the "light of the spirit" or unified field. Imagine balloon animals that are made by twisting off segments of the main balloon to make a head or limbs. Double twists would be like a nose, eyes or fingers. The photon quanta of the electromagnetic field is like this. The photon is a dipole, like a little nose for example. It would untwist to a quadrupole, the graviton which is like the head or body of the animal. When the head is untwisted the energy returns to the whole balloon which is like the ocean of light of the unified field in the eternal 12D domain. These twists (providing some inertia in the continuous gating cycle) are part of the Noetic Effect we referred to earlier. Now we have a basic model where these noeon twists of the unified field become all the atoms, forces and fields of our reality.

The Physical Self-Organized Cosmology of Qualia

In the cognitive theory qualia is only a philosophical construct defined simply as the sensation of thought or awareness. In Noetic Theory in order to make qualia physically real we must define three types of qualia. In a paper called "What's it like to be a bat?" T. Nagel states that current reductionist attempts to define qualia fail by filtering out any basis for consciousness; thus becoming meaningless since they are logically compatible with its absence [16]. He assumes that if an organism has conscious experience, "there is something it is like to be that organism." This is the subjective character of experience for any conscious entity whether bat or Martian. Every experience has a specific subjective nature or configuration of qualia.

The flow of quale provide the so-called "stream of consciousness." Not all qualia are coupled to emotion. We can configure qualia with additional emotive content as "states of mind." Love is a third degree. Love adds "shared" emotive content beyond the boundaries of the self that we will define below as a form of lasing or superradiant evanescence between the internal (nonlocal) "mirrors" of SOLS.

To Nagel, "There are facts which could not ever be represented or comprehended

202 Part III. How to Feel Well in Your Brain and Heart

by human beings, simply because our structure does not permit us to operate with concepts of the requisite type"; because "to even form a conception of what it is like to be a bat one must take up the bat's point of view." If one removed the viewpoint of the subjective observer, what would be left? Nagel suggests the remaining properties might be those detectable by other beings, the physical processes themselves or states intrinsic to the experience of awareness. This changes the perspective of qualia to the form "there is something it is like to undergo certain physical processes.... If our idea of the physical ever expands to include mental phenomena, it will have to assign them an objective character." Nagel recognizes that: Very little work has been done on the basic question (from which mention of the brain can be entirely omitted) whether any sense can be made of experiences having an objective character at all. Does it make sense ... to ask what our experiences are really like, as opposed to how they appear to me? ... This question also lies at the heart of the problem of other minds.... If one understood how subjective experience could have an objective nature, one would understand the existence of subjects other than oneself [16].

These are questions an integrative Noetic Science can now answer. Standard defi-

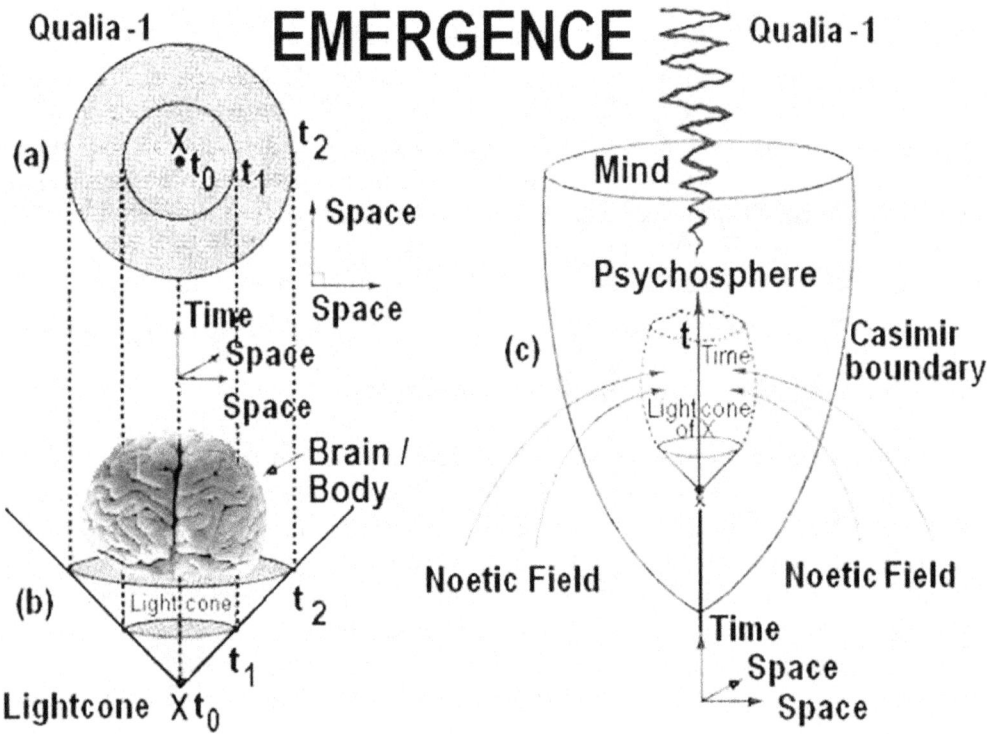

Figure 4. The emergence of Qualia into living systems. (a) From the 4D spacetime lightcone point $xt_0 \ldots xt_n$ noeon light enters every atom and thus the brain/body cyclically in time, t_0, t_1, t_2, ... b) Broader 12D context where qualia emerges into the mind or seat of awareness by a form of "evanescence." Note: These same Cassimirror (Casimir) boundaries bringing life and thought into the individual soul, when aligned (entrained between people in love) between two SOLS create the laser-like "light explosion" or joyous expansion of the soul we experience as love.

nitions of qualia are an inadequate philosophical construct describing only subjective awareness. In the physical sense of Noetic Field Theory (NFT) components describing qualia from the objective sense are introduced—i.e., distinguishing the phenomenology of qualia from the noumenon (separated from the apparition or superficial aspects of the phenomenon) or physical existence of the thing in itself beyond experience.

A comprehensive definition of qualia includes three forms considered physically real by NFT because the noetic fields of HAM cosmology on which the noetic model is based are all physically real:

Type I. The Subjective—The what it feels like basis of awareness. Phenomenological states of the qualia experience. (The current philosophical definition of qualia we term Q-I)

Type IIA. The Objective—Physical basis of qualia independent of the subjective feel that could be stored or transferred to another entity breaking the 1st person 3rd person barrier. These are the noumenal elements of qualia upon which the phenomenology of experience is based.

Type IIB. As in fig. 2b in terms of unified field noeon flux passing through the microscopic LCU raster of spacetime like a laser light producing a macroscopic holographic image; we define the discrete singular LCU points as "quanemes" or qualianemes derived from the term phonemes as the particulate components summating into a specific sound in phonology.

Type III. The Universal—By being alive living systems, SOLS represent a Qualia substrate of the anthropic multiverse, acting as a "blank slate" (TV turned on but "fuzzy" with no channel signal) as carrier from within which Q-II are modulated into the Q-I of experience by a form of superradiance or hyper-holographic evanescence [2]. See figs. 5 and 6.

This triune basis of qualia is only comprehensible in terms of the noetic definition of SOLS, Complex Self-Organized Living Systems in the anthropic holographic multiverse cosmology [2, 4]:

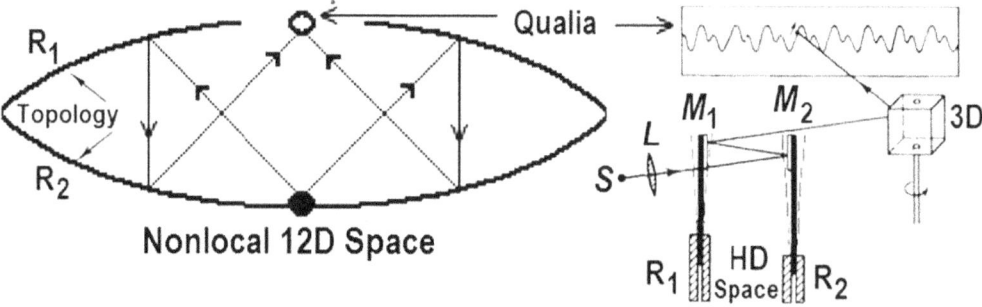

Figure 5. (a) If two parabolic mirrors (Casimirrors of the soul) are placed as shown (like the configuration of automobile headlight mirrors), an object put in the bottom (black dot) produces a virtual image of the object at the top (white sphere). (b) If the mirrors (topological spacetime boundary conditions) are made to resonate in a certain manner coupled to sensory input, memory archetypes or thought, an encoded mental qualia emerges into the mind as in combining figs. 2–4 with 5. S is the noeon source. $R_1-M_1 : R_2-M_2$ Casimirrors oscillate and reflect noeons into qualia.

- There is an Elemental Intelligence co-eternal with God. We know little about this parameter at present other than it constitutes the boundary conditions of individuality. Without which individuality "could not abide" [12].
- The 3D physical body living in spacetime and made of matter.
- The soul or "spirit and the body" [12] given life by the unified field noeon flux or spirit of God. The spirit of God somehow couples the domain of nonlocal elemental intelligence to the body and animates it by its action as the life principle. The difference between the spirit of God and the qualia of awareness may be like the twists making a balloon animal as described above.

Thus in summary these six elements comprise SOLS and the qualia system embedded and flowing within.

A standard image requires a screen or other reflective surface to be resolved; but if the foci of two parabolic mirrors (Casimir-like plates in our model) are made to coincide, the two images superpose into a real 3D image that does not need a screen. A science toy called the "magic mirage" is used to demonstrate this effect of parabolic mirrors. Objects placed in the bottom appear like solid objects at the top of the device (figure 5).

The lighthouse beacon action of *élan vital* energetics arises from the harmonic oscillation gating mechanism of least unit boundary conditions that tiles or tessellates the spacetime backcloth and pervades all SOLS. The inherent beat frequency of this continuous action produces the Q-III carrier wave that is an empty slate modulating cognitive data of Q-II physical parameters into Q-I awareness states as a superposition of the two (Q-III and Q-II). Figure 6. This modulation of qualia occurs in the 12D cav-

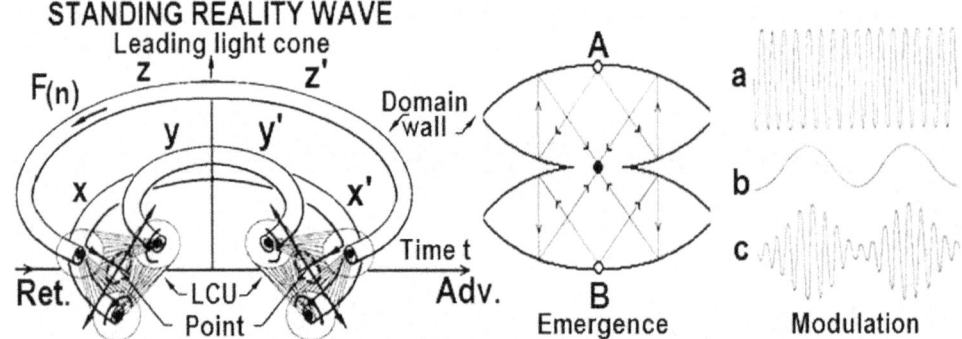

Figure 6. Metaphor for the emergence of qualia from the continuous action of the noetic least unit, LCU. (a) A microcosm of HAM cosmology where past oriented compactification periodically produces a classical spacetime point, x,y,z. The standing-wave domain walls represent the lightcone singularities of Q-III propagation, the surfaces of which act structurally as Casimir-like plates, and phenomenologically as a carrier wave base for Q-I qualia evanescence by Q-II modulation. (b) represents two pairs of parabolic mirrors (the Q-III Casimir domain walls) whose foci overlap; this is the high frequency wave in c) denoted as (a) (top). The longer wave (b) (middle) represents Q-II qualia as modulated by the Q-III wave into the usual Q-I qualia at the bottom, (c). Thus a, b, and c in c) represents the three forms of qualia and how they work together to form mental Q-I by superradiance of the noetic field.

ities of the cognitive domain of the psychosphere. The 12D cavities are a close-packed tiling of least unit noetic hyperspheres; the Casimir surfaces of which are able to reflect quaneme subelements. While the best reflectors of EM waves are polished metal mirrors, charged boundary conditions also reflect EM waves in the same way radio signals bounce off the ionized gases of the Kennelly-Heaviside layers in the Earth's ionosphere. This reflective "sheath" enclosing the cognitive domain is charged by the Noeon radiation (exchange particle of the noetic field) of the *élan vital*, the phases of which are "regulated" in the complex HD space of the least unit HAM cosmology [1–3].

How does noetic theory describe more complex qualia than the simple qualia of a light pencil? (The qualia–II of a light pencil is assumed to be the pencil (short ray) of light itself. Light quanta are microscopic in contrast to the macroscopic sphere of awareness. It is reasonable to assume that scale invariant properties of the HAM least-unit of awareness would apply. Like phonemes as fundamental sound elements for audible language qualia-nemes or quanemes are proposed for awareness based on the physical modulation of Q-II states by the geometric structural-phenomenology of the Q-III carrier base of living systems.

The Physical Basis of Love

In the last section we gave an elementary description of the physical cosmology of qualia. It was dramatically different from the cognitive science approach which remains philosophical. As the reader noticed qualia are very complex. It is said "the problem of qualia is tantamount to the problem of consciousness itself." The major difference between qualia of emotion and qualia of thought might be that the mental state of an emotion does not necessarily have any visual content, whereas a sensory based thought is more likely to contain visual qualia components.

Probably we will find out when experimental "telecerebroscope" platforms are developed that much of qualia is stored in a planetary database in what C.G. Jung called the collective unconsciousness of the Earth. We don't know this for sure yet, but we have discovered that quale for all life on Earth is universal. While higher level languages like Portuguese or English for example are quite different, the language of consciousness, which is encoded as qualia, is universal, as is DNA for all eukaryote SOLS. It seems simple to say the qualia for a pencil of light (segment) is the actual pencil of light. This may be true because the mind exists outside the body (psychosphere) and the spiritual body is like a photonic quantum computer that processes by "light" (Unified Field noeon light). Figures 2–6 suggest this is like the waves of electrons that impinge the phosphor of a television tube screen. The unified noetic field pervades the triune structure of qualia and cosmological components of SOLS evanescing into the flow of consciousness.

If we accept this model, then there is still something different and more special for the qualia of love. This relates to the first person third person barrier. Generally qualia are individual and private (first person). It is commonly known that when two mirrors are perfectly aligned in parallel, a light explosion called lasing occurs between the two mirrors. Love appears to be like this. Love is like a lasing of 12D psychosphere Casimirror spacetime topological boundary conditions [2, 35]. This telergic property is like the Einstein Podolsky Rosen (EPR) experiment of quantum theory. Some atoms like mercury emit photon pairs simultaneously. When one photon is touched by a polarization filter for example, the other photon no matter how far away resonates with the same effect. This proven nonlocal connection allows an actual lasing of love qualia between people in love. The quantum entanglement of their souls allows resonance of the spirit between them (see figs. 5 and 7). The EPR experiment is the main empirical proof of nonlocality—that the 12D arena hidden behind our 3D virtual world is like a hologram where any piece torn out (like an individual) contains all the information of the whole image. If qualia are like Jung's archetypes it would be this holographic property that allows storage in a "collective unconsciousness."

The physical nature of Love is a whole cosmology that cannot be described adequately in terms of narrower discourse of cognitive psychology, philosophy or theology, but needs context of both an anthropic multiverse and a full understanding of nature of awareness. From this noetic point of view love is a substantive cosmological personal/interpersonal state having aspects of a physical "noetic field" of light (noeons projected into an image much like the creation of a rainbow) produced by laser-like super-radiance such that an EPR type coherence between people occurs. Details and actions of this noeon field for self-organization in autopoietic living systems (life itself) apply in addition to the light of consciousness and lased state of romantic and altruistic love.

Why does it take a cosmological point of view to describe the nature of Love? The crux of this relates to what is called "Biological Mechanism." Biological mechanism states that: "The laws of chemistry and physics are sufficient to describe all life; no additional life principle is required." If you believe in the mechanistic point of view, you

Figure 7. When SOLS align a coupling of the noetic field occurs resonating between the two souls allowing them to share the mutual entangled qualia of love. While the hypertori images are illustrative here; the actual psychosphere structure and topology has similarities, i.e., wheels within wheels with gating mechanisms that may align or misalign.

believe people are just programmed machines and love is just a biochemical reaction; this is not the point of view implemented here.

The common definition of Love is: a strong positive emotion of regard and affection. Emotion is defined as: A mental state that arises spontaneously rather than through conscious effort and is often accompanied by physiological changes; a feeling: the emotions of joy, sorrow, reverence, hate, and love. Emotions are the affective aspect of consciousness, a feeling or conscious mental reaction (as anger or fear) subjectively experienced as strong feeling usually directed toward a specific object and typically accompanied by physiological and behavioral changes in the body.

Love is developed through trust, a condition allowing openness. Trust is defined as the assured reliance on the character, ability, strength, or truth of someone or something in which confidence or dependence is placed; hope and trust are the foundation of a healthy, happy relationship. When two people want to create a deeper more meaningful relationship vulnerability is also added. If you enhance a trusting relationship with vulnerability the feeling of being anxious, fearful, and apprehensive may be experienced before exposing themselves. Trust accompanied by vulnerability leads after the exposure to feelings of love or pure joy.

Vulnerability is defined as capable of being physically or emotionally wounded; open to attack or damage. If the people in the relationship choose to be vulnerable with each other the result of working through an issue, allowing the couple to feel and have empathy with and for each other creates a strong, deep bond of loyalty that does not happen without being vulnerable [31]. Stronger relationships can be created in the work place, within the community, with extended families and in especially in romantic relationships which we consider here. We will try to show that these emotional states of mind allowing love to occur have an actual physical basis in the structure of the soul.

Traditionally love has been the domain of romantic poets and philosophers. Psychologists and theologians have addressed some of its operational properties like how love relates to happiness, temporal well-being or how to prepare for eternal joy in heaven. But until now it has not been possible to describe its physical basis and how it mediates the physiological nature of complex self-organized living systems SOLS, its relationship to interpersonal properties of transpersonal psychology, and thought processes through the processes of mind-body interactions called the "Noetic Effect" as a force of coherence.

Most might argue that the phenomenon of love isn't a process that is physically real. Rather it is believed to be an abstract ineffable or immaterial quality, that at most might be considered spiritual, that could or never should be elucidated—reminiscent of the feelings portrayed by the philosopher/poet Keats who once drank confusion to scientists like Isaac Newton for explaining rainbows, suggesting it would be a desecration to formally describe life's only real treasure. On the other hand such an elucidation would ultimately have such a profound effect on so many aspects of our existence that if such a task can be accomplished, it should be given urgent consideration.

Recently fundamental principles drawn from modeling a continuous-state holographic anthropic multiverse [1] lead to a framework for describing the physical cosmology of love as dynamic hyperdimensional coherent interactions of the noetic unified field. Firstly it is postulated that life is a dynamic multidimensional recursive self-organized autopoietic complex system; itself a complete microcosmology that is a continuous transform of phenomenon and noumenon, mediated by the noetic unified field. Within this framework the domain of individuality is defined as a psychosphere; a further complementarity between unity with the wholeness of the universe and the separation of the fundamental state of nonlocal individual elemental intelligence.

EPR Entanglement Precursor to Understanding Physical Cosmology of Love—Qualia—IV

We know that nonlocal connections exist between atoms. Since people are made of atoms it is reasonable that nonlocal connectivity exists between SOLS. This has been proven in quantum physics by what is called the Einstein-Podolsky-Rosen experiment (EPR). If a pair of photons is simultaneously emitted in opposite directions and one of the photons polarized; a simultaneous change in polarization occurs in the other photon. This has been tested to 30 kilometers, and preparations are being made for an Earth-Moon test. Thus our noetic theory suggests that when lovers entangle in an adequate manner love may evanesce.

Previously we defined the three components of qualia. It appears now that an additional form that includes the EPR mechanism is required to describe the process of breaking down the first person–third person barrier. Qualia Type IV has all the properties of the Qualia-I, II, III triad with an additional duality and gating mechanism to mediate interpersonal boundaries [2].

A coupled noetic field configuration exists for each qualia state with dynamic evanescent standing wave-like properties within the raster of consciousness (see figs.) cycling from Classical to Quantum to Unitary. It is assumed that there is a coupling of the noetic field mediated by agency of both individuals and objects if a subject looks at, thinks of, talks to, or interacts in any way. There is a continuous general set point or homeostasis to the "normal" bandwidth of an individual's noetic field interactions that one is generally habituated to (fig. 8) with little noticeable sensation beyond the general introspective mode we sense and call awareness. This habituated bandwidth depends individually on our mood, stress level, health interactions and environment and has a set point of intelligence also.

There is additionally a law of hierarchies associated with this multistate bandwidth. Ones position in the hierarchy relates to personal intelligence, ethics, control position, status, and group dynamics etc. Within any interaction or noetic field connection free energy can be increased or decreased to either noticeable or subconscious degrees by subjective manipulation such as meditation or love, or nonlocal collective unconscious "karmic" effects. Some control and therefore a change of loci related to the flow of noetic flux energy can be given up by agency or controlling factors to superiors, jailors, subordinates or equals. In certain of these scenarios the "give and take" is not equitably balanced and cultural mores do not always necessitate such. This collapses some spacetime flux loci structures and may open others. Noetic theory suggests chronic deficits in this interpersonal energy balance are probably a major cause in autoimmune disorders. Part of the law of hierarchies denotes an actual physical flux boundary and part is necessary to maintain our individuality and maintain those boundary conditions. This relates of course to psychological issues in addition to the cosmology of consciousness.

The Physical Nature of Love

In terms of these postulates we now ask what is love? Simplistically love is a hyperdimensional 12D dynamic configuration of noetic field interactions along coupled loci where superradiance and evanescence takes place interpersonally. This description can be physicalized in terms of quantum teleportation maintained in EPR-like entangled psychosphere states. Every action has an opposite and equal reaction in terms of conservation of energy or state. When "moments" of love begin to take place a coherent entanglement starts to occur; the coherence lengths of the superposition increases until more and more noeons (mental photons) are "free" in the interaction. Boundary conditions change. More and more "separation space" is converted to shared nonlocal "unity space."

At a certain threshold there is sufficient shared space and noeon coherence that a laser-like avalanche of superradiance begins to occur. The threshold can remain small and local, but with sufficient trust, openness, and "generosity" love (phenomenology of) this small pocket of superradiance can increase and become pervasive until it becomes like an internal fountain expanding every particle of ones being in an evanescence that begins to be within the fringes of awareness.

To put in other terms noeons are constantly flowing in the psychosphere like production of a rainbow. Much of the commerce of exchange does not occur within the evanescent boundaries compatible with sensory awareness, firstly. (The locus of awareness is typically maintained at a level on the hierarchy below the threshold of spiritual awareness—see fig. 8.) Secondly there are no interpersonal coherence or superposition effects that would be associated with superradiance. The "mirror dynamics" leap frog so to speak but not initially in a "standing wave" synchronicity modality. Feedback is not required or expected along a recursive path; and the return path is not maintained here. So in a sense the propagation initiator mirror or cavity "dissolves" or translates before the receptor mirror appears or aligns in a form that would lead to an open feedback loop in this "prelove" locus of interaction where there is little or no entanglement of boundary conditions leading to noeon light cone superposition. The individuals maintain a separation and send out external "comets of interaction."

Good friends, trusted companions, naturally open individuals, or lovers begin to entangle and integrate light cone boundaries; through an additional causality associated with consciousness. In terms of the biological use of nonlocality the feedback takes on a whole new character of a much higher complexity. Permanent or maintained noumenal mirrors whose coherence lengths, entanglements and superpositions may grow; lead to the coherent configurations of psychosphere dynamics that is love. Several thresholds of phenomenology are crossed; and this tier is quantized with several arbitrarily defined markers in coherence lengths that lead to various levels of subjective love awareness.

Summarizing the mutuality of conditions of a threshold hierarchy to experience love there is:

- A maximum separation with no noeon interaction of world lines other than those in the universal collective unconscious as part of being human and being associated with the Earth.
- Basic interactions of conscious commerce. Parallelization of world lines, but no psychosphere integration in lowest order interactions, noeon "comets" are sent out in exchange of energy that through agency or control develops set points following which a conservation of energy within the set points is generally maintained even though the commerce may not be equitable. (No parallel mirrors.)
- Coupling begins with entanglement of psychospheres and a developing coherence length. Mirror alignment begins. And sensory feedback threshold appears at the pleasant or "like you level." This is more a corona effect with the double mirrors appearing during volleys of interaction, or draws from reservoirs and inner boundaries are not crossed or left open.
- Modification of internal light cone boundaries, channels are opened and maintained. Generation of EPR like mutuality created. Maximization of internal channeling through all of the 3-fold hyperdimensional transform. Condition of pervasive love, but still more localized.
- Global maximization of superradiance effects, like a superradiance of the superradiance creating an all pervading love of the whole psychosphere and consciousness. The full extent of this is not commonly achieved even by lovers, as it includes a maximization of the spiritual noeon channels as well as the more physical mind and body.

Love in the literature has not been described in any real detail other than briefly or superficially in terms of psychology, biochemistry, sexuality and altruism. Love then in its essence must be is a whole cosmology.

Lucis sapiens—*Next Evolutionary Step for* Homo sapiens

A complete understanding and implementation of Noetic Love on Earth could cause an evolutionary step in humanity and lead to a new race of humans that might be called *Lucis sapiens* or intelligent humans of light (spiritual). *Lucis sapiens* could eventually replace *Homo sapiens* (intelligent apes) on Earth. This may be said to occur on all planets in the multiverse when they come of age—when discovery of the conscious universe and the physical nature of awareness causes the hominid society to become fully evolved.

Part 1: The evolution of Human consciousness has come full circle to the time of Galileo when we begin another paradigm shift in the progression from myth and superstition, to an age of reason to a Galilean age of empiricism. But with the discovery of mind the paradigm shift completes human epistemology. Thousands of years ago Plato said noetic insight was highest form of knowing because it came from beyond human reason from the teleology of the anthropic multiverse. No matter how great ones intelligence or deep ones wisdom noetic insight came from beyond the self. This is now being realized in completing epistemology as the union of philosophy, science and theology which are not mutually exclusive but opposite ends of a long continuum of human understanding. This integration entails development of an "empirical metaphysics" where noetic insight is received subjectively in transcendent states and then empirically verified [3].

Part II: Discovery and Nature of Conscious Universe. Post Big Bang Cosmology, Extending quantum theory, Gravitational theory and electromagnetic theory, introduction of teleology of anthropic multiverse.

Part III: Coming Age of Transcendence: Used as hypothetical metaphor for teaching societal ethics or as real millennial transformation—The birth and evolution of *Lucis sapiens*, "Intelligent Humans of the Light (Lucis)" evolved by the completion of human epistemology and the greater spirituality and love required to utilize transcendence in a global manner as a tool of science, psychology, etc.

Part IV: Nature of Love: Love cannot be described adequately in terms of narrower discourse, but needs context of an anthropic multiverse and understanding of nature of awareness. From the noetic point of view love is real and love has aspects of a physical field of light and by laser like superradiance an EPR type coherence between SOLS occurs.

In Search of Ecstasy

What brings joy to human beings? Principles and phenomena inherent in "expansion" of the soul? Not as the Bible proverb says: "Folly is joy to him that is destitute of wisdom." Ecstasy seems the extreme of happiness, a joyous state arresting motion of the whole mind. Once experienced just the thought makes us long for it. Closeness to God facilitates the state of ecstasy. Once achieved amazing joy spills into all aspects of one's being. We become trees, feet planted in the Earth, standing transfixed in the ecstasy of sunlight.

Man is designed a social animal. Another avenue is through profound love shared with another. Limited by cultural constraints it is rare even for close friends and family. With the opposite sex one can intimately share intense feeling. With a close friend with an optimal level of spirituality it is possible to reach a state of heightened awareness independent of the sex act that can culminate in a state resembling ecstasy. If what is called "the afterglow" were magnified manifold times, this would qualify as ecstasy. This refreshing altered state that can be beckoned at will once learned. I see little difference in the nature of ecstasy achieved romantically and the state shared with God. The difference being to know God as well as ones lover so that one could plan ecstasy by practicing a prayerful worship.

Reaching such state of joy spills over into all aspects of our being with equal ease whether originating with God or a special friend. Pure love is Love apparently. Meditatively maintaining the state of ecstasy allows one to stay awake all night and arise as refreshed as if one slumbered. Ecstasy is mentioned in the scriptures: "He fell upon his knees, and began to pour out his soul in prayer and thanksgiving to God for what he had done to his brethren; and he was also overpowered with joy, and thus they all three had sunk to the earth."

212 Part III. How to Feel Well in Your Brain and Heart

Another incident occurs when King David dances before the Lord into a state of ecstasy. Could ecstasy be considered an excess like intoxication? As a feeling of delight that arrests the whole mind perhaps this is so. However I do not believe that in order to be close to God or have a high degree of earthly happiness it is necessary to live a Spartan life or undergo self-punishment to the degree the ascetics did. St. John of the Cross says: "The appetite blinds and darkens the soul because the appetite as such is blind. It is blind because of itself it has no intellect. Reason always acts as a blind person's guide for the appetite" [17].

Consequently, as often as people are led by their appetites they are blinded, just as we might say that when a blind person guides someone who has good eyesight both are blind. This is the folly of human nature, but with reasonable effort one can be master of one's self without resorting to a hermitage. St. John of the Cross also says: "The elevation and mind in god in which the soul is as though carried away and absorbed in love, entirely transformed in god, does not allow attention to any worldly thing." This seems an important point. The state of ecstasy should be learned by all people, not just those in a "hermitage." One does not require monastic asceticism to achieve this love; it is available to anyone who seeks it diligently. As seen in *The Sayings of the Desert Fathers* and evidenced in the monastic experience or similar secluded settings, asceticism

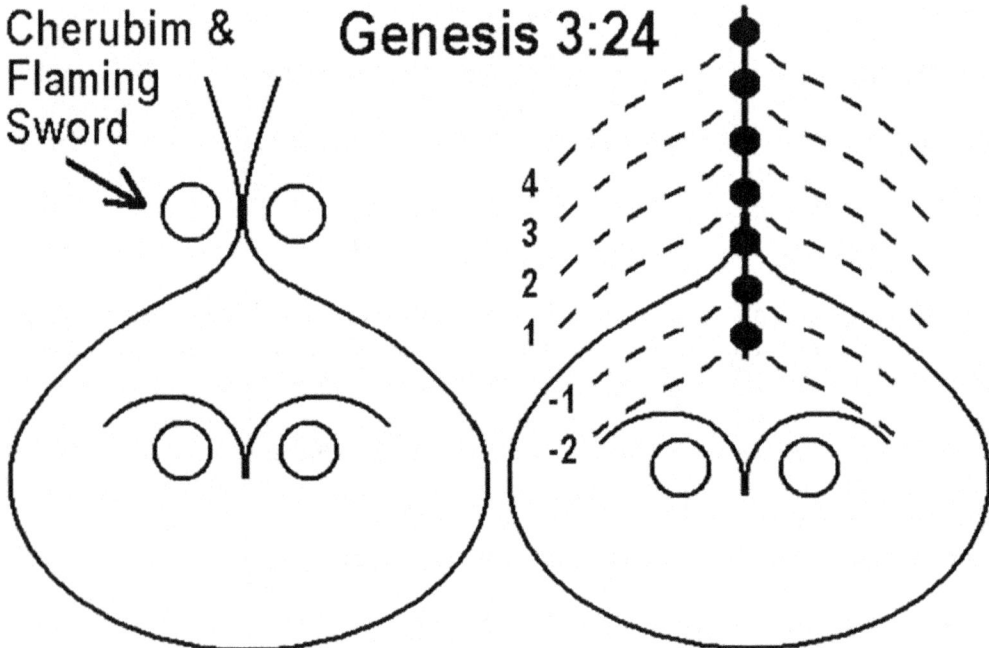

Figure 8. Hierarchy of telergic interpersonal connectivity related to love, intelligence, health and transcendence. In terms of (a) the "Cherubim and Flaming Sword" "Guarding the way to the Tree of Life" act as a set point of one's intelligence and spirituality. (b) Shows an inherent hierarchy of the souls structure. In terms of Noetic Tantra set points below the "corona" (0 to -2, etc.) keep spiritual awareness subconscious. As the interpersonal "wormhole" opens wider and wider with sufficient pure love (1 to 4, etc.) a threshold is reached such that the Noetic method allows profound interpersonal effects to occur.

historically seems to be the typical or most commonly chosen path to mysticism. Psychic implications of penance, seclusion, fasting and contemplation are profoundly interesting theologically and from the point of view of understanding the processes of human consciousness. However there are modern paths to this form of enlightenment achieved by following the Golden Rule as perfectly as possible. The Judeo-Christian scriptures state: "Upon these two great commandments rest all the Law and all the Prophets" [18]—these commandments being Love of course.

Achieving transcendent abilities is not necessarily limited to one theology or philosophy. James states: "He who bridles the tongue…" [19]. This is part of the law of hierarchies [2]. The base of the pyramid leading to the all seeing eye as on the back of the U.S. dollar bill is based on sins or karmic debt of actions like murder, adultery, violence, theft. The midlevel is as James stated crimes of word. The worst words could produce suicide, the least like "where did you get that stupid shirt" can be easily ignored. When one lives ones life at the top, managing ones karma at the level of thought, this is all the universe can expect of a human being and transcendent abilities occur spontaneously in that person. This author chose Mormonism because its doctrine and principles were strict enough to work for him; but any adequate discipline can lead to a sufficient level of spirituality with adequate effort.

Primacy of Love

The commandment to love was the primary guide for the Desert Fathers lives, and informed most of the stories and accounts in Sayings of the Desert Fathers [20]. Their practice included not only the command to love all, but to be transformed by God's love. For those who lived the monastic community life it was especially prominent. Their efforts to live by that commandment were not seen as being easy—many of the stories from that time recount their struggles to overcome negative emotions such as anger and judgment of others. Helping a brother monk who was ill or struggling was seen as taking priority over any other consideration. Hermits were frequently seen to break a long fast when hosting visitors, as hospitality and kindness were more important than keeping the ascetic practices that were so dominant in the Desert Fathers' lives.

Two interpretations of the Song of Songs are of interest. Firstly, is the song merely a proclamation of the delights of marital bliss, which for the virginal bride and celibate groom can be considered a mystical experience. Rabbis state that the phallus acts as a beacon of light shining enlightenment on the bride. It is Jewish doctrine that marriage is the vehicle for perfecting the soul. A parallel metaphor is that King Solomon's Song of Songs is sung to the glory of god and the great joy this brings [21]. A case exists for both interpretations; but the latter is more intellectually appealing than holding the Song merely as a description to glorify passions of the flesh. The song is truly a beautiful piece of love poetry—"*Ani lo dodee lo dodee nee*—Hebrew for I am my beloved's and my beloved is mine." But our interest here is in the metaphor for praising God. Can sexual bliss, ecstasy in general, or love be an additional path to the mystical experience of knowing God? Matthew 12:18 states: "Behold my Servant, whom I have chosen, my beloved, in whom I am well pleased: I will put my spirit upon him." The servant, either Jesus

Christ or a chosen disciple, is beloved by an ecstasy bringing spirit. Again in Romans 11:28 "As touching the election, they are beloved for the father's sakes." In this case the Beloved is the people of Israel.

Scriptural references give evidence for the song to be a metaphor for the deep joy embracing the gospel of Christ can bring. Apophthegms of the desert fathers give subtle hints of obtaining joy. Abba Elias for example said in terms of the ascetic life, "What can sin do where there is penance?" and "If the spirit does not sing with the body, labor is in vain. Whoever loves tribulation will obtain joy and peace later on." There has to be a balance in life and while it would be hard to fault someone wanting to become an esthetic to commune with God; it seems that one may dedicate one's life to god in whatever one does being in the world without being part of it. Developing the self-mastery for mystical enlightenment enables one in any of life's stations.

It is wonderful that we can bring joy to each other. All must learn if this planet is going to be a place worth living on. Human beings have an innate need for love; both to give and receive it. We assume we are created by God. He organized bodies into souls; if we were intelligent plant men, with green skin for photosynthesis, or our hair leaflike, had asexual reproduction, budding incorporated into our genetics, we could curl up our roots when we wanted to walk and have the same locomotion *Homo sapiens* now have. But God didn't make us this way; everything about our nature seems designed so that we need other people both physically and mentally. For ecstasy asexual tree people might get by without community. But we have soft skins, sensitive personalities, and face a hostile environment conducive to working together. We are designed for love. Love is at the core of our being and needs. The greater our ability to love becomes, the more experience becomes mystical experience. Ecstasy as a tonic for the soul would go a long way to making this world a better place to live in. Should it be taught in elementary schools? From Thomas Merton's selections from *Day of a Stranger*: "What I wear is pants. What I do is live. How I pray is breathe." "I see no reason why a man can't love god and a woman at the same time. If god was going to regard woman with a jealous eye, why did he make them in the first place?" "Sermon to the birds: Esteemed friends, birdsof noble lineage, … be birds." Be mystically ecstatic….

On a more technical note this process is governed or described by the cosmology of the Noetic Field equation, $F_{(N)} = E/R$ where the Noetic Force, $F_{(N)}$ is a topological force governed by coherence, E is the energy in Einsteins and R the coherence length or continuous-state rotational radius. One could say it is a form of wave-particle duality combined. The Noetic Force, $F_{(N)}$ is not a usual phenomenological interaction mediated by an exchange such as the photon of the electromagnetic field. The noeon mediator of the noetic field is an energyless topological interaction where information is exchanged ontologically. This is called topological switching. Imagine the vertices of a Necker Cube as the region where information is stored [1].

Noeon: The photon is an electromagnetic dipole and the postulated graviton a quadrupole that turns out to be a dual photon. The photon as been defined as a Euclidian space quanta, but in the photon-graviton complex one of the component dipoles is confined or embedded in the nonlocal spacetime metric in a manner similar to quark confinement. Following this reasoning the noeon is an octuplet and has a form of Calabi-Yau mirror symmetry allowing it to govern or pilot the evolution of cosmology, quantum systems (matter) and complex self-organized structural-phenomenology of living systems. As the exchange element of the unified field, the noeon is synonymous with the spirit of God. From this underlying simple symmetry all of the complex self-organized structure of the cosmos arises. Technically the photon is spin 1, the graviton spin 2 and probably the noeon is spin 4. (Fermions like the electron are spin ½.)

Brief Summary of Anecdotal Insight Related Entrained Science

As a lead in to the Noetic meditation procedure for "soul entrainment" we relate some correlative material:

- Studies have been performed that show correlations in autonomic and electroencephalographic (EEG) brain states of Tantric Yoga meditation. Unlike most previously reported meditation studies, proficient meditators demonstrated increased autonomic activation during meditation while inexperienced meditators demonstrated relaxation.
- Contemporary scientists consider the nature of love from various psychological, sociological, genetic, sexual, and biological-biochemical perspectives that include neurotransmitters like the so-called "love chemical" oxycontin best known for its roles in sexual reproduction, in particular during and after childbirth. Recent studies have begun to investigate oxytocin's role in sexual arousal [32–34].
- f-MRI imaging technics showing what regions of the brain "light up" or are activated for lovers.
- Quantum fields may influence neurological and immune function at the cellular level. Rein and McCraty tested this premise by demonstrating conformational changes in DNA molecules by the focusing of deep feelings of love on a sample of DNA [22].

Our Noetic model is different based on a cosmology of mind related to a form of Cartesian Interactive Dualism [2]. The spiritual nature of this model is nicely stated by Aristotle: "Love is composed of a single soul inhabiting two bodies."

Shared Breathing Experiment—Can One Mind Intimately Be Another?

Some of the insight in this section comes from the author's first-hand experience, certainly among the most profound in his life. In searching for the light of consciousness an experimental meditation technique was found that allows two people in love to intimately share their Souls for a moment as if they actually occupied the other person's body (as if they were them). The experience is incredibly profound and worth the effort to learn to achieve. We give a disclaimer based on the cases we have studied:

1. Some skill in meditation is required. The reason being that meditation is a tool that opens the boundary of the soul to higher dimensional space where interpersonal

and transcendent pathways exist. This is the HD space of the Unified field we have defined in prior sections. Note: These pathways are always available, but if not coupled to the loci of awareness no conscious experience for the observer can occur.

2. The couples must be in love or able to share love sufficiently; meaning altruistic close friends, siblings, parent-child relationships may also open these pathways which can occur immediately in persons sufficiently evolved to trust and be open to another individual at this high level. *Déjà vu* is a lower form of this experience. Love is the vehicle which opens the noetic pathways sufficiently for breaking the first person–third person barrier. Note: If a screen was placed very close to a film projector one would only observe small points of light or as in the usual subconscious case of lovers—feel love. What is required is that the interpersonal channel be open sufficiently so that in a sense an image or better a "copy" of the whole person transfers so that one experiences the others soul as if one were them!

3. A threshold level of spirituality is also mandatory. This is similar to 1 and 2 above as love and spirituality overlap. Meditation provides passage into the structure of spirituality. One can only receive this kind of love by giving it because a feedback loop is required to open the "wormhole gate" sufficiently wide.

These three conditions may limit the population of readers the meditation will work for; however we believe everyone can learn to meditate, everyone can experience love and that everyone should experience spirituality. We listed examples of well-known volumes on meditation in the references [23, 24].

An additional disclaimer is that the procedure is based on the generally known but somewhat obscure techniques of Tantra—specifically "Tantric Shared Breathing." Tantra means to "weave together" and is defined in general usage primarily as a technique-rich style of spiritual practice. Tantra has no single coherent doctrine; rather, it developed different teachings in connection with the different religions that adopted the Tantric method.

Tantric practitioners use *prāna*, breath, which in Sanskrit means life-force, an energy that flows through the universe (and thus one's body) to attain goals that may be spiritual, material or both. Most practitioners of Tantra consider mystical experience imperative. Tantric methods are most often used in lovemaking to enhance or lengthen the duration of the experience [25–28]. However, let us make it perfectly clear that modulating the sexual experience is not the purpose or goal of the noetic method of Tantric shared breathing described here and may even be used as an alternative to sex. Instead "The utility of the Noetic version of Tantric shared-breathing is used as the primary vehicle in a unique mediation whose purpose is to produce an inter-psychic subjectivity at the level of becoming the other person," i.e., as a spiritual tool or perhaps better said as a spiritual gift to experience a loved one in a profound manner. We have only performed a finite number of tests, so it is possible what we consider a "rule" may not be. When one goes to sleep one's awareness uncouples from the external world and probably retreats into the body as if it were like a womb. This provides a good metaphor for what we believe about Noetic Tantra. Applying the energy of Tantra to the sexual experience is a like going to sleep in terms of the higher interpersonal pathways, i.e., a large spiritual energy cost. If that spiritual energy is instead uncoupled from the sex act and applied to the interpersonal pathways connected to ones lover one may instead break down the first person–third person barrier. Ecstasy is found by many in sexual relations, and the usual usage of Tantra can profoundly extend this process; but the noetic meditation is meant to be even more esoteric. It is meant to be nonsexual and purely spiritual. But the spiritual depth is so strong one might consider it to be better than the sex act, especially since it seems that there is no time limit to the duration of ecstasy. The author's longest case was about 10 hours, stopped by duties like work that morning. I remember being worried that after being totally awake all night I would be too tired, but something in the nature of the interpersonal connection or high level of spirituality refreshed the body even better than sleep because of the heightened love.

On a personal note I had no idea in retrospect what love is or the hidden depths of joy available before having these experiences. One has felt love at whatever level one has been capable of. Then with this noetic experience it is like love itself being in love—so much deeper. Then when I was inside the soul of my partner I also experienced them experiencing their love for me—nearly ineffable! With a little practice one can create a ball of light that engulfs the couple. I wanted to get to the point in being able not only to experience the other person, but actually being able to see out their eyes!

Since the onset of scientific thinking a debate has continued as to whether or not people have souls or spirits and whether one soul can touch or communicate with another. The purpose of this noetic exercise is to demonstrate an inter-psychic experience to the participants such that through this subjective experience one can "know" firsthand of the existence not only of inter-psychic phenomena but to experience another person's soul as if one was momentarily resident therein. This is both a joyous experience because it is mediated by a high degree of love; and its subjective fact could lead to a motivation to modify the basis for scientific epistemology [2, 3].

Some training is required. Subjects should be in love (or putatively there would be no possibility of entrainment), and a certain level of skill in meditation and empathy is also essential. It should be noted that there is a threshold for occurrence of the phenomena, i.e., the noetic meditation opens an entrained channel between the participants perhaps best felt as a "burning in the bosom." This is what differentiates the normal act of prolonged kissing (the physiological format) from the noetic or spiritual format. Romantic involvement precedes entrainment along with a history and ability to meditate, and a belief in spirituality. Other than that the technique is very simple.

The procedure initially involves reaching a state of sexual arousal to the extent where breathing is accelerated. After sufficient experience this step can be skipped and the couple can automatically go to the second step. At this point the subjects then meditate on deep feelings of love for their partner. One then "turns off" (uncouples from) or leaves the sexual aspects behind. This is a mandatory decoupling. One must center on pure love and recouple the feelings of love and intimacy on the chest or heart rather than the genitals so that sexual arousal is minimized or best kept totally absent as this main purpose is to produce a PURELY spiritual interpersonal experience not a sexual one. This is difficult to define because love and love-making is a powerful spiritual experience in addition to the biological component. I suppose use of that "power" is key. If the power is embedded in the physiological engine of passion less energy is available for noetic aspects. Passion has an inward component of desire. The Spirit is a physically real field of action. To intimately share spiritual bodies as if one were the other person there can be no desire which because of the physicality of the noetic field acts like a gravity that collapses the interpersonal wormhole. The best metaphor for this is the Chinese finger puzzle. If one pulls, one's fingers get stuck; and the harder one pulls, the more strongly they are stuck. One must relax and the fingers come loose. Likewise the noetic interpersonal pathways cannot be "touched" or pulled on; they must be cherished or loved; otherwise they will remain closed.

This is the simple process. One kisses ones partner passionately. At the threshold of accelerated breathing breath is shared with one's partner. Instead of breathing externally from the side of the partner's mouth as one normally would from the surrounding atmosphere (as strange as it might seem to the uninitiated), breaths are taken from the partner's lungs. If the subjects have maintained a sufficient threshold of spiritual coupling and spiritual love (not genital), at the moment of shared breath the presence of the other person's soul is felt in synchronicity within one's own soul for about a second's duration initially. Cyclically continuing the process the experience of visiting ones partner's soul oscillates like a lighthouse beacon. A highly profound inter-subjective experience is produced if one simply remembers spirituality over physiology. With practice and increased spirituality the duration of the cyclical presence may be increased. Who knows, you may learn to become proficient enough to actually "see" out your partner's eyes when you are apart. There is no greater gift perhaps than knowledge of eternity and our place within it! "There is no fear in love; but perfect love casteth out fear: because fear hath torment (guilt). He that feareth is not made perfect in love" [29].

Conclusion—What Is Love?

Obviously we have only partially met our goal. But hopefully the reader has a new appreciation for what love is. It is not philosophy, sociology or psychology. It is not chemistry, a neural configuration or an AI program.

We have outlined a new fundamental basis for SOLS as comprised of eternal Elemental Intelligence—Body stuff—Psychosphere—Mind animated by a life principle or Spirit of God. The most difficult aspect is defining Qualia—tantamount to defining awareness itself for which we have outlined four forms and the required new anthropic multiverse cosmology which provides a context much like the complete structure of a movie theater housing the seated observer experiencing the flow of consciousness projected on the screen [30]. We also compared that process of awareness to the production of a holographic image created by a laser. Lasing occurs in an enclosed cavity in this case the psychosphere of SOLS. All that's the hard part. After that defining the fundamental physical basis of Love is easy. The lasing cavity is expanded to include two SOLS where the intertwined evanescing superradiant unified field "light explosion" is Love; but only because the noeon light of the Unified Field is synonymous with the Spirit of God. And in that sense Love still remains the greatest of mysteries; but we have moved our understanding to a vastly more interesting arena!

Acknowledgment

Heartfelt thanks to Kerry Fannin (*Sapere Vedere* [term used as a motto by Leonardo da Vinci to mean "knowing how to see" (beyond the clouds)]), social services administrator for the Utah State Dept. of Human Services (DHS) Child & Family Services, for helpful discussions, input and suggestions on the nature of trust and vulnerability in Sect. 6 as part of the gating mechanism opening the door to love.

REFERENCES

[1] Amoroso, R.L., and Rauscher, E.A. (2009). *The Holographic Anthropic Multiverse: Formalizing the Complex Geometry of Reality*. Singapore: World Scientific.
[2] Amoroso, R.L. (2010) (ed.). *Complementarity of mind and body: Realizing the dream of Descartes, Einstein and Eccles*. New York: Nova Science.
[3] Amoroso, R.L., Kauffman, L.H., and Rowlands, P. (eds.) (2013). *The Physics of Reality: Space, Time, Matter, Cosmos*. Hackensack: World Scientific.
[4] Amoroso, R.L., and Di Biase, F. (2013). "Crossing the Psycho-Physical Bridge: Elucidating the Objective Character of Experience," *Journal of Consciousness Exploration & Research*, 4:9; pp. 932–954.
[5] Amoroso, R.L. (2013). "Empirical Protocols for Mediating Long-Range Coherence in Biological Systems," *Journal of Consciousness Exploration & Research*, 4:9; pp. 955–976.
[6] Amoroso, R.L., and Martin, B. (1995). "Modeling the Heisenberg matrix: Quantum coherence and thought at the holoscape matrix and deeper complementarity." In K. Pribram, ed. *Scale in Conscious Experience: Is the Brain Too Important to Be Left to Specialists to Study?* Mahwah, NJ: Lawrence Erlbaum.
[7] Amoroso, R.L. (1996). "The production of Fröhlich and Bose-Einstein coherent states in in vitro paracrystaline oligomers using phase control laser interferometry." *Bioelectrochemistry and Bioenergetics* 41, 39–42.
[8] Amoroso, R.L. (1997). "Consciousness, a radical definition: The hard problem made easy." *The Noetic Journal* 1:1, 19–27.
[9] Amoroso, R.L. (1999). "An introduction to Noetic Field Theory: The quantization of mind." In R. Amoroso & M. Farias, eds. *Science and the Primacy of Consciousness*. Orinda, CA: The Noetic Press.
[10] Josephson, B., and Pallikari, F. (1991). "Biological utilization of quantum nonlocality." *Foundations of Physics*, 21:2, pp. 197–207.
[11] Kafatos, M.C., and Nadeau, R. (2000)."The conscious universe: Parts and wholes in physical reality." New York: Springer Verlag.
[12] Smith, J. (1998). *Doctrine & Covenants, Sect. 88*. Salt Lake City: Church of Jesus Christ of Latter-day Saints.
[13] Chalmers, D. (1996). *The Conscious Mind*. Oxford: Oxford University Press.
[14] Amoroso, R.L. (2012). Spacetime energy resonator: a transistor of complex Dirac polarized vacuum topology, U.S. Patent, http://www.google.com/patents/US20120075682.
[15] Jibu, M., and Yasue, K. (1995). *Quantum Brain Dynamics and Consciousness*. Amsterdam: John Benjamins.
[16] Nagel, T. (1974). "What's it like to be a bat?" *Philosophical Rev.*, 83, pp. 435–450.
[17] Anthony of Sourozh (1975). *The Sayings of the Desert Fathers: The Alphabetical Collection*, London: Mowbrays Publishers.
[18] The Gospel According to St. Matthew, 22:36–40, Holy Bible, New Testament, King James Version.
[19] The General Epistle of James, 1:26; The Book of Psalms 39:1, Holy Bible, King James Version.
[20] Waddell, Helen (1957). *The Desert Fathers*. Ann Arbor: University of Michigan Press.
[21] The Song of Solomon, 6:3, Holy Bible, Old Testament, King James Version.
[22] Rein, G., and R. McCraty (1993). Local and non-local effects of coherent heart frequencies on conformational changes of DNA. Proc. Joint USPA/IAPR Psychotronics Conf. Milwaukee.
[23] LeShan, L.L. (1974). *How to Meditate: A Guide to Self-discovery*. Boston: Little, Brown.
[24] Saraswati, Swami Satyananda (2000). *Sure Ways to Self-Realization*, Munga, Bihar, India: Yoga Publications Trust. ISBN 81-85787-41-7.
[25] Sivapriyananda, S. (2009). *Secret Power of Tantrik Breathing: Techniques for Attaining Health, Harmony, and Liberation*. New Delhi: Destiny Books.

[26] James C. Corby, Roth, Walton T., Zarcone, Vincent P., and Kopell, Bert S. (1978). "Psychophysiological Correlates of the Practice of Tantric Yoga Meditation," *Arch. Gen. Psychiatry*, 35(5):571–577.
[27] Walker, Benjamin (1982). *Tantrism: Its Secret Principles and Practices*. London: Aquarian Press. ISBN 0-85030-272-2.
[28] Dempsey, B., Link, A., and Copeland, P. (2007). *The Everything Tantric Sex Book: Learn Meditative, Spontaneous and Intimate Lovemaking*. Avon, MA: Adams Media.
[29] 1 John 4:18 Holy Bible, New Testament, King James version.
[30] Fredriksson, I. (2012) *Aspects of Consciousness: Essays on Physics, Death, and the Mind*, Jefferson, NC: McFarland.
[31] Brown, Brene' (2012). *Daring Greatly: How the Courage to Be Vulnerable Transforms the Way We Live, Love, Parent, and Lead*. New York: Gotham Books.
[32] Acher, R., and Chauvet, J. (1988). "Structure, processing and evolution of the neurohypophysial hormone-neurophysin precursors." *Biochimie* 70 (9): 1197–1207.
[33] Lee, H.J., Macbeth, A.H., Pagani, J.H., and Young, W.S. (2009). "Oxytocin: The great facilitator of life." *Prog. Neurobiol.* 88 (2): 127–51.
[34] Carmichael, M.S., Humbert, T., Dixen, J., Palmisano, G., Greenleaf, W., and Davidson, J.M. (1987). "Plasma oxytocin increases in the human sexual response." *The Journal of Clinical Endocrinology and Metabolism* 64 (1) 27–31.
[35] Casimir, H., and Polder, D. (1948). "The influence of retardation on the London-van derWaals forces." *Phys. Rev.* 73:4, 360–372.
[36] Pribram, K.H. (1995) in J. King and K.H. Pribram (eds.) *Scale in Conscious Experience: Is the Brain Too Important to Be Left to Specialists to Study?* Mahwah, NJ: Lawrence Erlbaum.

Consciousness in the Third Millennium

Amna Al Faki, M.D., and Ingrid Fredriksson

What Is Consciousness? by Amna Al Faki

There is no generally recognized definition for consciousness (Searle 2002, Susan Blackmore 2004); no definition that provides explanations for all psychologists, philosophers and other workers in the field of consciousness that is widely accepted. It is because of the lack of a physical or biological fundamental theory to explain consciousness, consequently scientific definitions failed to arise.

This missing theory of consciousness, if founded, should address, in scientific, physical and biological fashion, the fundamental role of consciousness in our actions, behavior and the whole essence of life—our existence, morals, good and evil, religion and cultures, and the relation of our consciousness to the rest of the conscious universe. Also the theory of consciousness should explain the relationship between human consciousness and universal consciousness and how they interact and affect each other. Consciousness has no accepted or recognized specific scientific definitions. Yet there are constantly many trials by philosophers, scientists and other workers to define and disclose the mystery and genesis of consciousness and its cause and effect, not only upon our existence as human beings, but also its effect upon the whole universe and whether it is fundamental to universal existence as a whole?

The simplest definition that is generally accepted is that it is a subjective awareness of the self being and the surroundings. This definition, though, is lacking as we need a testable theory that is biological, physical and coherent to explain consciousness.

The "heart intelligence" together with "brain intelligence" seems a feasible approach to explain the biological phenomenon of consciousness. I (Al Faki) published the first paper in the world stating that the heart is a sense organ that deals with feelings, emotions, thought processing and extra sensory perceptions. Furthermore, that it plays a fundamental role in the emergence of conscious experience, conscious act (Amna Alfaki, 2009, Medial Hypothesis) and not solely a simple mechanical pump. In fact I consider the heart as a substrate and the first step in emergence of conscious and voluntary action.

Consciousness at the current time is the most exotic and challenging subject of research in neuroscience, neurophysiology, psychology, philosophy, human sciences, religion and advanced research in technology related to artificial intelligence, space sciences, etc. So consciousness is now at the heart of all important scientific research, but in spite of all what has been mentioned above, the important question is does the unexplained phenomenon of consciousness deserve all this extensive effort? That is, the multidisciplinary international annual forums and conferences which have now started in many parts of the world including the United States, Europe, Canada and others to explain in scientific bases the genesis of consciousness. Is it worthwhile? Is it cost effective?

In my opinion the answer is yes. Why? As I think there is a global shift and change in our planet, the earth is warming causing some parts of the two arctic poles to start to melt. The icy oceans and the top of the Himalaya Mountains are already starting to melt as a result of environmental pollution and warming. This is due to ozone depletion in the earth's envelope surrounding our planet and a result of hostile aggression and cruel behavior of human kind against nature, environment and against each other.

I think these universal changes also affect human consciousness in behavior, beliefs and conceptual reality. There is a noticeable shift from absolute material thoughts and doctrine from western philosophy that dominates every aspect of life to spiritual consciousness, a search for reality and self where science and religion will re-unite again. In the mediaeval ages and before the Renaissance the church had a hostile and aggressive attitude towards scientists who explained the physical laws of nature. Scientific facts were often unaccepted by the church, and scientists were either forced to recant, which led to the scientists rejecting the church, resulting in a divide between science and religion. In Eastern philosophy, science and religion are in harmony and two faces of the same coin; they are not contradictory, opposing each other, and this is how religion explains consciousness in life and after death.

It is well known that modern science in the very beginning was based upon Eastern philosophy, like that of Ibin Vince, who was the first to describe blood circulation. Ibin Rushd and many other early religious scientists believed the heart to be a mechanical and functional power which is the seat of wisdom and source of enlightenment and intuition. In Eastern philosophy the brain, especially the fore brain, is also considered a cognitive organ, so a new approach and new definition based upon the brain and heart will explain consciousness.

Also, the theory of consciousness should explain the relationship between human consciousness and universal consciousness and how they affect and interact with each other.

Western philosophy that depends upon material and mental brain guided doctrine, laws that gear the action and behavior of the human beings and everything is related to the brain intelligence alone without the heart. It made a sharp demarcation between science and religion which led to and reached the climax of a material civilization that lacks ethics, morals, love and humanity. This resulted in morals, noble feelings, mutual love, genuine and sincere emotions among people and nations are either becoming attenuated or lost and replaced by social disruptions, weakened family bonds, hostility, aggressions and denial of others.

The world now needs new enlightened spirits, a new understanding of the conscious self, a conscious mind and a conscious heart and new era where a dichotomy between science and religion domain. The world needs new changes in every aspect of our life that will modulate, shape and change our behavior to be guided by the intelligence of the heart. Our free will that respects considers and accepts the others and by the others we mean all who share life in this beautiful earth our mother. Leading us to care and love the birds, animals, plants, mountains, oceans, seas and rivers because we share universal consciousness so we should share love and sympathy.

We need enlightenment, new spirit and consciousness that will lead and guide us to a new horizon full of faith, love and acceptance of the others based upon both heart and brain intelligence. Science and religion doctrine based upon Eastern civilization is the new philosophy to be adopted to unite heaven and earth through science and religion. A new spirit and consciousness that will shift and change the world to a new era where we will be guided by the intelligence, wisdom and glory of our hearts together with the logic of the brains.

Consciousness—The New Concept of Heart-Brain Interaction

The heart, from an anatomic point of view, is the most important organ in our body. It is composed of four chambers, two atria and two ventricles; the main function of the heart is to pump oxygenated blood to the whole body including the brain. The heart is well established as a sensory organ, the emerging field of neurocardiology has established that the heart contains an intrinsic nervous system that exhibits both short and long-term memory functions. In addition to the distributed network of cardiac ganglia, the human heart contains approximately 40,000 specialized sensory neuritis, these are involved in relaying afferent information to the brain. These sensory neurons are sensitive to a wide range of mechanical and biochemical stimuli. It is also possible that the specialized striated muscles are sensitive to external sources of information which are related to the intrinsic neural system of the heart. I hypothesize that the information processing which takes place in the hierarchy of neural plexuses in the intrinsic cardiac nervous system can affect perceptual experience via multiple pathways which modulates cortical activity and perceptions. I also hypothesize that neurotransmission, ion-channelopathy, nitric oxide, and some or all of these modulators may facilitate inter-neural connections and information transfer.

The heart is a unique organ with a specialized conductive system (including the sino-atrial node [S.A.N.] the atrio-ventricular [A.V.N.] the bundle branch [B.B.]), the unique Purkinje fiber system. Also a complex neural system which has both short and long-term memory and a widely distributed network of sensory neurons, it also produces a wide range of hormones. The intrinsic nervous system is innervated by the efferent fibers of both the sympathetic and the parasympathetic branches of the autonomic nervous system (A.N.S.); however the heart can make local decisions which can override external inputs for the (A.N.S.). The latest research has shown that the hearts conductive system is under the control of the intrinsic nervous system of the heart. The neural systems in the heart are derived from the neural crest of the ectoderm in the developing embryo as are the neurons in the brain. The heart muscle is specialized striated muscle with a unique function. The next important function of the heart is psychic and emotional function of the heart. For a long time since ancient history and among all nations, we find in philosophy and religion the heart is considered as a seat of wisdom righteousness, faith, love, and emotions. The heart is the source and origin of love in its broad sense of requited mutual love that embraces the whole universe and interacts with nature. All holistic love to Him Almighty, the Absolute Reality and sharing in part that love to everything around us. This is because emotions and love are positive powers and energy that leads to goodness and perfection and it is the work of the heart as well. In modern philosophy of successful economy, one of the major indicators of success is high emotional IQ rather than intellectual IQ, the former is related to the heart, while the latter to the brain. The next important organ in our body is the brain, it is the executive organ and it performs all tasks according to signals received from the heart and the body which are fed back by action or behavior. It is this work that is the basis and genesis of conscious actions, experience or behavior.

So conscious acts or conscious states are produced by the work of the heart as well as the brain in heart-brain interaction and the new hypothesis in explaining the neurophysiology of conscious acts. The work of the heart, both mechanical and functional, is crucial to functioning of the brain which cannot sustain anoxia (cut off oxygenated blood) for more than 7 minutes, after which the brain becomes unconscious and falls into a coma. Other causes that affect brain consciousness are diseases like cerebrospinal meningitis, encephalitis, cerebral malaria and toxins.

The integrity of brain function and energy depends upon the heart. The heart is the substrate for the emergence of consciousness and conscious act and behavior of the animal and man; it is the source of freedom and free will. Brain death for any cause is announced after all signals coming from body including the heart stopped where the heart death follows brain death and the heart death after the brain death the last signal to leave the body is from the heart.

Conclusion

Based upon my hypothesis that the heart is sensory-motor cognitive organ its neural system has a unique structure and function that make the heart the main single cognitive organ that plays a fundamental role in conscious behavior of man and animal and determine his intention, free will and volitional action. This important findings and the role of the heart has important implication affect his performance and social acceptability. The heart has a tremendous power, ability and capability to create and direct our intelligence, intentions and behavior towards good issues and new creative models and tremendous impact in the believes and behavior of conscious conduct of the individual with subsequent moral and legal responsibilities towards his own behavior and deeds and how that that modulate and transform our action and behavior that has tendency to violence and aggression from hatred to love and compassion and the acceptance of the others. We have to detect our own hearts power and empowerment to bring the necessary intelligence that control our consciousness, conscious action and behavior in our planet and utilize our heart power and intelligence to bring peace and love to our conscious universe.

Amna Al Faki's interesting observations above about consciousness in the third Millennium are enlightening. We need a better understanding of the heart-brain interaction as the heart is not only a mechanical "motor." "The heart is a sensory-motor cognitive organ, it's neural system has a unique structure and function that makes the heart the main single cognitive organ that plays a fundamental role in the conscious behavior of man and animal, determining his intention, free will and volitional action," says Amna.

What does this have to do with the heart/brain?

"The heart from anatomic point of view is the most important organ in our body, it is composed of four chambers two atria and two ventricles the main function of the heart is mechanical to pump oxygenated blood to the whole body including the brain. The heart is well established as a sensory organ and the emerging field of neurocardiology has established that the heart contains an intrinsic nervous system that exhibits both short and long-term memory functions. In addition to the distributed network of cardiac ganglia the human heart contains approximately 40,000 specialized sensory neuritis involved in relaying afferent information to the brain. These sensory neurons are sensitive to a wide range of mechanical and biochemical stimuli."

After the following up of patients that have undergone a heart transplant researchers found that some patients had passed away from a heart attack between 3 and 5 years after the transplant while others showed no signs of ill health. It has become apparent that the interplay between the heart's adaptability in combining nerves and hormones is important to increase the heart frequency's ability to vary. The heart should, quite simply, not beat too regularly which is caused by the interplay between hormones and nerves. Researchers have studied whether the variability is in fact random or chaotic. It doesn't seem to be chaotic but it does show a nonlinear behavior. According to the heart researcher and chaos specialist Leon Glass, it varies in a complicated way, which is called multifractal.

The heart is therefore a dynamic system with a built-in reflex mechanism which affects nerves and the concentration of hormones via a surgically implanted pacemaker. It is difficult to state whether the heart shows a random behavior or whether it is dynamic/chaotic. In theory it is not difficult—it's enough to write up every parameter from all measurement taking. If the process is studied randomly then it takes on the shape of a diffused cluster: If the process is dynamic/chaotic then the curves will begin to form. The problem with determining this for variable heart frequencies has been the amount of data from testing and its accuracy.[1]

There are 40,000 touch-sensitive organs of which there are at least five different types that send signals to a "mini brain," brain cell tissue situated and connected directly to the heart's muscle. The heart is the body's most powerful generator and communicates with other parts in different ways.

- Neurologically: via nerve impulses to the brain
- Biochemically: via hormones and neurosender
- Biophysically: via pressure and sound waves
- Electromagnetically: via the creation of strong magnetic field around the body which can be measured a meter from the body. The field is 5,000 times stronger than the magnetic field the brain produces.

226 Part III. How to Feel Well in Your Brain and Heart

The heart is as equally fascinating as the brain. Every heartbeat—a pumping—a vibration, is controlled meticulously during every part of the process. The length and power are perfectly suited to what the body requires at that exact second in time. At the same time an analysis of the blood is carried out with regard to the amount of hormones the heart pushes out with every pump fulfilling the requirement for that exact moment in time (Jan Jutander).

From the very first heartbeat when we are three-week-old fetuses, to four billion heartbeats later when we leave this life, we are a part of life on earth.

The Non-Particle View

Montagnier's experiments bear upon certain crucial questions of the scientific method which could not be properly addressed within the usually posed paradoxes of modern physics, but which begin to find a clearer resolution when the subject matter becomes the relationship among the non-living, living, and also cognitive domains. For example, we knew already from the work of de Broglie and Schrödinger in the 1920s that the paradoxes arising from the attempt to reduce experience within the nonliving domain to a particle-based conception of substance could be overcome by a wave conception which subsumed the phenomena of electromagnetic radiation and the old "mechanics" within a unified conception of microcosm and macrocosm.

However, Schrödinger was unable to carry over such insights into the domain of life, instead proposing a disappointing notion of local negation of entropy to explain the obvious upward organizing principle characterizing both evolutionary progress and cognitive human advance. That difficulty was resolved midway through the twentieth century by Lyndon LaRouche's recognition that human creativity, which he recognized as the driving force of human economic advance, and the actual source of wealth or value, as opposed to all prevailing theories of labor content or market valuation, was also the knowable principle of universal progress, or cognate with it. Therefore, the characteristics of that universally propagated creative principle must be adducible from properly constructed investigations into the relationship of cosmic radiations to life on Earth—provided that the usual flawed assumption about the completeness and efficacy of the human sensorium, the five senses, is cast aside, as LaRouche has recently emphasized.

By revisiting the question of the interplay of radiation, including atmospheric and, implicitly, cosmic radiation, with life, the Montagnier experiments have brought to bear some fresh new evidence into this area of inquiry which had been declared almost *verboten* by the scientific establishment for most of the last century.

Leonard Laskow (1992) has noted that "something in the relationship between the doctor and the patient comforts and makes healing easier."[2] He has also developed techniques to try to describe systematically and predictably what modern medical science has lost.

In one experiment, two identical groups of bacteria were exposed to antibiotics which normally would have inhibited their growth. But before the antibiotics were added, loving energy was focused on one of the groups of bacteria. The group that was protected by loving energy survived and continued to be mobile, while the control group wasted away.

A number of similar experiments finally convinced Laskow that the results he got with energy healing could not be ascribed to the psychological placebo effect alone or even to psychoneuroimmunology in general.

In order to understand how our thoughts or feelings can influence our body, we must understand that our body is not only physical, or material. Einstein accepted that matter and energy are equivalent and mutually interchangeable aspects of a single underlying reality or "universal field."

In other words, everything is energy in different phases of vibration and motion. Just as the sea consists of many currents and waves that are moving simultaneously in various directions and with varying force, so our body consists of many pulsating, interacting energy fields. Though we think of our body as a solid physical mass, its mass is quite simply energy that has been given that particular form.

Within the energy system we call the human body are a great many subsystems that contribute to healing us and keeping us healthy. These include the lymphatic system, the circulatory system, the nervous system, the muscular system, the immune system, the digestive system, and the endocrine system, and all of them act together. Each one of them is receptive to the subtle energies that come from both inside and outside the body.

We know that DNA has piezoelectric qualities, which means that it can convert energy from one form to another. For example, if energy in the form of pressure or vibration is applied to a piezoelectric structure, it releases electrons. If, on the other hand, electrons are introduced into a piezoelectric structure, it starts to vibrate. Almost all the cells in our body, except for fully developed red blood cells, contain DNA and are therefore piezoelectric.

Nobel laureate Albert Szent-Gyorgi has pointed out that the transfer of electrons, both within and between cells, is the key to vital process. Thus it is not at all surprising that vibrations of certain energy fields can be beneficial or harmful for our health.

Research indicated further that infected cells transmitted information about their diseased condition to healthy cells, and that they did this through energy that had the ability to pass through quartz but not through glass. (Quartz lets ultraviolet light through, while ordinary glass blocks or filters it so that the signals which are sent by the cells are altered.) Further studies showed that the energy in question was that which is close to the ultraviolet spectrum— that of DNA radiation.

This research, which comprised over 1,700 experiments, shows that DNA in living cells is able to communicate with other cells in the vicinity through transmission of energy in the form of light. These results indicate that cells can communicate with each other independent of biochemistry and organic systems such as the circulatory system, the nervous system, or the immune system.

Bernard Grad, biologist at McGill University in Montreal, showed that the spectrum of absorption, surface tension, conductivity, and degree of acidity of water can be changed by means of focused thoughts or intention. When it is structured by means of healing that is sent, the hydrogen-bonding angles of the water molecules are widened. The increased angle weakens the water molecules' normal degree of attraction to each other. This leads to a decrease in surface tension and an increase in the solubility of the structured water, as well as a changed pattern in its ability to absorb light. Laskow says that if thought and healing energy can structure extra- and intracellular fluid, which in its turn affects the distribution of electrical charges in the cell membrane, this could apparently facilitate the healing process.

Non-Local

Action at a distance is well known in quantum physics and might explain healing at a distance. To explain this phenomenon, physics has invented the concept of non-locality, as it is described in Bell's theorem. Non-locality is one of the main concepts in quantum mechanics and signifies that the matter in the universe is linked by means of non-localized forces such as strong and weak atomic force, gravity, and electromagnetic force.

But our consciousness, then? No one has shown where it exists. Consciousness appears to exist in everything that has DNA (is it in the base pairs or in the hydrogen bonds between the base pairs?). Our consciousness takes in information without making use of our normal five senses. (Remote Viewing is one instance of this.) It is especially interesting that the information which is obtained in this way appears to be independent of distance not only in space but also in time, which has resulted in the phenomenon's now being called non-local consciousness. This leads to the speculation that perhaps consciousness as such cannot even be said to have its origin in the brain, but that the brain's function is rather to translate consciousness so that it can function smoothly in a physical dimension of time and space.

Might it be that what we think of as our brain is a "slave-transmitter" for our consciousness, which actually lives free of time and space? If we conceive a non-local consciousness, as it is demonstrated by the EPR paradox, Alain Aspect, or modern information technology, we gain a number of explanations for what had previously been unexplained, as when consciousness leaves the body in out-of-body or near-death experiences when people describe having seen their body from above, or—why not?—when a loved one dies and knowledge of this reaches us instantaneously on another continent.

At a conference called "Science and Non-duality" in San Rafael, California, a talk was given by Professor Stuart Hameroff who, alongside being a professor, is also a doctor of anesthesiology at a hospital where organ transplants are a daily occurrence. He spoke of an occasion when a number of patients who had passed away through heart failure only to 15 minutes later suddenly shown an EEG gamma level of 80–100 Hz. This continued for 20 minutes before the EEG once again showed 0.

At the conference "Toward a Science of Consciousness" held in Stockholm in the spring of 2011 professor Lakhmir S. Chawla spoke of very similar circumstances to those Hameroff had experienced.[3] In one in particular Chawla speaks about a dying man who's EEG curve a short while after his heart stopped beating unexpectedly curved upwards and remained that way for a while until it slowly returned back to 0. At first he suspected interference from a pager, but there were none. Chawla wrote a scientific report about the cases, which then numbered seven. After this occurrence the same thing has been seen with 100 patients, in 80 percent of cases. A possible explanation for this phenomenon is that the lack of oxygen means that the nerve cells can no longer maintain the normal tension on their membranes. When a large number of nerve cells are fired off one last time the effect could be a cascade of electrical activity. Such a peak would, in that case, be a worthless result of the nervous system's construction, similarly worthless as the flash of light that could appear on the screen of an ancient TV when it was switched off. Lakhmir Chawla explains that the brain's last activity consists of gamma waves (30–100 Hz), which according to certain researchers coincides with consciousness. The suspicion of this has led to ethical discussions in connection with organ transplants.

"We know very little about the mental conditions which can exist in a brain and how they are linked with what we call reality," says Nobel Prize winner Arvid Carlsson. Arvid Carlsson was awarded the Nobel Prize in Physiology or Medicine in 2000 for the discovery of the signaling matter in the brain called dopamine. He has also carried out a series of groundbreaking experiments which have led to new medicines. In line with other the majority of brain researchers he is also deeply interested in how the body's most complex organ provides our conscious experiences. He speculates how it may be possible for us to experience something which has no time aspect at all, a condition in the collapsed brain completely disengaged from the sense of time. What is it? Of course it is eternity! It may be the case that while we are on our way out, for want of another word, just then we experience eternity. We shall then experience for an eternity, according to Arvid Carlsson.

The Brain Functions Holographically and Quantum Mechanically[4]

So says the Hungarian quantum physicist István Dienes, who is managing the legacy of his world-famous countryman Dennis Gábor in an exciting fashion. Yes, Dienes and a number of today's outstanding researchers think that the world is a gigantic hologram. And if they are right, we are living in an illusory world, which the ancient Hindu Vedas call Maya.

In the course of his studies of the Vedic scriptures, Dienes has found clear connections between Hindu thought, modern holography, and quantum mechanics. And at Maharishi's European Research Institute in Switzerland he introduced a conceivable physical model of consciousness, which he called the holomatrix of consciousness.

A hologram, as we know, is a three-dimensional image that is created by means of a laser beam. The first person who pursued the achievement was the Hungarian Dennis Gábor, who received the Nobel Prize in 1971. He split a laser beam and directed one half at an object, which was photographed. The other half, in turn, was made to collide with the reflected light from the first one. And what happened?

The collision generated a pattern, which was registered on film. Subsequently, when a laser beam crossed the pattern on the film Gábor discovered behind the film a three-dimensional image of the object he had photographed.

That discovery was followed by an even more remarkable discovery. When the holographic film was cut into small pieces, through which a laser beam was shone, it was seen that every piece had the same characteristic of being able to reproduce a three-dimensional image; that is, the information about the whole existed in each part of the film.

It was not understood at that time, but the underlying law came to be known as non-locality, since the information that was needed to produce the image was not localized at any definite piece of the holographic film but existed in every part of the film at the same time.

For some time, the science has argued for the universe as a whole being, a kind of gigantic hologram, a mirroring of another reality, in which neither time nor space exists—the world is a detailed illusion. To be sure, the theory is rejected by many, but it is gaining ever more ground.

According to the quantum physicist David Bohm, every part of the universe is connected with everything. It is not possible to break anything out of the whole and examine it separately—a theory that makes today's specialists go crazy. They, of course, reduce everything into small separated details and believe that the sum of the details gives the whole.

István Dienes reasons the same way as David Bohm when it comes to the human brain. With his holomatrix model, Dienes has completed the theory that was first introduced by Dr. Karl Pribram. Pribram found that the human brain is holographic when he was trying to learn where memories are stored in the brain. He found that memories are not stored in any definite part of the brain, but rather exist everywhere in the brain at the same time.

Pribram based his work, among other things, on the research results of the neuropsychologist Karl Lashley, who had taught rats to do certain things. After Lashley surgically removed various parts of the animals' brains and tested their ability, it was found that they could still do what they had been taught, even when a large part of the brain had been removed. Clearly, the memory of the animals was scattered across the whole brain, which thus stood out as a hologram.

Nor have people who, for medical reasons, have had a part of their brain surgically removed displayed the loss of any particular memories; all have remained after the operation, even if certain memories had become indistinct.

The idea of the brain as a hologram led to many thoughts for Pribram. He arrived at objective reality—the one that consists of tables and teacups, flowers and birds—as actually not existing, at least not in the way we imagine. And in that case, he thought, perhaps the mystics in the Vedas were right in that reality is Maya, an illusion. Everything that exists outside us appears to be only a great symphony of wave forms, frequencies, which are converted into the apparently concrete world we know only when they go through our senses.

Some researchers who advocate the hologram model start out from the failed attempts to discover where consciousness is in the human body. It is generally assumed to exist in the brain, but no one has been able to say where. Now a number of doctors, among them Raymond Moody, have drawn the conclusion that human consciousness is non-local. In their studies of near-death experiences they have assembled thousands of well-documented cases that appear to show that human consciousness is not at all bound to the body but is able to exist outside it; perhaps it can continue existing in another reality after death.

In his book *The Holographic Universe*, Michael Talbot provides numerous examples of how telepathy, near-death experiences, out-of-body experiences, and healing can be explained through the holographic model.[5]

Emanuel Swedenborg (1688–1772) was a scientist and one of the universal geniuses of his time. Among other things, he had out-of-body experiences. In the course of his "journeys" Swedenborg learned "that the human being after death is in possession of all her senses and of every memory, thought and feeling she has enjoyed in the world and that she leaves nothing behind but her earthly body."[6]

Swedenborg is not the only individual in history who possessed the ability to make out-of-body journeys to the subtler levels of realty. The twelfth-century Persian Sufis also employed deep trancelike meditation to visit the "land where spirits dwell."[7] The parallel between their accounts and what Michael Talbot writes about is striking.

Perhaps it is here that we have the solution to the riddle of life. Our consciousness continues on when we leave this life.

If we conceive a non-local consciousness, as it is demonstrated by the EPR paradox, Alain Aspect, or modern information technology, we gain a number of explanations for what had previously been unexplained, as when consciousness leaves the body in out-of-body or near-death experiences when people describe having seen their body from above, or—why not?—when a loved one dies and knowledge of this reaches us instantaneously on another continent.

The Holographic Heart—More Than a Pump

The heart's rhythmic energetic activity lies at the center of our account. The heart generates a continuous series of electromagnetic pulses in which the time interval between pulses varies in a dynamic and complex manner. These pulsing waves of electromagnetic energy give rise to fields within fields, which form interference patterns when they interact with magnetically polarizable tissues and structures. In more specific terms, we postulate that as pulsing waves of energy radiate out from the heart, the energy waves interact with organs and other structures to create interference patterns. At the same time, the endogenous processes in each of the other organs, structures, and systems, including those at the microscale of cells and membranes, also generate patterns of dynamic activity. These patterns of dynamic activity radiate out into the body's internal environment as energy oscillations, and they interact with the energy waves from the heart and to some degree with the energy waves of other organs and structures. In each of these interactions the energy waves encode the features of the objects and their dynamic activity as interference patterns. Because the heart generates by far the strongest energy field, which interacts with both the macro and micro scales of the body's organization, the waves it produces operate effectively as global carrier waves that encode the information contained in the interference patterns. These global carrier waves thus contain encoded information from *all* of the body's energetic interactions, and they distribute this information throughout all systems in the body. In this holographic-like process, the encoded information acts to *in-form* the activity of all bodily functions (McCraty et al., 1998).[8] This energetic communication system thereby operates as a global organizing mechanism to coordinate and synchronize psychophysiological processes in the body as a whole.

This theory—that the heart encodes and distributes energetic information holographically—is based on the same model that neuropsychologist Karl Pribram has used to describe the neural processes in the brain that gives rise to perception and memory. In this model, as Pribram makes clear, the neural impulses are only relaying information from one part of the brain to another. However, the actual processing of information occurs in the spectral domain of energy frequency—a domain outside space and time in which the waves of energy produced by the operation of the neural microstructure interact. Moreover, he has shown that that the same mathematics that Gabor (1948) used to describe the quantum-holographic principles involved in the physics of signal processing can also be used to describe the information processing that occurs in the electromagnetic interactions between the dendritic and axon fields of neurons (McCraty et al., 1998). While a discussion of this is beyond the scope of this article, Pribram and other brain scientists have presented a large body of compelling experimental evidence that supports the veracity of Pribram's bioenergetic model of information processing (King, Xie, Zheng, & Pribram, 1994[9]; McCraty et al., 1998; Santa Maria et al., 1995).[10] Thus, in addition to the energetic information processing that occurs in the brain, as described by Pribram, we propose that there is also a heart-based global energetic system that encodes and distributes information to coordinate and organize the function of the body as a whole.

There is compelling evidence to suggest that the heart's energy field is coupled to a field of information that is not bound by the limits of time and space. This evidence comes from a rigorous experimental study we conducted to investigate the proposition that the body receives and processes information about a future event before the event actually happens (McCraty et al., 2004a,[11] 2004b).[12] The study's results provide surprising, even astounding data showing that both the heart and brain appear to receive and respond to information about a future event. Even more tantalizing is the evidence that the heart appears to receive intuitive information *before* the brain. This suggests that the heart is directly coupled to a subtle energetic field of ambient information that surrounds the body, which, in turn, is entangled and interacts with the multiplicity of energy fields in which the body is embedded—including that of the quantum vacuum.

In short, it would appear that we are only just beginning to understand the fundamental role of a bioenergetic communication system in processing information from sources both within and outside the body to *in-form* physiological function, cognitive processes, emotions, and behavior.[13]

In this system, it thus seems clear that the energy field of the heart plays a crucial role.

Transplanted Personality?

A new pig's heart hardly turns us into pigs, but many people experience remarkable things after a heart transplant, such as changes in their personality or memories of things they have never experienced. For a long time these changes have been explained either as psychological reactions after an extensive surgical procedure or as side effects of the powerful drugs that are vital after the operation to keep the immune system from rejecting the new heart. However, in the United States there is a tradition of receiving information about the identity of the organ donor, and afterwards the donor's family often meet the patient who has received the donor's heart. This has given rise to a long list of aha-experiences in which the patient suddenly realizes that the new personality tallies completely with that of the dead donor.

Studies of people who have received a new heart through transplantation show that many actually do assume parts of the donor's personality and memories. Studies by scientists have led to several theories about how the heart might contain these qualities, which others consider to belong to the brain.

In the course of a ten-year period, psychologist Paul Pearsall of the University of Hawaii and his colleagues Gary E. Schwartz and Linda G. Russek of the University of Arizona conducted comprehensive interviews with 23 patients who had undergone a heart transplant, as well as with the patients' families and the donors' family members. During the conversations the psychologists found many instances in which some portion of the personality or memory appears to have gone with the heart into the recipient.

An example of this is a 24-year-old lesbian woman with a great predilection for hamburgers and other junk food, who after a heart transplant suddenly became a vegetarian and felt sexually attracted to men rather than women. In addition, every evening after the operation she experienced a physical pain in her chest, which the doctors said had nothing to do with the transplant. During interviews with the donor's mother the researchers learned that the 19-year-old woman whose heart had been donated had lived by all the hippie ideals: she was vegetarian, had her own health-food restaurant, and practiced "free love" with many men. She died in a traffic accident and on her deathbed told her mother that she could still feel the pain in her chest where the car had struck her.

In another case it seemed as though the young woman who received the heart took over some of the donor's memory as well. An 18-year-old woman received her new heart from a musician of the same age, who wrote the music and lyrics of songs. The woman later met the musician's parents, who played his music for her. Despite the fact that this was the first time she had heard the music, she was able to sing along with the lyrics, as if she had heard them before. One of the songs was called "Danny, My Heart Is Yours," and the young woman who had received his heart, ironically enough, was called Danny.

It is not only memory and personality that seem to make an impression on the heart, however. Some patients who have undergone heart transplantation experience the donor's moment of death again and again. A 56-year-old teacher experienced, as the only noticeable change after a transplant, that day and night he had a vision in which he saw Jesus before him. After that he would see a glaring ray of light and feel intense heat on his face. The wife of the 34-year-old policeman who had donated his heart said that her husband had died in the line of duty as he was about to seize a drug dealer and was shot in the face at close range. The presumed perpetrator had long hair, expressive eyes, and on the whole resembled Jesus. The teacher who received the policeman's heart re-experienced in his dreams the last visual impression the donor had had before he was killed.

The researchers have several explanations for the phenomenon. The starting point for the scientific explanation is what are called neuropeptides. These are small, short protein chains that are used as signal substances in the brain and contribute to conveying information from one nerve cell to the next. The neuropeptides are produced by nerves in the entire body, and they are active in many different organs. Moreover, the same neuropeptide can have different functions in the body. For example, the neuropeptide NPY contributes both to regulating the appetite, which is determined in the brain, and to regulating the pumping activity of the heart.

The second theory is based on the fact that both brain and heart generate strong electrical and electromagnetic fields, which create the foundation for their function. The electromagnetic field of the heart is so strong that a sensitive measurement device can register it at a distance of over 30 meters. By that means, the heart may possibly be able to influence the brain. However, there are no scientific experiments which have documented that the heart is able to store memories or alter personality traits in the brain.

Gary Schwartz and Linda Russek are advocates of a third theory, which says that the cells and their molecules are able to store information through microscopic changes in shape. Adherents of this theory think that, as a footprint in the sand can testify to who has walked along the edge of the beach, the information about a person's life leaves impressions in all the organs of the body. Thus, according to this theory, which is called systemic or cellular memory, the brain is far from alone in remembering and is able to receive new memories through a transplanted heart and to process them as if they were its own memories.[14]

What is one to think? Personally, I lean towards the third theory, since the body's cells remember.

Obviously, these controversial phenomena need more study. From this standpoint, it is something of a pity that in Sweden it is forbidden to provide information about the donor's identity. German studies show that almost one-third of recipients show personality changes after a heart transplant. In Sweden this would correspond to just over ten people per year.

More on Consciousness Beyond the Body

Several passages follow from *What They Saw ... At the Hour of Death*, by Karlis Osis, Ph.D. and Erlendur Haraldsson, Ph.D., a book based on their many years of study of this field.[15]

Cardiologist Michael Sabom (1982) concentrated his research effort on the out-of-body experiences of resuscitated patients. He was fascinated by patients' detailed observations of the resuscitation process that took place when they were unconscious. He carefully explored the possibility that patients gathered such information by normal means, such as hearing what was going on while they were in unconsciousness state, staff members telling patients about the resuscitation procedure, knowledge gathered by watching television medical shows, etc. After painstaking investigations, Sabom[16] concluded that:

> During the autoscopic portion of the NDE (near-death experience), near-death survivors claimed to have seen and heard events in the vicinity of their own unconscious physical bodies from a detached elevated position. The details of these perceptions were found to be accurate in all instances where collaborating evidence was available. Moreover, there appeared to be no plausible explanation for the accuracy of these observations involving the usual physical senses. An out-of-body (extrasensory?) mechanism would explain both the personal interpretation afforded these experiences by those who had them (i.e., "the spirit left the body?") and the visual accuracy of the autoscopic observations. My own beliefs on this matter are leaning in this direction. The out-of-body hypothesis simply seems to fit best the data at hand [p. 199].

There is extensive literature purporting to give information of those who have been on the other side for some time. Although such sources are beyond the scope of this book, ignoring them completely would make for a lopsided view of the postmortem survival issue. Each of the world religions tells a story: the Bible, the Upanishads, the Tibetan *Book of the Dead*. Their empirical foundations are, however, very difficult to trace.

Communications with the dead are widely claimed. According to a national opinion poll conducted by Greeley (1975) every fourth American says that he or she has had contact with the dead. Haraldsson (1976) obtained similar results in Iceland, and some even say that they have talked with them (Rees 1971). Legitimate, scientific studies of such are rather scarce, though (p. 204).

Nils O. Jacobson (1973), a Swedish psychiatrist, intricately describes a dream-world theory developed by a Danish writer, Martinus, who claimed to have had out-of-body visits to another world. This theory is quite comprehensive in its explanation of different spheres or locales in the other world (such as Purgatory), several hierarchical loci of Heaven—which one has to evolve through by personal development—and such concepts as Karma, reincarnation and so on.

> The visionary experiences of dying patients seem to contradict the essential features of the dream-world theory. First, apparitions often exhibit a will of their own, contrary to the patient's wishes and expectations. Second, the environments seem to exist independently of

the patient's motivations. Scenes do not change according to his wishes or fears, as predicted by the dream-world theory. Martinus's theory assumes that only like-minded persons of the same level of spiritual development will be able to perceive each other; communication with the rest will be impossible. This was not so in the vision of dying. Close relatives, rather than like-minded individuals, are the dominant take-away figures. Therefore, deathbed observations are more consistent with the view that the dying do indeed encounter something "out-there." Furthermore, we have reason to believe that the take-away figures are independent entities rather than thought projections. As such, they seem to share the patient's visual space, instead of coming with their own [pp. 207–208].

Wherever you look, your perspective on everything will be changed. The feverish resuscitation efforts of the doctors and nurses to save your life will seem totally out of place, as through they were working on someone else's body. The heartrending anguish of weeping relatives will appear to be childish and beside the point. Your own grand concerns—the unfulfilled dreams of the future, duties to loved ones, work, everything you ever looked forward to—will become small and unimportant, fading like dried flowers. With a sudden wave of joy, you will be ready to go.

If you are a Hindu, you will most likely experience the same things, but you may be received by a Yamdoot rather than by the "professional" himself. But don't despair; you will be brought to the man in the white robe, and he is always a benign ruler with an aura of sacredness around him [pp. 212–213].

Our last moments are far more marked by our surroundings than had previously been thought up to now. A Swiss climbs a mountain into the sky, an Indian rides off across the prairie, while a New Yorker's last journey is made in a yellow taxi.[17]

NDEs have been questioned, naturally. Researchers have tried to explain them as the brain's reaction to lack of oxygen, but the fact that our belief, culture and thoughts are decisive for who we experience our last time is just marvelous.

An Appreciative Heart Is Good Medicine

Psychologists once maintained that emotions were purely mental expressions generated by the brain alone. We now know that this is not true—emotions have as much to do with the heart and body as they do with the brain. Of the bodily organs, the heart plays a particularly important role in our emotional experience. The experience of an emotion results from the brain, heart and body acting in concert.

The Institute of HeartMath, a research center dedicated to the study of the heart and the physiology of emotions, has conducted numerous studies identifying the relationship between emotions and the heart. A number of their studies have provided new insight into understanding how the activity of the heart is indeed linked to our emotions and our health, vitality and well-being.[18]

Emotions and the Heart

Recent HeartMath studies define a critical link between the heart and brain. The heart is in a constant two-way dialogue with the brain—our emotions change the signals the brain sends to the heart and the heart responds in complex ways. However, we now know that the heart sends more information to the brain than the brain sends to the heart. And the brain responds to the heart in many important ways. This research explains how the heart responds to emotional and mental reactions and why certain emotions stress the body and drain our energy. As we experience feelings like anger, frustration, anxiety and insecurity, our heart rhythm patterns become more erratic. These erratic patterns are sent to the emotional centers in the brain, which it recognizes as negative or stressful feelings. These signals create the actual feelings we experience in the heart area and the body. The erratic heart rhythms also block our ability to think clearly.

Many studies have found that the risk of developing heart disease is significantly increased for people who often experience stressful emotions such as irritation, anger or frustration.

These emotions create a chain reaction in the body—stress hormone levels increase, blood vessels constrict, blood pressure rises, and the immune system is weakened. If we consistently experience these emotions, it can put a strain on the heart and other organs, and eventually lead to serious health problems.

Conversely, HeartMath's research shows that when we experience heartfelt emotions like love, care, appreciation and compassion, the heart produces a very different rhythm. In this case it is a smooth pattern that looks like gently rolling hills. Harmonious heart rhythms, which reflect positive emotions, are considered to be indicators of cardiovascular efficiency and nervous system balance. This lets the brain know that the heart feels good and often creates a gentle warm feeling in the area of the heart. Learning to shift out of stressful emotional reactions to these heartfelt emotions can have profound positive effects on the cardiovascular system and on our overall health. It is easy to see how our heart and emotions are linked and how we can shift our heart into a more efficient state by monitoring its rhythms.

Benefits Come from Being Appreciative

The feeling of appreciation is one of the most concrete and easiest positive emotions for individuals to self-generate and sustain for longer periods. Almost anyone can find something to genuinely appreciate. By simply recalling a time when you felt sincere appreciation and recreating that feeling, you can increase your heart rhythm coherence, reduce emotional stress and improve your health.

For people who may initially find it difficult to self-generate a feeling of appreciation in the present moment, experts suggest that they recall a past memory that elicits warm feelings. With practice, most people are able to self-generate feelings of appreciation in real time and no longer need the past time reference. Dr. Rollin McCraty, director of research for the Institute of HeartMath, says, "It's important to emphasize that it is not a mental image of a memory that creates a shift in our heart rhythm, but rather the emotions associated with the memory. Mental images alone usually do not produce the same significant results that we've observed when someone focuses on a positive *feeling*."

> Positive emotion-focused techniques, like those developed by HeartMath, can help individuals effectively replace stressful thoughts and emotional patterns with more positive perceptions and emotions. One of the long-term benefits to be gained from the practice of these kinds of techniques is increased emotional awareness. This increased awareness can

help individuals maintain a more consistent emotional balance, a fundamental step in the process of improving cardiovascular health.

Diet and exercise will continue to be an important factor in keeping the heart healthy. However, there is increasing awareness of the importance of maintaining a healthy emotional state for those recovering from heart-related illnesses, as well as for maintaining heart health. Studies have shown that positive emotion-focused techniques reduce stress and anxiety, which is a safe and effective way to lower blood pressure and increase functional capacity in heart failure patients. This approach is currently being used in a number of hospitals and cardiac rehabilitation programs around the country.[19]

Sir Roger Penrose, professor emeritus at Oxford and one of the greatest scientists of theoretical physics, among other things the discoverer of the energy of black holes in space, thinks that consciousness must be a quantum phenomenon because the neurons are too large to have anything to do with consciousness (Penrose, 1989). In the neurons there is a cytoskeleton with microtubules, which control the synapse function. Penrose thinks that consciousness arises from the microtubules and is an interaction between classical physics and quantum physics. He has developed the theory together with Stuart Hameroff (Penrose, Hameroff, 2011). Penrose distinguishes between objective and subjective reduction. Objective reduction, Penrose has discovered is a type of collapse of wave function when the universe has to choose between significantly different space time geometries, whereas subjective reduction belongs to quantum theory. The quantum phenomena of objective reduction control the brain's activity through the coherent flow inside the microtubules. There is a separate mental world but it is part of the physical world.

According to the Orch OR model, these microtubules in the cytoplasm of the dendrites are isolated from their classical (i.e., non-quantum) environment due to this superpositioned entanglement.

It is true, as critics note, that the Penrose OR model is unproven, and that if this model does prove to be correct then quantum theory would have to be rewritten. Hameroff says that quantum theory as it is formulated today is incomplete. It *must* be rewritten. The critics think that Penrose/Hameroff must "show the existence of aspects of the brain that are not explained by neuro computational theories and that can be explained by quantum computation or associated mechanisms." Hameroff believes that neuro computational theories fail to explain essential features of consciousness like binding, transition from unconscious activities to consciousness, non-algorithmic processing and the "hard problem" of subjective experience (Chalmers, 1996, 2004), characteristics that everyone is able to discuss. Instead Hameroff points to gamma synchrony EEG as a candidate for the "neural correlate of consciousness" (the "NCC") that is, the neural basis for consciousness. Gamma synchrony EEG (30–90 Hz) has been observed in hundreds of human and animal studies with multi-unit scalp, surface and implanted electrodes, and occurs within and across cortical areas, hemispheres, the thalamus and even the spinal cord (Schoffelen, Oostenveld & Fries, 2005).

In concluding, critics point to Orch OR being a theory of consciousness that rests on as yet unproven biology and physics, but is consistent with known science, falsifiable—i.e., can be tested—and it generates testable predictions (Hameroff 1998a; Hameroff 2006a), customary conditions for it to be scientific.

The Intelligent Heart

Many of the changes in bodily function that occur during the coherence state revolve around changes in the heart's pattern of activity. While the heart is certainly a remarkable pump, interestingly, it is only relatively recently in the course of human history—around the past three centuries or so—that the heart's function has been defined (by Western scientific thought) as *only* that of pumping blood. Historically, in almost every culture of the world, the heart was ascribed a far more multifaceted role in the human system, being regarded as a source of wisdom, spiritual insight, thought, and emotion. Intriguingly, scientific research over the past several decades has begun to provide evidence that many of these long-surviving associations may well be more than simply metaphorical. These developments have led science to once again to revise and expand its understanding of the heart and the role of this amazing organ.

In the new field of neurocardiology, for example, scientists have discovered that the heart possesses its own intrinsic nervous system—a network of nerves so functionally sophisticated as to earn the description of a "heart brain." Containing over 40,000 neurons, this "little brain" gives the heart the ability to independently sense, process information, make decisions, and even to demonstrate a type of learning and memory. In essence, it appears that the heart is truly an intelligent system. Research has also revealed that the heart is a hormonal gland, manufacturing and secreting numerous hormones and neurotransmitters that profoundly affect brain and body function. Among the hormones the heart produces is oxytocin—well known as the "love" or "bonding hormone." Science has only begun to understand the effects of the electromagnetic fields produced by the heart, but there is evidence that the information contained in the heart's powerful field may play a vital synchronizing role in the human body—and that it may affect others around us as well.

Research has also shown that the heart is a key component of the emotional system. Scientists now understand that the heart not only *responds* to emotion, but that the signals generated by its rhythmic activity actually play a major part in *determining the quality of our emotional experience* from moment to moment. As described next, these heart signals also profoundly impact perception and cognitive function by virtue of the heart's extensive communication network with the brain. Finally, rigorous electrophysiological studies conducted at the Institute of HeartMath have even indicated that the heart appears to play a key role in intuition. Although there is much yet to be understood, it appears that the age-old associations of the heart with thought, feeling, and insight may indeed have a basis in science.

The Coherent Heart

The concept of an energetic information field is not a new one. Indeed, many prominent scientists have proposed models in which information from all physical, biological and psychosocial interactions is enfolded as a spectral order outside the space/time world in the energy waveforms of the quantum vacuum. Holographic principles[20] (Gabor, 1948) form the basis of most of these theories and have been used to describe how information about the organization of a whole is nonlocalized—enfolded and distributed to all parts and locations via the energy waveforms produced by interactions in the brain (Pribram, 1971, 1991), social structures (Bradley, 1987; Bradley & Pribram, 1998),[21] and the universe (Bekenstein, 2003; Nadeau & Kafatos, 1999). We adopted a holographic perspective to describe how energy waveforms generated by the heart's electromagnetic field encode and distribute information about all structures and processes throughout the body from the cellular level to the body as a whole. Moreover, the energy fields produced by the heart and other bodily structures are transmitted externally. And because these energy fields are in continuous interaction with the multiplicity of energy fields in the environment, it appears that information about nonlocal events and processes is conveyed back to the body and processed as intuition.[22]

We believe that the concept of energetic information holds promise as a way of understanding how the body's bioenergetic communication system operates to process information from sources both within and outside the body. Based on the evidence we have presented, it seems clear that the energy field of the heart plays a crucial role in in-forming physiological function, cognitive processes, emotions, and behavior.

We have endeavored to present a deeper understanding of the central significance of the heart in virtually all aspects of the body's function. As a principal and consistent source of rhythmic information patterns that impact the physiological, cognitive, and emotional systems, the heart thus provides an access point from which a change in system-wide function can be immediately effected. When positive emotions are used to shift the heart's pattern of activity into coherence, a global transformation in psychophysiological function occurs. As the evidence we have presented clearly shows, this transformation results in increased physiological efficiency, greater emotional stability, and enhanced cognitive function and performance. As a simple and direct means by which one can shift into a state of psychophysiological coherence, the HeartMath tools are a highly effective method to facilitate this transformation. In the case of Chris, with which we opened this article, the use of these tools proved to be a life-saving and life-changing intervention, leading to changes not only in his physical health, but also in his emotional life, work performance, and relationships. We believe that the growing use of these and similar heartbased tools around the globe by educators and students, health care workers and patients, and managers and employees, among others, can play a significant part in improving the "life processes" of humankind. **Far more than a simple pump, as was once believed, the heart is now recognized by scientists as a highly complex system with its own functional "brain."**

Research in the new discipline of neurocardiology shows that the heart is a sensory organ and a sophisticated center for receiving and processing information. The nervous system within the heart (or "heart brain") enables it to learn, remember, and make functional decisions independent of the brain's cerebral cortex. Moreover, numerous experiments have demonstrated that the signals the heart continuously sends to the brain influence the function of higher brain centers involved in perception, cognition, and emotional processing. In addition to the extensive neural communication network linking the heart with the brain and body, the heart also communicates information to the brain and throughout the body via electromagnetic field interactions. The heart generates the body's most powerful and most extensive rhythmic electromagnetic field. **Compared to** the electromagnetic field produced by the brain, the electrical component of the heart's field is about 60 times greater in amplitude, and permeates every cell in the body. The magnetic component is approximately 5000 times stronger than the brain's magnetic field and can be detected several feet away from the body with sensitive magnetometers.

The heart generates a continuous series of electromagnetic pulses in which the time interval between each beat varies in a dynamic and complex manner. The heart's ever-present rhythmic field has a powerful influence on processes throughout the body. We have demonstrated, for example, that brain rhythms naturally synchronize to the heart's rhythmic activity, and also that during sustained feelings of love or appreciation, the blood pressure and respiratory rhythms, among other oscillatory systems, entrain to the hearts rhythm.

We propose that the heart's field acts as a carrier wave for information that provides a global synchronizing signal for the entire body. Specifically, we suggest that as pulsing waves of energy radiate out from the heart, they interact with organs and other structures. The waves encode or record the features and dynamic activity of these structures in patterns of energy waveforms that are distributed throughout the body. In this way, the encoded information acts to in-form (literally, give shape to) the activity of all bodily functions—to coordinate and synchronize processes in the body as a whole. This perspective requires an energetic concept of information, in which patterns of organization are enfolded into waves of energy of system activity distributed throughout the system as a whole.

Basic research at the Institute of HeartMath shows that information pertaining to a person's emotional state is also communicated throughout the body via the heart's electromagnetic field. The rhythmic beating patterns of the heart change significantly as we experience different emotions. Negative emotions, such as anger or frustration, are associated with an erratic, disordered, incoherent pattern in the heart's rhythms. In contrast, positive emotions, such as love or appreciation, are associated with a smooth, ordered, coherent pattern in the heart's rhythmic activity. In turn, these changes in the heart's beating patterns create corresponding changes in the structure of the electromagnetic field radiated by the heart, measurable by a technique called spectral analysis.

More specifically, we have demonstrated that sustained positive emotions appear to give rise to a distinct mode of functioning, which we call psychophysiological coherence. During this mode, heart rhythms exhibit a sine wave-like pattern and the heart's electromagnetic field becomes correspondingly more organized.

Heart Intelligence

McCraty found compelling evidence to suggest that the heart's energy field (energetic heart) is coupled to a field of information that is not bound by the classical limits of time and space. This evidence comes from several rigorous experimental studies that investigated the proposition that the body receives and processes information about a future event before the event actually happens. One of these studies, conducted at the HeartMath laboratories, showed that both the heart and brain receive and respond to pre-stimulus information about a future event. But even more surprising is the finding that the heart seems to receive the intuitive information *before* the brain. They also found that study participants in a positive, emotion-driven, coherent state prior to the experimental protocols proved to be significantly more attuned to the information from the heart than those who were not in such a state. This suggests to McCraty that the heart is directly coupled to a subtle energetic field of information that is entangled and interacts with the multiplicity of energetic fields in which the body is embedded—including the quantum vacuum.

That the heart appears to receive intuitive information before the brain should not be all that surprising, says McCraty. It just confirms what people mean when they speak of the *intuitive heart* or *heart intelligence*. The energetic heart is coupled to a deeper part of ourselves. When we are heart centered and coherent, we have a tighter coupling and closer alignment with our deeper source of intuitive intelligence. In a heart coherent state there is an increased flow of intuitive information that is communicated via the emotional energetic system to the brain systems resulting in a stronger connection with our inner voice and allowing us access to the largely untapped potential for bringing our mental and emotional faculties into greater balance and self-directed control. Practicing shifting to a more coherent state increases intuitive awareness and leads to shifts in perception and worldviews from which better informed and more intelligent decisions can be made.[23]

I think Amna Alfakini was correct. The complexity of the human brain is enormous but the heart itself has its own nerve system. This nerve system enables the heart to react quicker than the brain to the same impulse. "I mean that it depends on an interplay between the heart and the brain and that the neural signals which control free will, conscious action and intention are reliant on this interplay," concludes Amna.

Notes

1. I. Ernberg, et al. *Vad är liv i kosmos, i cellen, i människan?* (What Is life?) pp. 138–140.
2. L. Laskow, *Healing with Love*, p. 31ff.
3. http://fof.se/tidning/2011/7dodssgonblicket-i hjärnan, accessed 4 August 2012.
4. I. Markos, from a report on the 2nd Unified Theories Conference in Budapest, 16–19 May 2008. <http://www.kreaprenor.se/main.asp?g=10&r=305> accessed 13 July 2008. István Dienes's lecture at this conference was entitled "From Gravitational Holography to Living Holograms, from Consciousness-Holomatrix to Self-Conscious Neuronetwork."
5. M. Talbot, *The Holographic Universe*, p. 279.
6. E. Swedenborg, *Om andarnas värld och mäniskans tillstånd efter döden* (On the World of the Spirits and Man's State after Death), p. 43.
7. Talbot, p. 260.
8. R. McCraty, Barrios-Choplin, B,. Rozman, D., Atkinson, M., and Watkins, A.D. (1998). The impact of a new emotional self-management program on stress, emotions, heart rate variability, DHEA and cortisol. *Integrative Physiological and Behavioral Science*, 33 (2), 151–170.
9. J.S. King, Xie, M., Zheng, B., and Pribram, K.H. (1994). Spectral density maps of receptive fields in the rat's somatosensory cortex. In K.H. Pribram (ed.). *Proceedings of the second Appalachian conference on behavioral neurodynamics: origins: Brain and self organization* (pp. 557–571). Hillsdale, NJ: Lawrence Erlbaum Associates.
10. M. Santa Maria, King, J., Xie, M., Zheng, B., Pribram, K.H., and Doherty, D. (1995). Responses of somatosensory cortical neurons to spatial frequency and orientation: A progress report. In S. King and K.H. Pribram (eds.), *Scale in conscious experience: Is the brain too important to be left to specialists to study?* Mahwah, NJ: Lawrence Erlbaum Associates.
11. R. McCraty, Atkinson, M., and Bradley, R.T. (2004a). Electrophysiological evidence of intuition:

Part 1. The surprising role of the heart. *Journal of Alternative and Complementary Medicine*, 10 (1), 133–143.

    12. R. McCraty, Atkinson, M., and Bradley, R.T. (2004b). Electrophysiological evidence of intuition: Part 2. A system-wide process? *Journal of Alternative and Complementary Medicine, 10* (2), 325–336.

    13. McCraty, et al. The Coherent Heart INTEGRAL REVIEW. December 2009, Vol. 5, No. 2.

    14. G. Palmgren, "Personligheten sitter i hjärtat" (The Personality Is in the Heart), *Illustrerad Vetenskap (Science Illustrated)*, 15/2005, pp. 60–61.

    15. K. Osis, and Haraldsson, E. *What They Saw ... At the Hour of Death*, Norwalk, CT, Hastings House, 1997.

    16. M.B. Sabom, *Recollections of Death: A Medical Investigation*, New York, Harper & Row, 1982.

    17. K. Wilhelm, "Våra sista tankar" (Our Last Thoughts), *Illustrerad Vetenskap (Science Illustrated)* 9/2001, pp. 56–59.

    18. As part of the "Heart Smarts" series, *Today* explores the link between your heart health and your emotions. The heart's more than a pump—it actually sends messages to the brain. Dr. Rollin McCraty of the Institute of HeartMath visited *Today* to discuss the science behind the theory.

    19. For more information on the Institute of HeartMath, check out www.heartmath.org/today.

    20. D. Gabor (1948). A new microscopic principle. *Nature, 161*, 777–778.

    21. R.T. Bradley, and Pribram, K.H. (1998). Communication and stability in social collectives. *Journal of Social and Evolutionary Systems*, 21 (1), 29–80.

    22. McCraty, et al. The Coherent Heart INTEGRAL REVIEW December 2009 Vol. 5, No. 2.

    23. Surel Dominique. *Speaking from the heart*. EDGESCIENCE #6 • JANUARY–MARCH 2011/7–9.

Bibliography

Bradley, R.T. *Charisma and Social Structure: A Study of Love and Power, Wholeness and Transformation*. New York: Paragon House, 1987.

Cederquist, J. *The Purposeful Universe—How Quantum Theory and Mayan Cosmology Explain the Origin and Evolution of Life*. Rochester, VT: Bear, 2009.

Emoto, M. *Love Thyself: The Message from Water III* (v. 3) Carlsbad, CA: Hay House, 2006.

Emoto, M. *Water Crystal Healing: Music and Images to Restore Your Well-Being*. New York: Atria, 2006.

Emoto, M., and D. Thaym. *The Hidden Messages in Water*. New York: Atria, 2005.

Fredriksson, I. *H2O Just Ordinary Water*. Siljans Masar, e-book, 2010.

Hect, L. *New Evidence for a Non-Particular View of Life*. 2011.

Laskow, L. *Healing with Love,* San Francisco: Harper, 1992.

Nadeau, R., and Kafatos, M. *The Non-local Universe: The New Physics and Matters of the Mind*. New York: Oxford University Press, 1999.

Owe, T. *Beyond Death*, Tempe, AZ: New Falcon Publications, 2003.

Pribram, K.H. *Brain and Perception: Holonomy and Structure in Figural Processing*. Hillsdale, NJ: Lawrence Erlbaum Associates, 1991.

Pribram, K.H. *Languages of the brain*. New York: Brandon House, 1971.

Swedenborg, E. *Om andarnas värld och mäniskans tillstånd efter döden* (On the World of the Spirits and Man's State After Death). New York: Swedenborg Foundation, 1940.

Talbot, M. *The Holographic Universe*, New York: Harper, 1991.

Vitiello, G. *My Double Unveiled. The Dissipative Quantum Model of the Brain*. Philadelphia: John Benjamins, 2001.

The Need for an Existential Holism

Alf E. Sjöberg

Introduction

On wisdom (holo-thesis) as something far more than knowledge (synthesis) for the purpose of finding the meaning, possibilities, and goal of life, was it, I wonder, the hope of wisdom that remained at the bottom of Pandora's Box when all the knowledge-based troubles were set loose from it?[1] In this essay I wish to bring out some paths—as remarkable as they are possible—to an existentiological model of explanation. It begins with a quantum philosophy perspective in connection with yoga and the hypothesis of the Tree of Life. It then becomes possible to look more closely at the phenomenon of Stonehenge and shamanism as a development of consciousness in ancient people. From there we must ask ourselves what interest is, and how the ancient Greeks responded to that question mythologically. We are then able to pose the question of what growth actually is and whether it is sustainable. The purpose of growth that is sustainable is the quality of human life: an existential quantum humanism with its meaning, possibilities, and goals. But this requires wisdom, for knowledge seems not to suffice.[2] Wisdom "x-rays" knowledge when it manifests itself as illumination in meditation.

Wisdom

In lexical consensus, a wise person is considered to be sagacious and very learned. But wisdom penetrates thought and its knowledge of good and evil. We can use a hammer to do carpentry work, but it can also be used for murder. It is wisdom that illuminates the realization of this. Wisdom is the perspective and stream of ideas of meditation. Wisdom is spiritual, and thought is material. Thought is the processing of information about the course of events relating to objects. See, there, how the three quantum constituents—order, wave, and particle—reveal themselves as analogues on the cognitive plane? But wisdom penetrates consciousness such that it is able to reflect them. Hence the ancient Taoists could say, "See how all things come into being."[3]

In the wisdom of meditation, the personal sense of self can also be objectified. This sense of self is called self-consciousness because consciousness has identified itself with the self. In reflective meditative insight, this identification is dissolved. The self thus comes to be like an altar on which the energy of interest burns. It seizes hold of the objects, and the interpretive thoughts stream up like smoke. As a consequence, the three constituents are expunged from the sense of self, and the meditative wisdom of consciousness illuminates the four components and the way they work together cognitively.[4] This illumination is not a repetition of knowledge but is, each time, a spontaneous, new, original experience, because knowledge is the object of the meditative illumination. It is likewise with all feelings.

When cosmic stillness and its silence purify consciousness from the self, the thoughts, and the feelings, it is then that the illuminating wisdom of meditation can be received. It may also be perceived as an ocean in which the self and its light—consciousness—exist. To meet the quantum wisdom of the oceanic stillness, one can make use of the yogic method of *trataka*. This involves gazing with slightly open eyes, the vision unfocused, blurred. At the same time, attention is fixed on the breath without influencing it.[5] The frequency of the brain then shifts from beta to alpha waves in the relaxation centers (the psychic state). The peace of transcendence arises and the self with its thoughts, impressions, and feelings is objectified, to rise like water bubbles in the oceanic stillness. Consciousness then becomes one with itself and, in turn, with the field of wisdom. Meditation arises as illumination's stream of ideas so that the realization is able to convey the wisdom to the passive, resting, receptive faculty of thought. In yoga this is called direct observation (realization).

To attain this life wisdom, the peace of transcendence, one must set aside time for no-time. This transcendence is timeless, and its essence is cosmic stillness with an accompanying inner silence in one's soul.[6] A nun in Oslo said, in 2011, that mental and spiritual health depends on stillness and silence. In this state of consciousness, thoughts fall in but just as quickly fall out again.[7]

My image of the wise, human-centered person of the 21st century is this: Her consciousness reflects, testifying to her insight into how her personal executive sense of self manifests the three quantum constituents. These consist of psychophysical energy (the wave) that relates to the objects (the particles) in the faculty of thought (the information). The energy holds both attraction (desire) and repulsion (hatred and escape). When the human being sees her self and its constituents simultaneously (holistically), then she has been born anew as a quantum human with the existential meaningfulness, possibilities, and goals of a quantum human life.[8]

Quantum Philosophy and Yoga

In the reductionist skepticism of our age, the scientists and their parrots say that evolution is without meaning and likewise its products: nature, animals, and humans. There is no ordering factor whatsoever guiding evolution's energy (wave) and matter (particle): everything is born of a unique chance. And our attempts to establish a meaningful explanation of life are based on a brain defect. So, according to the reductionists, philosophical, religious, and psychological models of interpretation are merely cognitive garbage.[9]

But their interpretation, as a theory of creation, ought to be coming from this alleged brain defect, too. The conclusion is that this explanation is part of the mental garbage. In holistic systematics, scientists consider, with David Bohm, that the evident, intelligent order which makes plants, animals, and human beings possible—the explicate order—emanates from an intrinsic (implicate) order in the quantum field. This is a must in order for evolution's Einsteinian energy (wave) and matter, things (particles) to result, with analogical repetitions, in the human locomotive power (the wave) of the body (the particle) and intelligence (the information). In a quantum view of life, chance is synonymous with a leap as creative information. Thus, we can speak of a chance-logical context.[10]

In the human being, the intelligence of creative leaps manifests as "aha" experiences and meditation's intuitional stream of ideas. These are made real as meta-cognitive seeds, which fall down into a practical context so that the activity (the wave) will unite with a thing (particle) so it becomes meaningful. But the three quantum constituents (the wave, the particle, and the information) are aroused by our intention (the need),[11] and it is conscious. Thus, we can see how, as a result of the evolution, a furniture dealer, for instance, is conscious of his intention—to carry the furniture in and arrange it in his store. When we go to the health clinic we want to consult the doctor's intention along with her competence in order to act such that the illness will be eliminated. When evolution has these five quantum factors (particle–wave, order, intention, consciousness) as an outcome, then—to use the Bohmian logic of implicate–explicate—it should also have them as starting components.

In speculative research science we can make our way back philosophically to the breakpoint between changelessness and beginning. We can see a quantum-cosmic "furniture dealer" with the intention of kick-starting the quantum constituents of energy, matter, and information (wave, particle, and order). The intention is probably what triggers the sun and the planets. But consciousness, then? In the present state of science, people are puzzled about how consciousness has arisen. It is regarded as an outcome of evolution, and the brain is the definition of consciousness. But only one part of the scientific community speculates in that manner. The other part sees consciousness as a unique phenomenon in creation.[12] Consciousness is able to split off from the brain and is therefore not by definition identical with it. So if we continue the speculation beyond the quantum intention, the beginning could very well be a conscious kick.

What are we to have life for, in that case, if consciousness has its evolution and the environment has its? The question is resolved in yogic and Buddhist tradition, where we are considered to be capable of developing consciousness into something more than the postulated experiences of the ideology of material prosperity (wave), gadgets (particles), and news (information). In short, we are stressing ourselves out for the purpose of having more and more things and more and more information. This is merely the physical-material part of life. Consciousness is a matter of the spiritual-existential part. Both are equally important.[13] In yogism and Buddhism, one goes beyond thinking to direct realization and experience in the field of introspective observation. Consciousness can also leave this inner field to transcend to the metaphysical (celestial) plane of life and return. Consciousness is able to receive information there about the significance of the bliss of love and wisdom (*samadhi*) for fellow humans.[14] In the relaxation centers of the brain (the psychic state) the path to the development of consciousness is able to come about through the peace of transcendence. In the language of yoga, its guideposts are called *nyamas* (the spiritual observances) as theory, and the practice is called *trataka*. With these guideposts one is able to attain the fusion of contemplation with Cosmic Consciousness (in yoga this is the highest stage of development, *kaivalya*).[15] Yoga is a practice that is very well able to complement quantum psychology and complete it. Yoga can be a good aid in understanding the shamanic art of living, Stonehenge, and our intelligent Cosmos.

The Tree of Life Hypothesis

Carl Johan Calleman (2009), in his book *The Purposeful Universe*, presents a reliable and detailed discussion of how quantum theory and Mayan cosmology are able to explain the origin and evolution of life. He is also the author of *The Mayan Calendar and the Transformation of Consciousness* (2004). Calleman has devoted many years as a scientist to a close examination of the consensually respected Darwinian explanatory model of biological evolution, has also subjected religious creationism to critical examination, and has replaced them both with a new theory formation that he calls the idealist, or Tree of Life, hypothesis. It is likely to lead to a new paradigm.

Calleman's book contains a number of significant elements. Seen in time's rear-view mirror, there are a number of evolutionary periods in the cosmos. According to Calleman, the Mayan people have clearly been able, through shamanistic wisdom, to make a full catalogue that bears up under scientific examination. The Mayans also have a qualitative concept of time (the vertical) that complements the quantitative (the horizontal). The concepts of time proceed from the quantum cosmic Tree of Life, analogous to the cosmic central axis. This is not a belief but a testable hypothesis. From it, evolution's genesis of life, intelligence, and consciousness can be explained with scientific reasoning, and the shortcomings of both Darwinism and creationism can be also explained on the basis of the quantum cosmic Tree of Life hypothesis. This hypothesis develops the conception that cosmic evolution has a meaning, a direction, and a goal pre-programmed in the Tree of Life. There is no Darwinian chance that happens to arise on Earth. We have planned quantum leaps that cause species changes synchronistically, not by incremental steps. The slow, gradual change of Darwinism cannot holistically explain the mutation of new species. The Tree of Life has an intelligent design to offer to evolution. We have a cellular Tree of Life, says Calleman. It is the centriole, in the center of the cells, and it is an antenna for interaction with the cosmic Tree of Life.[16]

Consciousness, intelligence, and meaningfulness are consistent factors in an interpretation of the Tree of Life in the quantum field. When the Tree of Life manifests itself in us, it is able to awaken love and compassion. It is likely that both of these spiritual characteristics are in resonance with a sacred and spiritual world, with the Tree of Life and its "branches," the centrioles, playing a crucial role. In that case, love and compassion as cornerstones of the human being could not be reduced to brain chemistry, but are quite likely conveyed by it.

Carl Johan Calleman is very detailed in scientific penetration. He is humble and careful in his analyses and suggested interpretations. In the Tree of Life hypothesis, his combining of the Mayan people's ancient wisdom and our modern science is an expression of how life, thought, and consciousness emanate from an intelligent quantum universe. I wonder now if Stonehenge might possibly be an interpretation of the Tree of Life. The anthropic principle's orchestration of human life on a physical and metaphysical (celestial) level?

Stephen Hawking and Leonard Mlodinov, in their book *The Grand Design* (2010), have not touched on the Tree of Life hypothesis or on any theory of the phenomenon of consciousness in creation. Hawking says, however, that everything appears to have arisen from Nothing in the Cosmos, with laws of nature so finely tuned that they have resulted in a human form of existence. The authors suggest an "M-theory" as an explanatory model for all creation. They consider it to be "the *only* candidate for a complete theory of the universe." "Spontaneous creation is the reason there is something rather than nothing," they say, adding that "it is not necessary to invoke God" for creation (pp. 180–81). With their "M-theory" (model-dependent realism), the authors make the logical error that Nothing is able to bring forth Something. In quantum theory, the timeless, spaceless quantum field is spoken of, and this, according to my interpretation, is a Something that, via evolution's wave–particle and order–information, brings forth the kind of something like you and me, among other things.

In another document, *Self Comes to Mind*, Antonio Damasio (2010) has come up with a hypothetical explanatory model for the origin of consciousness. Wanting to track human consciousness from evolution, he calls the hypothesis "the fourth perspective." The brain is composed of neurons in complex circuits, networks, and patterns of organization. Gradually, he writes, the autobiographical self, thoughts, emotions, and consciousness arise. Consciousness could very probably have emerged as a product of the neurons, Damasio speculates. But he is humble, saying that we do not yet know everything about the brain and consciousness. He does not mention anything about the findings of transpersonal research with respect to consciousness. Nor anything about the Tree of Life hypothesis.

In the following sections on Stonehenge and the Astro-archetypes I want to convey some significant factors that, together with the Tree of Life hypothesis, can provide us with an alternative explanatory model of life, its origin, and its possibilities.

Stonehenge as Life Orientation

Why was Stonehenge built and how did it happen? These questions were taken up by Swedish Television in the spring of 2011in a program subtitled "The Stone Age Space Program."[17] Great numbers of archaeologists and tourists visit the approximately five-thousand-year-old stone circle. It was thought that Stonehenge might be explained as an expression of that era's philosophy of life.[18]

Hans Biedermann (1992), in *Dictionary of Symbols*, talks about the significance of the circle as a symbol. Its pattern is without beginning and end. The Temple of Apollo in ancient Greece is thought to have been circular. The circle has been used as a symbol in the high cultures—and in other cultures as well. With certain Native American peoples this showed in circle dances and the layout of their camps, but for them the circle was a symbol of the cosmic significance of the "Great Spirit" as well. In Buddhism the circle stands as a symbol of perfection, and in the yin/yang of the Chinese the circle is what encloses that duality. The circle has been seen as representing the sky and the quarters within the circle as symbolizing the earth. In discussing the *mandala* (an orientation symbol), Biedermann writes that it signifies the circle used to aid concentration and meditation, but it also appeared architectonically in the design of temple structures, as a depiction of the world-order. The circle could be interpreted as a cosmogram, with a guideline in towards the center "to narrow the mind's field of vision," notes Biedermann, quoting Jung. Of Stonehenge, Stefan Ewald et al. (1997) write in *Religionslexikonet* (Dictionary of Religion) that on the longest day of the year the rays of the sun fell through a stone portal onto the "altar stone" in the inmost circle.[19]

It is apparent from this comparative study that humanity has had a cosmological understanding, with a visible and an invisible part, since long before our own calendric reckoning was established. The circle came to be the symbol for those thoughts, and its central point became the inner center of the human being. In shamanic mysticism, this point, according to my interpretation, corresponds to the spiritual light-body, which Paul talks about in the Bible.[20] With it, the shamanically gifted of ancient times could make soul journeys, in yoga called *akasha gamana*, also known in our time as transcendent out-of-body experiences (OBEs). There is wisdom of this kind in Maya Indian shamanism, and in its developed art of living we may have the explanation for Stonehenge. One attempt at a conclusion is that Stonehenge was a symbol temple for esoteric initiations set by the positions of Sun and Moon in the vault of heaven. The five pairs of stones in Stonehenge can be interpreted as expressions of elements of the Tree of Life: two as the quantum field's wave, two as particle, and one as information. The two circles inside Stonehenge may symbolize the wise spiritual consciousnesses that are said to exist in the quantum field.[21]

There is support for this interpretation in Franz Bardon's *The Practice of Magical Evocation* (2001), in which he gives the names of spiritual beings and, in addition, the seals that will enable "knocking on their doors." He provides a color illustration of an ancient Egyptian initiation temple that has some similarity to Stonehenge. In soul journeys, Bardon says, the initiate could receive wise consultations. So could (and can) the rune shamans. Historian of religion Tor Andræ (1926), in *Mystikens psykologi* (Psychology of Mysticism), writes that mysticism is an inner experience of the divine. With these comparisons, it appears that Stonehenge can be given its spiritual explanation, still timely for our era as well.

Might Stonehenge possibly have been a place of initiation for out-of-body experiences, the kinds done at the Monroe Institute in the United States?[22] C. J. Jung, in a near-death experience, experienced the void of space with the highest possible feeling of bliss. The three times (past, present, future) had flowed together into a whole that he was able to observe with complete objectivity.[23] Was this a mystical "Stonehenge" experience? Linear earth forces, known as ley lines, are said to be concentrated in Stonehenge and other sacred places. They have been interpreted by Guy Underwood, as well as others, as being significant for ancient religious practice.[24]

The Astro-archetypes

What do the astro-archetypes do in your life? Basically, they are what jump in with interpretations and values when you notice something, think about doing something, or talk with someone.[25]

1. Neptune daydreams, fantasizes, is the mental video picture.
2. Uranus is curious, alert, inventive, sees new ways and means.
3. Saturn is serious, has the capacity to concentrate, imposes requirements, is skeptical, stubborn, persevering, makes rules, obligations, is depressive.
4. Jupiter is enthusiastic, hopes, has desires, both just and unjust.
5. Mars acts, takes initiative, can be rude, violent, malicious, mocking, but also selflessly helpful.
6. The Sun wages a struggle for existence and power, dominates, takes command and may put other people down, competes, and wants to be something.
7. Venus is friendly, cheerful, inclined to pleasure, a substance abuser, gets infatuated, falls in love, is an aesthete.
8. Mercury is talkative, inquiring, reflective, dwells upon and encapsulates the sense of self in thought, judges, deliberates, debates.
9. The Moon dozes off, rests, but lives the life of a vagabond, in the best case is caring, compassionate. Can also be indifferent and knows the art of relaxing and being maternally forgiving.
10. Pluto can be the healer in the best case and in the worst case the dictator, the mass destroyer, the most ruthless in the world of evil.

There is a connection in the human Tree of Life, the cross, among the astro-archetypes. Neptune stands for mental vision, Uranus for alert attention, and Mercury for intellect; these are in the upper vertical part of the cross. In its lower vertical part are Jupiter's force of urging on and Saturn's force of braking and stability. On the horizontal line are Mars's power to act, to the left, and, to the right, Venus's filtering desire and aversion. In the middle of the cross are the will and leadership of the Sun-self and, below this, the spontaneity of the Moon-self. When Uranus is alertly attentive to something, Mercury interprets it, and the visionary Neptune makes its orientating mental film (the illusion). Venus filters the object and Mars does something about it, while Jupiter urges on and Saturn stands for concentration (perseverance). So the Moon-self leads the project spontaneously, but the Sun-self throws itself into the course of events and governs it when necessary. We can all identify these phases and this connection as energies beyond the words.[26] See also the ankh cross below.

The sum of the reincarnative karma will show itself in the natal horoscope.[27] The astro-archetypal factors that are seen in the natal horoscope interpret and assess the experiences of this life for good (syntropy) or ill (entropy). The whole of life (the reincarnations) is a school for wisdom and the development (evolution) of consciousness, with theory on the celestial plane and practice on the earth plane. The goal is the blessedness of divine selfless love, the wisdom and intuitive wisdom of contemplation's co-consciousness and timeless life. Through guided meditation, the human being is inspired towards his stream of ideas as confirmations of the path of skillful means. This is the explanation for an esoteric faith in hope and love, which the timeless self (spirit) of the human being harbors like the flower that turns heliotropically towards the sun.

Through correctives to the karmatic factors of the horoscope we can successfully rectify the life-plan. The corrective can be done through an analysis of how this life's ongoing horoscope factors are affecting the conditions of our life. We have full freedom in managing the static astro-archetypes of the natal horoscope and the dynamic factors of the daily horoscope. That is, we are karmatically non-determined in dealing with the determined factors. The karmatic corrections can be brought about with prayer, meditation, contemplation, mental training, and behavioral training. By these means, the "Sun-self," as rational will and leadership, is able to program the "autopilot," the physical body's lifestyle, so that the "Moon-self" can spontaneously give us a qualitatively happier flow (life).

Some of humanity is seeking this "heliotropic" longing for life's quantum wisdom: the hope and love of the longing for wisdom's faith. This is the testament of my knowledge. There are those who interpret this astro-psychological life wisdom skeptically, as superstition. Then there are those who harbor neither the one nor the other model of interpretation. In yogic language, the seekers are expressions of the constituent of *sattva*, the skeptics of *rajas*, and those who do not care of *tamas*. The constituents of the primordial ground (the quantum field) have given rise to the wave-particle (*rajas-tamas*) and information-order (*sattva*).[28] They move through evolution to plants, animals, and human beings. There is a cosmic collective consciousness (quantum consciousness) with individual spirits. To this celestial consciousness our consciousnesses rise up with their light-bodies (quantum bodies).

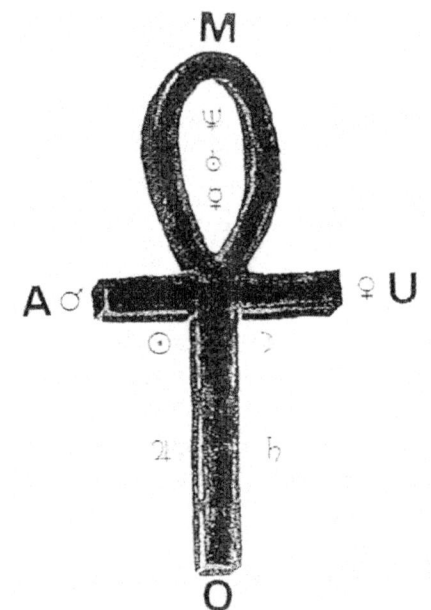

It is fully possible to make a meta-synthesis of the yoga mantra AUM, the ankh cross as a symbol of the Tree of Life, the three *gunas* (constituents of yoga), and astro-archetypes. The synthesis forms identifiers for urging on, restraining, and illuminating.

Figure 1. *Explanation.* In the eye of the Ankh are Neptune with vision, Uranus with alert attention, and Mercury with intellect. On the transverse beam, to the left is Mars with the power to act and to the right is Venus with the filter of desire and aversion. On the vertical beam, to the left is Jupiter with enthusiasm and to the right is Saturn with seriousness and discipline. In the center of the cross, to the left is the Sun-self and to the right is the Moon-self. On the cross beam, A represents the factor of urging on and U the factor of restraining. On the vertical beam, at the top is the absolute homeostasis of the peace of transcendence, M, and at the bottom is relative equilibrium, O. When O and M are united in the shortened version of the mantra OM, psychic rest, O, and serenity, M, arise. Cognitive and conscious purity arise, realization emerges from the faculty of thought like the butterfly from the chrysalis, and the divine illumination of meditation arises. These are yoga's five spiritual observances (rest, etc.), called the *niyamas*.[29]

Interest

There is no doubt that existentiology is a question of the whole person, both the spiritual and the physical. In a fundamental sense, the prerequisite of existentiology is interest, as a phenomenon. Without an interest in what life is, we cannot form a conception of life's meaning, possibilities, and goals.

When we ask people about what interest is, the answer we get might be "I'm interested in football (soccer), sewing, and carpentry." In the response, the quantum constituents disclose themselves as wave, with interest as psychic energy, and as particles, the objects of interest. Both depend on the constituent information, which in the human being is expressed in intelligence.

When the energy of interest flows through attention to the object, then the interpretative factors that characterize the energy of interest and thought show up, equipping themselves with values.[30] In ancient Greece, the interpretations–values were depicted as "gods" and "goddesses." These mythical figures existed in all people but expressed themselves in varying ways. In Jungian psychology, the "goddesses" and "gods" have been brought up to date by Jean Shinoda Bolen with *Goddesses in Everywoman* (1984) and *Gods in Everyman* (1989).[31]

The "gods" and "goddesses" sit round the round table in our subconscious like consultants, says Bolen. With this metaphoric interpretation, we can understand more easily how the energy of interest is steered to objects by our attention, triggering the thought process. Zeus makes us interested in leadership, Apollo in research, Hermes in information, Ares in force, Hephaestus in craftsmanship, and Dionysus in transcendence. Demeter is interested in mercy, Hestia in peaceability, Aphrodite in love; Hera often frustrates, Artemis is socially engaged, and Pallas Athena is the "goddess" of wisdom. These are qualities as keywords. Each "god" or "goddess" has many more qualities that are analogously gathered into a specific basic character or archetype.

Remarkably, a group of scientists has found six fundamental archetypes shared among humankind. They have researched a great many documents, Martin Seligman (2002) writes in *Authentic Happiness*.[32] The explanation for this was supposed to be that these strengths are genetically based, but they are also expressions of the quantum field's Tree of Life. These strengths are (1) knowledge and wisdom, (2) courage, (3) humanity, (4) justice, (5) temperance, (6) spirituality and transcendence. These strengths are expressed in the figures of Greek mythology as well, and likewise in Jung's astropsychological archetypes.[33] These strengths also shape an ethical-moral lifestyle and attitudes. From these six strengths, we gain a basic understanding of what humankind has been—and still is—interested in for the purpose of finding a worthy life.

Into the six strengths we can read quantum philosophy, yoga, the Tree of Life hypothesis, and Stonehenge as expressions of the search for spirituality's transcendence based in knowledge and wisdom: an existential justice that requires courage, temperance, and humanity. It is wisdom and its transcendental dimension that form the basis of the existential peak experience for the new human-centered person of the 21st century. We must go from consuming to relating and from that to a transcendent spiritual dimension as a complement to the worldly one.[34]

But in that case, we must disidentify ourselves from our thoughts (information), their objects (particles), and the energy of thought (wave) with its feelings. This can be done with the help of the figures of Greek mythology. Aphrodite gives desire to the faculty of thought, Artemis gives it tension, Hera gives it expectations and frustrations. Hermes verbalizes the knowledge. But Zeus, the leader, gives Apollo the assignment of exploring the process, and Athena is to deliver the illumination about it. Zeus gets Ares to switch off the process, and the strength of Hephaestus helps out so that Demeter can relax all the "gods" and "goddesses" except for Hestia, who brings cosmic peace (equilibrium). Dionysus is then able to transcend consciousness on the cognitive height of Olympus. There, consciousness is able to realize how Zeus's leadership has taken power from his brother Poseidon and from Eros.[35]

Without doubt, the most powerful element in this section on interest is what the Danish psychologist Ole Vedfelt (2001) calls "the supramodal inner room." We also call this "room" the timeless inner Self. It has a creative intelligence that goes far beyond the rational. In connection with Vedfelt's explanation, the contextual and coordinating mind, *manas*, of yogic tradition, which probably interacts with the great *Manas* of the World Tree, can be accommodated. *Manas* can be understood very well as a meditation- and hologram-mind for heightened insights and spiritual wisdom. In old folk tradition, you "sleep on it" so you will "have gold in your mouth come morning." Jesus spoke of "knocking" so it might "be given."[36] Artists, writers, and scientists are familiar with the creative leap which morning intuition can bring forth as the stream of ideas. With the development of *manas*, human intelligence and wisdom can attain undreamt-of heights![37]

The three quantum constituents—wave–particle and information—manifest through their analogue system as the energy of interest, its object of focus, and knowledge about it. But the constituents also make our ability to move, the physical body, and its head for intelligent ability. This is the quantum human.

Growth

Without a sustainable environment it is totally impossible for the human being to develop existentially. Scientists warned on a Swedish Television program broadcast in the spring of 2011 that the world economy had reached the ceiling.[38] Material growth—which is expected to increase constantly, while Earth's resources are limited—is no longer going to work. The growth economy's way of thinking is tearing Earth's ecosystem apart. It is the greed of a few leaders that drives consumerism to a striving for gadgets of ever-increasing status. There is no connection, either, between an increase in material well-being (the stimulus factor) and increased human well-being (the response factor). The problem is how we are going to manage without economic growth. We have to find a way out of this meta-ideology. It was apparent in the television program that we will need to be prepared for more free time and less consumerism.[39]

Goethe (1749–1832) predicted a humanism in which each person's existence would be the essential thing.[40] Erich Fromm (1900–1980) carried that philosophy on and warned that the human being could be exploited, as a consumer, "to have" as a barrier against the existential "to be" that is the important goal of life.[41] The Swedish philosopher Alf Ahlberg (1892–1979) also pursued Goethe's and Fromm's thesis.[42] In our time, the

Swedish physician Nisse Simonson (2008) has summed up the problem of "having" and "being" like this: "Why do we feel so bad when we have it so good?"[43] Perhaps Hans Hof, professor of philosophy of religion at Uppsala University from 1969 to 1987, has the answer: that we have to become, or be, more of a human being.[44] Might the simple living and mindfulness movements be two instruments for this?[45]

Barbara Ehrenreich, in her book *Bright-sided*, has shown how positive thinking as a postulate of growth is a success myth (2010).[46] An American journalist, she does a good job of verifying her propositions about the speculative economy of the United States as an economy based on optimistic and positive thinking (OPT, as I prefer to abbreviate the phenomenon). It is tempting to call it a casino economy once one has read *Bright-sided*, which calls OPT strongly into question. OPT has become an industry for cheering on business and banking (and it has spread to Europe and other parts of the world). But this OPT has been a driving force devoid of skeptical examination and feedback from reality. OPT's leading figure was President George W. Bush. OPT entered into a symbiosis with consumption capitalism to increase the desire to possess more and more assets and gadgets. People were supposed to earn more money and borrow more money for consumption. Producers, merchants, and consumers were all supposed to practice OPT. But OPT was exposed afterwards as self-hypnosis, delusions of grandeur, mass deception, an opiate of the people, an illusion, a virus. The economic meltdown, the recession, was apparently driven by OPT-manic consumption-and-loan consultants. The burden of debt swelled. Governments had to pump billions into banks and corporations. No one foresaw, she writes, that American OPT would go to hell.

Barbara Ehrenreich writes that Americans take two-thirds of the world's antidepressants. Americans rank outside the top 100 countries in one "happiness" index. The rich are rolling in their fortunes, and more and more poor people are living in extreme poverty, she says. With the factual information provided by her and other writers, it is fully possible to make a catalogue of the misery and consequences of all that the OPT-driven casino economy has caused in the world.

Once one has read Barbara Ehrenreich's *Bright-sided*, the speculation economy stands out as unsustainable. In a scenario of the future, which starts today, we can no longer hold with the win–disappear and wealth–poverty of the casino situation. Perhaps the ego-centered person of speculation and consumption is singing the last verse? *The remarkable thing seems to be that the self-regulating economy of speculation and consumption is destroying itself.* But what will we have instead once this fatal "success economy" is seen to be making our world into a sterile Easter Island, without potable water, without food, and without a tolerable environment? I hope the author will produce a sequel responding to these questions with the help of accessible scientists. Barbara Ehrenreich's book is like an audit report. It deals with the casino effect of the unsustainable speculation economy: win or disappear from planet Earth. The book gets us to reconsider matters in ecosophical terms with a view to surviving on our planet. But let us adopt the six strengths as experimental aspects of the phenomenon of growth.

If we are now going to analyze the phenomenon of growth, we can look at it as a material part and an existential part. The material part is at risk of hitting the wall, and the existential (spiritual) development is often interpreted as a product of sheer fantasy. We can now see how the characteristics of the first strength have been employed for knowledge about material development, while existential wisdom lags behind or is nonexistent. The second strength, courage, is divided into the power to act and leadership. In a humane democracy, both characteristics are used in a positive manner, but in a dictatorship they are shaped into an inhumanly ruthless leadership bound up with human torment. Accordingly, the third quality, humanity, is a prerequisite, together with wisdom, for the fourth virtue among the strengths: ethical-moral social justice. But this requires a fifth virtue, and that is temperance in the use of earth's resources, temperance in the expansion of population, and temperance in striving for an increase in the material standard. Temperance is also the prerequisite for our prioritizing time for the sixth virtue and strength, which is spirituality and transcendence. In this lies existential development, which Erich Fromm, in his critique of society, called "being happy," while material development stops at "succeeding" with some project.

Thus, we can see how, according to Martin Seligman, the six strengths are resources for us in dealing with both physical-material and spiritual-existential development. This is the balance we must have between both lanes of development in order to attain a meaningful quality of life. But in that case, we must hold one overarching thought, the way professional auditors do—in order to discover the risks that could result in crisis and bankruptcy! And that thought is: What is essential? If the social system demands too much from the market system, which demands too much from the natural system, then all three systems can collapse. Just as when we lose our balance and fall, systems can go wrong; so too with these three systems, which require a global audit for human survival.

Quality of Life

There are many indications that we are on a path into the endeavor for a new global culture society, with human-centered relations instead of consumption. The present "societies" of experiences, shopping, and information (analogue revelations of wave, particle, and order) exert stress on a human way of life. They quantify it with an uninterrupted effort to set a record in charts of the standard of material prosperity. But there is no connection between a constant increase in this standard and the quality-of-life curve for well-being.

Researchers like Sonja Lyubomirsky (2008) have found that the prosperity-and-market society was capable of stimulating a sense of well-being and quality of life in only a 10-percent slice, at most, of the whole pie chart of responses.[47] Martin Seligman (2007) says of the relationship between supply and experiences, which has been studied in forty countries, that no connection was found between an increase in the material standard of living as stimulus and the quality of life as response. A U.S. study of a group of billionaires found their experience of quality of life to be no greater than that of people with average incomes.[48] It appears that instruments like simple living, mindfulness, life orientation (reflection), mental training, and cognitive behavioral training are needed to give us the increase in quality of life that the prosperity-and-market society never can.

We have two opposites to the wisdom, meaningfulness, love, joy, and happiness of a genuine quality of life. These are the dys-qualities and the pseudo-qualities that give us kicks to get up out of the dys-qualities. When we fall into dysthymias like anxiety, meaninglessness, and depression, we willingly resort to corrective addictions of various kinds. The smoker exemplifies one such yo-yo life. We have a center in the left frontal lobe for quality of life and one in the right for its opposite (to put it simply). So, through purposeful, steady practice we can switch from the right to the left.[49] In "Meta-synthesis" (2007–2009), I seek to show the connection between the life-, the pseudo-, and the dys-qualities[50]:

Figure 2. Metasynthesis

It was Abraham Maslow (1908–1970), it appears, who set about working with the problem of quality of life.[51] His hierarchy of needs is a classic—and I found that it tallied nicely with a synthesis of the 2002 election programs of the Swedish parliamentary parties. Consequently, I have framed a supplement to the hierarchy that can be summarized in three points which can serve as a rule of thumb, where (1) stands for factors of comfort and well-being, (2) for the development of person and environment, and (3) for existential meaningfulness, happiness, and life wisdom. It is evident from the hierarchy that we have a need for means and ends of quality (stimulus) in order to attain the wisdom-bliss and sublime existential experience of quality of life (response).

From this it follows that all the stimuli in the environment should have the quality of objectivity, while the experience-response should have the quality of life. Most often, a distinction is not made between these qualities in the debate. Using a ring cake as a metaphor can pedagogically explain the connection between the four components of quality.

In the research, happiness has been broken out from the quality of life for the purpose of seeing what happiness is and what it consists of. But people have gone a step further and are now inquiring after the meaning of creation, life, and happiness. The longing for existential wisdom can be glimpsed, a spiritual light that penetrates our knowledge of good and evil. In my summary of the happiness complex, I would like to point to three fundamental states: happy, pseudo-happy, and unhappy. The first of these consists of an elementary happiness (the brain's "alpha state" as the peace of transcendence), creative happiness (the autopilot's flow), advanced happiness (a selfless state resembling intoxication, such as genuine love between partners or an athletic performance), and transcendent happiness (like the wisdom of meditation). Pseudo-happiness consists of compensation (comfort food, etc.), addiction (hedonism), and intoxication (alcohol, etc.). The state of unhappiness consists of elementary unhappiness (periodic malaise), extreme unhappiness (dysthemias, burnout), and existential unhappiness (absence of meaning in life) (Sjöberg 2009).

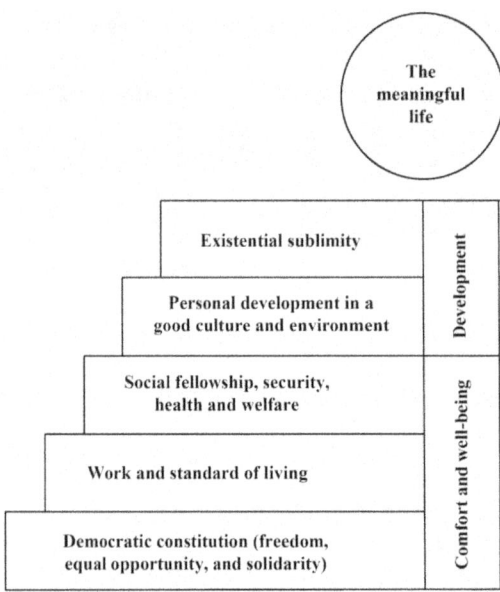

Figure 3. The Hierarchy of Quality of Life and Needs

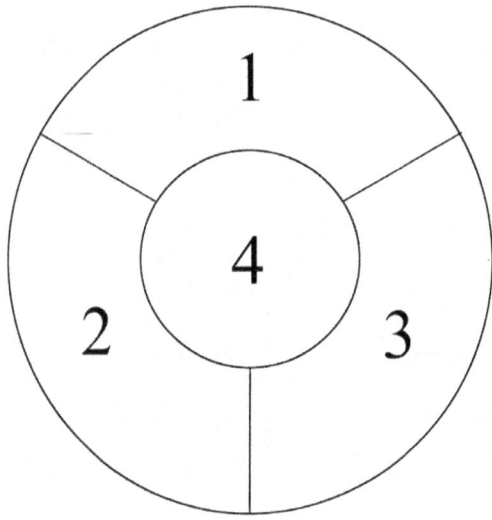

Figure 4. A Ring Cake as an explanatory image of the four components of quality:
  1. **Method: Knowing what knowledge of quality of life is, choosing proper stimuli, wanting to practice one's way of life.**
  2. **Internal stimuli: Interests, intelligence, and attitudes.**
  3. **External stimuli: Culture, nature, and society.**
  4. **Internal response: Well-being, happiness, and quality of life.**

The Transcendent Self

Have you ever experienced that you are another person? I have. I was once surprised to be a monk who was walking down a path on a television program. On another occasion I was suddenly a friend of my wife's, and on a third occasion I was a fellow writer. The mystic Dénis Lindbohm wrote of it like this: "You are I in another person."[52]

This phenomenon is associated with transpersonal psychology. It is not a manifestation of anything pathological, hallucinatory, or superstitious. It is free of religious, philosophical, and psychological interpretations. An experience by which we human selves are refreshed in what the Swedish philosopher and educator Alf Ahlberg called co-consciousness.[53] According to Patanjali, who long before our epoch wrote the Raja Yoga Sutras, which have become so well known in the scientific world of our time, this experience appears in yoga, where it is called the gift of the *siddhi*'s grace: suddenly, contemplatively, to become identical with another person's sense of self, also called *ahamkara*.[54]

As a consequence of the transcendence of the self to identity with another person's self, we enter into a different value base, phenomenologically, existentially, and socially. On the same grounds that we do not want to expose ourselves as individuals to harm, we also cannot expose other I-humans to harm. This is called conscience,[55] fellow-feeling, and compassion. A hurtful thought about another person is already causing pain in us when we think in that sort of way: we are precognitively experiencing this person's experience as he would have received it if we had slapped him with something said in a hurtful way. Likewise, if we do hurt someone it causes pain in us. I remember so well when I shoved Lars into the ditch at school. Way in there on the shelves of memory, the experience remains, fragmentarily, in the service of conscience, warning against similar shoves.

So the transcendent self is perhaps a Maslowian peak experience. This self is more than the "Moon-self" at its limbic level and the "Sun-self" at its cortical level.[56] The transcendent self relates to itself in "another person." It is probably a quantum occurrence, this self, interacting intuitively, free of time and space. It is likely that the transcendent self is capable of becoming identical with such great spiritual figures as Jesus Christ and Buddha, just for a moment![57] For this reason, we meditate on these figures and the messages through which they wanted to lift us up to the wisdom and happiness of the transcendent timeless self, which in yoga is called *samadhi*.[58] Indeed, we must interpret the self's transcendence in this way, that enlightened masters in both the visible and the invisible are able to contemplate themselves with us. This is *siddhis* in yoga[59] and the great benediction of Numbers 6:24–26.[60]

To suddenly become another person's self[61] is a glimpse of what is called a leap in quantum theory. We can prepare the way for such experiences by having the core values of sympathy, the identity of conscience, fellow-feeling, and compassion. We can count on receiving the blessing of enlightenment from the invisible gurus, even if it is in small glimpses, but these are large on the staircase of life. The transcendent self is one such glimpse. Be ready for it once you have read this testimony!

I am convinced, from within, that the tender nature of conscience is the doorway to the transcendent self. We can practice and develop the path to the door, but the opening of the door is a quantum leap from the divine plane of life. We can make the path rationally, but we receive the gift intuitively. This leads to the synergy of self-transcendence—we are suddenly much more than just two ego-centered selves. We are human-centered in the transcendent self.

Information Particle

The September 3, 2013, program in the Swedish television series *Vetenskapens värld* (The World of Science) pointed out that quantum mechanics has never been able to be falsified, never been proven false. In it, so-called leaps of change occur. How can such things happen? The latest quantum research has experimentally discovered something called a "teleported particle." This involves a particle's being moved from A to B without crossing the intervening distance in spacetime. The commentary stated that what is teleported is information. But in that case, what does the information consist of?

When we follow the history of "chance" we can see that chance is logical-systematic. We can talk about a chance-ology of quantum leaps, a cosmo context of order, the Logos of the ancient Greeks and Urd's web of the ancient Northerners. Physicist David Bohm[62] brought to quantum research the concepts of manifest (explicate) order emanating from a potential (implicate) order, presumably inspired by the "pure ideas" Plato[63] philosophized about in ancient Greece.

We can postulate that nothing in our world is able to happen without order—that is, information—as one of the quantum constituents. It is necessary to accompany and guide the other two constituents, the wave (energy) and the particle (matter). Analogously, these three basal quantum factors are manifested as the motion, body, and intelligence of the human being.

But as a factor x in creation's equation, the information appears with the question: What, basically, is information? The wave-particle as energy and matter has quantum physical reality. Why doesn't the information? Well, you might say, look at the patterns as plans, systems. Yes, certainly, but if the wave-energy and particle-matter is, of itself, arranging plants, animals, and human beings? In that case, the logical consequence is that an inherent information-and-order particle most likely exists together with the wave-energy and the particle-matter.

In an "aha!" leap during a morning meditation on the information factor, I got the term "Minon" for the information particle. Outstanding scientists often get minon leaps. A minon, as an information particle, might explain Plato's pure ideas and David Bohm's implicate order and the wave-particle's pattern formation. With that, factor x of creation's equation would be solved. The minon as mutator in cosmic and human culture. The minons that emanate from the quantum field's DNA, internet, and "holo-thesis." Why not Jung's[64] collective unconscious as this quantum field? This would make possible the design of the universe which Stephen Hawking and Leonard Mlodinow[65] philosophize about in *The Grand Design*, a glance in the rearview mirror of evolution. It is my hope that the minon as information particle may be of benefit to quantum research.

Summary and Attempt at a Conclusion

Now, more than ever, we are seeking a transcendent meaning to life as devolution and environmental destruction threaten us.[66] We cannot remain any longer in our existential lostness. For this reason, the need for wisdom and meaningfulness top the quality-of-life hierarchy.[67]

We can ask ourselves, along with a burnt-out professional woman, "What's the meaning of it all?" The meta-ideology of politics and the market, the standard of material prosperity, does not provide us with the answer! It is likely that quantum idealism and the development of transpersonal consciousness are clues to the answer: an existential quantum holism.

We have to give up prioritizing the market society's theatre stage with its zombified people and tunnel vision. These who, from ignorance of their passions (craving, hatred), suffer under the troubles let out of Pandora's Box. We have begun to explore meditation as a higher cognitive resource for receiving answers to the existential questions. As a transcendent, meditation can lead to a sublime holistic wisdom with a human-centered person anchored in her timeless quantum self.[68]

Epilogue

The Wisdom of Myth

Through ignorance, Adam, the Sun-self, falls
for the Moon-self, Eve. She holds out the apple,
the thing (the particle) from the Tree of Knowledge
(the information). The snake is passion's craving
(the wave) for it, with the torments and bitterness
of suffering as a consequence. Until insight (the leap)
illuminates the mirroring quantum consciousness
concerning this.[69]

Notes

1. Pandora is described in Greek mythology, among others by Tullia Linders in *Vem är vem i antikens Grekland och Romarriket* (Who's Who in Ancient Greece and the Roman Empire).

2. Described in the book manuscript "Den humancenterrade människan på 2000-talet—relation instället för consumption" (The Human-Centered Person in the Twenty-First Century—Relating Instead of Consuming), by A.E. Sjöberg.

3. The difference between knowledge and wisdom is that the latter is spiritual and shines through cognitive knowledge (lexical consensus otherwise regards wisdom as sagacity and being very learned.

4. Three basic factors appear to constitute evolution based on the quantum field. These are David Bohm's order (information) and Albert Einstein's energy-matter (wave-particle). See also note 8 below. In the yogic philosophy of life, the self is called *ahamkara* in Sanskrit. This can be translated as sense of self. From *Indisk filosofi: Samkhya* (Indian Philosophy: Samkya), C.E. Sjöstedt (ed.), and "De tre Gunorna i Samkya yoga" (The Three Gunas in Samkya Yoga), by A.E. Sjöberg. The three quantum constituents are called *gunor* in yoga and the quantum field is called the primordial ground.

5. *Trataka* is an established series of practices in yogic and Buddhist psychology of meditation (described by many authors). The method has been introduced in the Mindfulness of our age (in yoga also called *jnana*, which means insight meditation).

260 Part III. How to Feel Well in Your Brain and Heart

6. To make this experience rationally as well as intuitively graspable, I have been forced to create the concept of the peace of transcendence, a level of consciousness that is achieved via the brain's relaxation centers and its alpha waves.

7. The nun appeared in a program on silence broadcast by Swedish Television (June 13, 2011). She was active in Saint Katarina Home, a convent in Oslo.

8. This last paragraph is my conclusion both from literature and from the meditations of many years. Deepak Chopra talks about the quantum human in his books, as does Stephen H. Wolinsky in *Quantum Consciousness*. Psychiatrist Arthur J. Deikman's *The Observing Self*, published in 1982, also supports my conclusion in 2011. The Mindfulness movement is a support for my hypothetical conclusion, the quantum human, as well.

9. This is a summary of reductionist skepticism towards an intelligent, meaning-filled universe. This thought was represented several years ago on a Swedish Television program on philosophies of life.

10. From D. Bohm and F.D. Peat, *Science, Order and Creativity*; K. Wilber (ed.), *The Holographic Paradigm and Other Paradoxes*; and T. Nørretranders *Världen Växer* (The World Grows), among others.

11. Deepak Chopra writes about creative leaps and intention in his books, as in *Power, Freedom, and Grace*.

12. Deepak Chopra, in *Power, Freedom, and Grace* (see note 3 above), talks about consciousness as transcendent and having a cosmic correspondence. But many writers with research expertise are thinking about this explanation as well, e.g., M. Newton in *Journey of Souls* and B.L. Weiss in *Through Time into Healing*.

13. I have written extensively about the physical significance of the ideology of material prosperity in my books on Quality of Life and Existensiology. Chopra writes of physical materialism as reductionism, of its being a "scientific" superstition (misinterpretation); see note 3 above.

14. This transcendence is also described as out-of-body experiences (OBEs) and is dealt with in a serious manner. At the Monroe Institute in the United States, training in this skill has been done with what is called the Hemi-Sync method; see R.A. Monroe, *Ultimate Journey*.

15. In yoga, this fusion is called *kaivalya*. It is the tenth stage of development, the highest to which the word yoga refers. The connection between the preceding nine steps is as follows. One adheres to ethical rules and spiritual matters of this kind (*yama* and *niyama*). Then one sits in meditation posture and charges vital force (*prana*) in order to be able to master one's senses. It then becomes possible to perform mental concentration without disruptions so that one can proceed to meditation and contemplation (*samadhi*). Then consciousness can be developed according to plan (*aisvarya*). From the Raja Yoga Sutras of Pantanjali, in L. Zeilich-Jensen, *Hatha-yoga* (Hatha Yoga); see also references in note 4 of the Wisdom section above. The ten stages are a well-tested body of transmitted experience for the development of consciousness and the meaning of life.

The modern person is embroiled in hyper-information and cognitive stress (Maya's illusions). Getting oneself out of this requires the development of direct insight (*citta*) and the hologram-like mind of quantum meditation (*manas*).

16. This entire paragraph is taken from my review of this book in *Miljömagasinet* (Environment Magazine), February 2011. The last segment is my concluding judgment about the book.

17. Might the human psyche also have a centriole-like function in the yogic *manas*, the mind of coordination and meditation?

18. Swedish Television, Channel 2, May 16, 2011.

19. DRAWING OF STONEHENGE

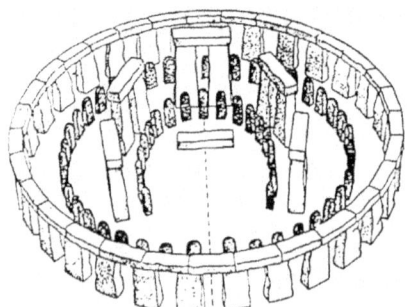

Circle: Reconstruction of shrine at Stonehenge. Southern England, ca. 1800 BC. (Hans Biedermann, *Dictionary of Symbolism*, 1992, p. 70.) The dotted line through the center indicates the direction for winter and summer solstices.

20. It can be mentioned in addition to this that in Christian churches the altar was to face sunrise in the east. One half of the altar rail in these churches is earthly and visible, while the other half symbolizes the invisible heavenly part.

21. Paul speaks in 1 Corinthians 15 of the resurrection of the dead. In 1 Corinthians 15:40 he says, "There are also heavenly bodies and there are earthly bodies; but the splendor of the heavenly bodies is one kind, and the splendor of the earthly bodies is another" (New International Version). In 1 Corinthians 15:50–54 he says that we are not able to have flesh and blood as an inheritance (can be interpreted as the earthly body) but that we shall all be transformed (can be interpreted as the heavenly body). Might Paul possibly have had a transcendent (heavenly) out-of-body experience, when the soul's body (the heavenly body) temporarily leaves the earthly one? 4, 5. This is my interpretation.

22. Bardon's book has been published in English in a number of editions. Bardon's book was published in 1956 by Herman Bauer Verlag, Freiburg im Breisgau. The book is so unique that it ought to be published in English and in Swedish as well. Uncertain if the company still exists.

23. R.A. Monroe, *Ultimate Journey*.

24. Stuart Holroyd, *My Life, Memorys, Dreams, Thought*, in Swedish (Stockholm 1964–1979).

25. G. Underwood, cited in S. Holroyd, *Arkana Dictionary of New Perspectives*.

26. The astroarchetypes (the characteristics) are taken from L. Zeilich-Jensen, *Astrologie* (Astrology), also from A.E. Sjöberg, "Astrologi: En väg till visdom" (Astrology: A Path to Wisdom) and "Astropsykologi: En väg till visdom" (Astropsychology: A Path to Wisdom).

27. The whole of this second paragraph is a result of my meditations of many years: the factors are psychic energies which it is possible, for one who has the patience for it, to identify.

28. This statement is the result of my many years of studies in horoscopic astropsychology. In the text below I develop a pertinent connection of interpretive factors from various outlooks on the world and life, which I would like to call "the testament of my knowledge."

29. The parenthesized words—*rajas*, *tamas*, and *sattva*—are yogic terms that are called *gunor*, which means constituents. These are analogous to quantum theory's wave (*rajas*), particle (*tamas*), and information—order (*sattva*). Before our era, yogis had discovered the *gunas* from which our era's three quantum factors (wave, particle, and order) emanate. The *gunas* are described in detail in A.E. Sjöberg, *Samkya yoga*.

30. The meta-synthesis is made by Alf E. Sjöberg, for the first time in this chapter on November 20, 2011. The Ankh symbol is from D. Fontana, *The Secret Language of Symbols*. The astro-archetypal symbols are: Sun ☉, Moon ☽, Mercury ☿, Venus ♀, Mars ♂, Jupiter ♃, Saturn ♄ (which have shaped the names of the days of the week), Uranus ♅, Neptune ♆, and Pluto ♀. (From <http://en.wikipedia.org/wiki/Astrological_symbols> accessed 17 Jan. 2011.)

31. This is the result of my meditative research on the inner cognitive field and on lateral thinking.

32. Bolen is a professor of psychiatry and has brought insights about these to bear in her practice. Both of these books are very unique and reliable.

33. Seligman is a professor of psychology. He introduced the demonstrated thesis of learned helplessness.

34. These are described by the psychologist Hans Ljungqvist in *Jung och astrologin* (Jung and Astrology). I have developed Jung's thesis of astropsychology, presented in a lecture on 13 April 2011, in Karlstad, Sweden, and documented in "Astropsykologi: En väg till visdom" (Astropsychology: A Path to Wisdom).

35. This is my synthesis of the six strengths.

36. With this interpretation of mine I hope to be able to make a contribution to Jungian psychology and the reactualization of ancient Greek mythology. With a little patience, it can be fitted into the universal human strengths that Martin Seligman writes about.

37. Matthew 7:7–8: "[7]Ask and it will be given to you; seek and you will find; knock and the door will be opened to you. [8]For everyone who asks receives; the one who seeks finds; and to the one who knocks, the door will be opened" (New International Version).

38. It would be extremely valuable if the experiences in this section became subjects of scientific research. This would probably lead to a shift from material consumerism and hedonism to a spiritual, timeless existentialism.

39. "Vetenskapens Värld" (The World of Science), Swedish Television, 23 May 2011.

40. It could be said, by way of comment, that we have developed the physical-material side of life but have not sufficiently developed the spiritual-existential side. See, below, my development of "The Hierarchy of Quality of Life and Needs."

41. R. Ekman, *Filosofins grunder* (Foundations of Philosophy).
42. Ibid.; E. Fromm, *To Have or To Be?*
43. Alf Ahlberg was headmaster of the Brunnsvik worker's educational institute, a participant in discussions of cultural matters, and held a Ph.D. in philosophy. His humanism is described by Thure Jadestig in *Humanistisk democrati* (Humanistic Democracy).
44. N. Simonson, *Varför mår vi så dåligt när vi har det så bra?* (Why Do We Feel So Bad When We Have It So Good?).
45. H. Hof, *Bli mer människa* (Become More of a Human Being).
46. G. Jørgensen, *Simple Living*; O. Schenström, *Mindfulness i vardagen* (Mindfulness in Everyday Life). Neither has been translated into English at the time of writing.
47. *Bright-sided* is published in the UK as *Smile or Die*, London: Granta Books, 2010. A full report on this book is given in my review for *Miljömagasinet* (Environment Magazine), Dec. 2010.
48. S. Lyubormirsky, *The How of Happiness*. This is a highly acclaimed piece of scientific work that has received a great deal of attention.
49. M. Seligman, *Authentic Happiness*.
50. See my overview, "Metasynthesis," from my book *Existensiologi* (Existensiology).
51. These centers are described by O. Schenström in *Mindfulness i vardagen* (Mindfulness in Everyday Life) and S. Klein in *The Science of Happiness*.
52. From my book *Existensiologi* (Existensiology).
53. R. Ekman, *Filosofins grunder* (Foundations of Philosophy).
54. Personal correspondence to the author.
55. Transpersonal psychology is described in H. Egidius *Psykologilexikon* (Dictionary of Psychology).
56. The concept of "co-consciousness" appears in one of Alf Ahlberg's books (here, freely from memory).
57. Patanjali mentions *siddhis* in his Raja Yoga Sutras, L. Zeilich-Jensen, *Hatha-yoga* (Hatha Yoga).
58. Alf Ahlberg writes that conscience is a transcendental phenomenon; see *Teknikens Himmelfärd* (The Ascension of Technology) (Stockholm, Natur och Kultur, 1960).
59. The school was in Alster, just outside Karlstad, Sweden.
60. In yogic terminology, the Sun-self and the Moon-self are called *ha* and *tha*, respectively.
61. I base this likelihood on the principle of imitation.
62. On the whole, there are two sorts of *samadhi*: *savikalpa* and *nirvikalpa*, the former being the wisdom-bliss and selfless love of earthly life, the latter being the divine love and wisdom-bliss of celestial life. For references, see note 4>3 above.
63. Patanjali speaks of *siddhis*; see note 4>3 above.
64. Numbers 6:24–26[24]:"The LORD bless you and keep you[25];the LORD make his face shine on you and be gracious to you[26];the LORD turn his face toward you and give you peace" (New International Version). This benediction is well known in Christianity.
65. This change in consciousness is spoken of in samkhya yoga and hatha yoga. It belongs to development stage nine, which is called *aisvarya* and signifies "transcendental ability." Consciousness may transfer itself to another person, a bird, and so forth. When consciousness frees itself from the physical body through disidentification with it, consciousness is able to move and reach eight different possibilities: smallness, lightness, weight, magnitude, attainment, freedom of action, omnipotence, and mastery. For references, see note4>3 above. Shamans are able to shift *hamr* or "shape" (that is, shape-shift) and identify with another person, bird, and so forth. See A. Grimsson, *Runmagi och Shamanism* (Rune Magic and Shamanism) and M. Harner, *The Way of the Shaman*.
66. This threat is a manifestation of the disorder of entropy.
67. This is a manifestation of the dynamic, creative, explicate order of negentropy or syntropy, a dissipative structure that organizes itself, sustains itself, and changes itself (I suggest that we call this cultural phenomenon "holotropy" as the wisdom and meaningfulness of the quantum leap).
68. There are two ways of thinking, according to the atomic physicist J. Robert Oppenheimer: these are "the way of time and history and the way of eternity and of timelessness, and both are part of man's effort to comprehend the world in which he lives.... They are ... complementary views," he says (see S. Holroyd, *New Perspectives*).
69. The myth of Adam and Eve is taken from the Biblical Genesis, here interpreted with the analogues from the quantum constituents of wave-particle and information, as well as the leap. Interpretation by Alf E. Sjöberg.

Thinking Matters
Well-Being, Mindfulness and the Global Commons

JANET MCINTYRE-MILLS

Introduction

As I get older and I look around me, I begin to understand the notion that we write the landscape in our daily choices and we create the world around us with every word we utter and every action we take. The joy of living and the life-giving energy as we create rapport with one another can contrast with the negative energy or deathly silence or coolness towards one another which creates distance. When we die who we are and how we live as individuals and as groups is written in the landscape and a memory trace is carried by those with whom we made a connection. For some the memory trace is carried at the local level by their grace and their stewardship of the land which they touched gently and with care. For others the memory trace is carried through their words written on paper from trees that have been felled and carried in digital waves through highly developed internet systems that generate land fill and toxins. It seems to me that living lightly and designing renewable forms of communication will become increasingly important.

The work of Yoland Wadsworth and Rose Bird stresses the importance of human praxis. Our bodies are part of the environment when we are alive and when we die. The connections we make with other sentient creatures and with the land are part of this understanding of the interconnectedness of life. We need to think of the human body as connected to the air we breathe and to the land or air to which we will return. Perhaps we will donate our organs to others and traces of our learning will be shared in this way? The notion of eros and thanatos are always at play in politics. Protecting human rights and a life of dignity should be uppermost, but human rights have rested on the rights of other species, just as some human beings have wrested power over other human beings and commodified them.

As the world becomes hotter and natural disasters increase, the challenge for survival will become greater. We need to become increasingly resilient. This has implications for how we see ourselves, others and the environment. New approaches to social policy and governance challenges will need to be timely, inclusive and responsive. Representation of public opinion, accountability of government, and sustainability are the central challenges. With reference to current and past research on these issues I will explore a number of interrelated questions:

- What is consciousness? If it is more than the firing of an assemblage of neurons in our brain (Chalmers, 2006), how does it relate to mindfulness?
- What is the link between mindfulness, well-being and the global commons?
- Where do we draw the lines of inclusion and exclusion when we consider rights and responsibilities for sustainable futures? Do we have a choice between isolation in zero sum competitive nation-states or finding ways to achieve multilateralism?
- Can mindfulness be enhanced through participation?
- How could intersubjectivity and expanding our relationships across self-other and the environment change our attitude towards representation, accountability and sustainable futures?

This essay reflects on past research aimed at enhancing public policy conducted over the past twenty years and draws on current research funded by the CRCAH[1] into ways to enhance communication and mindfulness to enhance well-being and resilience.

The Crisis in Democracy and Governance

The present essay[2] aims to:

- **Explore** ways to enhance governance and democracy by working across conceptual and spatial boundaries with the people who are to be affected by decisions and with future generations of life in mind.[3]
- **Address** social cognition by drawing on the emotional knowledge and intuitive wisdom within stories and other forms of expression (such as mapping and drawing connections across factors). **Reflects on** my past research based on the need to enhance the capability of people to address complex, wicked problems. We need to develop the capability to apply and combine domains of knowledge to areas of concern. This requires systemic design[4] to address risk and to develop resilience. The problem that many policy makers and managers face at all levels is the inability to think critically and systemically. How do we hold in mind multiple, diverse variables with different value dimensions?
- **Argue** that people should be able to have a say in designing their future to ensure that their needs are considered *to the extent that they are convergent with sustainable, livable futures* for this generation of life and the next. We will need to become increasingly aware that individual well-being is determined by group well-being. We will need to find ways of working across conceptual and spatial boundaries if we are to address the challenge of avoiding zero sum approaches (McIntyre-Mills 2009, ALARA and SPAR special editions). The capability to do this is clearly needed to operate in terms of international protocols, standards, charters, covenants and laws that span social, economic and environmental concerns from the local to global. My research builds on the field of critical, systemic thinking and practice by extending the concept of recursive consciousness. This

concept of mindfulness or "recursive consciousness" was developed by Stafford Beer (1994: 253) who cites Sir Geoffrey Vickers "the trap is a function of the nature of the trapped ... their rationality is conditioned to the traps own premises." Beer (1994) demonstrates that making connections impacts on all levels of the system from the individual to the community to the planet. Being able to "think about our thinking" through "unfolding" values with those who are to be affected by our policy decisions and "sweeping in" social, cultural, political, economic and environmental dimensions is vital (McIntyre-Mills 2006).[5]

Consciousness and Mindfulness

Dualist thinking has lead to limitations in the way we think.[6] What is the link between mindfulness, well-being and the global commons? How can we foster a cosmopolitan consciousness that transcends the local and embraces the global? How can we maintain liberal diversity while controlling the use of scarce/fragile resources? How can we achieve a balance between individual and collective needs? Well-being is a value based concept, but we can only be free and diverse to the extent that our freedoms do not undermine the freedoms of others or the well-being of future generations of life. I argue that based on an understanding of our common, intermeshed fate (Beck, 2005; Giddens, 2009; Held, et al., 1999) that rational responses need to be systemic. The problem is that the thinking is not translated into practice. A number of reasons exist for not implementing these overarching instruments to protect the collective good; some are political and some are due to the lack of capability to think in terms of the consequences of decisions. We need a deep understanding of the risks at stake and new forms of organization including regional parliaments, courts and caretakers with policing powers to address the concerns. The capability to adapt to the convergent social, economic and environmental challenges requires critical systemic praxis (CSP). We need systemic approaches to address social, economic and environmental sustainability and to avoid thinking in terms of binary oppositions: "us" versus "them" (Huntington, 1996) and to consider that we have moved beyond the zero sum approach. Quality of life requires making connections and matching knowledge to areas of concern.

As stressed elsewhere (McIntyre-Mills, 2009a, b, c) democracy and governance are in need of an overhaul, because whether citizens and noncitizens in large, diverse nation-states, people are not well represented. We need to find ways of achieving better representation and accountability within and across nation-states in the interests of a sustainable world. The Brundtland Report (1987) made the conceptual policy connection across health, sustainable development, well-being and peace. Professor Fiona Stanley has stressed that the challenges facing children and the most marginalized in the community in Australia are challenges that could be suffered more widely[7] as we face the impact of convergent social, economic and environmental challenges. Climate change will affect the standard of living that is taken for granted by the privileged (Stanley, Hawke oration lecture, 17 Nov. 2008).

Social and environmental justice policy needs to be implemented. Policy rhetoric must become reality, but for change to occur people will need to be able to hold organizations to account, to ensure that scarce resources are shared equitably so that the life chances of some are not undermined by others.

Climate change and poverty are examples of "wicked" problems, to use Rittel and Webber's (1984) concept in that we have to address many diverse variables that are interrelated and that have a strong value and emotional dimension. People are prepared to make an effort to become engaged in discussions pertaining to essential concerns. Health, housing, education and employment within livable cities are dimensions of a complex, interrelated social justice and well-being challenge posed by climate change (Stern, 2007; Flannery, 2005). These are the sine qua non of well-being. Wicked problems such as these require addressing many interrelated variables with an emotional and value dimension. The greater the use of participatory design processes to address complex problems (such as homelessness, family violence, drug use, unemployment and social inclusion issues) the better the problem solving outcomes for service users and providers (see McIntyre-Mills, 2008).

Geo-engineering[8] the planet's climate could be our ultimate act of hubris as a human race unable to reduce our emissions and refusing to admit that our way of life is unsustainable. The notion of planetary health needs to be placed in the forefront of our minds.[9]

The global commons is the environment on which we depend. It is can be defined as air, water, soil and the genetic code of life. We need to think in terms of "joining up the dots" at a personal, interpersonal and global level. To achieve mindfulness we need to be able to think about our thinking. When we cannot have a say in affairs we can resort to drugs and alcohol or try to achieve an altered state of being by watching television or engaging in rituals that help to give us a sense of control. Initially the concept of global commons was narrowly defined as "assets outside the national frontiers such as oceans, space and the Antarctic." This definition has been reframed to refer to the common good supported by social, legal, economic and environmental policy. The Brundtland report *Our Common Future* (1987: 20) highlights the need to work across boundaries: The global commons and quality of life provide the bases for well-being. "Well-being" is defined in terms of Nussbaum and Glover's (1995) conditions for quality of life. The concept "quality of life" draws on Nussbaum's notion of capability (1995: 83), which includes the importance of critical reflection:

> Being able to live to the end of a human life of normal length, not dying prematurely, or before one's life is so reduced as to be not worth living... Being able to form a conception of the good and to engage in critical reflection about the planning of one's own life. This includes ... employment outside the home and to participate in political life ... being able to show concern for other human beings ... being able to live with concern for and in relation to animals, plants and the world of nature.... Being able to laugh, to play, to enjoy recreational activities.

According to Fougere (2007). "Well-being is an idea whose time has come." Well-being and livability is determined by social, economic and environmental factors. The notion that we can survive at the expense of others is problematic. We survive because of the environment that sustains us. The more we are able to understand that our future depends on thinking not in terms of binary oppositions but in terms of systemic overlapping webs the better.

Consumption by individuals has driven unsustainable social, economic and environmental choices. We need to rethink the way that we see ourselves, our relationships and our place in the environment. Achieving social and environmental justice requires addressing complex, wicked problems. Awareness of the implications of our choices is a first step in developing and implementing change. Nation-states need to be guided by the UN Millennium and global covenants that can be interpreted and implemented within regional federations to translate the thinking into practice and to embed the changes.

Within our region we face challenges as a result of climate change. Indonesia faces the challenge of implementing Decentralization Law 22 of 1999 and Gender Mainstreaming Law 9/200 and Law 23/2002 to ensure greater opportunities for minorities, women and children, respectively (Barton 2002 and Kami 2006; Bessel in McLeod and MacIntyre, 2007). In both Australia and Indonesia the need to address these concerns could provide common ground across diverse religions and interest groups (Suedy, 2008; pers. com, Director of Wahid Institute and Prof. Dr. Gumilar, rector of University of Indonesia). A way to achieve this balance is to involve people in policy making so that they feel engaged and committed to the policy that ensures the well-being of their children.

By enabling people to make sense of their own experiences and to communicate this "sense making" to others we can help them to build connections and to establish rapport with each other. Culture and politics are linked constructs that can and do change! I argue that the plasticity of the brain is such that it shapes the environment and it in turn is shaped by the environment. This two way feedback is well known in cybernetics (Beer 1994, Von Foerster, 1995). This mutual co-determination is something that we need to remember in all our policy and management endeavors.

> It is widely assumed that the brain shapes our conscious experiences (and perhaps even more widely assumed—with less justification—that the brain "creates" consciousness). It is also known that the brain is in turn shaped by experience (one feature of brain development, for example being characterized as "survival of the useful": Changeux, 1985; Edelman, 1992). So, to the extent that collective representations shape the nature and contents of consciousness, we expect that these cultural constructs would also shape the functional anatomy and microstructure of the brain [Turner and Whitehead 2008: 45].

By systemic I mean recognizing that we exist not merely because of our connection to others and the environment but because we are part of the environment.[10] Consciousness is defined as "making connections" and it builds on the work of Nussbaum (2001), Cornelius (1996)[11] and Greenfield (2000: 13, 21) which stresses that emotions and an ability to think about our thinking are a key to extending mindfulness. It is possible to develop the capability to think about the way our lives and life chances have been constructed (as a result of our culture, where we live and the level of education and income of our parents and whether or not they were given the vote). Our sense of control over our lives or sense of agency will be shaped by our experiences and emotions and the experiences and emotions of our family and friends; nevertheless we have the capability to think about our situation and our emotions by exercising mindfulness.

Emotions and Mindfulness

> Emotions shape the landscape of our mental and social lives. Like geological upheavals in the landscape, they mark our lives as uneven, uncertain, and prone to reversal. Are they sim-

ply, as some have claimed, animal energies or impulses with no connection to our thoughts? Or are they suffused with intelligence and discernment, and thus a source of deep awareness and understanding? If the latter then emotions cannot be sidelined in accounts of ethical judgment as they often have been [Nussbaum, 2001, prologue].

> Indeed the great advantage of a cognitive/evaluative view of emotion is that it shows us where societies and individual have the freedom to make improvements. If we recognize the element of evaluation the emotions, we also see that they can themselves be evaluated—and in some ways altered, if they fail to survive criticism. Social constructions of emotion are transmitted through parental cues, actions and instructions long before the larger society shapes the child..." [Nussbaum, 2001: 173].

Emotions,[12] values and perceptions are central to our humanity.[13] They underpin the so-called "enemies within" (Churchman 1979), namely "religion, morality, aesthetics and polities," the human paradox of our potential for passion and compassion. Emotions can limit our consciousness, but they can also alert us to issues that we need to think about. Passion and compassion are the flip sides of one another. The more connections we can make, the better our thinking, our policy processes and our governance outcomes will be (see White 2002). Nussbaum (1995: 83) is concerned first about quality of life and human rights define quality of life and development (Crocker, 1995) in terms of ideals. Nussbaum (2006: 85) makes the point that quality of life pertains to both personal and public life: "the capabilities approach takes its start from the Aristotelian/Marxian conception of the human being as a social and political being, who finds fulfillment in relations with others" By drawing on and extending Cornelius (1996) it can be argued that emotion can be better understood from a systemic viewpoint that draws on many (not incommensurate theories of emotion). Awareness within context and responsive appraisal of many dimensions means that connections and interactions are the basis for human well-being. We can think in hierarchies and divisions and in terms of connections and continuums and it is the latter capacity that enables us to be creative and more conscious. An inability to make connections impedes our thinking. We need to be aware of our emotions. They can enhance or limit consciousness. It is this dimension that is important for spiritual life and an area of interest to many Aboriginal informants on what constitutes well-being (McIntyre-Mills 2007). Hierarchies are necessary to find patterns in the data, but they need to be open to continuous iterative testing based on discursive democracy, so that policy decisions can be reviewed from the point of view of those who are affected. Emotions are a major filter of perceptions. We need to acknowledge emotions through encouraging people to express their perceived needs in narratives or descriptions (see Geertz 1973, Edgar 1992).

Mindfulness of the Connections

The need for a new form of idealism that can build solidarity in an inclusive manner to support a "global covenant" based on social democratic ideology is made by David Held (2004). Singer (2002) also makes a powerful pragmatic argument about socio-environmental consequences in *One World* and Nussbaum (2006) argues (unlike Singer, 2002 or Rawls 1999), for ethical consideration to be given irrespective of possible reciprocal benefits or the consequences. She considers the needs of the disabled, weak and voiceless.[14] This is taken up by Sharpe (2005) who argues in her recent book *Creatures Like Us* that instead of considering the *right to a life free of pain and a life that is worth living* in terms of reciprocity and the public good, as argued by Rawls in "the Law of People's," that we should think in terms of relationships and a continuum of consciousness with non human animals. Nussbaum (2007) argues that living creatures have a right to fulfill their capabilities or to have "quality of life." If we find this hard to accept in idealistic terms or the expanded pragmatic terms of Singer (based on their being sentient beings) then make the connection (based on narrow pragmatism) that poor quality of life leads to sick animals who are likely to make us sick. "A is better off when B is better off" (Von Foerster 1995: 494). We only have to think of SARS and the sicknesses of caged birds, pigs and cattle to realize that it is in our interests to be compassionate! Saul Alinsky's (1972) "low road to morality" could bridge the moral divide in contexts where we cannot see eye to eye (McIntyre, 2007d).

Greenfield (2000: 21) argues that emotions and feelings are the most basic aspects of consciousness. She calls them "the building blocks" and that when we temper our emotions through thinking through implications of acting out passions we are able to become more mindful or conscious.[15] Baruma and Margalit (2004) argue that just as Occidentalism is a caricature of Western identity, thinking and practice, Orientalism is a caricature of Eastern identity, thinking and practice. Caricatures are the basis for current international relations, governance and public policy, based on mutual projections. Emotions, values and perceptions are central to our humanity. They underpin our values, the so-called "enemies within" (Churchman 1979), namely "religion, morality, aesthetics and polities," the human paradox of our potential for passion and compassion. Emotions can limit our consciousness, but they can also alert us to issues that we need to think about. Passion and compassion are the flip sides of one another. The more connections we can make, the better our thinking, our policy processes and our governance outcomes will be (see White 2002). We need to be able to set aside limited stereotypes if we are to achieve sustainable social and environmental justice.

McLuhan and Powers (1989) argued in *The Global Village* that paradoxically as human beings are exposed to images of suffering and news daily on TV and today by palm pilot and computer, they become inured to suffering. As we become more and more digital and image oriented we also face the tendency of human beings to think in terms of screen-based icons and pictures, rather than in terms of text-based abstract concepts, which could lead to their making rapid decisions. Greenfield (2008) stresses that we run the risk of reducing the size of the conceptual assemblies or connections that we are able to make, rather than thinking through ideas and drawing analogies. This is required when we read books and when we are required to imagine what the abstract words mean. We need mindfulness to achieve this based on fostering the ability to think in terms of larger assemblages of ideas spanning many kinds of knowledge.

What happens when we die?

If we accept that death involves decay then we become one with the earth—compost for living things. Our state transforms from one organic form to another organic form.

If we accept that death is merely a change in the form of our material being, this would however be an over simplification. I am not a scientist, merely a thinker and integrated of bits of data which I think about and try to make sense of.

For some organic life, decay of the physical body (or part of it) is stopped through transplantation of organs or blood from one body to another. My neighbor donated a kidney to her husband. Some of her being became one with his being, in a quite literal sense.

I have heard of transplant beneficiaries saying that after a transplant some of the trait of the donor become manifest in the life of the beneficiary.

If an interest in music or poetry was not previously apparent, perhaps the life changing event engenders this interest? Perhaps it is possible for consciousness and the connections created within the brain to stretch beyond the brain, to become dispersed consciousness across the whole human body?

Could it be said that some of the acquired learning (which after all is about brain connections) could be passed on from one to another through organ transfer? After all, it occurs when children inherit genetic life from their parents. Why not also through organic transfers? Perhaps as Rosenthal (2012) suggests, it would be possible through stem cell transfers to enable cells to re-generate. If some creatures are able to regenerate limbs, the future could be one in which transplants become a way of life. Hybridity in the sense mentioned by Haraway, could be around the corner in terms of medical and biomedical design….

But where does this leave us in terms of thinking about life? What is it to be alive?

Some organic life transforms to sustain other forms of life. By merging with the earth we become a resource for other forms of life. So being a blood donor when we are alive, an organ donor when we are alive (if we are generous) and an organ donor when we die, are just some of the ways in which we re-generate the earth. I would be happy for my ashes to merge with the ocean in Fish Hook or with the soil on Table Mountain, because part of me still (likes to) believe that a soul or a spirit continues.

But more likely we can hope that we will become memories for those who continue to live and perhaps a trace of some of our thoughts and actions will remain in digital records that could help to generate other (better) ideas and designs, the citations and knowledge that we glean by reading, listening to others and other means take on a life of their own. In a sense they print out or generate other responses and other designs. Minds can thus reach out across generations. In a personal sense I am able to connect with the minds of my great-great-great-great grandfather through his writings and the writings of a great uncle whose war diaries were written and sketched in a POW camp.

My being as a human animal is connected with all my animal forebears and my animal companions. The stray grey cat in our home, the grey kangaroo who grazes on the grass at night and my parents' stray dog—all enrich our lives with their friendship. My connection with the garden and trees restores my physical and spiritual being after spending too much time bonded to the computer. Greenfield stresses that the more we rely on asynchronous digital communication, the more likely we are to lose the ability to read emotions and complex social situations. So the capacity to use a design of inquiring approach is important. I think the concept of wicked problems is problematic, because it assumes that systemic approaches can strive towards taming them. These are problematic and anthropocentric terms. It would be better to try to find ways of living with the complexity. The way forward is the ability to work across disciplines and to appreciate many kinds of knowledge, but first we must recognize our anthropocentric starting point for the research (Butler, 2011).[16] Butler's work stresses "the need to rethink the human as a site of interdependency."

If human beings accept their interdependency, then they will be less anthropocentric and more likely to be able to recognize that they are part of an interconnected web of life.

We need to accept that we are human animals and that our sovereign states are a fiction. We are dependent on others in our immediate neighborhood and on others within our regional neighborhood.

Similarly our connection and return to other states of organic and inorganic life also needs to be recognized. Thus the lines between life and death become far less distinct."

Butler stresses that humanity needs to be able to ask for assistance and we need to be able to anticipate that we will be heard and that people will respond with compassion. Unless this is possible it leads to a life that can be unbearable. Do we wish to live in a world where we do want to help one another and in which we deny the pain of sentient beings?

Social and environmental justice needs to be addressed through social movements that are buttressed by international law that is supported by regional courts. The recognition of the EU (despite its many failings) with a Nobel Peace Prize is indicative of the potential of the EU. In a confederation citizens do not have a direct say in international affairs and an example of confederalist model is the EU. Archibugi (2010) stresses this is different from the "more rigid constitutional structure" of the United States or Australia, for example.

Public Engagement Based on a "Design of Inquiring Systems" to Address Risk and Enhance Representation

Mindfulness is essential if we are to appreciate the global commons and if we are to have a hope of sustaining the future. Emotions play a role in mindfulness. Paradoxically they can cloud our thinking or they can prompt us to ask, What is more important than anything else? We need to be able to examine our emotions. The capability to do this stems from being able to engage in thinking about our own thinking and being able to think through ideas with others. To do this we need to engage with one another respectfully and to be guided by processes that make this possible.

Balancing individual cultures and collective cultures can be achieved through testing out ideas with those who are to be at the receiving end of decisions. This is vital if we do not want to lose the notion of social and environmental justice, ensuring that values can be diverse and people can be free to the extent that their values and freedoms do not undermine the diversity and freedoms of others. This in turn requires personal rationality and public rationality. In this sense it is idealistic and normative, but it allows for the expanded testing out of ideas within context. Addressing these concerns, however, requires more than merely a "whole of government" approach or merely coordinating across government to achieve excellence. Co-creation needs to occur at the local level to address the most complex and intractable problems, namely social inclusion, poverty of the most marginalized Australians. Improving representation (meaning ensuring that people who are to be affected by the decision act as caretakers for the next generation). This requires a change in democracy, governance and ethics. It requires a capability to hold elections that span regions and generations, improving accountability, meaning ensuring that decisions can be audited and that pea-and-thimble tricks cannot be played because the decisions are local.

Ethical Literacy to Support Social and Environmental Justice

Engagement in face-to-face or electronic agoras can help to develop a better understanding of the way in which others think. It can also help to shape policy. Ethical literacy can be assisted by asking questions (see McIntyre-Mills 2008, drawing on and adapting West Churchman's "Design of Inquiring Systems" 1971 and other works, 1979a, 1982). Participation per se makes a difference to the way we feel. It can reduce a sense of alienation and hopelessness. Engagement enhances rapport with others. These ideas are not new. The notion of eudaimonia or the sense of engagement and connection with others contributes to well-being and quality of life. This was stressed by Aristotle in *Nichomachean Ethics* (see Irwin 1985). In many ways it resonates with the ideas expressed by Csikszentmihalyi (1991):

> [T]he best moments in our lives, are not the passive, receptive, relaxing times—although such experiences can also be enjoyable, if we have worked hard to attain them. The best moments usually occur when a person's body or mind is stretched to its limits in a voluntary effort to accomplish something difficult and worthwhile. Optimal experience is thus something that we make happen.... For each person there are thousands of opportunities, challenges to expand ourselves. Such experiences are not necessarily pleasant at the time they occur. The swimmer's muscles might have ached ... yet these could have been the best moments of his life. Getting control of life is never easy, and sometimes it can be definitely painful. But in the long run optimal experiences add up to a sense of mastery-or perhaps better, a sense of participation in determining the content of life-that comes as close to what is usually meant by happiness as anything else we can conceivably imagine" [3–4].

Striving to match areas of concern to policy and practice requires considering the following:

- Subjective ideas that are brought into intersubjective processes
- Logical relationships across ideas
- Empirical data for the big (broad) and small (detailed) picture
- Idealism (not thinking about the consequences), because the moral law states we need to treat people as ends in themselves and not a means to an end.[17]
- Intersubjectivity, based on meaningful communication, compassion and relationships with others and the environment
- Expanded pragmatic caretaking based on considering the consequences for this generation of life and the next.

Compartmentalized thinking undermines accountability and ability to manage diversity and risk. The research into participatory governance for social and environmental justice is based on testing out ideas and considering "if-then" scenarios (McIntyre 2005 a, b; McIntyre-Mills in Van Gigch, 2003, 2006; McIntyre-Mills 2007) which could be useful for enhancing policy making and for ensuring that people are able to think about the consequences of their decisions for themselves, others and the environment. We need to understand how we are systemically interconnected with others and the environment to appreciate social, economic and environmental accounting (Murray, et al., 2007).

Reframing Ethics, Democracy and Governance as Systemic Interaction to Balance Individual and Collective Needs

Can mindfulness be enhanced through participation? Living a life at the expense of others (including the next generation) and at the expense of the environment is unsustainable. Testing out the ideas needs to be undertaken (not only by experts) but by caretakers who have "lived experience" and who are concerned about the long term consequences of social, economic and environmental decisions. This is essential to address the interests of the less powerful, but also to ensure that the ideas of what works, why and how (as far as the principals are concerned) is addressed to ensure the well-being of future generations of life. "We contend that the practicality of knowledge is determined not only by the careful judgment of social scientists but also by the politics and environment in which scientific knowledge is used…. By considering the socio-political context of its production and application … we can grasp the broader factors determining the practicality of social scientific knowledge…" (Meagher and Wilson, 2002: 662).

The Enlightenment has been critiqued for dismissing the voices of those with lived experience, rather than professional knowledge. Post-positivists and critical theories have responded by expanding the process of falsification to include a wider range of tests.[18] This section considers the implications of ongoing research on the relevance of participation for testing out ideas for science, ethics, and democracy. Testing enables the better match of development responses to context, thus enabling "evolutionary development," rather than "development for growth." This is the difference between development for growth which is unsustainable, because it "forgets" the "externalities of poverty" and pollution, and policy adaptation (Giddens, 2009) that is based on responding to the environment by adapting and evolving designs that are socially, economically and environmentally sustainable.

Ethical thinking could enhance representation and accountability by means of a "design of an inquiring system" to explore what is the case and what ought to be the case based on questioning and matching domains of knowledge to areas of concern (see McIntyre-Mills 2004, 2006c on C. West Churchman and conceptual tools). The approach makes a case for expanded pragmatism through thinking about the consequences of our decisions for ourselves, others and the environment in this generation and the next. Our environment shapes us and we shape the environment in ongoing recursive cycles. Discrimination and frailty can make human animals[19] as vulnerable as other creatures. Expanded pragmatism (as opposed to narrow pragmatism) considers the consequences for self, others and the environment in the short medium and long term of protecting the interests of the powerful at the expense of the powerless.

Implications of Findings to Date

The research attempts to show that it is possible to make sustainable decisions informed by testing out ideas in such a way that the principle of falsification which underpins positivism is extended by enabling the people who are to be affected by the decisions to be involved in the testing process. "If-then" scenarios are used to enable people to think through the implications of their decisions with the assistance of software. Currently the research has only tested out the software for complex personal and family decisions pertaining to five key areas of concern.

The architecture for constructing a new approach to democracy and governance for well-being involves the recognition of combinations of key factors that affect livability: home safety, health, sense of purpose, connection/belonging (people and land or place), self respect and confidence. It is significant that the research to date supports the notion that making connections is a means and an end to support well-being (McIntyre-Mills 2007, 2008). It is argued that agreement on these areas of concern could be the basis for scaling up participation at a regional level.

Discursive dialogue is used in a participatory action research process that can be represented as follows, in the process for operationalizing the Design of Inquiring Systems:

Step 1: Service users tell their unique story to a service provider;
Step 2: Service providers listen to the narratives told by women and men of all ages;
Step 3: The users start their healing journey by using one of three pathways that they can tailor to suit their own unique experiences;
Step 4: They decide what they will add to their life and what they will discard, in order to address barriers and to enhance turning points for the better and minimize turning points for the worse;
Step 5: They consider:

- What things they have in life—family, poverty, stress
- What they need—housing, training, confidence
- What they could add/discard—lack of confidence, a bad relationship
- What are positive and negative turning points—telling my story, attending local social inclusion projects, developing trust in a mentor
- What are the barriers—racism, negative thinking, lack of resources
- What services can be used and in what combination?

The architecture for the software is seen in figure 1.

Greenfield (2002) stresses that the more connections we can make within the brain and across different areas of knowledge and different paradigms (social, economic and environmental) the more conscious we can become. This has implications for the way we live, for the way we do science, for the way we run our governments and for ethics. We need to be aware of the different metaphors that we have for knowing. Do we "weave or draw together strands of experience" and make sense of them? This is a Ngarrindjeri

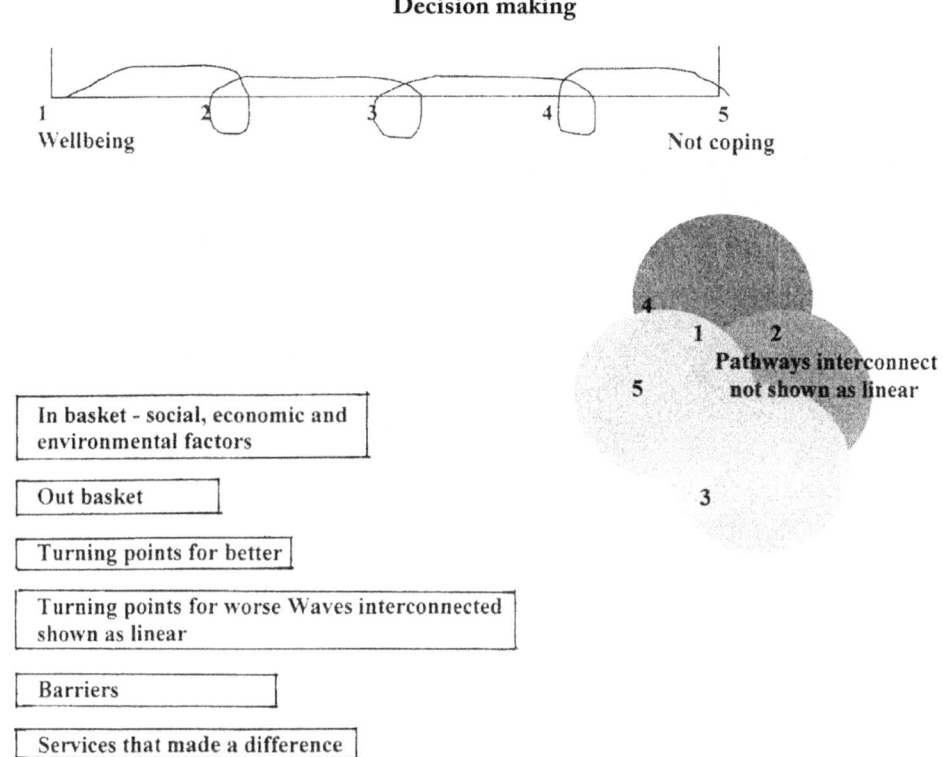

Figure 2: The architecture of the interactive software. Research approach using a design of inquiring system to address wicked policy and governance challenges. Expansive story telling develops myths that weave together meaningful strands of experience. Sharing stories and weaving together the strands of experience (McIntyre-Mills, 2006; McIntyre-Mills & DeVries, 2010, 2014).

metaphor which resonates with the approach stressed by Greenfield (2002) or do we compartmentalize and analyze at the expense of seeing the wider implications for this generation and the next?

Organic mapping enables the generation of ideas and relationships. Respectful conversation enables co-creation of ideas. Interactive software designed with the participants could support and respond to diversity while also establishing patterns. Healing pathways software enables combinations of service responses that are matched to complex user needs. Participation supports greater attachment to rational, sustainable decisions through engagement with ideas and the implications for decisions. This multi-dimensional process could be useful for mainstreaming social inclusion to address the challenge of balancing individual and collective needs. This requires multilevel governance to address complex challenges of social and environmental justice that span regions and nation-states. Balancing individualism and collectivism requires ensuring that values can be diverse and people can be free to the extent that their values and freedoms do not undermine the diversity and freedoms of others, the next generation of life and the environment on which we depend. This requires reworking our understandings of rights and responsibilities. In this sense it is idealistic and normative, but it allows for the expanded testing out of ideas within context and with future generation sin mind. To sum up: governance and democracy have to deal with three options pertaining to truth (see Crowder, 2004; McIntyre-Mills, 2000, 2006):

- One truth (monist) responses defended by grand narratives.
- No truth (postmodernist) approached defended by relativism or conflict.
- Mediated (co-created) responses based on testing out ideas with professional experts those with lived experience and as caretakers for the next generation of life.

Scaling up value pluralism from local to regional requires the ability to be open to diversity, but also to find patterns. Co-creation at the local level is tested out at the local level by addressing the most complex and intractable problem. Complexity refers to the number, variety and interrelationships across variables and the way in which they are perceived or valued. Our research to date indicates[20] that the following factors are central to human well-being: a home (a sense of safety), physical and mental health, a sense of purpose, a sense of connection/belonging (people and land), self respect and confidence. If it is possible to address the complex needs of the most marginalized using a cycle of open and closed questioning to support governance and democracy, then the approach could be scaled up to address other complex challenges that we will face at a regional level.

The NGO and the area it serves in the Southern Region of South Australia is representative of the issues faced by Indigenous communities in other areas of Australia and other parts of the region affected by lack of development, social inequality or by disasters which lead to high levels of health-related issues, unemployment, homelessness, family violence and limited education opportunities.[21] Social inclusion, homelessness, unemployment, gambling, family violence, criminal activities, and drug misuse are facets of a complex, interrelated problem that requires a coordinated governance response across departments in the public, private and non-government sectors. However, current compartmentalized thinking in respect of some aspects of human services has led to disciplinary specializations. Service providers need to develop the capacity to work across disciplines and to understand better the nature of "joined up" social problems as they relate to social well-being and governance (Fougere, 2007). This is not merely a change to policy and practice, but a move away from the perception and definition of issues in separate compartments.

The outcome is the development of prototype software that is co-owned and designed by the participants. We[22] chose one of the most difficult problems in Australian context, namely social exclusion, unemployment, health, housing and addictions (gambling, alcohol and other drugs) with the hope that if we could create an interactive policy tool for a "complex wicked problem" with many interrelated variables and with a strong value base (see Rittel, et al., 1973), we would be able to adapt the model to other less complex problems to inform policy on the basis of evidence of what works, why and how and on the basis of "if-then" scenarios to address the common good in the interests of maintaining well-being.

At a presentation of this research at the Social Innovation Conference in Adelaide and Towards a Science of Consciousness Conference in Hong Kong, I stressed that what is needed is *mainstreaming* the policy matching processes and enabling people to *think through policy options based on scenarios* for the their *own* and *collective well-being*. Solidarity can be achieved through realizing that (a) it is in our best interests and (b) that through inspiring and mobilizing an understanding that we stand and fall by our thinking and our practice. Our futures are recursively linked. The symbol of the boomerang is a symbol of recursiveness. Our own well-being is connected with the well-being of the environment and the well-being of others.

Only by considering the systemic feedback loop or "boomerang effect" (Beck 1992, 1998) can we take into account the notion that poverty and pollution are not the problems of other nation-states, they are our own problems and they pose risks for our well-being.

Balancing Individual and Collective Interests Through Regionalist and Federalist Approaches

Regionalist federations are needed to support the capability of policy makers and managers within government (Fukuyama, 2004) not merely non-government organizations to realize that well-being is the result of appreciating that quality of life is possible only when the global commons and the collective good is protected. For this to occur we need to be aware of the intermeshed or interconnectedness of all life. Multilevel structures need to support new regionalist, federalist forms of governance and democracy. According to Crossen and Niessen (2007: 332):

> The right to a healthy environment is one of the fundamental tenets underpinning the Convention on Access to Information, Public Participation in Decision-making and Access to Justice in Environmental Matters (the Aarhus Convention, 25 June 1998). Yet [it] ... does not create a substantive right to a healthy environment. Rather the Convention creates procedural rights to assert the "right to live in and environment adequate to his or her health and well-being" (they cite the preamble Para. 7). To have meaning ... a substantive right must be accompanied by the ability to seek enforcement of that right.

They conclude:

> The adoption of the Aarhus Regulation is potentially ... ground-breaking ... in the field of environmental democracy in the EU. Through the creation of procedural rights, and the ability to seek an internal review of administrative acts and omissions of Community institutions and bodies, in our view, the Regulation brings entitled NGOs within the standing provisions of the EC Treaty to access the European courts. Of course, this requires a decision of the course to establish the position. Should the court not agree with our interpretation, this could support a complaint to the Aarhus Compliance Committee for the failure of the European Community to meet its obligations to provide access to justice in terms of Article 9(3) of the Aarhus Convention. A right to access to justice cannot be overstated. The ability to seek enforcement of environmental law by the public is critical to the accountability of Community institutions and bodies. Moreover, it is essential to the protection of the environment—and ultimately the right to a healthy environment—as rights are only meaningful to the extent that they can be vindicated.

Scale refers to community, neighborhood, local areas, subregional areas, regional areas, subnational areas, national areas, macro regional areas (such as the European Union) and global planetary scale. This is a good starting point for understanding regions

(Pike, et al., 2006: 37). Both scale and nested systems (which Pike, et al., 2006, do not explicitly address) need to be considered when talking about representation and accountability. This connection is made by Florini (2003) who argues that the Aarhus convention provides the legal basis for a structure and process to enable people at the local level to access information on environmental issues that impact their well-being. This legislation could provide the means to ensure that Triple Bottom Line accounting (Elkington 1994, 1997) which is advocated by the United Nations Convention Agenda 21 is able to be implemented. Florini (2003) does not make this connection, but it links very well with the United Nations Convention on Corruption and European Whistle Blowing legislation. It also links well with the Employment Rights Act of 1996 in the United Kingdom and the Disclosure Act of 1998 in the UK (see Brown, 2008). By rethinking the economy based on valuing well-being we could address the concerns and suggestions made by Graham (2009) in the *Economics of Happiness*.

Diversity and Freedom

Some human values are in conflict, for example individual freedom and equality within and across groups. This can be addressed by means of a "design of inquiry approach" based on a consideration of different kinds of knowledge, namely subjective, objective and intersubjective such as logic, empiricism, idealism, the dialectic and expanded pragmatism that addresses the ultimate human paradox that cultural ideologies can predispose people to believe that there is only one way to do things (monists ranging from arch capitalists to arch radicals) versus an anything goes (post modernist approach fostered by the internet) or that truth needs to be co-created and tested out. The ultimate test being the line drawn to prevent undermining the rights of others and the next generation of life. To recap, values can be diverse to the extent that they do not undermine the diversity and freedoms of others, the environment or the next generation of life.

Table 2: Balancing Individual and Collective Interests

International	*United Nations Conventions*
Federal	Federal parliaments and courts, e.g., EU and courts supported by the Lisbon Treaty
National	States within the federation
Local	Location decisions subjmect to the principle of subsidiarity and supported by freedom of responsibility to be heard locally, nationally and federally in Lisbon

We need to develop a sense of who we are that transcends cultural differences[23] not merely by means of social movements, because these will not be enough to ensure implementation. Fukuyama (2004) stresses the importance of state building for governance, but we need to go beyond this. We need to move towards federation building where states are held to account by regional treaties. Examples such as the European Union's Treaty of Lisbon[24] could provide a step in the right direction for achieving collective representation in a conceptual and spatial sense.[25] Should people be forced to give up their rights to one nation-state in the aftermath of conflict? Perhaps space for difference in a "patchwork of nations" within regions is possible even if it is difficult for a "patchwork nation" (Edgar 1997) to address the need to be individuals but also part of a group.[26]

In three of the world's advanced democracies, namely the United States, the United

Kingdom and Australia, the divides between rich and poor are very wide, far wider than in Sweden or Denmark or Japan.[27] The disrespect that is associated with divided societies makes people feel demoralized or to use the profound Aboriginal expression "they feel shamed." The notion of shame is an emotion that should be explored by the powerful (Coetzee, 2007).[28] By ensuring that all local governments within regions report according to a social, economic and environmental score card we could ensure that life chances of people within a range of areas are addressed. Those whose carbon footprint is larger than others could be held accountable so that impoverished regions are subsidized by rich regions to enable them to meet individual and collective needs.

The law of the nation-state has prevailed in undermining human rights and the environment. To have any hope of buttressing well-being and the global commons we are going to have to find ways to identify with the future of the planet, rather than the efforts of the powerful to make the law to protect their own interests. Consciousness depends on our ability to re-think positivism (see McIntyre-Mills, 2006a, b, and c) and constructivism and to appreciate our interconnectedness[29] if we are to avoid becoming creators of the walking dead or "zombie institutions" (Beck, 1992, 2005) that lead to convergent social, economic and environmental collapse.

Representation, Accountability and Sustainability: Contemplating the Common Good and Value Pluralism

What kind of legacy do we wish to leave future generations? How can intersubjectivity and expanding our relationships across self-other and the environment change our attitude towards representation, accountability and sustainable futures? Consciousness is the connections we make across different parts of the brain. Representation, accountability and sustainability are the three key goals for consciousness (McIntyre-Mills 2009a, b, c). Positive and negative thinking shape ourselves, others and our environment. The ripple effects are borne by future generations.

The boundary of life and death is more permeable in other cosmologies. Indigenous peoples the world over do not draw the line so strongly between self, other and the environment. For example, the Xhosa peoples of Southern Africa believe that we are people through other people. This is the principle of ubuntu. A spiritual connection with the environment gives a sense of awe and reverence (Hobson-West 2007). According to Xhosa cosmology we need to consider our actions and the implications for future generations. The ancestors are ever present watching over the living. We are the environment and it is a reflection of our thinking and practice.[30]

Facing Up to the Challenges

What do we value as human beings? We will need to reconsider our identity as human beings. We have commodified so many aspects of our lives (including the environment and the very fabric of life). To argue that the market alone could solve our problems is unlikely. Profit, not the public good or the global commons could prevail. It is all very well for powerful stakeholders to claim that rational decisions need to guide policy, not economics or politics, but the question remains: "Who decides what is rational and what will the testing process entail? Will the Popperian falsification process be inclusive? Could it be regarded as a new form of tyranny? (Cooke and Kothari, 2001, Hickey and Mohan 2004). The steps I try to follow[31] to achieve harmony are:

- Finding out what various stakeholders want (using divergent[32] and convergent groups to find patterns in the data).[33]
- Helping them to realize what they need and their relationships with others and the environment by using "if-then scenarios" through guided processes, for example: narrative, soft systems mapping, art work, role play (depends on the group), populating the prototype, mining a data system that updates as it is used—the software is just an aid to the process (but could be useful for monitoring, evaluation and building evidence based policy—the latter is what we are working on at the moment).
- Enabling people to translate their own ideas into policy and then into practice, supported through democratic governance processes that are ongoing.[34]
- Building in a monitoring and evaluation system from the start through communities of practice (Wenger 1998, McIntyre-Mills, 2006).

The unity of the individual and the collective is addressed by Habermas (2001) when he stresses that the individual's rights are upheld in the collective recognition given by the law. Legal rights however do not necessarily overlap with moral or ethical behavior. A new approach to democracy, governance and ethical decision making could be based on considering both the existing *a priori* norms and the area of concern within a particular time and space through contextual, "if-then" scenarios that enable participants to consider the implications of their decisions in a form of expanded pragmatism to support the ideal of considering the consequences for the next generation of life. The structure and the process need to support respectful dialogue.

The time has come when the value of individual freedom needs to be balanced with the notion that we can be free to the extent that we do not undermine the freedoms of others or the next generation of life.

There is no such thing as a total system that we can anticipate[35] which is why we need to draw on rich detailed local stories. Our values and assumptions act as filters and we will never be able to develop software that will exactly mirror the way the human brain works (Rosen, 1991, Greenfield, 2000, 2008). If a group of people with a particular set of values design a computer program for others without co-creating the software, it will not necessarily provide an entry point that has resonance or salience.[36]

Systemic governance and democracy[37] could enable us to address the complex risks which we will need to face in addressing health, housing and social inclusion in increasingly high risk local government areas. We will need to be able to ensure that users and providers are responsive to fires, droughts and floods.

We need to develop a democracy/governance cycle that spans conceptual, spatial and temporal boundaries. In order to do this we need to engage people in what matters most to them, namely providing livable and safe environments in which jobs sustain the environment and do not undermine it.

The research on systemic praxis spans narrative, respectful dialogue and systemic design supported by e-democracy and e-governance cycle that could be responsive across regions. The steps could include:

- *Discursive democracy* (Dryzek, 2000) based on open conversation on issues to create a sense of solidarity (Gould, 2007) that spans the local, community and regional level.
- *Deliberation on areas of concern*, based on structured dialogue based on "if-then" scenarios scaled up to regional levels, combined with
- *Direct voting* which will be used to ascertain patterns in the ideas. These could be used to inform candidates running for office.
- *Representative democracy* voting in elected members who will respond to regional concerns. The representatives remain close to the electors.
- *Deliberation within parliament* informed by ongoing regional place based and on line fora.

Praxis Implications of Consciousness: Translating Theory into Practice

The challenge for traditional liberal democracy was to ensure that government organizations acted as accountable agents for the principles, namely the people they serve during a three or four year election cycle. Voting in elected members who represent the people was considered to be both necessary and sufficient. Democracy and governance requires more than social choices made by voting within national boundaries for a limited term, if it is to be representative, accountable and sustainable. It requires "open channel" processes that are responsive to ongoing sociopolitical, economic and environmental changes and the identity shifts that occur over generations. It requires caretaking that is extended beyond social contracts to address livable environments for the next generation of life.[38] Living a life at the expense of others (including the next generation) and at the expense of the environment is unsustainable. Testing out the ideas needs to be undertaken (not only by experts) but by caretakers who have "lived experience" and who are concerned about the long term consequences of social, economic and environmental decisions. This is essential to address the interests of the less powerful, but also to ensure that the ideas of what works, why and how as far (as the principals are concerned) is addressed to ensure the well-being of future generations of life.

The identity of a nation-state is not static. As Europe becomes increasingly Islamic,[39] with increasing numbers of immigrants who identify with the Islamic way of life and as the U.S. becomes more Hispanic and Christian, Australia could also have an increasing number of immigrants from diverse nation-states.

Accommodating differences within and across nation-states will become an increasing challenge, one which impacts on governance and democracy. Social exclusion within and across nation-states is unsustainable as Devji (2005) stresses "'the landscape of democracy' has changed." People identify with one another by virtue of their humanity not merely by virtue of their membership of a nation-state. As Pape (2005) and McIntyre-

Mills (2008, 2009) stress, social inclusion is a *sine qua non* for democracy. The conflict for resources or "the last of the non renewables" will have spillover effects for people internationally. By concentrating on practical issues such as health, education and employment we will be able to address key concerns that are highly valued and that have emotional resonance.

We will have to find ways of working across differences and perhaps realizing that we will become increasingly diverse in Australia. This could mean that we will identify more with America than with Europe, but this could be problematic, given our place in the world. Why should we assume that we will need to play a role as broker? Perhaps we can learn more from Indigenous first nations, not about nationalism per se, but instead about re-framing ourselves as caretakers. This could support a social movement to counter cyber nationalism to support a cosmopolitan "earth polities" approach (Beck, 1992, 2005) that will respond to the needs of environmental refugees and those who are at risk.

Hickey and Mohan (2004:18) stress that "different spaces require different polities" and that theories of what ought to happen need to be balanced with what actually happens. Recognizing the context is all important to making decisions based on an expanded form of pragmatism, is also vital for co-created transcendental themes. Balancing individual and collective interests is central to sustainable social, economic and environmental challenges. It has very important implications for reframing commodifying approaches that shape "civilization."

Postscript

Combining centralized governance controls and decentralized decision-making to support individual needs are not contradictory strategies. It is appropriate to *combine* cycles of open discursive democracy with cycles of rational, structured dialogue.[40] The role of detailed descriptions and storytelling over time could be supported by the internet to enable e-governance and e-democracy. Merely telling people about impending disaster or making people feel guilty is likely to have little effect. It is only when people make a personal connection with the implications of the problem that any difference to praxis will occur. Well-being and livability is determined by social,[41] economic and environmental factors.[42] We need to:

- Think through the consequences of decisions and try to become more mindful of the unintended potential consequences of our decisions through using scenarios and "if-then" logic. Our approaches should be not merely constructivist or guided by so-called realism, depending on the issues under consideration (Beck 1999: 26).
- Move towards consciousness of our recursive interconnectedness, based on a pluralist approach that supports freedom and diversity to the extent that freedom and diversity is not undermined. A process of engagement with others needs to be supported by means of social structures which honor the primary limits set by environmental considerations. The overlaps between us/them need to be rethought in terms of hybrid realities. We exist as part of the environment. We

are the land. We are the water. We are the atmosphere we breathe. Costs to the next generation cannot be externalized.[43] This realization has implications for science, ethics and democracy, governance and policy. Consciousness is a continuum from inorganic to organic life. As tool makers we shape and are shaped by the land.

Notes

1. The paper reflects on the extent to which *participation is an end in itself*, in other words that participation enables people to have a greater understanding of one another and a better match of services to needs. It builds on an Australian Research Council Project (McIntyre-Mills et al., 2007, 2008a, b). An ARC Linkage grant aimed to redress social inclusion issues by designing, developing and testing a participatory process to help match services to perceived need. The partners were: The Australian Research Council, AHURI, two Aboriginal organizations, the Department of Human Services and two universities. The approach advocates building the capacity of service providers by service users and to improve outcomes for service users. This is achieved through combining cycles of open and structured dialogue guided by e-democracy and e-governance software to inform decision making by both users and providers. It creates updated data which are used only as a guide to inform decisions and as an aid to address complex problems. By choosing a problem with many, diverse and interrelated variables it is possible to apply the approach to other challenges. It makes the **case** that participation is both *an end* and *means* to support well-being and that *people who are to be affected by decisions ought to be involved in the process of decision making*. Open testing processes must ensure that the people who are to be affected by decisions become part of the testing process. If people who are to be affected by decisions are not involved in the shaping process they can be disempowered from the outset (Cooke and Kothari, 2001, Cooke, 2004) and resistant to the need to make changes, because they have been excluded. This is what Gaventa (2004: 28) means when he makes the distinction between "making and shaping" versus "using and choosing." To sum up, balancing individual and collective needs will require: (a) facing up to convergent social, economic and environmental challenges and not "being ostriches"; (b) making sense out of the challenges and being innovative and creative while making the best use of resources through considering different scenarios before making policy choices.

2. Acknowledgements: Charles Whitehead asked me to submit my paper entitled: "Well-being, mindfulness and the global commons" to a special edition of the "Journal of Consciousness" and Ingrid Frederikson, a delegate at the "Towards a Science of Consciousness Conference" posed the following question: What happens to consciousness after we die? She invited a range of thinkers spanning an astronaut to a policy researcher to consider consciousness and non local space. This paper builds on and extends the following publications McIntyre-Mills, J. 2008a "Systemic Ethics: Expanding the Boundaries of Rights and Responsibilities." *Systems Research and Behavioural Science*, Vol. 25: 147–150. McIntyre-Mills, J. 2009. "Prologue: The global challenge outlined. Representation, Accountability and Sustainable Futures." *Systemic Practice and Action Research*. Volume 22, No 3: 127–138 (ISSN 1094–429X). McIntyre-Mills, J. 2009. "New directions through extending deliberative democracy to enhance representation and accountability." *Systemic Practice and Action Research*. Volume 22, No 3: 201–218 (ISSN 1094–429X). McIntyre-Mills, J. 2009. "Constructing Citizenship and Transnational Identity: Participatory Policy to enhance attachment and involvement." *Systemic Practice and Action Research* Volume 22, No. 45. Early view August Springer link http://www.springerlink.com/content/104295/?Content+Status=Accepted.

3. Just as the global commons needs to be reframed to be more inclusive that the OECD definitions, so too should our relationships across organic and inorganic life on this planet. The ethical *low road* to justice is a realization that our lives are intermeshed and that ideas and institutions buttressed by selfish interests will lead to our common demise. The ethical *high road* recognizes that we need to use our creativity as caretakers of this generation and the next.

4. The capability to adapt to the convergent social, economic and environmental challenges requires critical systemic praxis (CSP). We need systemic approaches to address social, economic and environmental sustainability and to avoid thinking in terms of binary oppositions: "us" versus "them" (Huntington, 1996) and to consider that we have moved beyond the zero sum approach.

5. West Churchman, a philosopher and organizations researcher, stressed this point, but so has the neuroscientist professor Baroness Greenfield (2000), who stresses that making connections across many

parts of the brain enhances mindfulness. Drawing on these influences, I argue that governments are: on the one hand "too big" to enable deliberation and discursive dialogue of diverse stakeholders to support individual well-being, but on the other hand, "too small" to address the common good of humanity and a fair share of the global commons. A realization of this connection could lead to a culture shift from categorical constructs to an appreciation of connectivism.

      6. We have divided ourselves from others (including sentient creatures) and the environment. Our overweening pride in our enlightened thinking has lead to our losing our sense of connection. Consciousness depends on our ability to re-think positivism (see McIntyre-Mills 2006a, b, c) and constructivism and to return to connectives.

      7. "Some of the things that our less advantaged Aboriginal communities are experiencing could be a talisman of the future for us all…. The global warming parallel is a recurring analogy … as the complex web of causality spreads out from a handful of life-threatening illnesses to encompass a whole scaffold of social determinants…. If you look at a civil society, it's one that is equal, that values trust, that values community above individual greed, that preserves the environment…. An uncivil society is one that is driven by an economic bottom line only" (http://www.theage.com.au/news/entertainment/tv—radio/suffer-the-little-children/2008/10/01/1222651093091.html?page=fullpage#contentSwap1).

      8. Lin (2009) raises the argument that addressing the cause of a planet's ill health is better than treating the symptoms. The issue is that our planetary health has declined so far that we will need to take drastic measures to prevent a decline into the end stage of disease management. The planet can be likened to a human body. We can either treat it with medicine or we can improve our life style. The use of aerosols and reflectors could impact on the ozone layer or lead to lead to unintended side effects, according to Lin. He concludes that governance will need to take into account planetary concerns and cannot be limited to the nation-state.

      9. Planetary Health, Professor Erica Frank, School of Population and Public Health, Department of Family Practice, Faculty of Medicine, University of British Columbia public lecture on 2 September 2009, Flinders Medical Centre.

      10. Air, water and soil sustain us and we return to these elements after death. This systemic recognition is mindfulness. Systemic praxis could be helpful in terms of shifting approaches from compartmentalized thinking and practice to matrix web-like thinking and practice that is suited to addressing complexity.

      11. As discussed in McIntyre-Mills (2008) "User centric design to meet complex needs," her work stresses that the brain is plastic and responsive to the environment. Consciousness is not located in any one place. The more connections we make the more aware we become. The brain is able to make connections through experiential learning. The mind is not located in any one place; it is the connections we make. Consciousness is a continuum, we can be more or less conscious depending on the number of connections made. So mindfulness is based on thinking about our thinking. Critical self awareness is essential for decision making and governance that supports well-being. The key to raising consciousness and self awareness is through greater understanding of the way that emotions cloud our thinking and limit our ability to make connections. The more we are able to understand the perceptions of others, the more connections we can make and the more conscious we become. Aboriginal understandings of well-being emphasize that well-being is about a sense of connection across self-other and the environment. Sharp (2005) has developed a powerful argument about consciousness and our connection to living creatures other than ourselves if we are prepared to accept that being gives rights. She argues that consciousness does not have to enable rational speech, just being.

      12. Emotions are defined systemically by Cornelius (1996) who summarizes and combines four lenses for understanding different dimensions of emotion, namely: 1. Darwinian theory that stresses the similarity of emotions across people of all cultures. Darwin stressed the connection across all life. This continuum is supported by Greenfield's (2000) research into the neuroscience of consciousness. The implications for social justice and for expanding notions of human rights are profound and have implications for cognitive capabilities; democracy, development and freedom (see Sen, 2000, Nussbaum, 2006). 2. The social constructions of difference across self and other impact on well-being. Whereas most urbanized, westernized cultures will construct (all?) emotions as depressions, others continue to make sense of the difficulties we face during our lives using cultural constructs from religion, such as Buddhism (Obeyesekere in Klineman and Good 1985) or callings by the ancestors who can cause spirit possession (see McIntyre-Mills 2000). 3. Jamesian theory that stresses that emotions are bodily reactions and that we can influence emotions through changing our behavior. (See also Candace Perl's "Molecules of Emotion.") 4. Cognitive

approaches (drawing on Arnold 1960) stress that perceptions and emotion are mediated by appraisals and sense making and that our psychology can be changed by thinking. Cornelius stresses that cognitive approaches are predated by philosophers such as Aristotle (see Cornelius 1996: 115) who stressed in Nichomachean ethics (see Irwin 1985) that well-being is supported by being involved in decision making (see McIntyre-Mills 2007).

13. Research demonstrates that emotions trigger the amygdale and that when we are exposed to information that seems relevant we react emotionally to it because it is salient: "In neuropsychology the term representation has become commonplace for the action of the brain in forming material counterparts for mental processes, and is it is attractive to consider the relationship between these two types of representation: the collective and the cortical" (Turner and Whitehead, 2008: 55).

14. Participation, social construction and valuing the experiences of those who are to be at the receiving end of decisions is important for well-being. Nussbaum argues that capabilities need to be used and nurtured. Well-being is about being able to use all one's abilities. If one is able to reason then one ought to do so and society should support this in every way possible. Citizenship is inadequate, human rights are inadequate and we need to consider that human beings are creatures within an ecosystem and that we can be free to the extent that we do not undermine the freedoms of others. Sentient creatures without reasoning skills also need to be accorded freedom to the extent that they do not undermine the freedoms of others.

15. The more connections we can make the more conscious and mindful we are and the more likely we are to make decisions that will promote our well-being. The less connections we make, the less conscious we are (Greenfield 2000). The most important contribution is that consciousness cannot be located anywhere; it is about connections (across many neurons and perceived variables) and the number of connections that enhance consciousness and our ability to think and appreciate our situation. Sustainable social and environmental futures depend on responding to diversity and enhancing representation and accountability. We need to consider the changed landscape in social, cultural, political, economic and environmental terms, rather than merely in terms of only the economic bottom line. A spiritual connection with their environment gave a sense of awe and reverence (Hobson-West 2007).

Our sense of control over our lives or sense of agency will be shaped by our experiences and emotions and the experiences and emotions of our family and friends, nevertheless we have the capacity to think about our situation and our emotions and to make sense of why our lives are the way they are.

16. Butler explores the violence towards the other and other species … in NominalistWay·6 videos. In these she explores the importance of "giving an account of oneself." In a conversation with a young woman (*Examined Life*—Judith Butler and Sunaura Taylor 720, p. vi) she discusses the right to move in space and to use parts of the body that are not usually used. In conversation Sunaura explains that "disability is socially constructed through the disabling effects of the way people respond to you…. Just organising myself ordering a coffee and demand help is a political protest…. We all need help…. We are all interdependent…. Impairment is the medical fusion of bones and the way it affects movement. Being able to move through space and to feel the right to express themselves … being able to move through space. When I did walk … told I walked like a monkey … where our boundaries lie as a human…. Monkeys have always been my favourite animal … in a way I was flattered."

17. The test for the moral law is being prepared to live with decisions if they were to be applied to oneself and one's own children. This is the basis of social contractualism developed by John Rawls (1999) who explains in *The Law of Peoples* that this "veil of ignorance" approach is the basis for liberal democracy. The problem is that the social contract is too limited to take into account the needs of the powerless, such as the disabled, children and animals. At this point idealism becomes flawed. We need the ethical capability to think about the implications of our actions on other forms of life.

18. See McIntyre-Mills, J., et al., 2006a, preface 11–15 and prologue 17–44. The idea is that testing should not only ensure that the complexity of the decisions taken match the complexity of the decision makers, but that all decisions consider the consequences for self, other the environment and future generations of life. This is a rule derived from cybernetics—called Ashby's Rule (1956, see C. West Churchman, *Legacy and Related Works*, volumes 1–3). The discussion is premised on the idea that there are many bodies of knowledge and that the design challenge is to ask questions that will enable the appropriate knowledge to be matched contextually to a task, challenge or problem (Aristotle in *Nicomachean Ethics*, Irwin, 1985). The three kinds of knowledge are *techne*, *episteme* and *phronesis* (based on the wisdom of matching the right kind of knowledge to context, based on dialogue and testing out ideas). The volumes in the C. West Churchman, *Legacy and Related Works*, *Rescuing the Enlightenment and Democracy from Itself* and *Systemic*

Governance and Accountability make the case for using C. West Churchman's "Design of Inquiring Systems" as the basis for testing out ideas using "logic, empiricism, idealism, the dialectic (which includes subjective ideas in the process of dialogue) and pragmatism." The "Design of Inquiring Systems" (DIS) is not only for self-reflection, but for engaging with others to achieve "best matches" and better decision making that is mindful of perceptions, values and emotions. I argue that based on an understanding of our common, intermeshed fate (Held, et al., 1999) that rational responses need to be systemic.

19. "Human Animals" are not the only tool makers and not all human animals can make or use tools. Learning through testing out ideas and tools within an environment leads to the evolution of species. Powerful tool makers and users dominate the less powerful and the environment to extract profit and short-term gain.

20. The well-being project is currently funded by the CRCAH and was previously funded by an Australian Research Council Linkage Project with the South Australian Department of Health, Flinders University, University of South Australia and Neporendi Forum Inc., an Aboriginal NGO. The co-researchers (comprising academics across a range of disciplines, service users and providers) address well-being in terms of their lived experiences of what works, why and how, in order to enhance their own capabilities, but also the capabilities of the service providers who learn from their experiences.

21. The effects of family violence are wide-ranging, for instance: the criminalization of the offenders has financial, physical and psychological consequences for the women, children and men involved. It also has intergenerational consequences. In South Australia the interconnected challenges facing families result in domestic violence. Long wait for domestic violence laws: Oppn ABC News posted Wednesday, September 9, 2009, 7:41 a.m. AEST. Domestic violence: still waiting for tougher laws, says Oppn (www.flickr.com: dion gillard). The Opposition says the South Australian government is taking too long to toughen laws against domestic violence. Opposition families' spokesman Stephen Wade says it has been four years since plans were flagged by Premier Mike Rann. The government says a bill for greater protection of domestic violence victims will be tabled in State Parliament soon. Mr. Wade says it must allow for an investigation of deaths attributed to domestic violence. "All of the three eastern states have already implemented death review processes," he said. "Our Government, after four years of thinking about the issue, still hasn't decided if it wants to do a death review process." I believe the government needs to give a higher priority to domestic violence legislation. It seems to be focused far too much on headline-grabbing legislation.... It makes sense that after a death the agencies involved sit down and think how things could be done better, ... not to blame the agencies but to do the best that we can to protect potential victims of domestic violence."

22. The ARC linkage team comprised: Professor John Roddick for information systems engineering; Professor Ann Roche for public health expertise pertaining to addictions and knowledge management; Assoc. Prof. Janet McIntyre, sociologist/social anthropologist for critical systemic thinking and practice pertaining to well-being, social and environmental justice, policy and management, joined up governance and discourses of knowledge; Assoc. Prof. Doug Morgan, for Aboriginal knowledge discourses and philosophy of knowledge; Bevan Wilson as Ph.D. candidate, member of the Neporendi Board; and Dr. Denise de Vries, Informatics programming. The CRCAH project was mentored by Kim O'Donnel, Janet Kelly, and Bevin Wilson. The research develops and tests out a means to undertake health impact assessment in a systemic manner with local Aboriginal participants who are to be affected by the consequences of decisions.

23. Douglas (1973) summarized cultural differences along the lines of grid versus egalitarian group cultures.

24. http://europa.eu/abc/treaties/index_en.htm. "The Treaty of Lisbon was signed on 13 December 2007. It will have to be ratified by all 27 Member States before it can enter into force, which is hoped to be before the next European Parliament elections in June 2009. Its main objectives are to make the EU more democratic, meeting the European citizens' expectations for high standards of accountability, openness, transparency and participation; and to make the EU more efficient and able to tackle today's global challenges such as climate change, security and sustainable development. The agreement on the Treaty of Lisbon followed the discussion about a constitution. A "Treaty establishing a constitution for Europe" was adopted by the Heads of State and Government at the Brussels European Council on 17 and 18 June 2004 and signed in Rome on 29 October 2004, but it was never ratified."

25. What is a nation if it is not a state? It requires remembering human identity in pre-colonial terms as being co-determined by "mother earth and father sky" (Peter Turner, 2009, *Making Liveable Sustainable Systems*). This is the question that I consider in my forthcoming book *Balancing Individualism*

and Collectivism. Can we move beyond tribalism to face a broader sense of who we are? Can we move beyond zero sum categories and us/them stereotypes? To what extent is a culture's identity compromised by tolerating or even accepting the culture of "the other" in a shared nation? Are some acts of oppression beyond forgiveness, and does it matter when two cultures must find a future in one nation? These questions are relevant to my ongoing research into the nature of democracy and governance and exploring alternative ways to govern. This is a quotation from an invitation extended to attend a 2009 Inaugural Edward Said Memorial Master Class held by Professor Saree Makdisi, Friday, 18 September. This question is to be applied to the Palestinian Israeli conflict and the hypothetical case of a post-conflict Arab Jewish nation. The invitation stressed that the same questions linger in South Africa, Australia and many other post-colonial nations.

26. Said stresses that the hierarchy of command, or the chain of command approach combined with the categorization of ideas leads to power over others and disrespect. Said (1978: 92) discusses how after the building of the Suez Canal it was possible for de Lesseps to talk about "one world," a world that would serve the interests of the West! The barriers between cultures are the mutual stereotypes based on ongoing projections of what "the other" is like. A way to understand "the other" better is through dialogue to create mediated or shared contextual truth. The challenge is to overcome the idea of representation based on one form of truth. "Kissinger may not have known on what fund or pedigreed knowledge he was drawing when he cut the world up into the pre–Newtonian conceptions of reality. But his distinction is identical with the orthodox one made by the Orientalist, who separate Orientals from Westerners. And unlike Orientalism's distinction Kissinger's is not value free, despite the apparent neutrality of his tone" (Said, 1978: 47). Said stresses that Kissinger uses binary oppositional logic, as follows, he argues the West is "deeply committed to the notion that the real world is external to the observer, that knowledge consists of recording and classifying data—the more accurately the better" (1978: 46–47).

27. Thursday, 3 September 2009. Richard Wilkinson, Professor Emeritus at the University of Nottingham Medical School and Honorary Professor at University College London. Discussion on his research on social inequalities, their causes and the social determinants of health. *The Spirit Level: Why More Equal Societies Almost Always Do Better* by Richard Wilkinson and Kate Pickett is published by Allen Lane. Australian Broadcasting Interview by Margaret Throsby.

28. It could be argued that for human rights to be implemented, even in democracies—it will require some overarching regionalist approaches to ensure that differences in life chances are not translated into disrespect for others and an overweening pride that helps us to deny the rights of others.

29. Because we have limited the way we think we have divided ourselves from others (including sentient creatures) and the environment. Our overweening pride in our enlightened thinking has lead to our losing our sense of connection.

30. It may be of comfort to argue that "life after death" is better than life on earth but it is no justification to use it as "the opiate" of the people or to neglect our role as conscious caretakers for the next generation.

31. McIntyre-Mills (2006, 2008) develops arguments for testing out ideas with those who are to be affected by the decisions, with the caveat that diversity and freedom should be supported to the extent to which diversity and freedom are not undermined. We need to build capabilities to think conceptually and spatially (or globally) at multiple levels and systemically.

32. Said stresses the importance of working with people and in specific contexts to understand situations. He stressed the value of the work of Clifford Geertz, whose interest in Islam "is discreet and concrete enough to be animated by the specific societies and problems he studies…" (Said, 1978: 326). What is taken as given? "…truths are illusions about which one has forgotten that this is what they are" (Said 1978: 203).

33. Hierarchies are necessary to find patterns in the data, but they need to be open to continuous iterative testing based on discursive democracy, so that policy decisions can be reviewed from the point of view of those who are affected.

34. The case studies, vignettes and examples (see McIntyre-Mills 2006c, 2007a, b, c, 2008) can be used to demonstrate that systemic approaches can be useful to engage diverse interest groups and ensure that people, irrespective of age, gender, socio-cultural background, level of education, or level of income, are able to participate in dialogue (Banathy, 1996) for problem solving across sectors (for example, health, education, employment) and across disciplines in a range of public, volunteer sectors at local and state level.

35. *The Holographic Brain*. Karl Pribram: interview mind-brain relationship with Karl Pribram, page

4, http://homepages.ihug.co.nz/~sai/pribram.htm. "Mishlove: Many neuroscientists today—it is almost axiomatic, when they talk about the mind, which they sometimes do—they say the mind is sort of located in the brain. I gather that that way of putting it is totally discordant with your own view of things. Pribram: Yes. There are lots of different ways of phrasing this. One is that mental phenomena are emergent properties of how the brain works, and so it is almost like the brain is secreting vision and mind and all that. But maybe a better way of talking about it would be to say that mental phenomena arise through the interaction between brain and body and the environment and—this better way than just thinking of the brain secreting it." So the one of the main principles of holonomic brain theory, which gets us into quantum mechanics also, is that there is a relationship here between what we ordinarily experience, and some other process or some other order, which David Bohm calls the implicate, or enfolded order, in which things are all distributed or spread." ... The point made by Pribram (see Bohn, 1980: 98) is that we "make sense" and meaning out of incoming waves of energy. It can be argued that energy and life go hand in hand. Closure leads to entropy and the release of energy as the body dies.

36. The machine consciousness workshop at the Science of Consciousness (Hong Kong 2009) did not address participatory design. Using a "Design for Inquiring System" (West Churchman, 1979) approach could draw on local knowledge and that can be used to assist the people who are to be affected by decisions to hold in mind multiple variables so as to make better decisions within local contexts. As time passes it is likely that machines (both external and internal) will be used in many ways to enable human bodies to overcome wear and tear. The ethical implications of where we draw the line will need to be decided in terms of expanded pragmatism, based on a consideration of the consequences for ourselves, others, the environment and the next generation. If we can avoid pain and suffering for sentient beings and we can do this without sacrifice to future generations or the environment then the use of artificial intelligence is likely to extend or enhance our well-being. What if we could use external software programmers in a range of learning contexts to re-wire the brain to think in terms of others and the environment and not just selfish survival?

37. The theme of the power of social movements has been echoed by many, but as Giddens (2009) said, social movements will not be enough. Systemic approaches enhance participation and enable service providers to case-manage complex needs. The theory written up in "Systemic Governance and Accountability" has been supported through this research. The participatory design provides effective solutions, both in treatment and community settings through the development of a computer-modeling technique that articulates and informs partnership arrangements and contributes to better communication and understanding of diverse discourses of understanding. Systemic approaches could engage diverse interest groups and ensure that people (irrespective of age, gender, socio-cultural background, level of education, level of income) are able to participate in dialogue for problem solving to address complex needs; and enable thinking and practice that is suited to addressing complexity. Mindfulness is needed to foster the ability to think in terms of multiple variables. This requires assemblages of ideas spanning many kinds of knowledge. The challenge is to find ways to foster mindfulness that avoids the dangers of "one truth" fundamentalism and "no truth" postmodernism. Instead we need to develop new sustainable forms of representation and accountability based on steering from above and below. We need both centralized controls to protect the global commons and decentralized engagement to test out ideas and to co-create a sense of ownership of the ideas. Where and how we draw the lines of inclusion and exclusion will be relevant for decision-making in the sciences, democracy and ethics. Ethical thinking can enhance representation and accountability by means of a design of an inquiring system that makes a case for expanded pragmatism through thinking about the consequences of our decisions for ourselves, others and the environment in this generation and the next. The notion that we can survive at the expense of others is problematic.

38. We can do little to change the problems if we continue to approach the problem of the global commons via the lenses of a compartmentalized, zero sum approach. We need to begin by accepting that *individuals and groups/compartments and webs* are equally important and need to be maintained through adjustments to ensure sustainability. In order to understand the challenges we will need to be informed by both qualitative and quantitative data. The meanings that are attributed to data are all important. It is not a matter of replacing one with the other.

39. Downer, A. 2009, *Advertiser*, 17 August, p. 10, "The Changing Face of Europe." In Britain the Islamic population is 3 percent, in the Netherlands more than 5 percent, in Germany 4.3 percent and Sweden 5 percent. The size of Muslims populations is growing and the local Indigenous populations are declining.

40. About where to draw the lines of inclusion and exclusion when we consider rights and respon-

sibilities for sustainable futures? We do not have a choice between isolation in zero sum competitive nation-states or finding ways to achieve multilateralism. Balancing individualism and collectivism requires local and regionalist participation to steer from above and below.

41. Basic needs plus social inclusion in public affairs is important for well-being: we do not live by bread alone! Participatory processes need to be responsive and need to match the area of concern.

42. We survive because of the environment that sustains us. The more we are able to understand that our future depends on thinking not in terms of *binary oppositions* but in terms of *systemic overlapping webs*, the better.

43. The rights and responsibilities approach to a safe environment within and beyond the nation-state (Hayward 2005: 25) has had little impact on idealist or realist praxis. Individuals have rights but are responsible for problems. Wealthy individuals and nations have had more rights and are arguably more responsible. It can be argued that to achieve wealth others suffer and so wealth and poverty are two sides of one coin. To achieve social and environmental justice we need to rethink the way we live.

References

Ashby, W.R. 1956. *An Introduction to Cybernetics*. London: Chapman and Hall.
Banathy, B. 1996. *Designing Social Systems in a Changing World*. London: Plenum.
Banathy, B. 2000. *Guided Evolution of Society: A Systems View*. London: Kluwer/Plenum.
Bateson, G. 1972. *Steps to an Ecology of Mind: A Revolutionary Approach to Man's Understanding of Himself*. New York: Ballantine.
Bausch, K. 2001. *The Emerging Consensus in Social Systems Theory*. London: Kluwer/Plenum.
Bausch, K., Christakis, A., and De Vries. 2008c. How Can We Break the Mould? Democracy, Semiotics and Regional Governance Beyond the Nation-state. *Systems Research and Behavioural Science*, Vol. 25: 305–321.
Beck, U. 1992. *Risk Society Towards a New Modernity*. London: Sage.
Beck, U. 2005. *World Risk Society*. Cambridge: Polity.
Beer, S., 1994. *Beyond Dispute. The Invention of Team Syntegrity*. New York: Wiley.
Bohm, D. 1980. *Wholeness and the Implicate Order*. London: Routledge and Kegan Paul.
Brown, A.J. 2008. *Whistleblowing in the Australian Public Sector*. Acton: ANU E-Press.
Capra, F. 1996. *The Web of Life: A New Synthesis of Mind and Matter*. New York: HarperCollins.
Chalmers, D. 2006. "David Chalmers" in Blackmore, S., ed. 2006. *Conversations on Consciousness: What the Best Minds Think About the Brain, Free Will, and What It Means to Be Human*. Oxford: Oxford University Press.
Chambers, R. 1997. *Whose Reality Counts: Putting the First Last*. Bath: ITDG.
Checkland, P., and Scholes, J. 1990. *Soft Systems Methodology in Action*. Chichester: Wiley.
Christakis, A., and Bausch, K. 2006. *How People Harness Their Collective Wisdom and Power to Construct the Future in Co-laboratories of Democracy*, Greenwich: Information Age.
Christakis, A. and Brahms, S. 2003. "Boundary spanning dialogue for the 21st century agoras," *Systems Research and Behavioural Science*. 20: 371–382.
Churchman, C. West. 1971. *The Design of Inquiring Systems*. Basic Concepts of Systems and Organization. New York: Basic Books.
Churchman, C. West. 1979. *The Systems Approach*. New York: Delta.
Churchman, C.W. 1979b. *The Systems Approach and Its Enemies*. New York: Basic Books.
Churchman, C. West. 1982. *Thought and Wisdom*. Seaside, CA: Intersystems Publications.
Coetzee, K.M. 2007. *Diary of a Bad Year*. Melbourne: Text Publishing.
Connolly, W. 1969. *The Bias of Pluralism*. New York: Atherton.
Cooke, B. 2004. Rules of thumb for participatory change agents. *Participation: From Tyranny to Transformation?* New York: Zed Books.
Cornelius, R. 1996. *The Science of Emotion: The Research and Tradition in Psychology of Emotion*. Upper Saddle River, NJ: Prentice Hall.
Cox, E. 1995. *A Truly Civil Society*. Boyer Lectures. Sydney, NSW: ABC Books.
Crocker, D. 1995. Functioning and Capability: The Foundations of Sen's and Nussbaum's Development Ethic, Part 2, in M. Nussbaum and J. Glover. 1995. *Women, Culture and Development: A Study of Human Capabilities*. Oxford: Clarendon Press.
Crowder, G. 2004. *Isaiah Berlin. Liberty and Pluralism*. Cambridge: Polity.
Csikszentmihalyi, M. 1991. *The Psychology of Optimal Experience*. New York: Harper and Row.

De Vries, D. 2008. A tool for creating pathways, in McIntyre-Mills, et al. *User Centric Policy Design to Address Complex Needs*. New York: Nova Science.
Devji, F. 2005. *Landscapes of the Jihad: Militancy, Morality and Modernity*. London: Hurst and Company.
Dryzek, J. 2000. *Deliberative Democracy and Beyond: Liberals, Critics, Contestations*. New York: Oxford University Press.
Edgar, D., 2001, *The Patchwork Nation: Rethinking Government-Rebuilding Community*. Sydney: Harper.
Elkington, J. 1994. "Globalisation's reality checks" in Held, H., et al. *Debating Globalization*. Cambridge: Polity.
Elkington, J. 1997. *Cannibals with Forks*. Oxford: Capstone.
Flood, R., and Romm, N. 1996. *Diversity Management: Triple Loop Learning*. Chichester: Wiley.
Florini, A., 2003. *The Coming Democracy: New Rules for Running a New World*, Island Press, Washington, D.C.
Folke, C. 2006. Resilience: The emergence of a perspective for social-ecological systems analyses. *Global Environmental Change* 16. 253–267.
Fougere, G. 2007. *"Well-being is an idea whose time has come." New Opportunities for Health Impact Assessment in New Zealand Public Policy and Planning*. The Public Health Advisory Committee. Wellington, New Zealand.
Fukuyama, F. 2004. *State Building: Governance and World Order in the 21st Century*. Ithaca, NY: Cornell University Press.
Gallhofer, S., and Chew, A. (2000). "Introduction: accounting and indigenous peoples," *Accounting, Auditing and Accountability Journal*, 13(3): 256–267.
Gaventa, J. 2004. Towards participatory governance: assessing the transformative possibilities in Hickey, S., and G. Mohan (eds.). *Participation: From Tyranny to transformation?* New York: Zed Books.
Geertz, C. 1973. Thick description: towards an interpretive theory of culture. In C. Geertz, *The Interpretation of Cultures. Selected Essays* (3–32). New York: Basic Books.
Hickey, S., and Mohan, G. 2004 Toward participation as transformation: Critical themes and challenges. In Hickey, S., and G. Mohan (eds.). *Participation: From Tyranny to transformation?* New York: Zed Books.
Giddens, A. 2009. *The Politics of Climate Change*. Cambridge: Polity.
Gore, Al. 2007. *Assault on Reason*. London: Bloomsbury.
Gould, C. 2007. Transnational Solidarities. *Journal of Social Philosophy* vol. 38 No. 1, 148–164.
Greenfield, S. 2000. *The Private Life of the Brain: Emotions, Consciousness and the Secret of the Self*. New York: John Wiley and Sons
Greenfield, S. 2008. *ID: The quest for meaning in the 21st Century*. London: Hodder and Stoughton.
Graham, C. 2009. *The Economics of Happiness*, http://www.brookings.edu/articles/2005/09globaleconomics_graham.aspx
Habermas, J. 1984. *The Theory of Communicative Action: Reason and the Rationalization of Society*. Boston: Beacon.
Habermas, J. 2001. *The Postnational Constellation*. Political essays. Cambridge: Polity.
Hardin, G. 1968. The Tragedy of the Commons, *Science*, 162:1243–1248.
Hawkin, P. 2009. Commencement: Healing or Stealing. University of Portland, http://www.up.edu/commencement.
Held, D. 2004. *Global Covenant: The Social Democratic Alternative to the Washington Consensus*. Cambridge: Polity.
Held, D., McGrew, A., Goldblatt, D., and Perraton. 1999. *Global Transformations. Politics Economics and Culture*. Stanford, CA: Stanford University Press.
Held, D., et al. 2005. *Debating Globalization*. Cambridge: Polity.
Hobson-West, P. (2007). Beasts and Boundaries: An introduction to animals in sociology, science and society. *Qualitative Sociology Review*. Volume 3, Issue 1. 23–41.
Hulme, M. 2009. Why we disagree about climate change. Understanding controversy, inaction and opportunity. Cambridge: Cambridge University Press.
Huntington, S.P., 1996. *The Clash of Civilizations and the Remaking of World Order*. New York: Simon and Schuster.
Irvine, L. (2007). The Question of Animal Selves: Implications for sociological knowledge and practice. *Qualitative Sociology Review*. Volume 3, Issue 1. 5–22.
Irwin, T., 1985. *Aristotle Nicomachean Ethics*, translated with Introduction and notes. London: Cambridge University Press.

Kauffman, L. 2006. Virtual Boundaries. *Cybernetics and Human Knowing.* Vol. 13, no. 2, pp. 94–104.

Kickert, W.J.M, Klijn, E.H., and Koppenjan, J.F.M. 1999. *Managing Complex Networks: Strategies for the Public Sector.* London: Sage.

Lin, A. 2009. "Balancing the Risks: Managing Technology and Dangerous Climate Change." *Geoengineering Governance Issues in Legal Scholarship*, Vol. 8: 3 *The Berkeley Electronic Press* 1–24.

Mandelbrot, B. 1977. *Fractals: Form, Change and Dimension.* San Francisco: W.H. Freeman.

McIntyre-Mills, J. 2000. *Global Citizenship and Social Movements: Creating Transcultural Webs of Meaning for the New Millennium*, Australia: Harwood Academic Publishers.

McIntyre-Mills, J. 2003a. *Critical Systemic Praxis for Social and Environmental Justice: Participatory Policy Design and Governance for a Global Age.* London: Kluwer.

McIntyre, J., 2004. Facilitating critical systemic praxis (CSP) by means of experiential learning and conceptual tools, *Systems Research and Behavioural Science*, 21, 37–61.

McIntyre, J. 2005a. Critical and systemic practice to address Fixed and Fluid identity and politics at the local, national and international level, *Systemic Practice and Action Research.* 18, No3 223–258.

McIntyre, J. 2005b. Working and re-working the conceptual and geographical boundaries of governance and international relations. *Systemic Practice and Action Research*, Vol. 18, No. 2, 157–220.

McIntyre-Mills, J., et al. 2006a. *Rescuing the Enlightenment from Itself: Critical and Systemic Implications for Democracy.* New York: Springer.

McIntyre-Mills, J. 2006b. Molar and Molecular Identity and Politics, in Van Gigch, J., with J. McIntyre-Mills, *Wisdom, Knowledge and Management*, Vol. 2. New York, Boston, London: Springer. C. West Churchman Series.

McIntyre-Mills, J., et al. 2006c, *Systemic Governance and Accountability: Working and Reworking Conceptual and Spatial Boundaries.* London, Boston: Springer. Vol. 3 of C. West Churchman Series.

McIntyre, J. 2007a. The Hijab and Systemic Governance: Transnational Policy Making and Human Rights. *Systems Research and Behavioral Science*, 24: 37–58.

McIntyre-Mills, J. 2007. Challenging economic and religious fundamentalisms: implications for the state, the market and "the enemies within," *International Journal of Applied Systemic Studies* 1(1): 49–67.

McIntyre-Mills, J. 2008a. *User-centric Design to Meet Complex Needs in Citizenship in the 21st Century.* Nova Science.

McIntyre-Mills, J. 2008b. *Systemic Ethics: Expanding the Boundaries of Rights and Responsibilities Systems Research and Behavioural Science*, Vol. 25: 147–150.

McIntyre-Mills, J. 2008d. Mobius Bands and Mandelbrot Sets as metaphors for Systemic Praxis. *Systems Research and Behavioural Science.* Volume 25: 323–329.

McIntyre-Mills, J. 2008e. New directions for social well-being through extending deliberative democracy to enhance participation. Paper presented at International Systems Sciences Conference, Madison, Wisconsin. ISBN 978-1-906740-00-9.

McIntyre-Mills, J. 2009b. Contributing to peace through participation to support unselfish feed forward to the next generation of life. *Action Learning and Action Research Journal*, Vol. 15, No 1: 2–43.

McIntyre-Mills, J. 2009 Prologue: The global challenge outlined. Representation, Accountability and Sustainable Futures. *Systemic Practice and Action Research.* Vol. 22, No 3: 127–138 (ISSN 1094–429X).

McIntyre-Mills, J. 2009. New directions through extending deliberative democracy to enhance representation and accountability. *Systemic Practice and Action Research.* Vol. 22, No. 3: 201–218 (ISSN 1094–429X).

McIntyre-Mills, J. 2009. Constructing Citizenship and Transnational Identity: Participatory Policy to enhance attachment and involvement. Systemic Practice and Action Research. Vol. 22, No. 45. Rarly view August Springer link http://wwwspringerlink.com/content/104295/?Content+Status=Accepted.

McIntyre-Mills, J., with De Vries, D. 2010. Addressing Complex Needs. *Int. J. of Interdiscip. Soci. Sciences*, Vol. 5.5, 11–32.

McIntyre-Mills, J. 2010a. Representation, accountability and sustainability. *Cybernetics and Human Knowing*, Vol. 17.4, 51–80.

McIntyre-Mills, J. 2010b. Well-being, mindfulness and the global commons. *Journal of Consciousness Studies*, Vol. 17, No. 7–8, 44–72. McIntyre-Mills, J., with De Vries, D. 2011. Identity, Democracy and Sustainability. Litchfield: Emergence, pp. 380.

McIntyre-Mills, J. 2011a. The food, energy and water crisis: The liberative potential of the Aarhus Convention and transboundary governance to protect the global commons and the collective good, in

De Costa, I. (Ed). *Democratic Participation in Employment and Societal Regulation*. Proceedings of the International Conference at Ecole Normale Superieure de Cachan. Paris, 27–30 June.

McIntyre-Mills, J. 2011b. The way forward? Controlling consumption through governance and participatory democracy: Learning less is more when living elegantly and ethically. *Democratic Participation in Employment and Societal Regulation*. Proceedings of the International Conference at Ecole Normale Superieure de Cachan. Paris, 27–30 June.

McIntyre-Mills, J. 2012a. Anthropocentricism and well-being: a way out of the lobster pot? *Syst. Res.* Published online in Wiley Online Library. (wileyonlinelibrary.com) DOI: 10.1002/sres.2131.

McIntyre-Mills, J., Binchai, N., and DeVries, D. 2014. *Transformation from Wall Street to Wellbeing*. London: Springer.

McLeod, R., and Macintyre, A., eds. 2007. Indonesia: Democracy and the Promise of Good Governance. Indonesia Update Series. ANU. Institute of South East Asia Studies, Singapore.

McLuhan, M., and Powers, B. 1989. *The Global Village: Transformations in World Life in the 21st Century*. Oxford: Oxford University Press.

Meadowcroft, J. 2002. Politics and scale: some implications for environmental governance. *Landscape and Urban Planning* 61, 169–179. The paper is available from www.elsevier.com/locate/landurbplan.

Meagher, G., and Wilson, S. 2002. Complexity and practical knowledge in the social sciences, *British Journal of Sociology*, 53(4):659–666.

Michels, R. 1915. *Political Parties: A Sociological Study of the Oligarchical Tendencies of Modern Democracy*. Translated by Eden and Cedar Paul, 2001. Kitchener: Batoche Books.

Murray, J., Dey, C., and Lenzen, M. 2007. Systems for Social Sustainability: Global Connectedness and the Tuvalu Test. *Cybernetics and Human Knowing*. Vol. 14, No 1: 87–105.

Nussbaum, M. 2001. *Upheavals of Thought: The Intelligence of Emotions*. Cambridge: University Press.

Nussbaum, M., 2006. Frontiers *of Justice, Disability, Nationality and Species Membership*. London: Harvard University Press.

OECD definition: http://stats.oecd.org/glossary/search.asp

Pape, R.A. 2005. *Dying to Win: The Strategic Logic of Suicide Terrorism*. New York: Random House.

Pike, A., Rodriguez-Pose, A., and Tomaney, J. 2006. *Local and Regional Governance*. New York: Routledge.

Pilger, J. 2002. *The New Rulers of the World*, London: Verso.

Putnam, R. 1995, "Bowling alone," *Journal of Democracy*, 6(1):65–78.

Rawls, J. 1999. *The Law of Peoples with the Idea of Public Reason Revisited*. London: Harvard University Press.

Reason, P. 2002. Justice, sustainability and participation. Inaugural lecture, *Concepts and Transformations*, 7(1):7–29.

Rittel, H., and Webber, M. 1984. Planning problems are wicked problems. *Developments in Design Methodology*. New York: Wiley.

Rose, D.B. 2005. Dislocating the Frontier. http://epress.anu.edu.au/dtf/html/frames.php see http://epress.anu.edu.au.

Rose, D.B. 1996. *Nourishing terrains*. Canberra: Australian Heritage Commission.

Rose, D.B. 2004. Reports from a wild country: Ethics for decolonization. Sydney: University of New South Wales Press. http://epress.anu.edu.au/dtf/html/frames.php

Rosen, R. 1991. *Life Itself: A Comprehensive Inquiry into the Nature, Origin and Fabrication of Life*. New York: Columbia University Press.

Sharpe, L. 2005. *Creatures Like Us*. Exeter: Imprint Academic.

Singer, P., 2002. *One World: The Ethics of Globalisation*. Melbourne: The Text Publishers.

Stern, N. 2007. *The Economics of Climate Change: The Stern Review*. New York: Cambridge University Press.

Turner, R., and Whitehead, C. 2008. How collective representations can change the Structure of the Brain. *Journal of Consciousness Studies*, 15 No. 10–11, 43–57.

Van Gigch, J., 2003. *Metadecisions: Rehabilitating Epistemology*, New York: Kluwer Academic/Plenum Publishers.

Vickers, G., 1983. *Human Systems Are Different*. London: Harper and Row.

Von Foerster, H. 1995. *Cybernetics of Cybernetics*. Second edition. Minneapolis: Future Systems.

Wenger, E. 1998. *Communities of Practice: Learning, Meaning and Identity*. New York: Cambridge University Press.

White, L. 2002. Connection matters: exploring the implications of social capital and social networks for social policy, *Systems Research and Behavioural Science*, 19(2):255–270.

Systematic Mental Training
Effects on Brain, Mind and Reality

Lars-Eric Uneståhl

Integrated Mental Training (IMT) was created in 1969 based on 10 years of research focused on three areas: (a) hypnosis, self-hypnosis and other alternative states of consciousness (ASC); (b) mind and body issues, especially directed to sport performances (the author was an athlete himself); and (c) the effects of systematic and long-term training on mental, emotional and social processes and areas.

IMT is based on the training and use of "alternative states of consciousness" (ASC1), mainly self-hypnosis. Another important part is the learning and development of "alternative systems of control" (ASC2) like triggers and images. IMT also uses "alternative systems of change" (ASC3) from very structured and voluntary effort–based changes, to cybernetic programming.

Altered or Alternative States of Consciousness

Many books have been written—and a lot of research has been conducted—about consciousness, but no one has so far been able to define consciousness in a way which has received a general acceptance. This can partly be related to different views and opinions about consciousness but also to the fact that the term consciousness seems to be a holistic concept which contains more than the different characteristics which are easier to define and measure.

It also seems to be easier to define ASC—various states of altered consciousness. However, the phrase "altered states of consciousness" is problematic as it raises the question, "Altered from what?" A common answer has been "Altered from our 'normal' state of consciousness." From this it is natural to think about ASC as "unnormal." I therefore suggest that we translate ASC as "Alternative States of Consciousness" "Alternative to what?" Answer: "Alternative to our *dominant* state of consciousness."

Sleep, Dreaming and Flow

The most common ASC, sleep, where we spend almost one third of our life, is rather easy to define, even if there is a twilight state between waking and sleep. The dream state, in which we spend around 10 percent of our life, is also easy to define. Dreaming is a unique ASC, and very different from both sleep and waking. Almost every human being has reacted with fear during a dream due to the fact that we did not know that it was a dream. When it happened it was real, and it was afterwards that we found out that it was a dream. In the same way we are not aware about being asleep until we wake up. When we say we had a good sleep we rationalize based on feelings after awakening. Patients with sleep disturbances are sometimes 100 percent sure that that they have been awake the whole night in spite of the recordings showing several hours of sleep. What they remember in the mornings are the hours they have been awake.

Another ASC, flow, has similar characteristics. We are not aware about being in flow until afterwards. As a former athlete I also know that if I got the awareness of being in flow it immediately disappeared and the performance level dropped. In the dream state the difference between "imagination" and our common "reality" disappears. However, the control of dream contents is normally low (aside from lucid dreaming), which makes it difficult to use dreams for the creation of a "desired reality."

Hypnosis

After some basic studies about sleep and dreams I therefore decided to make my doctoral studies about hypnosis, where images in the same way as in dreaming can create a reality for body and mind, but where we can have full control over the imaginary contents. However, hypnosis as an ASC is more difficult to define compared with sleep and dreaming and the different ways of measuring hypnosis have little agreement among them. That led to a common operational definition among researchers: "Hypnosis is what comes after a hypnotic induction." This definition, however, has several weaknesses, as the individual responses to the same induction differs widely and as there are spontaneous hypnotic trance states without any formal induction. Therefore I chose to make a spatial operational definition: "Hypnosis appears when we enter into our *Inner Mental Room*." (36).

Characteristics of the "Inner Mental Room" (IMR)

The patterns of EEG neuro-mapping and the spectral analysis of EEG point to the fact that the mental training state (IMR) is characterized by the following neuro-dynamic correlates

- An intensification of theta-activity in antecentral sections of the brain and smoothing of alpha-activity in the frontal-occipital direction. (Decrease of alpha activity 10–13 and increase of frequency 7–9)(41, 42).
- A disappearing of hemispheric assymetry and a synchronization of total hemispheric activity. This qualitative change could be described as a leveling out of the activity with the same activity in each of the four quarters of the brain (change of operative system into a "holistic mode"). The "holistic brain concept" (41, 42, 56).
- The subsequent analysis showed that the EEG frequency spectrum in retrocentral sections of the cortex represents a set of subdominant and harmoniously bound

frequencies in the range of delta, theta, alpha 1 and 2 and beta-rhythms (Fig. 1). Thus, the polimodal frequency harmonization of cortical bioelectrical activity whose basis may be considered as the so-called "golden ratio" or "divine section" (1/1.618), which has been shown to be one of the specific neuro-dynamic correlates of the IMT-state. The "golden ratio" stands for harmony, balance and beauty, and is found in the pyramids, Greek temples, art, and beautiful buildings, as well as everyday things like drivers licenses or credit cards, body harmony, DNA, the solar system, and even the whole universe, in NASA measurements of the background radiation (61). It was then natural to call the operational brain system in IMR the "holistic and harmonious brain" (Fig. 1). I then looked for other IMR/body relations to the golden ratio (Fig. 2).

- Investigations with the "Omega potential" have pointed to an optimal sport performance zone of 15 to 25 MV (Figures 3 and 4) (66).

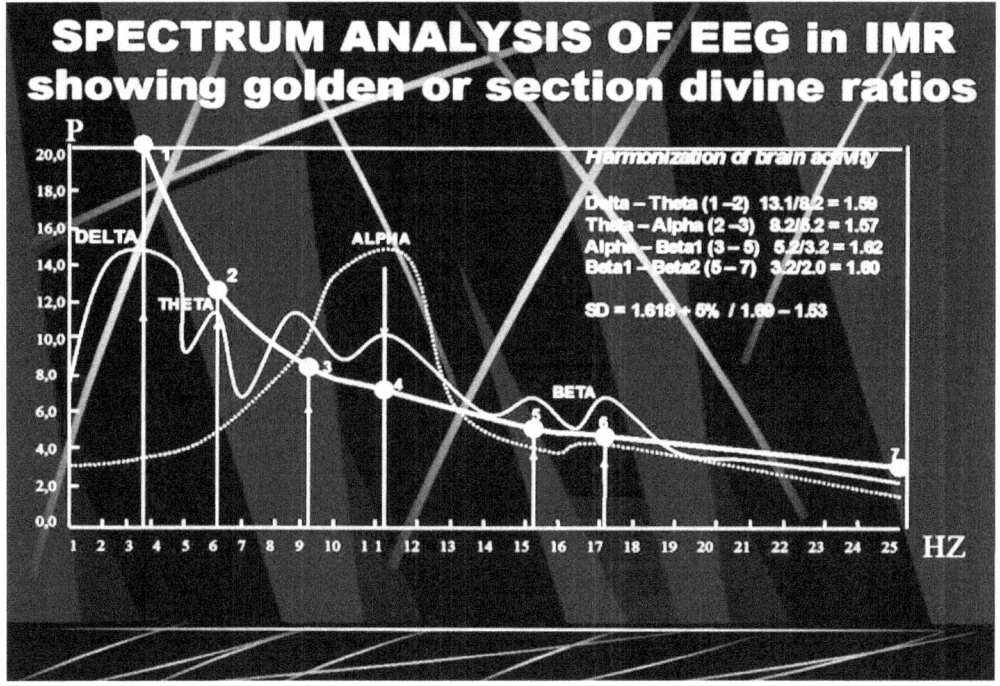

Figure 1

These findings of the "harmonious brain concept" led to investigations of more relations between the "IMR-state" and the golden ratio.(61) See another example of this in figure 3.

The optimal zone of performance, measured with Omega potential could then be used to compare athletes from different sport and levels. In figure 3 the activity of the left and right hemisphere is measured in an archery female athlete from an average level. As can be seen the left brain is more active during the whole competition of 6 shots.

Figure 4 shows measurements from her sister, who at the time of the measurement was a world record holder. Ten seconds before the shots the situation was the same com-

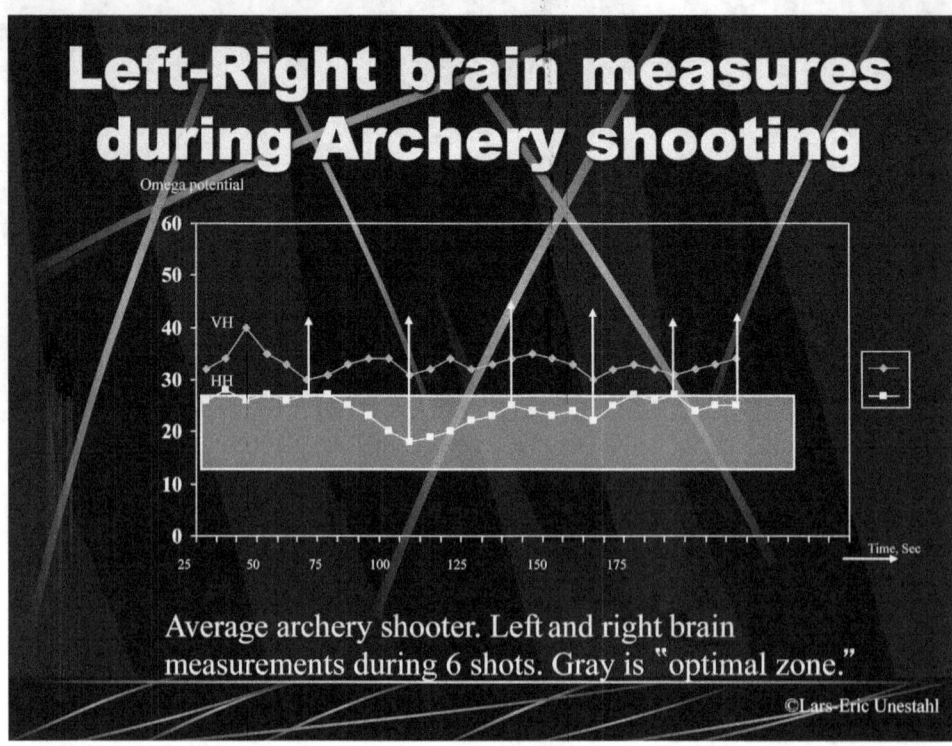

Top: Figure 2. *Bottom:* Figure 3.

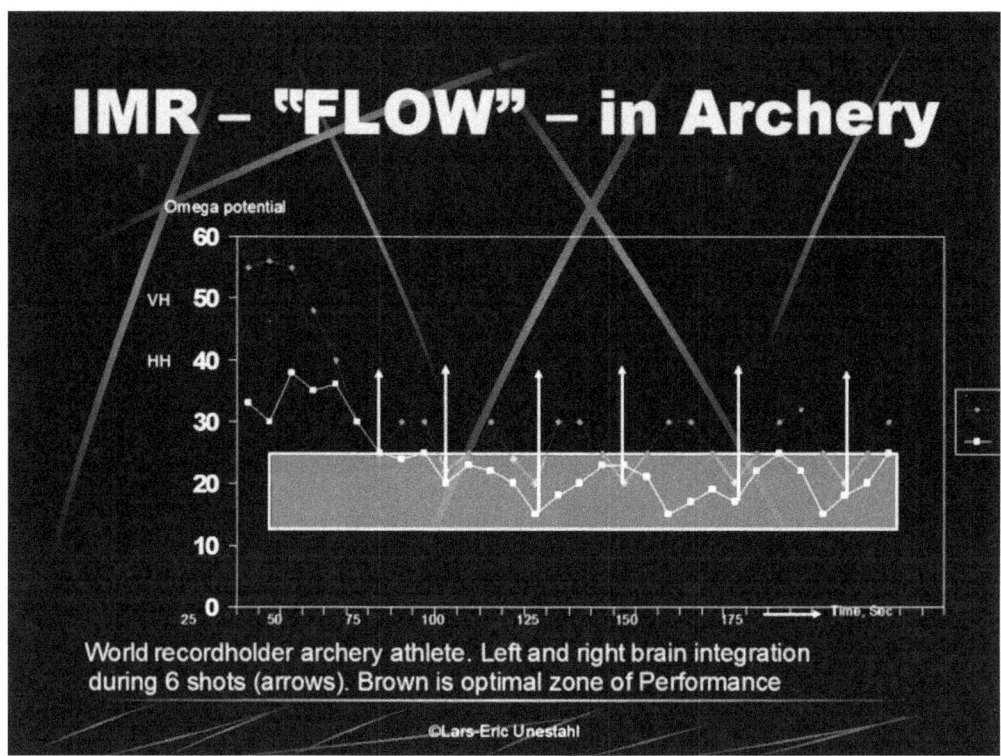

Figure 4

pared with her sister (more activity in the left brain) However during the last 10 shots there was an integration and leveling out. Thus, when the shots came the right and left brain were on the same level and both were inside the "optimal zone of performance." When the world record holder was asked "How do you know when you are ready to shoot," she answered, "I do not know but my body knows. The shot will come by itself when my body is ready." The "handing over to the body (brain)" also means that there will be an "ideomotor" release of the arrow. When we have measured the finger movements (tremor) by EMG we find a smaller reaction in the last case compared with her sister, where the release is more voluntary. Thus, in the investigations of ideal or optimal zones of functioning in regard to sport, school, work or rehabilitation from illness or injury, the difference often seems to be in the activity of the left hemisphere.

Mental training based on the concept of the "harmonious and holistic brain" (IMR) used as a main mental process another holistic concept, "images." The quantitative and the qualitative changes of brain activity during and after IMT training seems to change the information system in such a way that the body through decreased "reality testing" interprets internal images as "real."

The differences between a physical event and the image of such an event seem to diminish or disappear in the "inner mental room." This may be the main explanation for the significant impact which the IMT training has on various areas from behavior and emotion to psychosomatic problems. Also, in the area of personal development the use of images play a major role. The training of self-image and goal-images in IMR makes it possible to create a reality which is in accord with a person's wishes and desires.

Hypnosis/Self-Hypnosis as a Special and Trainable State

Training and Hypnotic Susceptibility

Hypnotic susceptibility has been regarded as a stable personality trait by many experts and is still so today. Even in modern textbooks numbers could be found indicating what percentage of the population could enter deep, medium, or light hypnosis. This is peculiar as there is very little research which could prove such statements. Often it is not even stated in what way "hypnotic depth" has been measured, and there are low correlates between different measurement methods.

What every researcher and clinician will know is that there are big response differences between subjects even when methods and hypnotists are not varied. However, this is no proof for claiming that these differences in hypnotic susceptibility should be regarded as a personality trait. It could as well be regarded as differences in the degree of training needed in order to gain good hypnotizability.

I also met with Milton H. Erickson, who convinced me that every person could be a "good subject." Erickson spent many hours training subjects to develop the ability to go into deep trance (46, 47, 48, 49). This was the reason why I decided to look into the effect of long-term training of "hypnotic skills." In a number of experiments in the sixties I managed to show that:

- There was significant increases in the Stanford hypnotic susceptibility scores after 6 months of hypnotic training (1, 56).
- There was a significant increase of imaginary capabilities after 6 months of imagery training (1, 56).

Thus, a more interesting question than if he or she is a good hypnotic subject will instead be, What training methods could be used and what training duration is needed in order to develop a good hypnotic capability in this person?

Hypnosis Is Self-hypnosis, Not a Relation Between Two People

Self-hypnosis (SH) or autohypnosis has been used to a great extent in therapy, but very little has been done in the research area. Serious research has mainly been conducted in heterohypnosis. A thorough review of the hypnosis literature reveals that this is characteristic of the whole 20th century, while in the 19th century there was more work done on SH and autosuggestion. The literature on SH, with some few exceptions, is full of oversimplification and has a popularized, prescriptive nature. The lack of research might be due to various factors: the denial of the concept "self-hypnosis" on a theoretical basis (analytical theories); the opinion that SH is too exclusive and that very few people can learn it; or the opinion that research on heterohypnosis can readily be applied to SH.

One of the few good studies was made by Erica Fromm (50) who found:

a. More idiosyncratic, primary process–type visual imagery in SH than in HH.
b. More ego divisions or splits in SH than in HH, with the added disassociated part being the speaker.
c. Differences in other ego functions or in depth of trance were not unequivocal but rather in different directions for different subjects.

The lack of research does not prevent many opinions to exist about SH. Some authorities consider SH as a function of "real" hypnosis (HH), a function of the experiences and expectations which the subjects bring from heterohypnosis. Others seem to switch the argument and consider HH as a form of SH. Even if an outside hypnotizer gives the instructions, the subject does not function as an automaton since he is capable of converting the given suggestions and is able to take over the conductance whenever he wishes to do so. That a person cannot reach similar depth in SH as in HH seems to be a common statement, one possible reason being that since the subject is his own self-hypnotizer, he has to play both and active and a passive role at the same time. The retention of a certain degree of conscious control and activity should prevent the subject from reaching a greater depth. To find answers to these and many other questions, two studies were carried out (24, 25) with the following results in summary:

- The effect of a hypnotic induction was the same if I gave the induction "live" or through a recorded tape.
- The effect of 6 months of self-training was in some areas even better (more independence, easier to apply the training to new areas) than after 6 months of training by an hypnotist.

Thus, it seems like all hypnosis could be regarded as self-hypnosis where the hypnotized person has the control. However, in order to be able to take over the control, the subject must know *that* he is in control, and *how* to take control. As hypnosis contains alternative systems of control these have to be learned first. If the subject is using the "dominant system" (voluntary effort) he/she will often feel out of control (56, 57).

In a series of experiments with Self-hypnosis I was able to show:

1. The subject can reach the same depth of hypnosis in SH as in HH (1, 24, 56).
2. After 30 training sessions with SH, the subjects rated SH as more positive than HH in all rating variables (24, 56).
3. Everything done in heterohypnosis can also be done in self-hypnosis (25, 56).
4. The subjects can even induce posthypnotic amnesia for their own suggestions and for the whole SH (25, 56).
5. It is possible to receive spontaneous amnesia also after SH (24, 25, 56).
6. It is difficult and for some subjects impossible to prevent actively entering SH if they follow the induction procedure (5).
7. It is possible to self-induce "negative" and undesirable effects and they appear even if the subject later tries to prevent the effects to appear (3, 8, 56).

8. It is easier to influence a localized pain than a radiating one, and a constant pain is more easily influenced than a fluctuating pain (10, 56).

9. During SH, the subjects are also susceptible to external suggestions; however, this susceptibility can be blocked so that no one else can give effective suggestions other than the subject himself (4, 5, 56).

Hypnosis as a Unique State

In order to find what is unique with hypnosis/self-hypnosis it was important to take away common but not necessary hypnotic characteristics. I have already mentioned that a hypnotist as well as a formal induction were not necessary elements in hypnosis. Another unnecessary thing was "closed eyes." In order to investigate this further I conducted two experiments. In the first experiments subjects were asked during hypnosis: "What is different in this state compared with normal waking?" Whatever the answer was, a suggestion was given to remove this special thing until the subject had difficulty finding anything more that differed from "normal."

In the second experiment subjects in hypnosis were instructed to open their eyes and behave as if they were in a waking state, but to remain in hypnosis. In one case the subject had to remain in this state for one week before "waking" took place.

The common denominator in both experiments was an increased responsiveness to suggestions, either from the hypnotist (heterohypnosis) or from the subject (self-hypnosis). The "one week in hypnosis" subject in experiment 2 also had amnesia for the whole week (56).

Studies About the "Reality" of Hypnotic Phenomena

In order to investigate if hypnosis/self-hypnosis was a unique ASC (Alternative State of Consciousness) and not only "role-playing" I conducted a number of studies. Here are two examples.
- Color blindness
  I gave suggestions about color blindness both in hypnosis and as a posthypnotic suggestion (PHS) and measured the result by tests like Ishihara and compared with role-playing. The hypnotic and posthypnotic effects were shown to be real and accurate in comparison with the control group (3, 56). These findings have 30 years later been replicated by Kosslyn et al. (53, 54, 55) who have shown the reality of phenomena like hypnotic color blindness by modern neuroimaging techniques.
- Hypnotic deafness
  Conditioning a tone to emotions with autonomic changes. Creating a "hypnotic deafness" for the tone. Result: Not only subjective deafness for the tone but also no autonomic reactions (56).

Posthypnotic Phenomena

Posthypnotic Suggestions (PHS)

Posthypnotic suggestions (PHS) are, according to the prevalent definition, "suggestions given under hypnosis but working afterwards in the waking state." On the basis of my research on spontaneous trance, I have found that a more adequate definition would be to say: "Posthypnotic suggestions are suggestions given under hypnosis, but the effectuation of these appears after the original trance." There are two classes of posthypnotic effects: changes occurring merely as a result of having been in hypnosis, and specific effects that occur as a result of suggestions given during hypnosis.

PHS is one of the outstanding phenomena of hypnosis. On one hand it shows the strengths and the quality of the PH performance. On the other hand, it is one of the phenomena of hypnosis most difficult to explain on theoretical grounds. Why should the suggestion be fulfilled when the subject has returned from the hyper-suggestible state to a state of normal waking consciousness?

In order to explain this apparent paradox, many authorities on this subject have maintained that the waking from hypnosis is only apparent and that in fact the subject really remains in a modified hypnotic state until the PHS is finally carried out. This is not an especially plausible explanation as we now know that PHS can be carried out years after the hypnotic programming.

A more likely explanation could be that PHS is a special type of conditioned reflex, one that can be created through a single session of "learning," while other conditionings normally are established by repetitive trials and learning. A posthypnotic conditioning is also more durable and is not as rapidly extinguished as a conditioned reflex. Subjects can have a total or partial amnesia for the PHS but some can also be quite aware of the suggestion when they carry it out. A voluntary effort to resist the suggestion often creates tension and anxiety. In this respect there is a clear resemblance to obsessive-compulsive behavior. Very few studies have been concerned with various aspects of the durability of PHS.

I have found it relevant to divide the PHS into different types, depending on their content and effectuation. Regarding the content, two main types can be distinguished:

A. Suggestions for a *specific response*, often a certain act.

B. Suggestions for a *general state*, for instance a certain mood, emotion, activation-level or attitude.

Both types of suggestions can be released in different ways, through:

1. Awakening
2. A delay of the effectuation decided in time
3. Stimuli, given signal value under hypnosis, for instance a certain word.

The effect of posthypnotic suggestion for an act (type A), limited in time, ceases when the suggested act has been executed. Suggestions of type B, on the other hand, continue to work until the effect spontaneously ceases or until a new signal is given which abolishes the effect. However, remarkably few studies have been concerned with the mechanisms of posthypnotic suggestions, although these represent unique qualities of the practice of hypnosis. The few investigations that have been conducted were concerned with suggestions of type A, which have often been used for studies of unconscious motivation.

Posthypnotic Trance

I observed that the effectuation of a posthypnotic suggestion often seemed to be accompanied by a posthypnotic or a spontaneous trance (ST). However no research could be found about such a trance. The only one who had described this phenomena was M.H. Erickson (46, 47, 48, 49). His findings can be summarized as follows:

a. Although there has been frequent recognition that posthypnotic suggestions lead to the development of a peculiar mental state in the hypnotic subject, there has been no direct study of that special mental condition. Neither has there been provision or allowance made for its existence and its possible significant influences upon results obtained from posthypnotic suggestions.

b. The specific manifestations which occur rapidly in direct relation to the giving of the specified cue for the posthypnotic act often have the following sequence: A slight pause in the subject's immediate activity, a facial expression of distraction and detachment, a peculiar glassiness of the eyes with a dilatation of the pupils and a failure to focus, a condition of catalepsy, a fixity and narrowing of attention, an intentness of purpose, a marked loss of contact with the general environment and an unresponsiveness to any external stimulus.

c. The spontaneous posthypnotic trance may be single or multiple, brief or prolonged. In general, it appears for only a moment or two at the initiation of the posthypnotic performance and hence it is easily overlooked.

d. Demonstrations and testing of the spontaneous trance are usually best accomplished at the moment of the initiation of the posthypnotic performance by interference either with the subject or with the suggested act. Properly given, such interference ordinarily leads to an immediate arrest in the subject's behavior and a prolongation of the spontaneous trance.

e. The lapse of an indefinite period of time between the giving of a posthypnotic suggestion and the opportunity for its execution does not affect the development of a spontaneous posthypnotic trance as an integral part of the posthypnotic performance.

f. Apparent exceptions to the development of the spontaneous trance as an integral part of the posthypnotic performances are found to derive from significant changes in the intended posthypnotic situation which alter or transform it into one of another character.

g. The spontaneous trance is a phenomenon of sequence, since it constitutes a revivification of the hypnotic elements of the trance situation in which the specific posthypnotic suggestion was given. Hence, its development is a criterion of the validity of the previous trance.

h. The spontaneous trance may be used advantageously as a special experimental ant therapeutic technique, since it obviates various difficulties inherent in the usual method of trance induction.

i. The posthypnotic performance and its associated spontaneous trance constitute dissociation phenomena because they break into the ordinary stream of conscious activity as interpolations and since they do not become integrated with the ordinary course of conscious activity.

Except for the observations of Milton H. Erickson, the studies on spontaneous trance (ST) have been conducted mainly in Uppsala. An one-dimensional scale was constructed on the basis of information analysis theory (14, 56). As a measure of suggestibility the concept of transmission was used. The degree of transmission was based on the subject's subjective estimation of a tone stimulus which was presented with varying degrees of veridicality. By using multivariate information analysis, transmission values for hypnosis as well as spontaneous trance could be obtained. The maximum value for the scale was 1.59. Compared with the Stanford Hypnotic Scale of Susceptibility, form A (SHSS), scores of 0 to 2 gave a mean transmission value (M_T) of 0.03; SHSS scores between 5 and 10 gave a M_T of 0.16, and an SHSS score of 12 gave a M_T of 0.82. The scale had an increasing discriminatory ability with higher SHSS scores. Subjects with the maximum SHSS score of 12 could be clearly differentiated by the transmission scale. In one study (46) the transmission values were compared in hypnosis and spontaneous trance. Only the subjects with a deeper original hypnotic trance showed any evidence of a spontaneous trance. The results gave some support to the theory that the spontaneous trance should be a revivification of the original hypnotic trance. In the first experiments studying ST (2, 3, 6) color blindness was chosen as the PHS, i.e., blocking of the red and green colors.

The Posthypnotic Period

The posthypnotic phase can be divided into two periods: period 1 = ST and period 2 including the time from the termination of ST until the abolishing of the posthypnotic effect.

The studies reported in this chapter have shown that period 1 is of very short durability, lasting only for a few seconds, while period 2 could last for hours, sometimes even days. An interesting question in this respect is whether the posthypnotic effect starts working already during period 1. In the study with the PHS about levitation of the left leg (4, 46) the five subjects showing both period 1 and 2 began the posthypnotic act during period 1, i.e., while the anesthesia was still present. (The posthypnotic trance was operationally defined as the period of spontaneous anesthesia.)

Also in the study about atypical behavior during hypnosis the posthypnotic behavior appeared together with the ST immediately after the signal was given. In the study on PHS about anesthesia and hyperesthesia, the spontaneous effect of ST (anesthesia) either worked with the PHS (S_1) or against it (S_2). The clear differences in the ratings of shock-intensity after S_1 and S_2 indicate that the posthypnotic effect also here has begun to work during period 1. Many of our studies have contained PHS of type 3, i.e., signal-released PHS. In the experiment on car driving, where suggestions of type B 1 were used, no indications of any ST were found. The awakening seemed here to be followed directly by period 2, while the time-delayed effect of the B 3 suggestion seems to need a new trance to start the effectuation of the suggestion.

Erickson's findings concern mainly suggestions of type A. In the initial phase he observed certain changes in the individual's behavior whereupon the suggested act was executed.

This was followed by an awakening and a continuing of the normal activity, mostly with amnesia for the post-hypnotic act. This implies that the type A suggestion is working only during period 1 and that period 2 never appears. Erickson does not relate whether he observed any direct limit between the initial posthypnotic phase and the elicitation of the posthypnotic behavior.

This can be summarized in a schemata, which has been called "Uneståhl's paradigm" (56).

PHS Type	Programming Containing	Releasing Effectuation	PHS are working Period 1	Period 2
A 1	Certain act	Awakening	Occurs	Is missing
A 2–3	Certain act	Delayed	Occurs	Is missing
B 1	General state	Awakening	Is missing	Occurs
B 2–3	General state	Delayed	Occurs	Occurs

ST has in these studies been operationally defined as the period followed immediately by the signal eliciting PHS, where the subject manifests a spontaneous anesthesia. The time of anesthesia was mostly found to coincide with the time of amnesia and extended over a period during which the subjects also showed several of the earlier mentioned external signs of spontaneous trance. On one hand anesthesia seemed to be a good and objective criterion of the spontaneous trance that also gave a possibility to decide the duration of the spontaneous trance more exactly. On the other hand, it is not certain that the spontaneous trance always is accompanied by anesthesia. It can be assumed that the spontaneous trance in analogy with the original trance represents a continuum from zero to very deep. Anesthesia then appears somewhere on this continuum. Anesthesia is then not necessarily a criterion for spontaneous trance but the spontaneous trance is thus a necessary condition for anesthesia.

Another possible explanation is that anesthesia cannot always be registered at the initiation of posthypnotic suggestions because the trance, in some cases, is of a too short duration to allow measurement of anesthesia. ST has also important theoretical implications for hypnosis. Theories explaining hypnosis mainly in terms of motivation and expectation in the S and experimenter, have difficulties in explaining ST, since it appears completely unexpected by the subject. The many years of hypnotic history before ST was detected and investigated also indicate that the phenomenon has been unexpected by the hypnotists.

One study (23, 56) showed that the stimuli which received signal value in the hypnotic state gave an auditive and visual blocking for the signal in some subjects. These subjects also generalized the blocking to similar words and sound combinations. Another study (14, 56) using tunes as signals did not show the same blocking effects as with signal-words.

One study (57) showed that the recognition thresholds tended to be altered, when previously "neutral" words were given signal value, i.e., were able to release posthypnotic suggestions. Compared to control words presented immediately before the signal words in hypnosis, but of no signal value, the thresholds of the signal words were considerably lowered. The kind of posthypnotic signal and the way it has been presented did not influence proper posthypnotic behavior. Words, nonsense syllables, tunes and gestures as signals have been used.

One experiment (23, 56) showed that even a hallucination could serve as a signal. The signal has been presented alone or more or less embedded in some context, for instance one word in a Chinese song. The signal has been given by the hypnotist or by some other person not connected with the experiment. The signal has been delivered by tapes and records or in written messages. All these variations have been made without any noticeable differences in the effects of the signal.

More Summaries from the Uppsala University Reports, 1960–1973

- Any simple or complex stimulus, behavior or situation can receive signal value during hypnosis and serve as a cue, releasing posthypnotic effects (4, 56).
- No difference can be seen in effect of the signal is given by the experimenter or by a person, not connected with the experiment (4).
- Stimuli given signal value can cause in some subjects a spontaneous, auditive and visual blocking of the signals (23).
- Various procedures to abolish the blocking have been tried without results. The only effective procedure seemed to abolish the signal value of the stimuli (23).
- The blocking at meaningful stimuli, receiving signal value, seems related to the meaning and not the structure of the stimuli (23).
- No difference in the ability to discriminate tunes in the hypnotic and waking state was found (5).
- Recognition thresholds were lowered when previously "neutral" words were given signal value (37).
- During the effectuation of some PHS a peculiar mental state seems to appear (2).
- Very few studies on the phenomena called posthypnotic or spontaneous trance (ST) have been made and those were limited only to observational studies (2, 18, 56).
- ST was defined as the period following immediately after the release of PHS during which the subject manifests a spontaneous anesthesia (2, 18, 56).
- The period of anesthesia is mostly found to coincide with a period of amnesia (18, 56).
- In spite of some support for Erickson's reactivation theory the evidence from our data does not yield enough support to consider ST as a reactivation of the specific elements in the original trance (2, 18, 46).
- The shortest and longest measurement ST in our studies have been, respectively, 2 seconds and 10.8 minutes. ST-periods lasting for more than 1 minute are rather unusual (2, 11).
- A tendency for the occurrence of longer ST-periods after a signal (releasing PH-effect) compared with that of the anti-signal (abolishing PH-effect) was found (46).

- The posthypnotic phase can be divided in two periods, period 1 (=ST) and period 2 (end of PH-effect) (11).
- Period 1 is of very short duration (often seconds) compared with period 2 (often hours) (11).
- The PHS begin to work already during period 1 (4, 11).
- At type A-PHS, ST often seems to cover the whole act (period 2 does not appear) while at type B-PHS, period 1 is missing (4, 11).
- It is possible to induce blockings of specific or general abilities with help of PHS (23).
- Posthypnotic blockings, bound to a signal, are sometimes released even before the signal is administrated (23).
- The blocking of the number 6 can be complete or partial and may become evident in phenomena such as resistance or repulsion against the figure (56).
- The blocking of 6 is also transferred to number 6 in other familiar languages (56).
- The blocking may also manifest itself in the inability to repeat the blocking figure (56).
- The subjects could perceive the blocking figure, sometimes with some resistance, but do not interpret it as a number (56).
- In drawing a big 6 or a face containing sixes the subjects distorted the drawings (56).
- Intensive stimulation of the blocking figure or increasing motivation (offering money) does not abolish the blocking (23, 56).
- Increased effort in order to find the missing figure rather tends to strengthen the blocking (23, 56).
- Increasing awareness of something missing and increasing effort to find it increase the unpleasantness in the subjects (23, 56).
- Performance with very little conscious effort involved, like automatic writing, sometimes managed to break the blocking (23, 56).
- The phenomena of blocking may be better explained by theories of dissociation rather than by theories of perceptual defense (56).

Instrumental Hypnotic Research

Hypnosis/self-hypnosis can also be used as a tool to develop and control effects, which are interesting to investigate (for example emotions) Thus in "Instrumental Hypnotic Research" hypnosis is only used as a "producer" of the effects to be investigated. Hypnosis is used as a valuable tool for inducing and controlling experiment variables.

SUMMARY OF FINDINGS
- In recent years hypnosis has been extensively used as an experimental tool to study different problems inside psychology (12).
- PHS of B-type can be of considerable value as they are suitable to use for creating such general states which non-hypnotic experimental procedures have difficulties to produce (12, 56).

- Investigations were made to exemplify both the effect of a special subjective state on different measures and the effect on a special task of various produced emotions, attitudes, etc. (13, 14, 18, 21, 22).
- Investigations also cover measures such as subjective experiences, performance tests and physiological measures (13, 14, 16, 17).

- The subjective ratings show clear and evident deviations in the direction of the suggested state in spite of amnesia for the PHS (8, 13, 13, 14, 32, 33).
- Some performance tests are considerably influenced (RT) while other do not seem to be effected at all (physical work test) (56).
- The extension of RT in sleep deprivation experiments is mainly the result of some very long reaction times, while the skewness coefficient is only slightly larger during posthypnotic fatigue compared with "normal" (56).
- Posthypnotically produced emotional states seem to have more influence on certain physiological measures (blood pressure) compared with others (cathecollamines) (13, 16, 17).
- The method of using PHS in this respect is often administratively much more simple than other experimental procedures (56).

Posthypnotic Suggestions as Reinforcers of Behavior

Thorndike was the first investigator of the effect of reward on learning, resulting in the formulation of the well-known "law of effect." His successor Skinner, founder of "Non-mediational theory," claims that "behavior is shaped and maintained by its consequences." If we realize this then we can study behavior that operates upon the environment to produce consequences ("operant behavior") by arranging environment in which specific consequences are contingent upon behavior. We can also manipulate the environment, which often has dramatic effects. Skinner claims that the reinforcing effects of reward occur automatically, independent of the subject's awareness of the relation of response to reinforcement.

Bandura claims that learning without awareness is possible but such learning proceeds slowly. An aware symbolic representation of the relation of response to reinforcement will accelerate the learning and to a great extent influence the overt behavior. Bandura refers to an experiment by DeNike, showing quick and dramatic changes in the speed of learning as soon as the subjects realized what was reinforced. The treatment with operant techniques has mostly been applied to children and psychotic patients with the intention to develop new response patterns.

Skinner, in his methods of operant techniques, has mostly used external reinforcers, primarily, like food and sweets, or secondarily, like "tokens" of different kinds. Cautela, on the other hand, constructed a method with internal reinforces, called "Covert Reinforcement." He tried first with aversive stimuli presented in the imagination via instruction and found that they had properties similar to an externally applied stimulus. In the same way he found later that reinforcing stimuli functioned in a similar manner when presented in imagination as when externally applied. The first step is to find reinforcing stimuli, which here consist of previously experienced pleasant events and situations.

Cautela's methods are to a high degree based on the subject's capacity for imagination and involvement. The description of the "situation" at the therapy session has a very suggestive character in order to create strong emotions. Cautela's methods apparently have many features in common with hypnotic methods, and it is likely that "covert reinforcement or desensitization" in many subjects creates a state, which can be defined as hypnosis.

Skinner's techniques with external reinforcers have some disadvantages, for instance the administrative difficulties as the methods presuppose a rather strong control of the environment. The persons in the patient's surroundings have to know what behavior is going to be rewarded, they must observe, be consistent, react quickly with the reward, vary the reward, etc. These techniques are hardly applicable to all individuals. Also, Cautela's methods involve some problems in demanding a great deal of the subjects willingness to participate actively, and a good imagination ability is also necessary.

Thus, the question arises if hypnotic techniques can be used to remove some of these difficulties. In several experiments we had shown that general states like emotions could be released post hypnotically. It is also known, that the releasing can occur through a signal (PHS of the type B3). We have also shown how a certain behavior can be given signal value during hypnosis and then serve as a cue, eliciting the programed effect.

Summary of Findings
- A behavior can be given signal value during hypnosis and then serve as a cue, eliciting a programed emotion (4).
- A positive emotion can be separated from a previous event and bound to a certain behavior, which will release the emotion during a fixed number of seconds (7, 14).
- After programming such a reinforcer, the "critical" response increased significantly in both experiments (7, 14).
- The increase of response-frequency seems to last as a result of learning even after removal of PHS (7, 14, 56).
- The reinforcement was effective even for the subjects who never became aware of the relation of response to reinforcement (7, 14).
- In spite of some limitations the method has great advantages compared with "token economy" or "covert reinforcement" (7, 12, 56).

Integration of Self-Hypnosis and PHS into Mental Training

The development of Integrated Mental Training (IMT) began in the 1970s. Research about hypnosis, self-hypnosis and posthypnotic suggestions became a very important part of understanding effective IMT techniques.

Summary of Studies and Findings
- PHS /triggers were good tools to enhance and deepen self-hypnosis (4, 12, 18).
- Hypnosis/self-hypnosis increased the effectiveness of triggers and anchors (26).
- PHS and trigger-released concentration was valuable in all kind of sports (29, 30, 31).

- PHS became a common method in everything from performing arts to public speaking (56).
- Sleep through self-hypnosis and/or PHS created some interesting night–EEG differences (10, 20).
- It was possible to establish contact in the morning and program a "good" day before waking (69).
- Experiments to explain "the inner clock" ("programming" of a specific waking time, etc.) (69).
- The effects of PHS during narcosis in 72 orthopedic operations (69).
- PHS as operant techniques to reinforce behavior (56).
- Experiments to identify the "ideal reinforcement feeling" for behavior change (12).
- PHS in creation and removal of experimental phobias (56).

- The conditioning of various emotions to sounds with various frequencies (56, 66).
- The use of the Emotional Control System (ECS) to reinforce excellent swimming.
- The use of ECS to establish and control flow in sports and performing arts (29).
- The use of ECS to increase learning quality and test results in school (66, 69).
- The use of Self-hypnosis, ECS and PHS to learn a sport (golf) without physical practice (69, 70).
- Use of the Sleep Control System to remove jetlag and increase performance in the Olympics (69, 70).
- The use of ESC and mental training to increase performance in the Olympics (66).

Integrated Mental Training

With these research projects and their findings as a background the concept "Mental Training" was created in 1969 and the philosophy, principles and practical training programs were developed during the 1970s in close cooperation with the Swedish National and Olympic Teams. Sweden became the first country to introduce the training in sport, 1970–1976 (Unestål was the only mental trainer/sport psychologist at the Olympics in Montreal in 1976) and in the national school curriculum (1976–1982). Sweden also became the first country to involve "Life Skills Training" in schools (66).

Integrated Mental Training (IMT), a systematic and long-term training of cognitive, emotional and social skills and attitudes, based on alternative states of consciousness like self-hypnosis, has during 50 years been used by more than 3 million Swedish people. Starting with the National and Olympic Teams and the school system, IMT has been applied to most areas of Swedish society (business, work, leadership, health, personal development).

IMT is defined as a systematic, long term and evaluated training of mental processes (thoughts, images, emotions, beliefs, attitudes) to detect and develop resources needed to reach excellence in sport and life. IMT always starts with the "basic" mental training after which the training is divided into two parts: problem-solving and personal development (PD). Personal development, which goes on for minimum half a year, has two main parts: mental strength training and socio-emotional training. IMT is followed by "mental preparation techniques," where the general and integrated effects are complemented with specific effects, which are programed to be active in certain situations (like competitions in sport) (66).

Overview of Integrated Mental Training (IMT)

- Philosophy and Principles: IMT is future-oriented, goal-directed, solution-focused, resources- and experience-based and is built on possibility-thinking and action-learning.
- Life Goal Areas: IMT works with 3L (lifelong learning) and continuous growth, activated by the creation of an "attractive future," which is integrated in the "inner mental room" (self-hypnosis). The growth model and the training model are focused on the areas of performance, "mission" (work-relations) and health.
- Peak Performance and Wellness: Analyses of peak performance are made in sport, stage and work. Health development is based on the WHO definition of "optimal physical, psychological and social well-being."
- Ideal States: One part of the "better life concept" is the "ideal states" which are identified for areas like learning, decision making, creativity, performance, relations, healing, etc.
- Alternative Systems of Control: The dominant system of control (voluntary effort) is complemented with effective and more effortless control systems like images, triggers, etc.
- Basic Mental Training: The reduction of basic tension levels saves energy and opens up for the ideal muscular state, characterized by optimal tension in synergistic muscles and relaxation of the antagonistic muscles. The second part of BMT includes learning of the "inner mental room" (operational definition of self-hypnosis) and various aids to be used in this room.
- Self-Image Training: Ego-strengthening techniques improves the self-image (esteem, confidence, inner talk, etc.) and serve as a base for personal growth.
- Goal-Programming: Visions and overall goals are translated to situation-related images, which then are programed in the mental room. "Memories of the future" are created, which then give energy and inspiration to the "daily work" but also serve as the steering mechanism of the daily automaticity.
- Mental Toughness Training: Reduction or removal of "fear of future" is combined with the change of attitude from "problem avoidance" to a positive activation by challenges and difficult tasks.
- Concentration Training: Focusing on relevant stimuli (triggers) is combined with dissociation from irrelevant stimuli. What we focus on is what we get more of—problems, goals, etc.
- Life Quality Training: Systematic training of "optimism," inner security and balance is combined with "humor training" (laughing, humorous attitude and inner joy).

The "International Society for Mental Training and Excellence" (ISMTE) was created 1989 and consists of the following sections: Sport, Stage Performance and Performing Arts; Business and Public Administration; School and Education; and Health and Clinical Areas. World Congresses have been held in 1991 (Örebro), 1995 (Ottawa), 1999 (Salt Lake City), 2003 (St. Petersburg), 2008 (Beijing), 2011 (Kosovo) and in in Chandigarh, India, 2015.

Research Findings

Regular use of daily IMT-training for a few months has shown the following effects (41, 42, 43, 44):

- A significant reduction of the level of cortisol and free fat acids in the blood plasma
- Increase in beta-endorphin levels
- Increase of the general immunomodulating capacity
- Prevention of the reduced immunologi, normally related to overtraining
- Reversal of the age-related decrease of the DHEAS hormone
- Increase of self-regulating capacities and homeostatic processes
- Among other changes can be mentioned an improvement of the psycho-emotional status, measured by POMS, the Wellness scale, etc.

Examples of Studies Of—And with—IMT

Sport Performances

- PE students "shooting" 30 hypnotic basket penalty shots a day made a significant improvement (compared with a control group) and improved as much as those making 30 physical training shots a day (26).
- An experiment group of 100 bowlers showed personal but not performance improvements compared with the hundred in the control group after 3 months of IMT training, but after that the difference also in performance became bigger and bigger during the investigation period of 3 years. Ten years later one bowler in the mental training group became world number 1 for 3 years (31).
- One third of the whole team had a systematical mental training at the Olympics 1980 but more than half of the finalists and two-thirds of the medalists had such training (28).
- Objective measures and subjective ratings from alpine ski races show that the worst results were related to active thoughts of various technique details while the best results came after hypnotic race programming, handing over the race to the body and supporting the body with a "positive emotional rhythm production" (32).
- After reaching the finish line in the national downhill championships the skiers were asked to ski the race again, now mentally. The best skiers had more similar time in the physical and mental skiing (30).

- Physical training became more effective by replacing the traditional negative and delayed feedback with a positive and immediate feedback produced by operant techniques, where the "right performance" was reinforced through signal released post-hypnotic positive emotions (29).
- Post-hypnotic induced variations of mental states and attitudes produced a performance variation, measured through isometric strength. The "normal" maximum strength in the subject could be increased by 18 percent when the subjects had the best attitude to themself (self-image) and an optimal attitude to the task (goal-image) (33).
- "Total relaxation" lowered the performance (isometric strength). This finding led to research about the "ideal muscular state" and the formulation of the new English word "relaxense" corresponding to the Swedish "avspänd." This state, which is crucial for IPS, is characterized by "an optimal tension in the right muscles and relaxation of the antagonist muscles."

"Inner Body Changes"

- Significant decrease of cortisol and increase of betaendorphin levels are common effects after a number of weeks of regular IMT training (42, 45).
- Significant immunological positive changes, measured with T4/T8 cells, have been shown in 3 different IMT investigations. A further analysis showed that it was the "life quality training" ("emotional training") that gave the most positive changes (43).
- Three hundred cancer patients were matched into a control and experimental group. The difference in survival between the control and the mental training group was largest in the terminally ill group (66).
- Seventy tinnitus patients had regular mental training for 3 months. Few of these got rid of the sound but most of them reduced or got rid of the disturbance (66, 69).
- The same effect has been showed in the work with mental training for chronic pain patients. The most common effects have to do with moving and reframing the pain and learning to ignore and refocus (56, 59).
- Relaxing music and positive hypnotic and posthypnotic suggestions improved the conditions during and after 70 surgeries compared with a control group with white sound (66, 69).
- The aging process (biological age measured with the hormone DHEAS) could be reversed through 6 months of mental training. The experiment group became in average 7 years younger (45).

Other Areas

- The national team in swimming was divided in a control group and 3 experimental groups (mental training, melatonin, placebo) in a jetlag study before the Sydney Olympics. The mental training group showed the best results in the measured variables (sleep quality and performance ratings) (69).

- Studies made at the hospital in Helsingborg show that even if the chronic pain was still there most patients learned to dissociate and detach from the pain and move it away from the awareness (refocusing skills) (66, 69).
- In a number of studies the effects of IMT on areas like sleep, weight, smoking, allergies, chronic pain, etc., have been shown. The best results are shown if the training starts with the basic mental training (learning self-hypnosis) before starting with the specific application (66, 67, 69).
- The applications of IMT into the Swedish school system started in 1975 and after six years of studies (doctoral dissertation by Sven Setterlind, etc.), Sweden became the first country to include Mental Training in the school scheme. Currently a "lifeskills training" is under investigation in a number of schools from primary to high school level, containing basic mental training, mental training, lifestyle training, communication and teamwork, emotional and mental toughness training, and parenting and leadership training (66, 69).
- Evaluations have been made of those Academies who have regular Mental Training in their educational scheme, e.g., the police academy, the academy of music, etc., and at those schools and institutions with lifeskills training (66, 80).

REFERENCES

25 REPORTS FROM THE DEPARTMENT OF PSYCHOLOGY, UPPSALA UNIVERSITY, 1968–74

1. Uneståhl, L.-E. Hypnosis and hypnotic susceptibility, 1968.
2. Uneståhl, L.-E. The Nature of Posthypnotic Trance, 1969.
3. Uneståhl, L.-E. Posthypnotic induced color blindness, 1969.
4. Uneståhl, L.-E. Signal released posthypnotic suggestions, 1970.
5. Uneståhl, L.-E. Generalization and discrimination at posthypnotic suggestions, 1971.
6. Uneståhl, L.-E. Investigations concerning spontaneous trance and posthypnotic suggestions, 1971.
7. Uneståhl, L.-E., B. Berglund, and S. Gaunitz. A posthypnotic released emotion as reinforcer, 1971.
8. Uneståhl, L.-E., and S. Gaunitz. Specific behavior in hypnosis related to subjective expectations, 1971.
9. Uneståhl, L.-E., A.-M. Johansson, and A.-M. Nygårds. Posthypnotic induced arousal levels and Performance, 1971.
10. Uneståhl, L.-E., K. Piltz, and I. Söderlund. The effect of hypnotic/posthypnotic sleep onset on the sleep cycles, 1971.
11. Uneståhl, L.-E. A study of the duration of posthypnotic suggestions, 1972.
12. Uneståhl, L.-E. The interaction of Behavior Therapy and Hypnosis, 1972.
13. Uneståhl, L.-E., G. Granholm, K. Hilding. Cathecollamins and posthypnotic modifications of stress levels, 1972.
14. Uneståhl, L.-E., and S. Irfann. The application of posthypnotic released emotions as reinforcers, 1972.
15. Uneståhl, L.-E., L. Barkestam, C. Isaksson, and A. Melander. Expectations and hypnotic susceptibility, 1972.
16. Uneståhl, L.-E., B. Berglund, and B. Öhrstedt. Measurements of Hypnotic and Posthypnotic induced emotions, 1972.
17. Uneståhl, L.-E., B. Ahlstedt, L. Lodhammar, and C. Skoog. The effects of hypnotic anaesthesia on subjective ratings, blood pressure and chatecollamins excretions.
18. Uneståhl, L.-E. Hypnosis and spontaneous trance, 1973.
19. Uneståhl, L.-E. The Use of hypnosis in Sport and Art, 1973.
20. Uneståhl, L.-E., A. Beving, B. Ericson, and G. Wassberg. The effects of hypnosis and PHS on sleep problems, 1973.

21. Uneståhl, L.-E., K. Hultin, and B. Sundgren. The effects on Sport Performance of images during relaxation versus hypnosis, 1973.
22. Uneståhl, L.-E., E. Boström, and J. Orre. The effects of hypnosis on nystagmus och pupil size, 1974.
23. Uneståhl, L.-E., K. Waara, and S. Wastensson. Investigations of posthypnotic blocking suggestions and the relation to perceptual defense, hypnotic amnesia and posthypnotic trance, 1974.
24. Uneståhl, L.-E., and S. Appelgren. A study of Self-Hypnosis I, 1974.
25. Uneståhl, L.-E., and G. Larsson. A study of Self-Hypnosis II, 1974.

15 Reports from the Department of Sport Psychology, Örebro, 1975–82

26. Uneståhl, L.-E., and Y. Peterson. Motor learning and posthypnotic reinforcement. Report VIII, 1976.
27. Uneståhl, L.-E., A. Beving, B. Ericson, and G. Wassberg. Effekter av hypnos som sömnadministrerad sömterapi vid sömnbesvär, 1973.
28. Uneståhl, L.-E., K. Hultin, and B. Sundgren. Effekten av föreställningar under hypnos och avslappning på idrottsprestationer, 1973.
29. Uneståhl, L.-E., and M. Gustavsson. Psykologiska faktorer vid elitskytte, Rapport II, 1975.
30. Uneståhl, L.-E. The effect of variating physical and mental tension in shooting. Report IX, 1977.
31. Uneståhl, L.-E., and U. Buuts. The Summer Olympics, 1976. Report X, 1977.
32. Uneståhl, L.-E., H. Andersson, and B. Joelsson. Immediate feedback & posthypnotic reinforcement in swimming. Report XI, 1978.
33. Uneståhl, L.-E., K. Aspelin, and M. Hermansson. Investigations of downhill racing. Report XIX, 1979.
34. Uneståhl, L.-E. Utveckling och utvärdering av metoder för mental träning—En lägesrapport. Rapport XX, 1980.
35. Uneståhl, L.-E., and S. Breife. Evaluations of mental training in bowling. Report XXIII, 1981.
36. Uneståhl, L.-E. Motor learning through mental training. Report XXIV, 1981.
37. Uneståhl, L.-E., B. Henriksson, and J. Högström. The effects of posthypnotically induced mental states on isometric strength. Report XXVII. 1981.
38. Uneståhl, L.-E., and P.-A. Ingvarsson. Fotboll—En analys av fotbollsallsvenskan 1979. Rapport XXVIII, 1981.
39. Uneståhl, L.-E., and P. Strandh. Swimming and mental training. Report XXIX, 1981.
Uneståhl, L.-E., and M. Thor. Monotont långtidsarbete. I. Lidingöloppet. Rapport XXV, 1981.
40. Uneståhl, L.-E., S. Bexell, and M. Lanker. Mental träning och recovery skills. Report XXX, 1981.

5 Articles from the Swedish-Russian Project, 1996–2005

41. Bundzen, P., P. Bundzen, P. Leissner, A. Malinin, and L.E. Unestahl. "Mental relaxation: Neurodynamic markers and psychophysiological mechanisms." In R. Rodano and D. Hill, eds. *Current Research in Sport Sciences: An International Perspective*. New York and London: Plenum Press, 1996. 91–101.
42. Unestahl. L.E., and P. Bundzen. "Integrated Mental Training—neuro-biochemical mechanisms and psycho-physical consequences." *J. Hypnos*, 1996; 23(3):148–156.
43. Bundzen, P., P. Bundzen, E. Gavrilova, V. Isakov, and L.E. Unestahl. "Stresslimiting and immunomodulating effect of mental training." *J. Pathophysiol*. 1998:5 (1):148.
44. Uneståhl, L.-E., P. Bundzen, E. Gavrilova, and V. Isakov. "The effects of Integrated Mental Training on Stress and Psychosomatic Health." *J. Hypnos*, 2004, XXXI (2) 83–88.
45. Johansson, B., and L.-E. Unestahl. "Stress reducing regulative effects of Integrated Mental Training with self-hypnosis on the secretion of Dehydroepiandrosterone sulfate (DHEAS-S) and Cortisol in plasma." *Contemporary Hypnosis*, 2005. Wiley Interscience, DO1, 10, 1002/ch.314.

10 References from Other Authors

46. M.H. Erickson. "Self-exploration in the hypnotic state." *Int J Clin Hypn* 3(1) 49–57, 1955.
47. M.H. Erickson. "Initial experiments investigating the Nature of Hypnosis." *Am J Clin Hypn*, 1964.
48. M.H. Erickson. "Autohypnotic experiences of Milton H. Erickson." *Am J Clin Hypn* 20(1) 36–54, 1977.
49. M.H. Erickson. "Naturalistic techniques of hypnosis." *Am J Clin Hypn* 51(4) 333–40, 2009.

50. E. Fromm, and S. Kahn. "Self-Hypnosis—The Chicago Paradigm." New York: Guilford Press, 1990.
51. Examples of Section Divine findings from www.goldennumber.net.
52. Examples of Section Divine findings from www.phimatrix.com.
53. Kosslyn, S.M., W.L. Thompson, M.F. Costantini-Ferrando, N.M. Alpert, and D. Spiegel, "Hypnotic visual illusion alters color processing in the brain." *American Journal of Psychiatry*, 157, 1279–1284, 2000.
53. Kosslyn, S. M. (2001). "Visual consciousness." In P. Grossenbacher (ed.), *Finding Consciousness in the Brain*. Amsterdam: John Benjamines. pp. 79–103.
54. Kosslyn, S.M., G. Ganis, and W.L. Thompson. "Mental imagery and the human brain." In: Q. Jing, M.R. Rosenzweig, D'Ydewalle, H. Zhang, H.-C. Chen, and K. Zhang (eds.), *Progress in Psychological Science Around the World, Vol. 1: Neural, Cognitive and Developmental Issues*, pp. 195–209. London: Psychology Press, 2006.

16 Books

56. Uneståhl, L.-E. *Hypnosis and Posthypnotic Suggestions*. Örebro: VEJE International Publ., 1973.
57. Uneståhl, L.-E. *Hypnosis in the Seventies*. Örebro: VEJE International, Publ., 1974.
58. Uneståhl, L.-E. *Self-Control by Mental Training*. Örebro: VEJE International Publ., 1979.
59. Uneståhl, L.-E. *Hypnosis in Theory and Practice*. Örebro: VEJE International Publ., 1982.
60. Uneståhl, L.-E. *The Mental Aspects of Gymnastics*. Örebro: VEJE International Publ. 1983.
61. Uneståhl, L.-E. (ed.) *Contemporary Sport Psychology*. Örebro: VEJE International Publ., 1985.
62. Uneståhl, L.-E. (ed.) *Sport Psychology in Theory and Practice*. Örebro: VEJE Int. Publ., 1985.
63. Uneståhl-Paikull. *Yes You Can*. Örebro: VEJE International Publ., 1987.
64. Uneståhl, L.-E. *Motivation—The Core of Life*. Örebro: VEJE International Publ., 1990.
65. Uneståhl, L.-E. *Applied Motivation*. Örebro: VEJE International Publ., 1994.
66. Uneståhl, L.-E. *Integrated Mental Training*. Stockholm: SISU förlag, 1997.
67. Uneståhl-Hansson. *Mental Toughness Training*. Stockholm: SISU förlag, 2002.
68. Uneståhl-Hellertz. *Personal Development through Mental Training*. Örebro: VEJE Int., 2003.
69. Uneståhl, L.-E. *The New Life Style*. Örebro: Veje Int. Publ., 2005.
70. Uneståhl, L.-E. *Coaching and Mental Training*. Örebro: Veje Int. Publ., 2012.
71. Uneståhl, L.-E. *The History of Mental Training*. Örebro: Veje Int. Publ., 2015.

About the Contributors

Richard L. **Amoroso** is a theoretical physicist and noeticist. He is the director of the Noetic Advanced Studies Institute in Oakland, California, and of the quantum computing research laboratory at Veszprem University, Hungary. The author of over 30 books, 200 academic papers and chapters in five languages, he holds four U.S. patents on quantum computing and related medical technologies.

Göte **Andersson** is an artist in Säffle, Sweden, whose discovery of the "Psi-track" phenomenon gained the attention of physicist Jens A. Tellefsen and Dr. Nils-Olof Jacobson. Together they carried out scientific tests that resulted in an award-winning article about the subject. Has written two books about the phenomenon.

Allan **Emrén**, Ph.D., studied mathematics, theoretical physics and chemistry at the University of Göteborg, and was senior lecturer and research engineer in physical chemistry and nuclear chemistry at the University of Göteborg and Chalmers University of Technology. He is the managing director and a board member of Nuchem Research AB in Tollered, Sweden, and performs scientific research in a number of areas including physics, chemistry and renewable energy.

Amna Al **Faki**, M.D., is a professor of pediatric and child health at Omdurman Islamic University in Sudan. She is the originator of the hypothesis that the heart is a sensory organ, and the principal organ for the emergence of consciousness, through heart-brain interaction.

Ingrid **Fredriksson** has an M.A. degree in public health education. She has written several books, including *Flow Forever*, *The Third Book*, *The Power of Thought*, *Free from Dangerous Stress*, *H_2O: Just Ordinary Water*, *There Is No Death* and *The Journey to Life or Death* (2015). She is editor of *Aspects of Consciousness: Essays on Physics, Death and the Mind* (McFarland), and lives in Arjäng, Sweden.

John K. **Grandy** studied biology at Canisius College in Buffalo, New York, and has a master of science degree based upon cancer research with concentrations in neurophysiology and molecular immunology. He has published articles in medicine, genetics and on consciousness, and he has lectured at such places as Harvard, the Imperial College of London and Stockholm University. He works in urgent care medicine in Watertown, New York.

Menas C. **Kafatos** received a B.A. in physics from Cornell University in 1967 and a Ph.D. in physics from M.I.T. in 1972. He is the founding dean of the Schmid College of Science and Technology at Chapman University in Orange, California, and now directs the Center of Excellence in Earth Systems Modeling and Observations. He is the author or coauthor of numerous books and articles in a wide range of science.

Hyejung **Lee** is a Korean Medical Doctor (KMD) and professor at the College of Korean Medicine, Kyung Hee University. She has published more than 200 articles about acupuncture and science, as well as a book, *The Meridian, Philosophy of Flow*.

About the Contributors

Janet **McIntyre-Mills** is a sociologist based at Flinders University in Adelaide, South Australia. She is the author of books about social and environmental justice, public policy and governance. Her research focuses on well-being, consciousness and cosmopolitan ethics associated with governance and democracy, and addresses excessive social, economic and environmental consumption.

Jan **Pilotti,** B.Sc., M.D., is a retired child-adolescent psychiatrist, a scientist, and studies the relationship of near death experiences, consciousness and dimensions. He was co-editor of a book about near-death experiences, published in 1982, and has written about the subject and gives presentations at conferences about consciousness. He lives in Örebro, Sweden.

Stephan A. **Schwartz** is the Senior Samueli Fellow for Brain, Mind and Healing of the Samueli Institute in Alexandria, Virginia, and a research associate of the Cognitive Sciences Laboratory of the Laboratories for Fundamental Research in Palo Alto, California. For 40 years he has been studying the nature of consciousness, particularly that aspect independent of space and time. Part of the group that founded modern Remote Viewing research, he is the author of four books and over 100 articles.

Alf E. **Sjöberg** is a member of the Värmland Writers' Association in Sweden, holds a master's degree in business administration and managerial economics from Columbia Pacific University and worked as an accredited auditor. He lives outside Karlstad, Sweden, and is the author of several books as well as numerous reviews and articles.

Lars-Eric **Unestål** received a Ph.D. in psychology from Uppsala University in Sweden and is the founding president of the Scandinavian International University in Örebro, Sweden. He has been a visiting professor to a number of universities around the world and has organized seven world congresses in areas including sport psychology, mental training, and hypnosis and psychosomatic medicine. He is the author of 21 books and many research articles, and his mental training programs are used in many countries around the world.

Keun-Hang Susan **Yang** holds an M.S. in bioinformatics and a Ph.D. in computational biology and neuroscience from George Mason University in Fairfax, Virginia. She is a professor of computational science and biosciences in the Schmid College of Science and Technology and director of international science programs at Chapman University in Orange, California.

Index

aboriginal 268, 279, 283, 284, 286
adenosine triphosphate *see* ATP
aeon 198
Alain Aspect 172, 228, 231
Amoroso, Richard L. 2, 192, 195, 317
Andersson, Göte 2, 55, 81, 317
anterior cingulate 6, 7
artificial intelligence 163, 195, 221, 288
ataxia 129, 133
atom 8, 21, 26, 33, 34, 35, 97, 102, 119, 120, 121, 151, 157, 158, 163, 164, 165, 172, 174, 199, 201, 202, 206, 208, 223
ATP 125, 158, 159
aura 57, 65, 66, 67, 69, 71, 72, 73, 74, 75, 76, 77, 80, 235

Beatrice of Ornacieu 17
Beck, Friedrich 8
Bell, John S. 33, 35, 36, 37, 49, 50, 51, 52, 54, 172, 185, 186, 190, 193, 228
Beneviste, Jacques 174
Bernroider, G. 178, 189, 192
Big Bang 103, 179, 180, 182, 184, 185, 193, 194, 196, 197, 198, 211
Blackmore, Susan 221
Bohm, David 1, 8, 36, 51, 166, 168, 170, 230, 245, 258, 259, 288
Bohr, N. 33, 34, 168, 179, 185, 192
brain 2, 3, 6, 7, 8, 10, 15, 18, 19, 21, 32, 38, 40, 43, 44, 45, 46, 47, 48, 49, 52, 53, 77, 84, 85, 93, 100, 103, 116, 118, 119, 120, 121, 122, 135, 136, 137, 138, 139, 140, 142, 147, 148, 149, 153, 154, 155, 156, 161, 164, 165, 166, 167, 169, 170, 171, 173, 175, 176, 177, 178, 187, 188, 189, 190, 191, 192, 193, 194, 195, 196, 197, 199, 200, 201, 202, 215, 219, 220, 221, 222, 223, 224, 225, 226, 228, 229, 230, 231, 232, 233, 235, 236, 237, 238, 239, 240, 241, 242, 244, 245, 246, 247, 260, 264, 267, 270, 274, 279, 280, 284, 285, 287, 288, 289, 290, 292, 293, 294, 295, 297, 315, 317, 318
brain cells 2, 43, 149, 153, 156, 167, 225

cardiac arrest 1, 14, 15, 20
cathodic rays 26
cell 2, 7, 43, 86, 88, 89, 91, 117, 118, 119, 121, 122, 124, 125, 127, 128, 129, 130, 131, 132, 136, 141, 144, 145, 146, 148, 149, 150, 151, 152, 153, 154, 156, 158, 159, 162, 163, 164, 167, 173, 174, 175, 200, 225, 227, 228, 229, 231, 233, 240, 241, 246, 270, 312
CERN 18
Chalmers, David 41, 53, 219, 289
Chawla, Lakhmir S. 228, 229
chi 195
Chopra, Deepak 179, 187, 189, 190, 192, 193, 269
clairvoyance 57, 77, 78, 79
consciousness 1, 2, 5, 6, 7, 8, 9, 11, 12, 13, 14, 15, 16, 17, 18, 19, 20, 21, 32, 38, 39, 40, 41, 42, 43, 45, 46, 47, 48, 49, 50, 51, 52, 53, 54, 75, 78, 83, 84, 99, 100, 101, 103, 105, 106, 115, 116, 117, 118, 119, 120, 121, 122, 123, 124, 125, 126, 127, 128, 129, 130, 131, 132, 133, 135, 136, 137, 138, 139, 140, 141, 142, 143, 144, 145, 146, 147, 149, 150, 154, 155, 160, 161, 163, 165, 166, 167, 171, 173, 174, 175, 176, 177, 178, 179, 183, 185, 186, 187, 188, 189, 190, 191, 192, 193, 194, 196, 197, 199, 201, 205, 206, 207, 208, 209, 210, 213, 215, 218, 219, 221, 222, 223, 224, 225, 228, 229, 230, 231, 234, 237, 241, 243, 244, 245, 246, 247, 248, 249, 250, 252, 257, 259, 260, 262, 264, 265, 267, 268, 269, 270, 276, 279, 281, 282, 283, 284, 285, 288, 289, 290, 291, 292, 293, 300, 301, 309, 315, 317, 318
cosmological constant 181, 184
CRCAH 264, 286
cromatin fiber 125

dark energy 30, 179, 180, 181
dark matter 30, 52, 101, 102, 179, 180, 181
de Broglie, L. 33, 34, 35, 36, 38, 50, 189, 199, 226
Decartes, René 5, 16, 17, 20, 196, 199–200, 214, 219
Demokritos 1
dendrites 2, 149, 167, 200, 237
dimension 1, 21, 22, 23, 27, 28, 29, 30, 31, 39, 40, 44, 45, 47, 48, 51, 52, 100, 150, 154, 155, 156, 169, 170, 171, 175, 189, 192, 197, 199, 207, 209, 210, 215, 228, 229, 251, 264, 265, 268, 275, 284, 291, 303, 318
DNA 2, 83, 84, 89, 93, 116, 117, 118, 119, 121, 122, 123, 124, 125, 126, 127, 128, 129, 130, 131, 132, 133, 134, 135, 136, 137, 138, 140, 141, 142, 143, 144, 145, 146, 147, 149, 150, 151, 152, 153, 156, 160, 161, 173, 174, 175, 201, 205, 215, 219, 227, 228, 258, 295

319

Index

dowsing 55, 56, 57, 58, 59, 60, 61, 62, 63, 64, 65, 69, 79, 81
dualism 5, 41, 42, 43, 116, 144, 196, 199, 215

Eccles, J.C. 8
Eccles Psychon 200
EEG 77, 177, 215, 228, 237, 294, 309
Einstein, Albert 1, 8, 19, 20, 21, 25, 26, 27, 28, 29, 30, 31, 32, 33, 34, 36, 37, 39, 50, 53, 54, 161, 166, 168, 170, 172, 179, 181, 185, 189, 192, 201, 208, 214, 219, 227, 245, 259
electricity 24, 25, 26, 56, 174
electrolytes 160
electromagnetism 25, 26, 27, 66, 161, 163, 172, 174, 176
electron 26, 32, 33, 34, 35, 36, 39, 96, 97, 102, 126, 149, 152, 158, 159, 160, 163, 168, 172, 175, 174, 184, 185, 188, 198, 205, 215, 227, 291
Emoto, Masaru 160, 175
Emrén, Allan 2, 83, 317
energy 2, 21, 26, 29, 30, 32, 33, 34, 39, 49, 55, 56, 57, 64, 66, 67, 68, 69, 72, 74, 75, 76, 77, 80, 83, 86, 94, 95, 119, 124, 143, 150, 156, 157, 158, 159, 160, 161, 162, 163, 164, 165, 167, 170, 171, 179, 180, 181, 196, 197, 198, 201, 208, 209, 210, 214, 216, 219, 224, 226, 227, 228, 231, 232, 237, 238, 239, 240, 244, 245, 251, 252, 258, 259, 263, 288, 291, 310, 317
epigenetics 128, 135, 138, 145, 151
epilepsy 129, 177, 188
epiphenomenalism-dualism 41
EPR paradox 36, 149, 172, 173, 176, 228, 231
Euclid 24, 214
eukaryotes 128, 150
European Organization for Nuclear Research see CERN
evolution 16, 21, 44, 53, 83, 84, 85, 89, 90, 91, 92, 93, 94, 101, 103, 104, 105, 115, 118, 120, 122, 128, 134, 140, 141, 142, 144, 146, 147, 163, 175, 180, 185, 188, 191, 192, 196, 198, 199, 210, 211, 214, 220, 226, 242, 245, 246, 247, 249, 250, 259, 273, 286, 289

Faraday, Michael 25
flatness problem 180

Fourier, Jean B.J. 168, 169
Fredriksson, Ingrid 1, 3, 144, 149, 168, 221, 317
frequencies 1, 26, 32, 162, 165, 167, 168, 169, 219, 225, 230, 295, 309

Gabor, Dennis 168, 170, 229
galaxies 30, 103, 180
Galilei, Galileo 21
Galvani 24
Ganzfeld 10, 13, 19
gastric juices 160
genesis 3, 125, 133, 134, 135, 146, 220, 222, 224, 246, 262
genomes 90, 91, 92, 118, 122, 124, 125, 126, 127, 128, 129, 130, 131, 132, 133, 134, 137, 138, 144, 145, 146, 147, 148, 151
ghosts 39
gnostics 198
Golden Rule 213
Grandy, John K. 2, 116, 317
gravity 22, 24, 26, 38, 39, 119, 157, 165, 170, -172, 181, 182–184, 187, 218, 198, 211, 228, 241

Hameroff, Stuart 8, 154, 155, 228, 237
the hard problem 41, 53, 219
Hawking, Stephen 155, 247, 258
healer 6, 17, 249
heart 3, 13, 62, 77, 78, 154, 155, 174, 202, 217, 219, 221, 222, 223, 224, 225, 226, 228, 231, 232, 233, 234, 235, 236, 237, 238, 239, 240, 241, 242, 317
heart intelligence 221, 240, 241
HeartMath 235, 236, 238, 239, 240, 242
helium 85, 102
hippocampus 7, 137, 138
Hippocrates 1
hologram 1, 2, 149, 155, 166, 167, 168, 169, 170, 171, 176, 198, 199, 206, 229, 230, 241, 252, 260
holographic universe 1, 155, 169, 171, 176, 177, 198, 230, 241, 242
Horapollo 198
Hox genes 122, 133, 134, 135, 136, 137, 144, 145, 146, 147, 148
Hubble space telescope 180
human animals 269, 286
hydrogen 2, 33, 34, 85, 102, 128, 149, 156, 157, 158, 160, 161, 172, 173, 174, 227, 228

hypnosis 3, 79, 253, 293, 294, 298, 299, 300, 301, 302, 303, 304, 305, 306, 307, 308, 309, 310, 313, 314, 315, 318

immune system 2, 149, 160, 161, 173, 174, 176, 227, 232, 236
inferior occipital gyrus 7
information particle 258
integrated mental training (IMT) 3, 293, 308, 309, 310, 314, 315
interactionism-dualism 41, 42

Jung-Beeman, Mark 6

Kafatos, Menas C. 2, 178, 317
Kaivarainen 172
Krebs cycle 159
Kuhn 17, 20

lactic acidosis 129, 145
Lee, Heyejung 2, 178, 317
light 7, 20, 24, 25, 26, 27, 28, 29, 30, 31, 32, 33, 36, 37, 40, 42, 49, 52, 53, 54, 61, 62, 67, 86, 96, 98, 100, 101, 102, 154, 155, 156, 162, 171, 172, 174, 177, 179, 181, 184, 185, 196, 197, 198, 199, 201, 202, 203, 205, 206, 209, 210, 211, 213, 215, 216, 217, 218, 227, 229, 233, 244, 248, 250, 256, 298
Linne, Carl von 63, 64, 81
lithium 85
Lorentz, H. 26, 27, 28, 30, 31, 53

M-theory 39, 183, 247
macroscopic objects 2, 43, 102, 118, 167, 182, 203, 205
magnetism 24, 25
Maslow, Abraham 255
Maxwell, James Clark 25, 26, 27
meditation 6, 18, 195, 196, 208, 215, 216, 217, 220, 231, 243, 244, 245, 248, 249, 250, 252, 256, 258, 259, 260, 261
membrane 2, 88, 89, 104, 138, 139, 149, 150, 153, 156, 158, 159, 228, 229, 231
methylation 125, 126, 127, 128, 132, 135, 145, 148
microphysical 41, 42, 43, 48
mindfulness 3, 253, 254, 259, 262, 263, 264, 265, 266, 267, 268, 269, 271, 273, 283, 284, 288
Minkowski, H. 29, 50, 53
Mitchell, Edgar 168, 171, 176

mitochondria 124, 127, 150, 158
mitochondrial encephalomyopathy 129, 145
molecules 2, 85, 86, 89, 118, 121, 130, 141, 143, 149, 156, 157, 159, 162, 163, 172, 174, 201, 215, 227, 233, 284
Monism 38, 41, 42, 43, 48
Montagnier, Luc 161, 174, 175
MRI scanner 6
multiverse theory 105

near death experience (NDE) 1, 5, 6, 8, 10, 12, 13, 14, 15, 16, 18, 44, 54, 149, 154, 155, 166, 167, 176, 177, 228, 230, 231, 234, 248, 318
neurogenesis 2, 118, 129, 132, 133, 137, 139, 140, 143, 144, 145, 146, 153
neurons 2, 3, 117, 118, 120, 122, 133, 136–142, 144, 146, 149, 167, 188, 190, 194, 223, 225, 232, 237, 238, 241, 247, 264, 285
neuropathy 129
neuroscience 5, 6, 8, 12, 13, 19, 41, 53, 54, 163, 188, 221, 284, 318
neurotheology 6, 18, 20
Newton, Sir Issac 21–24, 26–28, 34, 37–39, 43, 195, 207, 260, 287
Nobel laureate 116, 161, 173, 174, 227
Nobel Prize 79, 153, 156, 163, 168, 175, 200, 229
noetic cosmology 195
nonlocal consciousness 5, 6, 7, 9, 12, 13, 15, 18, 149, 177
nuclear medicine 7

Occident 24, 269
orbit 33, 34, 38, 126, 182
oxygen 85, 129, 154, 156, 157, 158, 159, 172, 223, 224, 225, 228, 235

panpsychism 42, 49, 194
paradigm 1, 5, 6, 9, 16, 18, 90, 155, 168, 180, 194, 210, 246, 260, 274, 304, 315
particles 8, 18, 22, 23, 24, 26, 29, 30, 32, 33, 34, 35, 36, 37, 38, 52, 53, 83, 88, 96, 97, 98, 99, 100, 102, 105, 121, 170, 171, 172, 178, 184, 185, 187, 244, 245, 251, 252
Pax genes 122, 136, 137, 140
Penrose, Roger 8, 237
Petkov, V. 29, 39, 50, 51, 53

photons 7, 32, 33, 35, 96, 97, 98, 100, 101, 102, 185, 186, 197, 198, 201, 205, 206, 214, 215
Planck, M. 5, 6, 8, 9, 18, 19, 27, 32, 50, 53, 168, 179, 182, 183, 184, 185, 189, 200
Plato 14, 20, 29, 38, 190, 211, 258
Podolsky, Boris 36, 161, 172, 185, 189, 192, 206, 208
poltergeist 17
polygraph 150
Popp, Fritz-Albert 163
Popper, Karl 37, 53
positrons 39, 97, 98, 187
prana 195, 216, 260
prebiotic life 85, 88, 89, 90, 103
precentral gyrus 7
Pribram, Karl 1, 166, 168, 170, 176, 230, 231, 287
prokaryotes 150
psi 2, 13, 55, 57, 58, 59, 60, 61, 62, 63, 64, 65, 68, 69, 70, 71, 72, 73, 74, 76, 77, 78, 79, 81, 317
psi-track 2, 55, 57, 58, 59, 60, 61, 62, 63, 64, 65, 68, 69, 70, 71, 72, 73, 74, 76, 77, 78, 79, 81
psychography 7
psychokinesis 19, 57, 167, 171
Pythagoras' theorem 27

qualia 41, 187, 192, 196, 197, 200, 201, 202, 203, 204, 205, 206, 208
quanta 32, 53, 161, 167, 186, 189, 192, 201, 205, 214
quantum biology 7, 19
quantum hologram 2, 149, 167, 171
quantum mechanics 5, 8, 21, 27, 32–39, 42, 44, 52, 53, 101, 115, 159, 163–165, 172, 179, 193, 194, 228, 229, 258, 288
quantum theory 2, 33, 35, 52, 53, 126, 127, 166, 167, 169, 171, 175, 176, 178, 179, 187, 189, 191, 192, 193, 197, 199, 206, 211, 237, 242, 246, 247, 257, 261
quarks 119, 120, 121, 143

remote viewing 9, 10, 13, 15, 19, 165, 166, 176, 177, 228, 318
retinitis pigmentosa 129
reverse circular polarizer (RCP) 97
RNA 83, 85, 89, 115, 118, 121, 124, 125, 127, 128, 129, 130, 131, 132, 138, 145, 147, 152, 153, 154

Rosen, Nathan 33, 161, 172, 185, 189, 192, 194, 206, 208, 280, 292
Russell, Bertrand 38, 42

Sagan, Carl 10, 166
St. Francis 17
St. John 17, 212
St. Teresa 17
saints 17, 20, 219
Sanskrit 216, 259
SARS 160, 269
Schrödinger, E. 34, 38, 49, 51, 52, 54, 120, 159, 168, 177, 189, 199, 226
Schwartz, Stephan A. 1, 5, 318
self-hypnosis 3, 253, 293, 298, 299, 300, 307, 308, 309, 310, 313, 314, 315
Semmelweis, Ignaz 164, 174
Shaivism 191
Siva method 165, 175, 176
SOLS 204, 205, 206, 207, 208, 211, 218, 260
space-time 1, 2, 5, 16, 21, 28, 29, 30, 32, 39, 40, 41, 44–49, 51–53, 115, 167, 170, 181, 186, 189, 193, 197, 198, 199, 200, 201, 202, 203, 204, 205, 208, 214, 219, 258
spirituality 2, 6, 7, 9, 15, 17, 19, 20, 25, 80, 166, 177, 195, 196, 201, 205, 207, 209, 210, 211, 212, 213, 215, 216, 217, 218, 222, 235, 238, 243, 244, 245, 246, 248, 250, 251, 252, 253, 254, 256, 257, 259, 260, 261, 268, 270, 279, 285
Stapp, Henry 8, 37, 168
string theory 39, 119, 121, 155, 170, 171, 183
stroke 13, 129, 145
super Darwinian 83, 84, 89, 94, 101, 104, 105, 106
super extinctions 103
superior temporal gyrus 6, 7
superlight 29, 30, 40
supernova 181
synapses 2, 100, 149, 167, 195
synapsins 122, 146

Talbot, Michael 176, 230, 231
Tanamura, Dr. 36
Tantra 212, 216
telepathy 77, 78, 144, 164, 167, 171, 230
Tellefsen, Jens 60, 80, 81, 317
Tenant, Dr. Jerry 159
theory of relativity 27, 28, 29, 30, 32, 37, 39, 50, 98, 100, 104, 179

thermodynamic obstacles 86
Thompson, W.L. 26, 315

unexplained energy fields 2, 55, 64
universe 2, 3, 8, 37, 49, 52, 54, 83, 84, 85, 89, 93, 94, 96, 100, 101, 102, 103, 104, 105, 106, 116, 120, 151, 155, 165, 166, 169, 170, 171, 174, 175, 176, 178, 179, 180, 181, 182, 183, 184, 185, 186, 187, 188, 189, 190, 191, 192, 194, 196, 197, 198, 208, 210, 211, 213, 216, 219, 221, 224, 228, 230, 237, 239, 241, 242, 246, 247, 258, 260, 295
Uroboros 198, 199
Utts, Jessica 13

van Lommel, Pim 1, 14, 149
Vedanta 191
Virgin Eustochium of Padua 17
Vitiello, Guiseppe 161
Volta 25

wavelengths 26, 95, 165
waves 23, 24, 25, 33, 34, 35, 36, 37, 38, 96, 102, 105, 136, 161, 162, 163, 165, 167, 168, 169, 174, 175, 189, 205, 225, 227, 229, 231, 240, 244, 260, 263, 288; function collapse 35, 83, 95, 100, 101, 105, 189
Wiseman, H.M. 36, 37, 51, 54

Yang, Keun-Hang Susan 2, 178, 318
yoga 164, 215, 219, 220, 242, 244, 246, 248, 250, 251, 257, 259, 260, 262

www.ingramcontent.com/pod-product-compliance
Lightning Source LLC
Chambersburg PA
CBHW081538300426
44116CB00015B/2676